*American Panorama*
*East of the Mississippi*

# AMERICAN PANORAMA

# PANORAMA

## EAST OF THE MISSISSIPPI

### A HOLIDAY MAGAZINE BOOK

DOUBLEDAY & COMPANY, INC.

Garden City, New York

The illustrations in this book are the work of the photographers
listed:

Following page 52: John Lewis Stage—3 photographs
Following page 148: Pinto Studios, Lawrence Lowry, John
Lewis Stage
Following page 244: Elliott Erwitt, Lawrence Lowry, Tom
Hollyman
Following page 404: Tom Hollyman, Slim Aarons, David E.
Scherman

# Contents

Part II   *The Mid Atlantic States*

Here is the 99% of the state beyond Broadway—a journey
into an amazing and wonderfully varied land by a favorite
York State author.

There are green farm lands, forests and fabulous beaches
behind its crowded cities. A new look at a much misunderstood state.

For patriot or vacationer, for the sportsman or the traveler
with an eye for scenery, no other state offers more of the
good things of American life.

The amazing story of the tiny state where things have always happened in a big way—from high deeds in the Revolution to the fantastic growth of the Du Pont colossus.

Part III   *The East Central States*

Green woods and blue lakes are only one part of the Badger
State, industry and ideas are the other.

The nation's hub, and to many the most American of all the
states. A discerning portrait.

From dynamic Detroit to the great open country to the
north—a remarkable state, rediscovered by a distinguished
historian and native son.

# Introduction

The twenty-six states east of the Mississippi are the older half of the Republic, a series of regions within a region whose boundary lines are a great ocean and our greatest river. When we use the expression "Eastern United States," we are knowingly imprecise, for this land mass with its patchwork of history and manners and folklore is an arbitration of geography. New England, the industrial Middle Atlantic states, the sensitive South, the Middle West: to the Westerner, with his feeling of living in a growing-up land, all this is the East. Yet the difference between Boston and Miami, between Kentucky and the Pennsylvania Dutch country, is as deep-seated as it is dramatic. The climate varies sharply, so does the topography, even more do the people.

Besides a common purpose, the people of this region share a consciousness of living in the crucible of American history. Here are the landmarks, the monuments, the scars of a noble experiment. Here the past envelops, as in the West the future beckons. Another past is here, too, the past of Europe, for this is the region watered by the streams of immigration, in which hundreds of thousands from old countries found promise and fulfillment in the new, as did the original settlers before them. These ties to Europe, financial, cultural, emotional, remain strong and persistent. Finally, the East is the seat of our government, the center of commerce and industry, the marketplace where much of our money is made and many of our goods manufactured and dispersed.

This book is a gallery of portraits of the Eastern states, including Washington, D.C., and is part of Holiday's continuing coverage of the United States. They were drawn by some of the country's most distinguished writers. Together with its companion volume, *American Panorama: West of the Mississippi*, it provides a quilted pattern of this country—its people, its character, its beauty, its hope.

The Editors

*American Panorama*
*East of the Mississippi*

# PART I *New England*

# aine

## by ARTHUR BARTLETT

When the District of Maine was separated from the Commonwealth of Massachusetts in 1820, a Maine man under the spell of the mother state's ponderous phraseology proposed that it set itself up as the Commonwealth of Maine. A more typical Maine man, serving as a delegate to the convention, promptly objected. "It'll be called a state, wun't it?" he demanded. "What's the sense in naming it Jonathan if it's alluz going to be called just plain John?" This realism prevailed, and Maine became the State of Maine. Moreover, the decision so won the approval of a people to whom pretentiousness is at once the most amusing and the most unforgivable of foibles, and whose pride in the lack of it sometimes seems pretentious, that, to this day, State of Maine is the common usage. It is spoken almost as if it were one word, and a Maine man is invariably a State-of-Mainer.

In these days, when an average summer finds more than a million paying guests swarming into Maine, whose year-round population is something less than a million, the stubborn insistence of the typical State-of-Mainer on being himself, and his amused disdain for people who talk big, often tend to conflict with his pecuniary instincts. Some years ago, for instance, some publicity-minded individuals hit upon an idea for getting Maine's tourist and resort business some free advertising, and persuaded the legislature to decree that all the state's automobile registration plates, except those issued for hearses, should have the word Vacationland on them. This boosterism offends the natural conservatism and sense of dignity of many State-of-Mainers, and a determined attempt was made in the legislature to put an end to it.

One prominent legislator, noted for his dry, down-East manner of speech, declared that he had formed the instinctively defensive habit of approaching his car from the front, where there is no plate. "Seeing that thing," he announced solemnly, "always induces a mild attack of nausea."

The principal argument of those opposing the tag line on the plates was that it created the impression that Maine is *nothing but* a vacationland. The naïveté of the occasional outlander who thinks that moose roam constantly on the streets of Maine cities and that everything north of Portland (actually near the southern tip of the state) is uncharted wilderness produces the same combination of amusement and irritation in many State-of-Mainers that many Midwesterners feel from hearing of Europeans who think that Indians and cowboys still ride wild just west of Jersey City.

The question, "What on earth do you do here after the summer people leave?" is another frequent irritant; and the late Shavy Noyes, the town of Norway's favorite sidewalk philosopher for many years, gave a lady summer visitor the classic answer: "Oh, we jest fumigate." The summer visitors are an important source of income for the state, however, and the anti-Vacationlanders lost their fight to purge the registration plates of the boosterism. Indeed, so thriving is the business of accommodating tourists and vacationers, particularly during July and August, that one somewhat sour motorist who had driven into the state on U. S. Route 1, expecting to house his family for the night in one of the many tourist-cabin establishments along the road, stopped finally at the headquarters of the State of Maine Publicity Bureau, on the outskirts of Portland, and suggested an additional phrase for the registration plates: making them read: Vacationland—No Vacancies.

Maine is nearly as large as the five other New England states combined, and can suit almost any topographical taste, whether for seacoast, woods, lakes, streams or mountains. Its mountains, admittedly, are less grandiose and concentrated than the White Mountains of neighboring New Hampshire; but it is nevertheless a definitely bumpy state, with hundreds of protuberances ranging from good-sized hills to the 5267-foot Mount Katahdin, which compilers of Maine's triumphs claim as the first spot in the United States to feel the morning sun. More than four fifths of the state is still wooded; and—to dispose immediately of as many statistics as possible—it has 2465 lakes and ponds, ranging from millponds to forty-mile-long Moosehead, one of the largest lakes completely within one state; five large rivers and 5147 smaller rivers and streams; and a direct coast line of nearly 250 miles, so notched with bays and inlets that its tidal line is nearly ten times that long, and equal in length to one half the whole Atlantic coast line of the United States.

With all this to offer, plus a northern climate which assures moderate summer days and cool summer nights, Maine has been in the vacation business for more than a hundred years, ever since a group of rich New Yorkers discovered Mount Desert Island before the Civil War, and started the Bar Harbor summer colony. The father of Mrs. J. Pierpont Morgan, Sr., was one of the original summer settlers, and Bar Harbor has thrived, through the years, on the patronage of such wealthy families as the Rockefellers, Vanderbilts, Whitneys, Stotesburys, Pulitzers and McCormicks. It was, however, the late Henry Ford, who put cars within reach of families of moderate income, who made recreation Big Business for Maine. The state today has perhaps half a dozen big summer hotels where the rates tend to limit the clientele to the wealthier classes, and Bar Harbor has branches of the New York shops; but it is the thousands of smaller hotels, overnight cabins, sports camps, tourist homes, roadside lunches, and all the service-of-supply businesses dependent on them which bring in the bulk of the $250,000,000 or more which is Maine's recreational income in a good year.

Joe Doakes, on a two-weeks vacation with his family, or on a fishing or hunting trip with some cronies, is the man who supports these institutions, and who eventually often buys a cottage or an old farmhouse where his family can spend the whole summer. A superhighway, built at great cost with private capital and running from Portsmouth, New Hampshire, to Portland and on up to Augusta, makes it easier for him to get into the state.

Yet the tourists and vacationers are not quite so important to the state's economy as they seem during the brief summer season when they outnumber the natives. Industry still puts more money into

Maine pockets than summer visitors. Agriculture ranks second to industry. The recreation business comes in third, ahead only of commercial fishing among Maine's four major ways of making a living.

Maine's two major attractions for vacationers, the seacoast and the
woods, were the mainstays of the state's earliest economy. Into the
many harbors formed by the undulating coast line, ships began sailing
as early as 1497, when the Cabots explored the coast. In 1607, the
first ship ever built by Europeans on this continent, the "Virginia,"
took shape under the hands of the ill-fated Popham colonists at the
mouth of the Kennebec River; and by 1642, when Sir Ferdinando
Gorges converted, at least on paper, the little fishing hamlet of
Agamenticus (now York) into the first chartered city in this country,
both fishing and trading vessels were plying the Maine coast in substantial numbers. The Maine woods provided cargoes of furs for the
earliest trading ships. They soon provided, too, the raw material for
more ships; and dozens of little coastal villages, with lumber from
the back country, built and manned ships that sailed all over the
world. Lumber became the principal cargo that they hauled out of
Maine, and lumbering the state's principal industry.

Sailors, fishermen, woodsmen and, as some of the woods were
cleared, farmers were Maine's founders and builders. Most of them
came down from Massachusetts. (Maine is always down, no matter
how it looks on the map, because the prevailing winds along the
coast made it usually a down-wind sail from Boston.) They were virtually all of English stock, of course. With the exception of a few
landed proprietors—and most of those preferred to stay in Boston or,
even better, in England, and administer their settlements at long
distance—they had no claims to aristocracy and no backlog of wealth.
They were isolated and on their own, and acutely aware of it. If
their cousins of Massachusetts Bay thought of them as rough backwoodsmen, they thought of those cousins as inflated characters whom
it was prudent and not unenjoyable to remind, from time to time,
that hard-working and self-respecting backwoodsmen had the same
rights as anybody else.

They insisted on having not only elementary schools but a college
of their own, and got Bowdoin, which was chartered by the Massachusetts General Court in 1796 and opened in 1802; and after they
got it, they bedeviled the legislature for being too generous toward
Harvard and slighting Bowdoin. Sometimes their Yankee wariness of

being victimized led them into ingenious arguments, as when the
General Court imposed an excise tax on rum. The people of Cumberland and Lincoln counties demanded special consideration because they lacked good orchards for cider, they said, and were, therefore, "under the necessity of using more rum than their brethren to
the westward."

Early Maine, as a matter of fact, was a notoriously hard-drinking
area, as might have been expected of a place where nearly everybody was a sailor or a woodsman. As the farm population increased,
however, a strong temperance reaction set in, and in 1846 the state
passed one of the earliest prohibition laws in our history. It was
officially dry, with only minor interruptions, from then until it voted
wet again after the repeal of national prohibition. Authorities differ
as to how dry Maine actually was during the three quarters of a
century when the law forbade the sale of liquor—"not including cider,"
according to the terms of its constitutional amendment. Most State-
of-Mainers, however, live in small communities where sinning in
secret is difficult, go to church as a matter of course, and tend to
conform to a moral code which, though somewhat liberalized now,
still bars excesses. "Even if you aren't worried about going to hell,"
a Maine judge recently admonished a young man brought before him
for continued drunkenness, "you'd better begin to worry about how
much it's costing you to do it. I'll give you thirty days to think it
over."

With only about as many people as live in the city of Boston scattered over the state's spacious area, Maine has only twenty-one communities which call themselves cities, and several of them seem to
be stretching a point to do it. On the other hand, there are over 400
incorporated towns, which govern themselves at town meetings,
sixty so-called plantations, too sparsely populated to maintain a town
government, and 395 completely unorganized townships which are
just lines on the map, and in most of which nobody at all lives. Many
of these are in the Big Woods, which cover the northwestern corner
of the state, but some are in other areas, and serve, as Maine people
like to say, "to hold up the road" from one place to another.

Ever since the early part of the last century, when so many people
left Maine for the newly opened lands of the West that the contagious restlessness became known as the Ohio fever, the rate of desertion has been high, and Maine has supplied so many citizens for

other states that its own population growth has been in driblets. Many of those who left at the time of the Ohio fever were farmers, who sold their farms and goods at public auctions—and even auctioned off the care of elderly relatives and other dependents unequal to the migration by taking bids on their room and board for the rest of their lives and turning them over to the low bidders. Since then, however, the migrants from Maine have been largely young people, looking for wider occupational opportunities, and the tendency has been for those with family farms, businesses or other property interests to remain. This selective process has no doubt accentuated the already strong sense of property of the average Maine Yankee and his personal and political conservatism. A lobsterman of the town of Friendship was admittedly expressing an extreme view, yet one indicative of the average State-of-Mainer's attitude toward governmental interference with what he considers his rights, when he cussed out a state official not long ago, and insisted that all regulations about lobster fishing ought to be repealed.

"If God wanted them lobsters protected," he declared, "He'd send somebody to do it. So long's He don't, a man ought to be allowed to sell any of 'em he catches."

The present population of Maine is preponderantly of the old Yankee stock—at least sixty per cent, by most estimates. Most of the non-Yankees are Canadian, by birth or ancestry, and a large proportion of them French Canadian. The representation of other races and nationalities in the state is fragmentary. Only about one tenth of one per cent of the population, for instance, is Negro—a proportion equaled by the Indians still surviving on the Penobscot and Passamaquoddy tribal lands at Old Town, Eastport and Princeton. In the 1920's, when the Ku Klux Klan was driving hard for members, its greatest successes in Maine were in rural areas where the organizers' scare stories about Catholics and Jews were the more readily accepted because their prospects had never had any firsthand acquaintance with either. The French Canadians, or, as many of them prefer to be known, Acadians, are Catholic, of course, but most of them live in industrial cities, like Lewiston or Biddeford, or along the St. John River, which forms part of the northern boundary line with Canada. Maine industry relies heavily on them for labor, and since the pulp-and-paper industry is by far Maine's greatest, and is based on the continuing exploitation of the forests, the proficiency of French Canadians as lumberjacks is one of the state's major human assets.

With so much of the state's land surface still in timber and wood lots, including ten million acres in the Big Woods, the largest area of unbroken wild land in private ownership in any state in the country, the cutting of trees for lumber remains an important industry. Many factories around the state, mostly small plants, also use State-of-Maine wood for a multiplicity of products: clothespins, spools, bobbins, tool handles, skewers, heels, toothpicks, tongue depressors, stoppers, bungs, barrels, boxes, casks, hoops, ladders, sleds, paddles, pickle crocks, meat blocks, coat hangers and lollipop sticks, to name just a few at random. One factory uses 40,000 cords of wood a year solely for clothespins. Much the greatest part of the wood cut in Maine, however, is reduced to pulp for the manufacture of paper, and the big paper companies employ more labor and turn out more dollars' worth of product than any other single industry. Modern mechanical contrivances have taken some of the Paul Bunyan flavor out of logging. Lumberjacks, their axes on their shoulders, used to go into the logging camps and stay all winter; they now use automobiles and come out to town at least once a week. The ax and saw remain essential tools of the trade, and while trucks haul out a considerable amount of lumber, millions of logs are still driven down the rivers and lakes, with lumberjacks deftly hopping the booms to keep them going. One lumberman with a long-log mill at the mouth of the Saco River, is of the fourth generation of his family in the business. He still drives logs down the river under rights granted his family in colonial days.

The manufacture of textiles, a business which came into the state in the middle and latter part of the last century, primarily because of the water power generated by the many rivers and streams, ranks second among Maine industries. The cotton mills are mostly large plants, around which typical small mill cities have grown up; but most of the more numerous woolen mills are smaller enterprises, more typical of Maine, operating in semirural villages.

The manufacture of machinery and other metal products and of boots and shoes follow, in that order of importance, the textile industry, and also make use of the water power of the rivers. Auburn, on the Androscoggin, is the principal shoe-manufacturing center, while Waterville and Augusta, on the Kennebec, make a considerable part of the machinery. Maine's other important industry, canning, is closely related to its agriculture and its fishing, though several big canners now reach far beyond the borders of the state for their raw products. California pea beans, for instance, come to Maine in huge quantities to become New England baked beans, and State-of-Mainers take great delight in the fact that many of them then go all the way back to California to be eaten. For the most part, however, Maine canneries are situated in small towns near their source of supply, whether sweet corn, the most important single canning crop, blueberries, fish, or something else; and they play an important part in the economy of those areas, both as markets for farmers and fishermen and as employers of labor. Many of them operate only seasonally, relying largely on farm and small-town women who take time out from their household duties to add their bit to the family incomes.

It is typical of the Maine pattern of life for people to turn their hands to different kinds of work as varying opportunities arise. Many winter sawmill workers, for instance, are farmers in the summer; many men who act as guides in the summer, work in the woods or go trapping in the winter. During World War II, as during the previous one, when the normally small shipbuilding industry had to be tremendously expanded almost overnight, thousands of Maine farm people and others who knew nothing of ships but did know how to handle tools were quickly converted into skilled shipyard workers. A large proportion of factory workers live on small farms, and have their own gardens, and, perhaps, a cow. So do many fishermen, and one of them recently described his technique of shearing a sheep this way: "I grab him by the starboard aft leg and work for'ard." Chamber-of-commerce people and others concerned with trying to attract new industry to Maine make a big point of the versatility and stability of Maine workers. The executive secretary of the Associated Industries of Maine, put it this way: "Suppose John Jones works in a woolen mill. He owns his own house, and pays his bills. He is a good mechanic, and has always made a good living, whether in the mill or some other way. He can walk down the street in his town, and people speak to him with respect. He is a successful man. He can call the banker Fred, the lawyer Bill, and the owner of the mill where he works Charlie, and he probably plays whist and goes fishing with them. He has his vote in the town meeting, and may be elected selectman. He may join a union, but he isn't going to be pushed around by agitators. We haven't had a serious, crippling strike in Maine in a long time."

One of the weaknesses of this small-town economy is that the loss of a single small industry on which a town depends can be critical; and scattered about Maine are dozens of towns with beautiful and impressive old houses, evidence of an earlier prosperity, which have fallen into disuse, been sold to summer residents, or converted into tourist accommodations. The town of Cherryfield, on the Narraguagus River, once had fourteen sawmills in operation, but as the near-by timber on which they depended became less plentiful the town's reason for existence all but disappeared; hunters, fishermen and summer visitors are now a major factor in keeping it alive. Industry has been growing, however, rather than declining in recent years, as the national trend toward decentralization has strengthened; and many small communities which seemed in danger, during the depression, of becoming ghost towns, have come to life again as new industries have supplanted old ones. The little village of Mechanic Falls is an example: the paper mill and the shoe factory which used to support it had both become vacant before the war, and the mechanics of Mechanic Falls became farmers; today a big national cosmetic company is using the paper mill for the manufacture of facial tissue, the shoe factory has become a wooden-box factory, a machine shop is making precision machines, and the mechanics are all busy being mechanics again.

If a man has three acres or more of land and gets as much as $250 of agricultural income from it, the Census Bureau counts him as a farmer, no matter what else he may do. Under this definition, Maine has some 43,000 farms, but less than half of them are full-time commercial farms in the Midwestern sense. Most of the rest are pieces of land on which people live and do a little farming while also turning a penny by other means.

The fisherman-farmer previously quoted on the subject of shearing sheep, who stoutly maintains that the island where he keeps his sheep is so rocky that he has to go out and file down their noses so they can get at the grass, has a whole fleet of lobster boats and an interest in a shipyard. The fact that many Maine farm owners have a similar eye to other business, as well as an ingrained thriftiness, may be part of the reason why Maine farms are less burdened by mortgage debts than those of any other Northern state. Many a Maine farm has been passed down free and clear by previous generations. So long as it provides enough cash income to pay the taxes and to buy the few essentials of life that it does not grow, its owner is satisfied. It was the late Ed Allen, a philosophic farmer of the town of Stoneham, who stopped his Model T one day in 1930 to talk with a friend about the stockmarket crash, and said, "I feel awful sorry for all those city folks. They got used to thinking they had a lot of money, and now it's gone, and they don't know what to do. I figure I'm pretty lucky. I never had any money, and things are just the same as they always were."

However, up in Aroostook County, which produces more potatoes than any single state except its own, the attitude toward money is different. About half of the state's farm income comes from potatoes, and Aroostook grows over eighty per cent of them. Many farmers grow more than 100 acres, some more than 500, and a few more than 1000. This is big business, and the average Aroostook potato farmer is as acutely market-conscious as any stock speculator. During the war, the Government supported the potato market, to assure adequate supplies, and most growers were assured of reasonable profits; but in other years, the fluctuations of prices have been so violent that Aroostook farmers were commonly said to ride in Rolls Royces one year and go barefoot the next. A big national crop would send prices down, often to disastrous levels. In 1934, for instance, when potatoes sold at an average of fifty-five cents a barrel, Aroostook growers lost heavily. On the other hand, in 1925, when Aroostook had a good crop but the crops over the rest of the country were very poor, Aroostook had the wildest boom year it ever knew. Potatoes went to ten dollars a barrel, and everybody got rich. One farmer, with about 100 acres in potatoes, sold just enough of them at the early-season prices to pay his bills, and held the rest for the killing. He still had 10,000 barrels when the price hit ten dollars, making a clear profit of $100,-000. He built a new house with six baths, and a big barn, and began planting more potatoes. A few years later he lost everything and had to go to work as a hired hand. It is a story that has been repeated, with varying details, many times in Aroostook; though many shrewder men are able to hang on to their fortunes, making it one of the wealthiest farming counties in the country.

Unlike farmers of the philosophic Ed Allen school, who try to make the soil provide directly for as many of their wants as possible, most Aroostook farmers stand or fall on their potatoes. The county grows some grain, has recently grown enough peas to keep a freezing plant supplied, and some farmers vary their farm programs by raising livestock; but the more typical Aroostook farmer likes to be free to go to Florida in the winter if he feels like it—and if it is one of the years when he can afford it. Aroostook is the northernmost county in the state, jutting well up into Canada, so this craving for warmer climes in winter is, perhaps, understandable. Temperatures of twenty below are commonplace, and snow that fails to reach second-story windows is considered trifling by Aroostook veterans. Two thirds of Aroostook is still in the Big Woods, and logging and pulp operations along the St. John River constitute an important industry, but otherwise even the industry of the county is based on the potato: canning plants, starch mills and a distillery making potato alcohol, which has recently started producing gin and, of all things, a State-of-Maine vodka.

Elsewhere in Maine, dairying, poultry raising and apple orchards account for a large part of the farm income. These are types of farming which require little extensive cultivation of the soil. The Maine landscape is checkered with picturesque stone walls built by earlier generations of farmers who laboriously dug the rocks out of the earth to make cultivation possible, but modern Maine farmers find it more practical to do their farming on a sod basis, and let the cultivated crops be grown somewhere else. Ed Allen used to like to pick up odd-shaped rocks in his fields, and he had one, shaped like a human heart, which he called Pharaoh's heart, and which he showed visitors as proof that his farm was "the original Eden Spot." Such romanticizing of the rocks on Maine hill farms is hardly usual, however, and the more common attitude is one of resignation, as expressed by another Maine farmer, possibly apocryphal, who was asked by a summer visitor how there happened to be so many rocks on his farm. "Glacier brought 'em," he said. What was he going to do about it? the summer visitor asked. "Wait for another glacier to take 'em away again," he said.

Maine soil is by no means all rocky, but some of it is worse, and the thrifty stubbornness of State-of-Mainers keeps some of the most unlikely soil producing. Years ago, great fires swept some of the coastal counties, in the wake of lumbering operations, reducing large areas to barrens. The only thing edible the thin, acid soil would grow with any success was blueberries, which came in wild, and the picking of blueberries became a major means of livelihood for people in the area. Every few years they would burn part of the barrens over again, as the simplest way to prune the bushes and get rid of other growth, and the blueberries would come back as thick as ever. Presently a Yankee entrepreneur built a blueberry-canning plant, and others followed. Today there are seventeen, and Washington County leads the world in blueberry production, and, with two or three other Maine coastal counties, supplies the country with virtually all its canned blueberries and a large proportion of its fresh and frozen ones.

In a good year, the barrens may produce over three million dollars' worth of blueberries. The blueberry farmers still burn over portions of the land every three years, and, at harvest time, rake in the berries, literally, with specially designed wooden rakes. The canners admit that, until they perfected their machinery and equipment in recent years, the popularity of their product was considerably affected by the inclusion in the cans of leaves and sticks that had been raked in with the berries—everything, according to a common saying, "from cordwood to Christmas trees." This hardly constitutes full-time work, and since general agriculture is still unrewarding on the barrens, the blueberry growers have plenty of time, during the year, to exercise other talents. That may be one reason why sometimes more deer are shot in Washington County than in any other county in the state. Summer visitors help to provide seasonal work and income, and one blueberry grower in Columbia Falls, who also runs a summer hotel, rounds out his year as principal and (half the faculty) of the local high school. Obviously such opportunities are limited, but what with wood to be cut, boats to be built, and other odd jobs, State-of-Mainers are seldom idle, even on the barrens.

Most Maine farms, having been carved out of the woods in the first place, are still more or less wooded. About half the total farm acreage of the state is in woodlots; and cutting wood in winter is a conventional farm operation. Many farms and many rural villages off the main lines of transportation rely on wood for fuel, and a big pile of wood beside a one-room schoolhouse is still a common sight on country roads (to the chagrin, it may be said, of state educational officials, whose efforts to persuade Maine communities to consolidate their schools make little headway against the Yankee determination to hold on to what they already have, even if it is a poor thing). Most of the farm-cut wood, however, is sold for lumber or pulp, and provides a substantial part of farm income. Maine farmers also harvest a considerable quantity of maple sap for syrup and sugar, though some is suspected of finding its way to Vermont, which has a bigger reputation for this product, and whose labels accordingly command a better market.

If Maine contributes its bit to the Vermont maple-syrup output, it can be safely assumed, though it is a very hush-hush matter in Maine, that Canada similarly contributes to the volume of Maine lobsters supplied to the nation. Such Canadian lobsters as go to market through Maine shippers, and thus masquerade as Maine lobsters, are, in any case, the same kind of lobsters, *Homarus americanus*. The unforgivable sin, as Maine lobstermen see it, is to sell crawfish as lobster, as is done in Florida and California. The sale of crawfish from Africa in the state, in fact, has been forbidden by law, and may be punished by a fine of as much as $1000.

Even without benefit of Canadian assistance, Maine lobstermen catch eight of every ten lobsters taken in this country (always bearing in mind that the only real lobster is *Homarus americanus*), and this does not include any of illegal size that may get eaten without passing through the regular channels of trade. Under Maine law, only lobsters measuring no less than $3\frac{1}{16}$ and no more than 5 inches from the rear of the eye socket to the end of the body shell may be kept, on the theory that the short ones should be left to mature and the big ones to breed, and the restrictions are reasonably well respected. It requires considerable strength of will, however, for a State-of-Mainer to part with a perfectly good lobster merely because it happens to be a fraction of an inch too short or too long. The story is told of two Bailey Island lobstermen who worked their traps together, one hauling, the other measuring, with a firm understanding that whenever the one who was measuring found an illegal lobster, he automatically forfeited his whole share for the day. The story illustrates the reluctance of many lobstermen to take their measuring sticks too literally, and it is no secret that many of their families and neighbors find short lobsters both succulent and nourishing.

The lobstermen tend to be extremely independent-minded citizens, even for the State of Maine. Efforts to organize them into cooperatives have invariably failed. "I guess I'll sell my own lobsters," one man told an organizer, "and sell 'em to anybody I please, or give 'em away if I have a mind to." When prices dropped one fall, however, so many of them took their guns and went hunting that it had the effect of an organized strike—an action which, by that name, they would never have considered. During the war, when prices soared, some lobstermen made as much as $20,000 a year, though poor seasons may find them barely making a living. "I always guess wrong," moaned one lobsterman who quit just before the war and took a job in a sea-moss plant. "I've done it ever since I was twenty-one, and decided to be a Democrat."

The pride of State-of-Mainers in their possessions is seldom expressed in direct boasts, but nevertheless displays itself unmistakably, and the state's pre-eminence in the lobster business provides a good example of this quirk of character. Most Maine people like to believe that the Maine lobster is the best in the world, but they instinctively shy away from the extravagance of such a bald statement. Instead, they talk at great length about whether Maine lobster is better boiled, broiled or in a stew, just how it is best prepared in each case, and how to eat it. The Brunswick *Record* recently recommended lobster stew for breakfast, asserting, "we can think of nothing tastier on a subzero morning," while dismissing lobster Newburg, thermidor and even broiled-live as "effete and tasteless versions." Directions for eating lobsters (boiled-live) have been given as follows:

1. Twist off the claws.
2. Crack each claw with a rock, or what have you.
3. Separate the tailpiece and break off the flippers.
4. Insert a fork where the flippers broke off, and push.
5. Unhinge the back from the body, and eat the green parts.
6. Suck the small claws, drawing out the meat like sipping cider with a straw.

Clam chowder is another dish which gives State-of-Mainers an opportunity to boast, by indirection, about their sea-food resources. Maine clam chowder is made invariably with milk, and the watery Manhattan version, using tomatoes, is universally scorned as a glorified vegetable soup, probably so made because of the inferiority of non-Maine clams. Some years ago a member of the State Legislature drew up a bill forbidding the manufacture or sale, as clam chowder, of any concoction with tomatoes or other vegetables in it, and specifying as a penalty that the offender should be forced to dig a barrel of clams at high tide. The bill, though never formally introduced, was given wide publicity, which the author of the bill, with Yankee cunning, no doubt anticipated. Several canners, just at that time, had an oversupply of Maine clam chowder which they were anxious to move.

Maine clam diggers are as characterful as its lobstermen, and have shared with them the prosperity of peak prices. A good clam digger can get from two and a half to three barrels of clams a day, and the prices have fluctuated from a low of about a dollar and a quarter a barrel to sixteen and, at one time, even twenty dollars.

Nearly half of all the fish landed by Maine fishermen are herring, which are canned as sardines. Eastport (incidentally, the eastern-most city in the United States) is the center of this industry, and has been periodically rich and poor for many years, as Maine sardines have had good and poor markets. During the war the Maine canners both increased their output and took the opportunity to move into a higher-quality field previously more or less monopolized by the for-eign packers. The bulk of the Maine output used to be a cheaper product, usually packed in cottonseed oil, tomato sauce or mustard; and one of the lowest points in the industry's history came when National Prohibition cut off a major market by putting an end to free-lunch counters at bars. It was at a meeting of the packers during this period that the late Chief Justice William R. Pattangall, a man whose dry, sarcastic wit so pleased State-of-Mainers that he has taken rank with their favorite legendary characters, indirectly offered the advice which the packers have since taken. After listening to much moaning about the way Prohibition had ruined their business, and to many expressions of helplessness in meeting the situation, the judge arose and remarked, modestly, that he had little knowledge of the business, but that one question had occurred to him. "I have just been wondering," he said, "if any of you gentlemen ever thought of packing a sardine a man could eat when he was sober."

Whoever eats sardines, State-of-Mainers eat a lot of fish chowder, and are as didactic about it as they are about clam chowder or lob-sters. Most connoisseurs specify haddock as the proper fish to use, and Maine fishermen take large quantities of this fish from the ocean, as well as even more cod and substantial quantities of other varieties. Yet the fish that ranks next to herring in total poundage taken, and even exceeds herring in dollar value to the fishermen, is one that State-of-Mainers practically never eat: rosefish. Just as most Maine inlanders refuse to eat the common yellow perch, which insists on getting caught in most of the lakes and which summer visitors usually eat with relish, Maine coastal people have long been prejudiced against the redfish, as they prefer to call it, and fishermen always used to throw it out with skates and other trash fish until it was discovered that the fish had a ready market in other parts of the country. It is, in fact, one of the five leading fish in national sales, and the only one of the five that is taken in New England waters; but the Maine coast attitude is still as expressed recently by a Portland fisherman: "I'll catch them and take the money, but you couldn't pay me to eat one of those things."

The largest fish commonly taken off the Maine coast, tuna, are of minor importance among the state's commercial fish, but many fishermen have discovered that by fitting out their boats for the accommodation of summer visitors eager for big game, they can make more money than by taking the tuna themselves. Accordingly, a number of fishing skippers at Bailey Island, Boothbay Harbor, Portland, Ogunquit, York Harbor and Kennebunkport have embraced the Vacationland idea, and equipped their boats, as the state's official publicity puts it, "with every convenience for the comfort and enjoyment of their patrons." This includes a fishing chair and tackle for sportsmen who want to try for quarter-ton fish with rod and reel, a procedure which seems slightly insane to the average commercial fisherman.

This big-game fishing is a development of the last few years in Maine waters, and few State-of-Mainers have yet become addicted to it, yet fishing and hunting are the state's favorite sports. One year, for instance, the resident fishing and hunting licenses issued amounted to one for approximately every five men, women and children in the state, despite the fact that veterans got permits free and no license was required for anybody under sixteen. Without counting the veterans or the youngsters, this adds up to more than three times as many State-of-Maine hunters and fishermen as those coming in from other states, and would seem to indicate that most adult males went fishing, hunting or both sometime during the season. They usually do.

Fishing along the coast is mostly a matter of dangling a line from a dock for cunners and flounders or deep-sea fishing with a hand line for cod and haddock, though some fishermen go after pollack and mackerel with rod and reel, and striped bass are taken in some Maine waters. The seagoing fish that most stimulates Maine's pride of possession, however, is the Atlantic salmon, a great game fish which visited many rivers on the eastern seaboard to spawn a half century ago, but which has been so discouraged by obstructions and pollution elsewhere that Maine now has the only rivers in the country where it can be caught. One of these is the Narraguagus, which is a boon to the old town of Cherryfield; another is the Dennys, way down East; but it is the Penobscot, one of the state's largest rivers, which provides the occasion for a typical Maine indirect boast every year about its pre-eminence in this respect. A pool at the head of tidewater in the Penobscot, lying within the city limits of Bangor, has been designated the Bangor Salmon Pool, and the first fish taken out of it every spring is sent ceremoniously to the President.

There are fish of some kind in virtually all of the state's many lakes and streams; and fishing, both by natives and by visitors, runs the gamut from the bamboo-pole variety to the highest rites of the fly rod. The Big Woods still have waters that have never been fished at all, because of their inaccessibility, though a few ardent sportsmen have flown in, with pontoons on their planes, in recent years, and come out with tall tales of the big ones to be caught there. Most of the state's other waters have been fished, some of them intensively, for years; but the Inland Fisheries and Game Department restocks them every year with more fish than are taken out. Landlocked salmon in the lakes and square-tailed brook trout in the streams are the favorites of most serious anglers, but black bass, lake trout (usually called togue in Maine) and white perch are also widely distributed, while pickerel and the ubiquitous yellow perch usually assure the smallest and most inexpert fisherman something to catch. The state has also introduced a number of non-Maine fish to its waters, such as chinook salmon, brown trout and rainbow trout, though the average State-of-Maine fisherman finds it difficult to grant them equality with Maine's own landlocked salmon and squaretails.

Approximately four out-of-state visitors get fishing licenses in Maine in an average year to every one who gets a hunting license, probably because the fishing season runs through the summer vacation period, but more resident State-of-Mainers go hunting than go fishing—or, at least, take out licenses for the purpose. They start in October, shooting partridge, woodcock and ducks; hunt deer during the open season, which starts on October twenty-first in some counties, on November first in others; go coon hunting until the middle of

December, fox hunting until the middle of February, and shoot bears and bobcats whenever they can find any to shoot. Deer hunting is a major preoccupation throughout the state. One year recently deer were shot in nearly every town in the state—though it is *not* true moose roam constantly in the streets of Maine cities—even within the geographical limits of most of the cities: seven in Lewiston, for example, twenty-eight in Bangor, and 248 in Ellsworth, which has more woods than city proper. The total for the state was 32,000 deer.

Incidentally, there is some slight justification for the moose stories. Moose have been increasing in numbers in the state for several years, and they do occasionally stumble into a town or city, but, this is usually because they are sick and know no better. Few realize this, however, and the appearance of a moose always creates excitement, and usually gets into the newspapers. State-of-Mainers nevertheless pooh-pooh all stories of moose attacking human beings.

There is no open season on moose in Maine, though several are killed every year by being struck at night by automobiles and, more particularly, trains, in the headlights of which they stand transfixed. Experts know approximately where the moose herds are at any given time of year, and when they will change from one feeding ground to another. Signs are put up to protect them, like one on U. S. Route 1, near Waldoboro: CAREFUL—MOOSE CROSSING. Bears have also been increasing in recent years, and the state now pays a bounty of ten dollars on every bear killed in municipal or state-sponsored territory, such as cities, towns, townships, and plantations. Bears kill some sheep and game, break down apple trees in trying to get at the apples, and are general nuisances.

The typical Maine sports camp, at which many visiting fishermen and hunters stay, is a rustic hotel with a central dining hall and detached cabins for parties. Camps of this sort are scattered over the state, in the various regions where fishing and hunting are major attractions. Usually available are guides who will act as boat-rowers, camp-pitchers, outdoor cooks, storytellers and, if desired, instructors or coaches, but who, like most State-of-Mainers, take their own equality for granted, and are unlikely to engage themselves a second time to anyone who takes an employer-servant attitude toward them. Many a Maine guide has rowed clients back to shore and left them when he found them trying to order him around too loftily. They know their own superiority in their own field and way of life, and see no reason to be awed by a client's superiority in some other.

Many sportsmen become so attached to particular guides, once the man-to-man basis is established, and so addicted to their conversation, that they go on hiring them year after year, even if they do not particularly need their professional help. Old Man Farnham, for many years a famous Belgrade Lakes guide, used to have a regular client with whom he almost invariably got into a shouting argument as soon as they began to fish, either as to the lure to be used or some other fishing technicality. After some mutual bellowing, they usually settled down and fished all day without speaking to each other again; and when they came in at night, they both usually vowed they would never go out together again. The next day they would start all over again, and the next season.

Supplying sportsmen is a major Maine business in itself, and hardware stores and general stores all over the state, and even some drugstores and grocery stores stock sportsmen's supplies. There are also many specialized sporting-goods stores, and it is not at all unusual for a log cabin in a town of two thousand population or less to have a stock of rods, reels, rifles and gear rivaling the big-city stores. The log cabins are modern, and therefore somewhat phony, but the proprietor is usually so genuine an expert and enthusiast that he spends a considerable amount of time practicing what he preaches, and can stand storekeeping only because it gives him an opportunity to be surrounded by his favorite articles. L. L. Bean, the mail-order sporting-goods tycoon of Freeport, has made a fortune out of his ability to communicate his enthusiasm for the things he sells; and several others, in recent years, have moved into the mail-order field. Some, like the D. T. Sanders & Son Company of Greenville, on Moosehead Lake, which started as a general store in 1857, make a point of supplying not only sporting equipment, in the narrower sense, but everything people might need on a fishing, hunting or camping expedition. They engage guides, rent cottages, plan trips, and see that the cottages of their regular customers are stocked with wood during the winter, and cleaned up for occupancy in the spring.

One authoritative estimate places the annual volume of sporting-goods sales in Maine at $10,000,000. In addition, Maine manufactures many of the goods sold. Old Town canoes and Bass moccasins, for instance, are well-known trade names. An example of the way the interests, aptitudes and opportunities of State-of-Mainers have coincided to develop this field is the town of Norway, which turns out, in a factory, more snowshoes than any other town in the world. What modern industrialists like to call the know-how came from hand craftsmen to whom the knack of making snowshoes had been passed down by earlier generations to whom snowshoes were a necessity. One such Norway craftsman of a generation ago was Mellie Dunham, a white-whiskered old State-of-Mainer who made snowshoes during the long winter months on his farm on Crockett Ridge. During the course of a lifetime of snowshoe making, Mellie's talents became so well recognized by explorers like Peary that they had him make the snowshoes for their expeditions. Incidentally, Mellie was also a fiddler, and toward the end of his life was proclaimed by the late Henry Ford, after a contest, as the champion old-fashioned fiddler of the country. This brought him much publicity and a brief vaudeville contract. It also brought a comment, not too inaccurate, on the vagaries of modern publicity from one of his neighbors: "Mellie's the best damn snowshoe maker in the world, and there don't hardly anybody know it; but now the newspapers have made him famous as a fiddler, and he can't fiddle for sour apples."

Artists and writers have been discovering Maine for years, and it is a poor literary season when less than a couple of dozen books glorify the woods, the coast and the rocky hills. To the average State-of-Mainer, these gifts are just part of the everyday scene, like the Empire State Building to a New Yorker, yet they have their effect on the naturally philosophical, and most Maine towns have their village characters who roam the woods or beaches communing with Nature. One such character once startled a summer visitor, whom he met on a hillside clearing, by opening and closing a conversation with the following words: "That mountain over there don't give a damn for you or me."

A somewhat more orthodox State-of-Mainer who has been deeply impressed by the state's natural grandeur is former Governor Percival P. Baxter of Portland, who has devoted most of his life, since retiring from the governorship in 1925, to buying up, with his personal fortune, the whole wild area of Mount Katahdin and its surrounding mountains—an area of some 150 square miles—in order to present it to the state, to "forever be left," as his deed of gift specifies, "in its natural wild state, forever be kept as a sanctuary for wild beasts and birds, and forever be used for public forest, public park and public recreational purposes." Mr. Baxter is a thrifty Yankee, who is proud of the fact that he put a gift of eighty dollars in the bank at the age of seven and watched it grow to $583 in fifty years. He is also a bachelor, with no immediate family to inherit a fortune which has similarly grown since it was left to him; and he conceived the Katahdin project as a way to save for the state a legacy which he was afraid might be squandered.

Climbing Katahdin is a rigorous sport, but many do it every year. The wildness of the terrain is indicated by the fact that when an eleven-year-old Rye, New York, lad, Donn Fendler, got separated from a mountain-climbing party near the summit, several years ago, searching parties were unable to find him, and it was only because he made use of his Boy Scout training, lived on berries, and kept moving for eight days, following a stream, until he finally came to a sports camp, that he survived.

More than 200 boys' and girls' camps in Maine initiate youngsters into the wilderness life, but most of them are in the tamer wildernesses. Many of the older boys and girls are taken on canoe trips down the Allagash, a rugged, 150-mile excursion through the Big Woods, or are otherwise given a sampling of the real wilds; while younger ones may, as in one Maine camp, be safely supervised in an outdoor "Pooh Corner." Very few State-of-Maine boys and girls are deemed by their parents to need such organized camping experience.

The gratifying income from the summer recreational business has whetted the appetite for more, and some efforts have been made, in recent years, to add winter sports to the state's attractions. The distance and the lack of direct transportation from principal out-of-state cities to the points most favorable for such development have kept the number of winter resorts limited, but the promotional agencies of the state are now urging people to come to Maine for winter vacations. To travel from Boston, say, all the way into the interior of Maine just for a day, or even a week end, of skiing, would seem an unreasonable extravagance to the average State-of-Mainer, and he would much prefer to deal with people who planned to stay long enough to get their money's worth.

State-of-Mainers tend to disapprove of people who seem to them, in the Yankee phrase, to have more money than brains, and some people get the impression that they dislike all outsiders. This is erroneous, except for the occasional misanthrope who appears in any society. What makes it difficult for a State-of-Mainer to judge the common sense of a visitor fairly, however, is the weight he subconsciously gives to the obvious fact that the visitor chooses to live, during a large part of the year, somewhere else than in the State of Maine. "How did you like the city?" a friend asked a Maine outdoorsman, just back from the Sportsmen's Show in Boston. The traveler shook his head disparagingly. "You can't see nothing but houses," he said. "Beats me how anybody can live in a place like that."

# New Hampshire

## by DONALD WAYNE

Some people insist you can tell the difference as soon as you cross the state line. This—and people say it about other states—is purely a mystical notion, because the country looks at first exactly the same as that you left in Vermont or Maine or Northern Massachusetts, but before long you know you're in New Hampshire, and you know that it's different.

It isn't simply that you've seen the "Old Man of the Mountains" in Franconia Notch, or the colonial houses of Portsmouth, or smelled the Berlin pulp mills. There's something else. New Hampshire is a sort of effulgence. There's a reason why more poetry has been inspired by this little Yankee state than any other: why New Hampshire can't always be counted on to vote Republican; why the devil was afraid to come back after Daniel Webster kicked him out. Don't ask me what it is; it's partly scrutable, partly something in the air.

Think of New Hampshire as a slab of northern granite shaped like a sitting bunny, its ears pointed into Canada a little way, about 180 miles long and half as wide across the paunch. It is nearly landlocked, but it clings to a small pucker of seacoast in the southeast corner—the place where it was born. Yet New Hampshire is the highland "mother" of at least five important Yankee rivers, has 1300 lakes and fishing ponds, and its White Mountains bulking across the upper part of the state are the tallest, loveliest and most storied mountains of the U.S. Northeast.

All this plus superb summer climate foreordained New Hampshire's pre-eminence as a resort state. At Wolfeboro they show you the site where the colonial governor John Wentworth built the first summer home in America, in 1768. The modern tourist was born when F. O. Stanley, inventor of the Stanley Steamer, drove one of his contraptions up the carriage road to the top of Mt. Washington in 1899. Today summer visitors, counted in the millions, add up to New Hampshire's second industry, smaller in dollar volume than the industries making shoes, textiles and wood products, but bigger than farming. In human volume recreation is biggest, for the visitors, at the season's end, have outnumbered New Hampshire's 590,000 population by something like four to one.

When you cross from Massachusetts into New Hampshire you're in the New England "upcountry," a significant word, for its implications are as social as they are geographical. Locally, a New Hampshire Yankee goes "upcountry" for the good hunting and fishing, and when he says "downcountry" he may mean New England as far south as Boston. But New Hampshire itself is all "upcountry"—closer, that is, to its Yankee origins. It has the look of the frontier as the frontier must have been in colonial days. Of course the Indians and forts are gone, and descendants of the French have trickled back from Canada to work in the northern logging camps and the factories of Manchester, Nashua and Laconia. (These cities, as a matter of fact, have an average 50 per cent French-Canadian population.) There is also nothing frontierlike about Wilder Dam on the Connecticut River below Hanover, or the Rockingham Park race track. But the New Hampshire countryside is raw; it looks untamed. It looks old—not only in the colonial-looking Yankee towns but in the thickly wooded hills and vales where the green is a lush, fast-growing green. You tramp through the woods and come upon some small, forgotten graveyard among the trees, or stub your toe on some chimney remnant near the traces of an obliterated wagon path, and you wonder about these people and how long it took for the earth to wipe them out.

You part the weeds to read the names on the weathered stones, and the chances are a hundred to one you'll find the same names on nearby rural mailboxes. Yankees are a stubborn, imperishable people.

Concord, the state capital, is the crossroad of New Hampshire's paunch, lying spang in the Merrimack Valley, about as central to things as a capital can be. It is a gray little city of granite govern-

ment buildings and elm-shaded streets, austere and bleak even in
the August sun. The first thing to be cleared up about Concord, for
the edification of muddled tourists, is that it hasn't any "rude bridge"
where minutemen fired the opening shots of the Revolution. That
Concord is in Massachusetts. "But," a member of the State Planning
Commission told me, "it was here that the United States was tech-
nically created. New Hampshire was the ninth state to ratify the
Constitution, and that was the deciding vote." The date was 1788.

Spending the day in New Hampshire's capital I had a ramble
through the Statehouse, which drowsed in echoes and summer torpor.
The Statehouse, a bleak pile of Concord granite with a green dome,
has been classed with America's ugliest state capitols, an effect of
mood, I think, rather than architecture. It has seen a lot of Yankee
weather and maybe a surfeit of governors and legislatures. It is a
tired-looking Statehouse, not an ugly one. This fatigue may also be
due to gross weight, for New Hampshire has the largest state legislature in the United States—a General Court, as it is called, of about
400 lawmakers, or roughly one for every 1300 people.

If New Hampshire has progressive ideas about the world—and they
tell you it has—it hates to make internal changes. (Not until 1950,
for example, did the voters get around to changing the official legal
tender from pounds and shillings to dollars and cents, and scrapping
its militia—that is, its minutemen. And don't get the idea the vote
was unanimous!) The way representatives are chosen is by towns,
according to a population denominator. This system was smooth and
ultrademocratic back in 1784 when it was adopted, but New Hampshire has since had to remodel the Statehouse twice to accommodate the growing legislature.

A lot of New Hampshire's history centered on Concord, which has
been the capital since 1782. The character of this history is reflected
in the four bronze statues on the Statehouse green: there's the Revolutionary soldier-blacksmith, General John Stark, who beat the Hessians at Bennington; there's Daniel Webster; and Franklin Pierce,
who was New Hampshire's only President (and a Democrat); and
John P. Hale, whose main distinction was that he was the first U. S.
Senator to oppose slavery. If they suggest a theme, it is a Yankee
single-mindedness.

"Just don't say John Stark was an 'obscure Revolutionary patriot,' "
I was warned. "A writer used that phrase in a national magazine

once, and if he is ever caught in New Hampshire some uncontrollable
elements will give him the ducking stool. You can't say that about
John Stark."

You learn before you leave Concord that this is where Mary Baker
Eddy, who was born at nearby Bow, founded Christian Science,
though in the mode of the times she established the Mother Church
at Boston. You also see the name Rumford around town, a name
fancied by business establishments. (The Rumford Press, for instance, is one of New England's biggest printing houses.) Rumford
was an early name for Concord when it belonged to Massachusetts—
and it tells the famous story of a Yankee count.

Benjamin Thompson was a farmer's son who came up from Massachusetts as Concord's schoolteacher. He was a dashing, brilliant
young man with aristocratic fancies. In a short time he wooed and
won Concord's wealthiest lady, the widow of Colonel Benjamin Rolfe,
and plunged into the high life of Tory society. When the Revolution
broke out he left his wife and hied himself with his royalist friends
to England, where George III gave him a knighthood. He became
a celebrity of European courts, a famous inventor and physicist, the
Bavarian minister of war, and finally a count in the Holy Roman Empire.

"What title do you choose?" he was asked.

Thompson thought back to his beginnings, his Concord days.
"Count Rumford," he replied.

And Count Rumford it was. Thompson never came back to America, though he founded a Rumford professorship at Harvard. His
daughter Sarah rode the streets of Concord a bona fide New Hampshire countess, and when she died a Yankee stonecutter carved the
title on her tombstone. For many years the Rolfe-Rumford house on
Hall Street has been used as an orphan home for girls.

North of Concord on the Daniel Webster Highway, as Route 3 is
called, you soon emerge into open resort country, the so-called lakes
region, and directly north of that are the White Mountains. A good
starting point for touring either area is the town of Plymouth, which I
reached on a rainy Sunday afternoon, only a couple of hours from
Concord. Plymouth's hotel, perched on a hilly street above the business section, is the Pemigewasset House, a rather grandiose re-
minder of a bygone tourist era.

New Hampshire has a bevy of famous old hotels that find it tough
competing these days with motels and auto courts; but they manage

somehow to maintain an air of pedigree. I was moderately disillusioned to learn that this "Pemi" House is not the original where Nathaniel Hawthorne, that inveterate New Hampshire tourist, died, but a later edition, the old one having burned down about sixty years ago. The room clerk was almost apologetic about it; but from the pictures I decided this second "Pemi" House to be much more attractive and comfortable. The morning was clear and lovely, and before nine o'clock I was headed north into the White Mountain National Forest.

Touring the White Mountains is largely a tour of the White Mountain National Forest, a 700,000-acre scenic and recreational demesne that spreads over the greater part of the mountains, spilling briefly into Maine. You follow a serpentine route roughly in the shape of the letter *N*, passing in turn through the three popular notches—Franconia, Crawford and Pinkham—then looping up through the North Country where the hills fall away toward Canada.

I timed myself to get to Franconia Notch in the afternoon. In Yankee mountains a notch is simply a pass or gap, and here jutting from the steep cliffside of Profile (i.e., Cannon) Mountain is New Hampshire's famous landmark—the "Old Man of the Mountains." The afternoon sun, dipping behind the mountain, throws the face into perfect relief, and from the little clearing on the shore of Profile Lake you look up and remember Hawthorne's schoolbook classic *The Great Stone Face.* This is it. I looked up and made a discovery. The Old Man has an Adam's apple. Now, I don't claim to be the first to see such a self-evident detail, but nobody, as far as I know, has bothered to mention it before. The Adam's apple simply gives the Profile its startling verisimilitude, and just to be sure I wasn't imagining things I checked it with a man standing next to me. "Looks a little low," he said. "Could be a goiter."

The face, 1200 feet high above Profile Lake (referred to as the "Old Man's Washbowl"), is a miniature cameo to the naked eye, but I dropped a coin into one of the binocular machines in the arena, which blew him up to postcard size. The Adam's apple was still there.

The Profile was discovered in 1805 when a pair of road surveyors washing in the lake looked up toward the setting sun and thought they saw the image of Thomas Jefferson, who was then President. Since that time the Old Man has been identified with an interesting genealogy of resemblances, most persistent of which are Uncle Sam, Ernest (the hero of Hawthorne's story), and of course Jesus Christ.

The religious note, always strong in New England, inspired the majority of fancies. When Daniel Webster, with his flair for dedicating whatever he laid his eyes on, saw the Profile he called it God's shingle hung out in the hills of New Hampshire to show that His trade is making men.

In Franconia Notch, which is run as a 6000-acre park, you visit the Flume, an incredibly lovely gorge in the woods near the base of Mt. Liberty; or ride to the top of Cannon Mountain via the aerial tramway—one of the numerous ski lifts doing double duty for summer tourists. In this neighborhood there's an interesting side trip to Lost River, where I spent a morning going through caverns and rocky slots with such fanciful names as the Judgment Hall of Pluto, the Cave of Lost Souls, the Human Sandwich and the Guillotine. Lost River lies in beautiful mountain scenery between Mt. Moosilauke and Kinsman Notch, and after the gorge tour the head guide, and the director of the reservation, told me about the Society for the Protection of New Hampshire Forests, which owns and operates the place.

The SPNHF saved the White Mountains. Fifty years ago, when it was founded, private owners were lumbering the hills to death, and it was mainly through the fight led by the Society that the land was bought and set up as a National Forest in 1911. Not all the hills could be included in the purchase, however (the White Mountains are still a hotchpotch of private and public properties), and in 1925 the Society waged a "buy a tree" campaign to save Franconia Notch from being reduced to slash.

The policy of the SPNHF has been to aid, not to keep. It bought, developed and then turned over to the state such valuable and scenic areas as Crawford Notch, Mt. Sunapee and Mt. Kearsarge— all parks now—and will probably in time turn over Lost River and the piece it owns today of Grand Monadnock, a mountain in the southern part of the state.

The day was lovely and I paused for a look northward at Kinsman Notch. A party of "goofers" (as tourists are called) shambled in bright shirts and summer prints along the gravel path toward the Bear Crawl, the Elysian Land, the Center of the Earth. "Before we start down the gorge," the green-shirted guide said, "it might be a good idea to check your cameras, loose change, car keys, or anything that might fall out of your pockets. This is an absolutely safe tour, but . . ."

The Willey Slide is a famous bit of mountain history you come across in Crawford Notch. Landslides are occasional commotions of the White Mountains—you see old scars and fresh scars in every range in the hills—but you have to imagine the one on Mt. Willey.

A landslide is usually caused by a heavy, soaking rain after a long dry spell. Rocks, soil and trees tumble down with the rushing noise of an express train. The Willey family heard such a noise on a stormy August night in 1826. A huge hunk of mountain roared down toward their flimsy cabin. They rushed out—nine of them, including the children and two hired men—heading for a shelter down the Notch, but none of them made it. Some of the bodies were never found. The tragic irony was that a huge boulder above the cabin parted the slide into two streams and the cabin was untouched.

The irony so intrigued Hawthorne, who heard the story one night at the old Crawford House, that he used the Willey Slide as the basis for *The Ambitious Guest,* a story in *Twice-Told Tales*. A state park has been created around the site.

Crawford Notch is part of Hart's Location, a town that has an odd tradition. On election day, Hart's Location is the first U.S. town to announce its returns. "Hart's Location, First in the Nation" is almost a political motto.

"It started accidentally about fifteen years ago," a local inn-keeper explained. "We had only a dozen voters in the town. Most of them worked for the railroad (the Maine Central) and were afraid of losing pay if they took time out to vote. So I said, why not meet at my house for a six o'clock breakfast and cast our ballots at the same time? Well, we did, and the newspapers picked it up and made a thing out of it." Hart's Location has been first ever since.

I stopped at Bretton Woods to drop in at the Mount Washington Hotel, a modern Xanadu impressively set against a backdrop of the Presidential Range. This is where the international money conference met in 1944 with Henry Morgenthau, Jr., representing the United States. The hotel, easily the most sumptuous and expensive summer caravansary in New England, struck me as rather flashy. "You'll see more mink and diamonds here on a Saturday night," said the manager, "than on opening night at the Met." I didn't stay for that. The scenery was really terrific, and from the porch, I contemplated the Presidential peaks with Mt. Washington's monarchial bulk rising above them all. It looked like a perfect day to visit the sum-

mit, and a half hour later I was buying a ticket at the base station of
Colonel Teague's cog railway east of Fabyan.

Mt. Washington, with an altitude of 6288 feet, is the highest peak
east of the Rockies and north of the Carolinas. To the Abnakis it was
the sacred mountain of Agiochook, the dwelling place of the Great
Spirit. One of their legends told how the great Chief Passaconaway
rose to heaven from its windy summit like Elijah, on a fiery sledge
drawn by wolves. They said the mountain twinkled from a "great
carbuncle." A man named Darby Field of Portsmouth thought this
might be diamonds, and in 1642 became the first man to climb the
White Mountains, a feat that has been called the beginning of outdoor recreation in America.

Today the mountains are threaded with over 1500 miles of climbing trails and shelters, huts and camps maintained by the U. S.
Forestry Service in collaboration with private organizations like the
Dartmouth Outing Club and the oldest and best known of all, the
Appalachian Mountain Club. The great Appalachian Trail, which
comes up from Georgia, crosses the White Mountains from Dartmouth's Mt. Moosilauke over into Maine; but that is a mere artery in
this large intricate pattern. You can visit National Forest camps like
the Dolly Copp, Campton Pond or Zealand—there are maybe a
dozen all together—and see where summer visitors pitch tents and
rough it in the great outdoors.

These Great White Hills are mountain climbers' mountains. You
see the hiking fraternity all over the place, along the roads, in the
inns and taverns, and of course at favorite rendezvous like Gorham,
Franconia, and Pinkham Notch, headquarters of the Appalachian
Mountain Club.

What was the carbuncle? Hawthorne—bless the fellow—got out a
story about *that*, too, without explaining it. The phenomenon is supposed to be a trick of light (though I've yet to nail down an actual
eyewitness), the way the sunlight hits the snow or, more likely, the
sun glistening on the tumbling rivulets of Tuckerman Ravine.

You can drive to the summit of Mt. Washington on the auto toll
road from Glen House in Pinkham Notch, an eight-mile spiral of
successively wonderful mountain views, or go up, as I did, on the cog
railway. You are nudged three and a half miles up the steep slope
of the mountain and nudged down again, a round trip of about two
hours. I got rather used to it part way up the mountain and found it

created a certain lugubrious camaraderie in the car; something like being trapped in a fun house. The amusement-park effect is heightened by the toylike appearance of the locomotive, a pusher type with a slanted boiler (tilted so as to be horizontal on the mountainside); but the grime it threw in the windows was the real McCoy.

I was curious about the cog railway and later, talking to its vice-president and general manager, learned that it is one of the oldest and shortest and safest railroads in the world. (Also the most expensive, at something like sixty cents a mile.) It was invented by Sylvester Marsh, who let Swiss engineers copy it free of charge for the Alps. Old Peppersass, the original engine, made the first ascent to the summit in 1869, and the cog railway, except for intermissions during the two world wars, has been carrying passengers ever since. The railway's only serious accident involved Old Peppersass. In 1929, at the age of sixty, she was taken out of moth balls for a big celebration; she climbed the trestle in fine style. But on the way back something broke. The antiquated engine started down the trestle like a bat out of hell, jumping the track at the steepest grade, Jacob's Ladder, and killing the only man who failed to jump, a publicity photographer named Rossiter. Rossiter had his revenge. Old Peppersass was reassembled and is on display at the base station, evidently under a photographic curse. All day long tourists use it as a background for snapshots.

The summit of Mt. Washington was blanketed in fog, so I missed seeing the panorama that Barnum called the "second-greatest show on earth." On a clear day you look off, I am told, at a vista 130 miles in any direction. But you're on surer ground picking winners at Rockingham Park than gambling on Mt. Washington weather.

This is one of the world's stormiest mountains, and you hear about climbers who froze to death in the middle of summer or wandered lost in fogs and gales; you hear about the wind that blew 231 miles an hour in April, 1934—the biggest wind ever recorded. Mt. Washington has a weather of its own, which explains why I ran into fog. All the way up, the day was clear and lovely. On the rocky plateau of the mountaintop the wind blew the fog in swirls; and it was cold. Mt. Washington has a few buildings: a summer hotel called the Summit House or Mount Washington Club run by the cog-railway people, an Air Force icing-research station, and a weather observatory. The men in the observatory work for Harvard and the U. S. Weather Bureau and live on Mt. Washington all year round, which isn't so dull or lonely as it sounds. The boys tuned in their TV set and we watched half an inning of a Red Sox ball game. When I left, the Red Sox were up, one out and none on. They won, I heard later.

The North Country, as you leave the mountains, is New Hampshire's forest primeval. For long stretches in this lonely rolling country yours is the only car on the road. Occasionally a loaded lumber truck goes by headed south, and you pass log-cabin homes with the day's wash hanging out on the porch and the woodpile in the yard and the inevitable flower garden—I've never seen such flower-loving people as the New Hampshire Yankees—and all around is the great silent wilderness. Once I stopped to look across a valley at the rolling meadows backed by a great forest of hemlock and spruce and gleaming white birch. And across the valley from one of the farms drifted the clear, casual tones of a man's voice. I'm sure it came a good half mile. It doesn't seem the place for a man who wants to keep things to himself.

There aren't many places to visit here in upper Coos County unless you're a serious sportsman or an apprentice hermit. The Connecticut Lakes—First and Second in particular—are the finest fishing waters in the state, and if you're curious to see the source of New England's great river, the Connecticut, you climb to a small beaver-dammed tarn, called Fourth Connecticut Lake, almost touching the Canadian border, where the mighty stream that journeys all the way to Long Island Sound begins as a trickle in the reeds. You pause at Pittsburg, New Hampshire's northernmost settlement, a rugged frontier village where practically everyone in town is a guide and kids cut their teeth on venison and bear meat.

I stopped at the Balsams in Dixville Notch, a town-size luxury hotel where rumba lessons start right after breakfast and you play golf on top of a mountain. I will always love this hotel because the breakfast I had of steamed finnan haddie with eggs was a gustatory revelation I have since rejoiced in at home on alternate Sundays.

Coming down the Androscoggin, a river of floating logs, you hit Berlin (accent on the first syllable, to distinguish it from all other Berlins in the world). This is New Hampshire's wood-pulp metropolis where the Brown Paper Company each year transmutes hundreds of thousands of cords of wood into things like paper towels, playing cards, and wood fibers that go into a variety of industrial products. This is done in part by boiling, and when you boil trees you produce a stink that, on dank days, is strong enough to fell Paul Bunyan's blue ox.

"It's better than it used to be," natives say cheerfully, and at the Brown Company—which for a hundred years has meant Berlin—they wage unremitting chemical warfare against the whiff.

Coming back south through the mountains, this time down the Eastern Slope, you visit North Conway. The town is so full of summer people that if you see a native you're allowed to make a wish—a custom that used to apply to maidens gazing up at White Horse Cliff. A century ago North Conway supported a summer art colony that turned out some famous canvases—one hangs in Windsor Castle —but North Conway today is, in a manner of speaking, the town that Harvey Gibson built.

Gibson was a local boy who became a famous New York banker and came back to his old home town to end his days. But Gibson was a hard man to retire. Instead, he promoted North Conway into a bigtime skiing and summer-resort center.

You come down to the Ossipees, where the mountain country peters out and the lakes country begins to spread itself in a great belt across the state, but as long as you can see Chocorua it commands your attention. Chocorua, they say, was an Indian chief who, pursued to the top of the mountain, pronounced a curse on the white man before he leaped to his death. After that the cattle of surrounding farms mysteriously sickened and died and for generations people said it was Chocorua's curse—till scientists found it was a noxious element in the water, muriate of lime, that poisoned the cows. It still makes them sick, but farmers cure them today with a home remedy of soapsuds.

According to a precise friend of mine who used to teach Arthurian legend at Harvard and had been a summer resident of Chocorua since the '90's, the curse itself is a bald piece of fiction.

"Then there's no curse?" I said.

"My boy," he said, "do not despise legend. It is often a way of revealing truth. You know the story of the Holy Grail." He sat back and gazed thoughtfully at his favorite mountain. "Chocorua's curse is simply a demonstration of due respect."

New Hampshire has, incidentally, a kind of grail legend of its own that grew out of a notorious historical episode. In 1759 Rogers' Rangers went up to wipe out the St. Francis Indians in Canada—you may remember the episode in Kenneth Robert's *Northwest Passage* or the movie version with Spencer Tracy—to stop raids on the Vermont settlements (Vermont being then the divided property of New York and New Hampshire). Caught by surprise, the Indians were massacred, their village sacked, plundered and left a smoking ruin. Part of the loot the Rangers carried off was a pair of golden candlesticks and a silver statue of the Holy Mother, stripped from the Indian chapel.

The expedition, pursued and broken up into wandering parties, was one of the most ill-fated of the French and Indian Wars. Only a pitiful number, including the indomitable Major Rogers himself, survived the escape down the Connecticut Valley, and for years the people of upper Coos would come across skeletons of the lost men with wampum and silver buckles and other telltale evidences of their swag. Legend says the Rangers were so starved they ate their moccasins, powder horns and even their own dead—which one may reasonably doubt. Good woodsmen don't die of starvation; it was probably the cold and exhaustion that did them in.

In 1815 the golden candlesticks were found near Lake Memphremagog, but the silver statue vanished into the White Mountains. The nine men who had it in their possession were last heard of around Crawford Notch. Years afterward a hunter related a strange experience. He was caught in a storm on Mt. Adams. Suddenly, as if in a Bible tale, the storm parted and a vision rolled out of the mists. He saw a stone church and a candlelit chapel with Indians kneeling in prayer. Then, as the church faded, the Indians filed down the mountainside in a solemn procession led by the silver statue, which vanished into a ledge of rock. People say this ledge is where the miraculous statue (it is said to weigh about eight pounds) will probably be found some day—by a Parsifal, of course.

Lake Winnipesaukee, translated as the "Smile of the Great Spirit," has a mainland shore line of 183 miles. It has 274 islands that are big enough to hold summer estates, boating colonies and children's camps, and it is, as any local booster will tell you at the drop of a popcorn ball, one of the largest intrastate lakes in the United States.

You take the sixty-mile drive that circumscribes the lake, passing through relatively peaceful lakeside hamlets like Moultonborough and Alton Bay and Center Harbor with their sunny little docks and fishing cottages and summer inns; through Wolfeboro (named for the general who took Quebec from the French), the town that started as America's first summer resort—and finally you arrive at The Weirs. The Weirs, where the Indians of pre-tourist days laid their salmon nets, is a Sunday driver's heaven of cruise boats, outboard races, water carnivals, casino dances, parachute jumps, fishing contests and a bathing-beauty pageant whose winner is crowned Miss Winnipesaukee. Shutting my eyes to the honky-tonk (though I unbent to gorge myself on lobster rolls and taffy candy), I found the lake really very nice.

Endicott Rock, close to The Weirs on the channel leading into Paugus Bay, is a state park built around the marker of the old Massachusetts boundary. I found Winnipesaukee to have other interesting historic high lights. Guernsey Island, for instance, now shrill with the voices of boy campers, is where Guernsey cows were introduced into America in 1831, and where Harvard and Yale held their first crew race in 1852. Harvard won.

Speaking of Guernseys, you'll find the American Guernsey Club at Peterborough, organized, the man there told me, in 1877 and keeping file on 550,000 registered contemporary Guernseys. Oddly enough, Guernseys are not the favorites of New Hampshire farmers, who prefer Brown Swiss and Durham. Milk is New Hampshire's biggest farm product, and practically all of it goes to Boston.

Yankee soil never made anybody rich—it was the shipbuilders and rum sellers and slave traders and millowners and land-grabbing politicians who got rich—and you'll find many a New Hampshire farmer these days who gets up with the sun to milk his cows, drives to a factory for the seven o'clock shift and gets back around four-thirty to milk again and do the rest of his chores.

They don't get rich that way either, of course, and don't particularly care about it, because Yankees place a high premium on their independence and self-assertiveness. If you do run across a well-to-do New Hampshireman you'll rarely know it by the way he lives. He'll run his old car till the wheels wobble off and drop his fifteen cents (maybe a quarter nowadays) in the collection plate on Sundays, whittle his own fence posts and collect rusty nails in an old tobacco can; but he might have enough credit at the town bank to float a small war loan. They tell a fable about a frostbitten old native who lost all his friends. A stranger inquired why everybody had stopped talking to the old boy. "He dipped into his capital," was the indignant answer.

Newfound is often said to be a "picture-postcard" lake but I don't think it has anything on Squam and Winnisquam, which seemed to me livelier and more interesting. There are snooty summer colonies hidden among the trees, and the inevitable moppet charivari of the children's camps. Back in 1888 an avuncular genius named Ernest Balch, whose smile evidently emulated that of Winnipesaukee's Great Spirit, opened what many aver to be America's first children's camp on Squam's Chocorua Island. Today the lakes region abounds in more than 200 of them.

The Ossipee hills entertain the whiskered ghost of John Greenleaf Whittier, the Quaker poet who eulogized the Bear Camp country, though he traveled over and wrote much about the state. Like Hawthorne, Whittier died as a summer tourist—at Hampton Falls near the seacoast, in 1892. A town and a mountain in the Ossipees are called Whittier, New Hampshire's way, and a rare one it is among states, of returning a writer's compliment.

At Sunapee State Park, newest but one of New Hampshire's twenty-four state parks, I took the chairlift ride to a festive lobster-clambake on top of Mt. Sunapee.

Sunapee is a typical New Hampshire park, which is to say it amounts to a complete summer resort. There's an annex on the lake shore with a beach and boathouses, but the main part of the park sprawls at the foot of the gentle wooded mountain in a dell that used to be a rendezvous for Rogers' Rangers in the bloody Indian raids on the Connecticut Valley forts.

The park is beautifully kept, and the State Forestry and Recreation Department wisely lets park managers do things without interference.

Portsmouth, New Hampshire's once-great seaport and provincial capital, lives on two things: "The Yard" and memories of its opulent past. It is still a bustling little city and has such a compelling 18th Century atmosphere that I half expected along the neat, winding, lane-like streets to run into Wyseman Claggett, the King's Attorney, or the pretty barmaid Martha Hilton who scandalized society by snagging Governor Benning Wentworth for a husband.

Benning (whose name lives in a couple of Benningtons) was an amiable guy. He handed out grants till his plump arm ached, but always kept a little piece for himself—just in case the woods turned into real estate. You won't find many New Hampshire towns that don't bear some mark of the Wentworths (there were three of them governors), but Benning was an ardent patron of Dartmouth and cut the famous College Road up to Hanover to attend the first commencement. Sections of this road are now tourist highway.

Portsmouth hasn't worked seriously at being a seaport since the whaling industry petered out and Boston copped most of the maritime trade. But it's still a sea town. Bridges span the Piscataqua to the Portsmouth Navy Yard—which is actually in Kittery, Maine. The river mouth broadens out to sea, and you stroll along the harbor where fish-market smells pay court to the onetime mansions of merchant princes, shipbuilders and governors.

Portsmouth, whose Navy Yard now builds submarines, was building fighting ships during the Revolution. On Badger's Island in the river, Tobias Lear built the *Ranger* which John Paul Jones—flying a flag made of the gowns of Portsmouth's belles—sailed to France in 1777 with the news of Burgoyne's surrender. The Yard was the scene in 1905 of the historic Treaty of Portsmouth by which Teddy Roosevelt put an end to the Russo-Japanese War. The delegates, and the toothy Trustbuster himself, stayed at the huge genteel summer hotel at New Castle, the Wentworth-by-the-Sea, where I stayed myself as I toured the seacoast. The hotel is huger now and genteel enough to have entertained a recent Governors' Conference.

A ramble around Portsmouth is an 18th Century stroll (though the town goes much farther back—it was New Hampshire's first settlement in 1623) along streets with original cracked flagstones and narrow brick sidewalks and colonial doorways flush with the lane. Television antennas seem incongruous. The streets are dead quiet except for the sounds of boat horns in the morning fog. All the Historic Houses are in the general area of the harbor save for a couple that are over in Kittery.

These were the homes of early famous men, and I'm told that architects and designers come here to study them as examples of Georgian elegance. Today they are mostly kept up by such ministering guardians as the Colonial Dames and the Society for the Preservation of New England Antiquities.

You visit St. John's Church in Chapel Street, which claims to have one of the four American copies of the Vinegar Bible, and where "it is impossible," wrote Thomas Bailey Aldrich, "to walk anywhere (in the graveyard) without stepping on a governor." Aldrich, incidentally, was raised in his grandfather's house on Court Street—the

Nutter House of his *Story of a Bad Boy*—which is included among the Historic Houses. Aldrich is Portsmouth's literary figure. He came back in the 1880's and wrote his nostalgic ramble, *An Old Town by the Sea*, which ought to be required reading if you want to enjoy Portsmouth.

Bad weather killed my trip out to the Isles of Shoals, which are a group of tiny barren islands ten miles offshore and part of which belongs to Maine.

But I did hear some of the Shoalers' tales—about the pirate Philip Babb whose ghost walks at Babb's Cove (guarding a treasure, they say), and the famous murder at Smuttynose which the late Edmund Pearson, that eminent scholar of homicide, saw as a study in violence brought on by the sea.

Captain John Smith, browsing around the Yankee coast in 1614, discovered the reeflike islands and they were first called Smith's Isles. They have lent themselves to holy and devilish purposes. Successors to the pirates were the rumrunners of the '20's who hid out in the rocky and often fogbound coves. Today Star Island is the scene of Congregational and Unitarian-Universalist religious conferences. It is the only occupied island, the only one with a dock for the daily tourist steamers from Portsmouth.

New Hampshire's coastline is only eighteen miles long. From Portsmouth to Seabrook it extends in a stretch of rocky sea-sprayed coves and jetties and curving beaches, and dispenses as much social rank as it does sunshine and sea air.

From the snooty beach colonies of Rye and Jenness and Little Boar's Head with their wealthy estates and fancy clubs you drive down to Hampton Beach, which, during Carnival Week in August, is New Hampshire's answer to Coney Island. Hampton Beach, which has a little boardwalk and a big state park right on the ocean and a kind of midway of hot-dog stands and incessant music, draws heavily on the working classes of Boston and Lowell, especially week ends. Then there are the independent souls who picnic on the rocks by their own spot of beach and let the rest of the world go by.

A historic spot on the Rye coast is Odiorne's Point, which is the New Hampshire equivalent of Plymouth Rock. Settlers landed here in 1623, three years after the *Mayflower* dumped its Pilgrims farther south. New Hampshire had the bad luck of playing stepchild to Massachusetts on other counts. Paul Revere galloped in a mad dash up to Portsmouth on a cold December day of 1774. He streaked into the New Hampshire capital announcing—exactly as he did later on when the historians were listening—that the British were coming. A Portsmouth mob swarmed over to New Castle and stormed Fort William and Mary (now Fort Constitution), where it carried off the gunpowder supply and some spare muskets.

This should have been the opening gun of the Revolution, but the garrison surrendered without firing a shot. The gods were waiting to give the nod to Massachusetts, and Paul Revere had another try the following April.

Traveling over the state I kept casual score on the number of artists I observed sketching and painting covered bridges, old mills, pastorals, seascapes, barns and hills. I counted forty-six (including a water-color class near Center Sandwich). Of course there must be hundreds.

Lincoln's two most conspicuous memorials have a New Hampshire connection. Daniel Chester French, the state's outstanding sculptor, made the statue for the Lincoln Memorial in Washington. The other is the standing Lincoln of Augustus Saint-Gaudens in Chicago's Lincoln Park.

Saint-Gaudens was looking for a model, the story goes, when a friend told him that in New Hampshire he would find "plenty of Lincoln-looking men." He came up to Cornish, a little town on the Connecticut River below Hanover, and stayed there the rest of his life.

Today his studio is run as a memorial, and every summer the curator and his wife put on a few art shows. You might walk in on an exhibit of Charles Platt, or Paul Sample, or Maxfield Parrish.

The Cornish colony never had any motive. The MacDowell Colony at Peterborough has. It's a retreat for writers, artists and composers who want to work without distractions.

Edward MacDowell, the composer, found creative inspiration among the cool birches and water lilies under the benign eye of Mt. Monadnock, and after his death Mrs. MacDowell, who really founded the Colony, developed it into something. Over the years it has helped writers like Willa Cather, Thornton Wilder, Edward Arlington Robinson, composers like Aaron Copland and Lukas Foss.

From late September through October, when the town fairs are over, when Old Home Week is over, when driving along a New

Hampshire road is that sheer experience of flaming fall colors labeled a "foliage tour"—when the turning leaves reach a high mark of brilliance and there are baked-bean suppers and real barn dances by the natives (now that most of the summer folks are gone) and bird hunters in red caps tramping in the woods, the smell of wood smoke and fallen apples and the grass with early-morning frost, and over the rivers the first geese coming down from Canada—why it's enough to bring out the artist in any man.

You can understand then why New Hampshire has a growing crop of fall tourists.

# ermont

## by DOROTHY CANFIELD

When you pass the state-line marker, you may hear someone in your car say, "Oh, can't you just *feel* that now you are in Vermont? What a difference!" If it is your first trip, most likely you look out on the mild, home-like landscape and think that there is nothing in sight to get excited about. Agreeable, yes, and varied. Certainly not spectacular. Even disappointing. Compared with the Alps or the Rockies, these tree-covered, rounded Green Mountains would hardly rate as foothills.

Yet if you stay a while, and later come again, you may be surprised to hear your own voice murmuring, "There certainly is a difference, as soon as you cross the state line." Something about the country has a quality of its own. You can't put it into words. If you have a traveled person in the back seat, he may give you a clew. "It's like the Westmorland lake country in England," he says, or, "You'd think you were in the Vosges, in France."

He may be stretching a slim resemblance to show off his tourist experiences, but he is right. The resemblance is there. That is what makes Vermont look different from the wilder parts of Canada, or the Adirondack country or our own West. Odd that one of the most intensely American corners of our country should bring Europe faintly to mind. Probably it is because the countryside has been mellowed and visibly molded by the humanizing influences of the men,

women and children who have lived, are still living, close to those
hills, those slanting fields, those tumbling streams. Not many people.
Never more than enough to make up one fair-sized modern city, and
spread thin over some six million acres, but fairly evenly distributed,
and (most important of all) with the sort of character needed to
put their special mark on the background.

So when we say "Vermont is different," part of what we mean is
that a distinctive way of life has been worked out there. Like most
generalizations, this is debatable. It makes many of our young folks
impatient. "Oh, that's the bunk," they say. "We're just like anybody
else."

I see their point. They go to schools neither better nor worse than
the U.S. average. They read national magazines. They pore over
mail-order catalogues. They share all the rest of fashion-regulated
modern life. Just the same, no generation can throw off the past like
a suit of old clothes.

Just the same, there is such a thing as Vermont personality. One
of the first visible marks noticed by visitors is orderliness. Henry L.
Mencken, of Baltimore, some years ago motored down the length
of our shoestring-narrow territory, perhaps two hundred miles as the
north-south roads wind. Writing about it afterward, he spoke of the
"old-maidish neatness" of Vermont villages. We knew very well that
he did not mean it as a compliment. But we took it that way. We
figured that what a man from Maryland called old-maidish neatness
was just about what we could call decent-looking.

Another thing you'll notice at once is that these clean-raked, lawn-
mowered, syringa-and-lilac-and-elm-adorned villages rarely have big
handsome houses. Few Vermont homes look (as many older American houses look, elsewhere) as though they had been planned for a
sizable staff of servants to take care of. Some of them are roomy
enough, evidently built to shelter a lot of people. But those people
were the children of the family and their parents, maybe some step-
children, too, and grandparents and spinster aunts and invalided
uncles and assorted cousins. Ask to see the "servants' room" in such
a house, and you will more than likely get a queer look from a
Vermonter.

A tall man can touch the ceilings in any of those older houses, a six-
footer can put the flat of his hand against them. Like much of what
you see in Vermont, this building habit did not just happen. It is
functional. It tells of long winters and people who do not expect

to run away to Florida when the first snow flies. Like other functional elements in life, it also shapes the character of its background, for it is practically impossible to put on style and "live handsomely" in a house with very low ceilings.

It is only little by little that you realize how the Vermont landscape with its homes, barns, shops, churches, fields, is a vessel for human life as carefully, minutely, purposefully shaped to hold exactly what it does hold, as any receptacle modeled by a creative hand in porcelain, silver or pottery. It is folk stuff, not mass produced.

The first look at the landscape and buildings of a new region reveals the material background. Most travelers next turn their eyes to the inhabitants. And of course the quality most apparent to the newcomer is the "general attitude" of the people with whom he comes in contact. According to some, Vermonters are sharp-spoken, unaccommodating, with a remarkably well-developed gift for being disagreeable. Yet other visitors are touched that, in the hurly-burly of the modern world, there are still Americans with time to be kind, to be aware in the old neighborly way of the existence of other human beings in the same world with them. Both these impressions are accurate. I've taken both "attitudes" myself in the same half hour, moved by impulses far too deeply rooted for me to resist.

Probably the explanation lies far back in our history. Vermont alone, among the older states settled before the Revolution, never had two kinds of inhabitants—gentry and plain folks. Even New Hampshire and Maine had, in their colonial days, a few who were gentry of a sort, people in prosperous seaports, whose money came from trade. They wore good clothes all the week around, their wives did not wash their own dishes, their children had nursemaids. Between them and the rough inland farm and forest folk, there was a relationship not at all mutually admiring or friendly.

Nathaniel Hawthorne, describing the students of Bowdoin College in his day, makes a distinction between the well-dressed, sophisticated young men from the seaports, and the "inland rustics," who yet were, he mentions casually, remarkably vigorous intellectually. Massachusetts always had the same division between the well-to-do tradesmen's families in Boston, and the farmers and small handworkers of the western end of the state. Connecticut had its bookish Yale academic world as well as prosperous merchants on the seacoast, in contrast to its rustics. Just look back at elegant tidewater Virginia, set against its primitive hill people; at the white-pillared

bluegrass Kentucky big house, so different from the ignorant hillbilly's shelter; at the patroons of the Hudson Valley, detested generation after generation by the farmers.

Of course, even in Vermont, there were born a certain proportion
with a taste for being gentry. But they went somewhere else to live,
if they possibly could. And, at the other end of the social scale, there
never were any slaves in our history. Vermont had the first constitution on the continent which forbade holding human beings, black or
white, as chattels.

The state has always belonged to all of us. There has been nobody
to condescend to anybody else—except to the shiftless, on whom we
all look down with un-Christian intolerance. But they are not helpless, and they don't look up to the thrifty. That's a vital point. The
mark of a caste system is not that some individuals look down on
others. What, in our Vermont opinion, makes caste deadly, is that
it creates a class that looks up to another, just because they themselves are looked down on.

Neither of these two attitudes ever marked any class in Vermont.
The reason is historical. Vermont was settled soon after 1763, at the
time when the younger generation all over the western world was
rising in hot rebellion against fixed old social and economic lines—
the rebellion which made the success of both the American and
the French Revolutions. The first Vermonters *were* young genera-
tioners. Our first census showed an astonishing proportion under
thirty-five. Our ancestors were the flaming youth of their period.
They detested the idea of any ruling class, whether clerical, aristocratic or economic.

Consequently they were much disapproved of by the clerical
powers in the older colonies which they had left behind. Timothy
Dwight, of Yale, said of our first Vermont forefathers, "A considerable
number of those who have influence in the State of Vermont are men
of loose principles. We cannot expect to find the public measures of
Vermont distinguished by any proofs of integrity."

Some of the "loose principles" reprobated by the 18th Century
gentry, we especially glory in upholding. One that meets with our
whole approval is lack of deference for social rank. As evidence, let
me tell you one of the old-time stories, which constantly reappear
in our casual talk.

During the Colonial days and immediately after them, governors were grand officials. They and everybody else felt that to uphold their social status they must live in state. You've seen pictures of them in American history textbooks—velvet coats, satin breeches, coaches with footmen, their wives with serving maids, and all the rest.

The first governor of Vermont was Thomas Chittenden. He was a farmer who worked his own farm. The Chittendens lived for a while in Arlington, my own home town, which lies near the New York State line. One day Mrs. Chittenden had visitors from Albany, elegant ladies, wives of York State officialdom. They were surprised to see their hostess bustling about, cooking dinner, with the help of a neighbor's daughter. Still more surprised to see her, when the meal was ready, step to the door and ring the big bell to call in the hired men. In response to their look of astonishment, Mrs. Chittenden said (her words have come down to us verbatim, in oral tradition, and you will notice the typically dry turn of her ironic phrase), "Yes, I know it must seem queer to you, for us to eat at the same table with the haymakers. They've been working hard mowing out in the hot sun, while we've been comfortably in the house. By rights, of course, they ought to eat first and we ought to wait for a second table. But I thought since you're company, we'd make an exception and all eat together."

I present that to you as a distilled drop of the tradition which is the essence of our "attitude."

The Vermont farmer of whom, leaning from your car, you ask road directions, is saturated in that distilled essence. An autoist recently said to a neighbor of mine, who was raking stones from the road, "My man, we want to go to Rutland." My neighbor replied with gentle, slow precision, "I haven't a mite of objection." Naturally some people think that Vermonters are cussedly cranky. They are.

On the other hand, it is seldom that anybody is refused who asks for help. That is, if it is asked as you'd appeal to somebody who lives next door to you, not as you'd ask somebody who lives in a shanty across the tracks. Not long ago a motorist from Illinois, driving through Vermont, told me that he had slid into a deep mudhole on a solitary and very muddy road, and asked for help from a farmer passing by in an old buggy. The Vermonter gave up his own business for over an hour to contrive and heave and finally to cut young tree trunks for levers (on somebody else's land, but he said nobody would mind under the circumstances). When the Illinois car stood once more in the middle of the road, the Vermonter said quietly, as he wiped his muddy hands on his worn overalls, "No, I don't cal'-late to charge you anything. Might have happened to me," got into his buggy, clucked to his horse and went on his rattling way.

Now it is all very well in theory to feel that you are anybody's social equal, and that anybody who is decently clean and self-respecting is your social equal. But in actual practice this theory is closely tied to your economic security. If you absolutely depend for your livelihood on another man, it is hard to feel yourself his equal. Here is a theme—let's call it economic life—which profoundly influences the Vermont attitude towards our summer and our winter visitors. You probably think of Vermonters as poor people. Up here, we don't call any man poor who is pretty sure that he can always get his bills paid, without being forced to take orders from somebody else. The key word in that sentence is *"forced."*

In my youth, when a Vermont man or woman was asked to work for somebody else, the answer was always, "Well, I'll do it to accommodate you." Nowadays we have become aware that this formula is considered rustic and queer, not to say infuriating, by people from the outside. They have back of them the industrial idea, a century and a half old now, that there is no difference between buying a human being's time and buying a pound of butter. So the old phrase, worn as smooth by usage as a pebble in a brook, is now not often heard. But for the Vermonter, it is still the tacit basis of his working for somebody else. He doesn't need money to bet on the races, his wife can get along without a fur coat; but both of them are silently willing to buy, at no matter how high a price, the absence of compulsion in their daily life.

It's true this complicates the economic life in Vermont. For example, our game laws permit the hunting of deer for a week or ten days in the early winter. During part of that time factories might as well close, farm work is cut to the barest minimum, offices and stores are undermanned, senior classes in high schools are thinned, the streets of towns and villages look as though the able-bodied men were off in a war. There are plenty of Vermonters, of course, who don't care for hunting, but they stand up as firmly as those who do for a man's right to decide whether he wants to work or to amuse himself. "Deer week" is an affirmation of that right.

There have been times, naturally, when one of our factories had a rush order to be filled, and the men gave up their cherished week in the woods, to sweat long hours at lathe, press or saw. But when that happened it was "to accommodate" the management, and so understood all around.

Vermonters are not more courageous than other folks who need to make their livings. They are just not so hard put to it—even though they may look to you like poor people. There is nearly always, for any family not made up of half-wits, some money in the savings bank, some potatoes in the cellar of the self-owned house, firewood available to anybody with an ax. Many observers have said of Vermonters that they know nothing, nothing whatever, about the black hopelessness of the average modern urban wage earner, who, when his job is lost, can only sit in his tenement-house flat and wait for the rent collector to come around.

In other words, when a Vermonter feels himself "economically secure," as he generally does, he does not at all mean that he has money enough out at interest so that he can be sure he will never have to work again. We see economic security, not as a cushioned armchair into which we can sink with all our weight, once and for all, but rather as sufficient skill in balancing on a tightrope so that we are not in much danger of falling off.

Do you ask how young widows, left with little children to support, balance on that economic tightrope? Or the sick, or infirm old people? The sad answer is that they can't. The Vermont scheme of life is fine for able-bodied, hard-working people sound in wind and limb, and with good headpieces; but it is very hard on the sick, the old, the helplessly dependent, and tragically hard on the mentally subnormal. Vermonters know that, and regret it. We've made a start at social welfare service. But we have not been able, as yet, to do as much as is needed. Perhaps a community can't have things both ways at once, any more than an individual can.

What is surprising is how many of us do manage. Talking the other day with a venerable teamster who was hauling firewood to accommodate me, I was surprised to have him speak of a great-uncle of mine. I said, "Why, Mr. West, can you remember my Uncle Niram? He died so long ago—when I was a little girl." Mr. West said, "Yes, I remember him. We were neighbors. You see, I'm eighty-three years old." I exclaimed in surprise, "Really? I'd no idea of it. Why, it's wonderful that you can still drive a big pair of workhorses into the woods, and handle logs." Mr. West took up the reins to go on, dropping over the wheel to me, "I may be eighty-three years old, but I don't aim to do no settin' down on the Old-Age Pension Act."

Along with such self-dependence necessarily goes a certain hardness in judging others who are not so enduring, also a practiced and skillful sharpness in expressing such hard judgments. A farmer I know, living in the next town to ours, has considerable skill as a carpenter. He has been working at that trade, lately, for a city man, who took his silent employee for just an employee, not for a fellow human being. When the "employee" came into our general store, a group of neighbors asked him, "What kind of man *is* the fellow that's bought the old Perkins place?" To which the Vermonter, who had been good at mathematics in high school, answered gently, "Well, I should say he's kind of an imaginary line drawn through a suit of clothes."

In general, though, Vermonters keep their opinions to themselves. But sometimes silence is impossible. The big automobile draws up to a farmhouse and honks a loud imperative horn to summon somebody to a parley. It sounds several times before the door opens, showing a farmer in overalls and shirtsleeves. With no courteous preliminaries of salutation, the man behind the wheel calls out, "I understand you take orders here for fireplace-length firewood." The answer is, "Well, yes, I do have some wood cut the right length for fireplaces. And I do sometimes sell it. But," as the door quietly narrows its opening, "I don't take orders from nobody." The period at the end of that sentence is the click of the latch as the door shuts.

There is a common misapprehension about Vermonters. They haven't much money, and they are very careful with what they have. Often their thrift is mistaken for something else—for sharp, grasping ability to bargain. The usual Vermonter does not enjoy either buying or selling, though he is entertained sometimes by swapping. In general, he is a poor businessman.

One of the innumerable stories about this trait tells of a Vermont grocer, playing checkers with a friend in the back room of the store. His friend says, "A customer has just come in." The storekeeper answers, "Sh! If we keep quiet, maybe he'll go away." And with my own ears I heard the elderly proprietor of a grocery in our town (he was a relative of ours) say impatiently over the counter, "No, I have *not* got that kind of crackers. I'm not going to carry that brand any more. People buy it so fast I can't keep it in stock."

A French friend of mine, spending a vacation up here, told me rather casually, "Vermont is rather like France; it is the only place in the United States where I ever hear thrift spoken of with respect." But I have never heard anybody admire Vermont ability to run a business. Indeed most Americans when they hear how we do run the finances of our farms, towns, villages and state, marvel that we are solvent at all. A man from Iowa, looking around him at the small stony fields and thin pastures, said wonderingly to a Vermonter, "I shouldn't think it would pay to try to farm such land. I'm surprised that anybody tries to." To which the Vermonter patiently answered, "Does seem queer, don't it, that we can make a living out of it, and save enough to invest in mortgages on Iowa farms."

Of course, the normal number of people must be born in Vermont who like gambling better than hard work, and have a hankering for diamonds and drink and flashy ladies. Jim Fisk, that gaudy, successful confidence man, was a Vermonter born. But he didn't stay here. You know where he went to live.

Another aspect of Vermont tradition is the fact—maybe it is important enough to call a phenomenon—of nonviolence in the state's past and present. The rifles and shotguns you see in every house up here are not for shooting people but for hunting. Vermont has, and always has had, one of the lowest homicide rates in the country (in the world for that matter). Yet the state was settled at almost exactly the same date, and by almost exactly the same kind of "old-American-stock" people as the Kentucky and Tennessee mountains, where the homicide rate has always been extremely high. Vermonters aren't pacifists. The state has taken a little more than its full share of every war our country has been in. One of Vermont's most prized inheritances is a saying that, by tradition, comes from a big battle in the Civil War, when a general, directing the order of men being sent into the fight, said, "Put the Vermonters in the front line." And few outsiders know the quaint item that Vermont declared war on Germany and Japan before the Federal Government did. Fact. What was at issue was paying the State Guard, called out for duty, but (since they could be legally paid only in wartime) not getting any pay checks. So the Vermont Legislature very sensibly and realistically voted that "since a state of war really existed" those men should be put on a wartime basis. Vermonters fight in wartimes; but there are no personal shooting feuds in our mountains.

We like to think our nonmurderous tendencies are due to the fact that Vermont is the only state which never had any trouble with Indians. Never have I seen in print any adequate recognition of this prodigious stroke of good luck for our ancestors. We can't claim that it was more than good luck. It was not a blessing earned, like the Quakers' steady, purposefully friendly relations with the Indians. It just happened that way here. The deeply forested, well-watered, tumbled mountainous country which became Vermont had been for Indians since time immemorial a hunting field, not a staked-out, fought-over place of habitation. Several different tribes had the habit of roaming around in that region; but the game was of such pro-digious abundance there was little need for any one tribe to try to keep others out. There was enough for everybody.

Our Vermont forefathers displaced nobody, burned nobody's te-pee, had nobody's wrathful resentment to fear. They could and did live in peace with the land to which they were wedding themselves. Not fearing the Indians, they did not hate them, and not hating them, neither killed nor were killed by them. From old-time Vermont talk, no hideous axiom has come down about the only good Indian being a dead Indian. Probably those long-legged, good-natured, lively young folks from way down south in Connecticut, who came up here after 1764, would have killed Indians to avoid being killed by them, like other white settlers elsewhere. But not one recorded instance is in our history of an unprovoked Indian attack on white settlers in Vermont. There have been raids, yes, and scalpings and prisoners taken—but every such incident was part of a white man's war, was a regular military maneuver, and every such expedition was led by white officers in one or another army.

Our forefathers no more thought of shooting Indians than we think of shooting gypsies. It took white settlers in other parts of our continent more than a hundred years after the settling of Vermont to reach this state of mind.

And after Indians? I know you have heard about the Green Mountain Rangers and Ethan Allen and their fight for our land against grasping York State. (Give me credit that till now I haven't mentioned Ethan Allen.) No matter where you studied history, I am sure you have some notions about that fight. Probably when you think of it, you see fierce, powerful, unruly, buckskin-clad guerrilla fighters, every one a sharpshooter, every one armed with his own rifle, with Ethan Allen swaggering and cursing as he led them into the fight. Right. But did you ever hear that not one of those rifles ever killed a human being in battle? The only actual physical violence done any man during those guerrilla years was some floggings—a taken-for-granted procedure in those days—and that one man's thumb was put out of joint. They didn't like York State officials, but they didn't shoot any of them.

And after the Green Mountain Boys? No record of any mob violence in our history. No building ever burned by angry crowds. Feeling ran high in the U.S.A., you may remember, in the early '40's when nobody knew whether our country would enter the war. Some isolationist propagandists came into the state then. (Maybe they were communists; this was when Russia was still an ally of Germany.) We never did know exactly what they were up to. They had a little puppet theater, with which they gave a play attacking President Roosevelt for what they called "warmongering." (You wouldn't think that criticism of President Roosevelt would be much disapproved of in Vermont. Yet I never heard F.D.R. spoken of here with the ugly resentful hate of many rich people elsewhere.) In addition, there was a distinctly pro-Russian communist slant to the play. It was shown a couple of times, greatly to the distaste of the audience.

Then a small mountain town prepared to resist. The people who gathered to see the play in the little wooden theater set up on the village green consisted only of men and boys. They listened to every word in that profound attentive silence which is one of our Vermont social gifts, and very intimidating to outsiders. At the end, without a word, they slowly walked forward in a mass. Those who had been giving the show probably thought that they were to be lynched, or physically attacked, and took to their heels, leaving the marionettes and their little theater behind them. They barricaded themselves in a house. But the "mob" did not go near them. It carried the little theater out to a vacant lot, burned it to ashes and went home.

Sober, responsible people all over the state were shocked by "mob violence" appearing within our boundaries. Property had been destroyed illegally. (As I remember the amount, it was between thirty and forty dollars.) Restitution must be made. A collection was taken up, every county in the state being represented in the sum raised. It was forwarded to the puppeteers, with a letter which read about like this: "We do not like your ideas. We are sorry you came to Vermont. We hope you won't come again. But we regret that your property was destroyed here, and we are sending you enough money to pay for the damage done." Traditions are lasting in Vermont.

But why *should* anybody go to Vermont for his vacation, or be interested in a state where the people are so standoffish and taciturn and so crabbedly independent; where living conditions are pretty plain, where a newcomer is likely to stub his toe any minute on a granite ledge of an unsuspected "tradition"? Well, to tell a truth seldom mentioned, Vermonters themselves sometimes wonder why people who, as the phrase goes, "have everything," leave their comforts and come up to a land where everybody gets along with mighty little.

We are in this matter rather like the family who have in their living room an old chair, come down from a great grandfather. They sink down into it after a hard day's work for an evening's look at the newspaper. They are genuinely astonished (although they would not show this for the world) to have a visitor exclaim about it as a fine antique, point out its "good lines," admire the "sturdy workmanship" which stands up to more than a century's hard use. After the visitor goes, the family look hard and wonderingly at the old chair, which they had always taken for granted.

We do know several reasons why you might like to come to our plain old state for your vacations. One is that Vermont is beautiful. The word "beautiful" is in itself a superlative, and Vermont tradition is against superlatives in speech. But I not only let it stand, I add to it "lovely," "harmonious," "exquisite," "graceful." Please note I do not say "sublime," "magnificent" nor above all "gorgeous" or "spectacular." When you feel like looking at landscapes to which such adjectives can be applied, turn your automobile towards the West and the Rockies, where, as you gaze, your ears ring with the resounding brass of Wagner and Berlioz.

When you climb to the ridge of a Vermont hill pasture and find yourself before the spaciousness of what we call "a four-town view," your inner ear doesn't hear anything loud at all, at first only a gentle inner quiet. From your seat on such a pasture rock, continue to look at the flowing lines of the blue mountains, rhythmically meeting,

**MASSACHUSETTS** Stacked rifles on the village green at Lexington, scene of the opening battle of the American Revolution.

**CONNECTICUT** (*center spread*) *The Charles W. Morgan*, last of the wooden whaling ships, lies peacefully at anchor in the Mystic River.

**RHODE ISLAND** Some of the many 18th Century houses surviving along Academy Cove, a resort on Narragansett Bay.

crossing, parting, carrying your spirit far into the still sunlit distance. Presently you become aware of the shapely, symmetrical (but discreetly unobtrusive) pattern of the green or tawny rectangles of the fields, drawn in with gray-golden stone walls, or with feather-light, green, wild hedgerows. And when, as all this and the blue radiance of the summer sky move together in a perfect composition, your vision centers slowly on a noble ancient maple thrusting its great roots into the earth with such power that it strengthens you to see it— it's not Wagner's percussion bangs and trumpet shrieks you hear, it is perhaps one of those persuasive, mild-seeming Mozart passages which, as you listen to them, sink deeper and deeper into your heart; or maybe one of Beethoven's later quartets, purified of all but heart-shaking emotion.

You probably think that a very purple passage? It's nothing to what I could do, to what I am moved to, as I lift my eyes to what I see all around me, as I move here and there about my daily work. For instance, an incredible miracle of color sometimes blooms on the mountain range on the other side of our valley, on a clear midwinter afternoon. For about twenty minutes, just as the sun sinks behind the mountains back of us to the west, some heavenly quirk of slanting light rays casts a great transparent cloak of glowing color over the eastern slopes.

When it comes, we stop our work for the brief time it lasts, pull the kitchen curtains to one side, or stand knee-deep in the snowy woods to watch it slowly come to life, and then as slowly, as imperceptibly, subside through a million shades of stained-glass mauve to the cold, ringing blue of the winter twilight, with the first star showing.

And the warm, mellow, deep blue and gold of a summer night, as you walk back over the short upland grass, after a picnic on Gravel Pit Hill. And the flooding electrifying splendor of a July morning when you look out from your bedroom window to see what the weather is. And a zero night when the Northern Lights flicker and burn in long rays over the mountains.

Every place has weather, landscapes and light effects, and many places lots more than Vermont. There is the thundering magnificence of Niagara, and the epic glory of the Grand Canyon, and the slam-bang melodrama of the rocks at Bar Harbor where the sea surges up with sullen, terrifying force and breaks into tall geysers of white foam; the great forests of the Western Coast, and the illimitable spacious ground swell of the Wyoming plains, and the jagged snow-topped peaks of the Sierras.

To such gorgeousness, a Vermont landscape with its intricately interlaced lines of mountain slopes, tilted fields, brooks, roads, with its hundreds of transparent colors, every one of them gently tempered to a harmony with the others by the gentle light—it is like a little plain rustic Greek temple, compared to a Gothic cathedral. But there, that's enough about Vermont's looks. I must remember the austere adage on which we are all brought up:

*Praise to the face*
*Is open disgrace.*

I meant only to suggest that one reason why people do come to Vermont may be the serene, unobtrusive, harmoniously composed Vermont landscape.

Another reason may be Vermont standoffishness. This is a trait of great value to newcomers who have a lot of work to do, such as painters and writers. Vermonters don't know much about what an artist or a writer does, but it seems natural to them that he should work very hard at it for long hours, and be tired when he gets through. They put on him no spoken or unspoken social pressure to more liveliness than comes natural to him.

And they do not pry into his affairs. They detest anybody's prying into their own affairs—this is part of the "tradition" of stubborn independence and not depending on others. Shortly after Sinclair Lewis had gone to live in a Vermont town, he said that he had known all kinds of American communities, but never a place where folks were so little nosy about their neighbor's business as in Vermont. Perhaps this, in addition to the calm classic beauty of the landscape, is one reason why Norman Rockwell, John Atherton, Mead Shaeffer, Luigi Lucioni, Dorothy Thompson, Vincent Sheean, Robert Frost and ever so many other such working people are drawn to live in Vermont.

Perhaps another reason is that Vermonters came away from the Puritanism of older New England, intending to enjoy life, as their elders did not. They have kept on enjoying life. They have always danced with abandon and zest. Vermont is one of the few places where the old square dances never went out of fashion. Now one special feature of square dances is that everybody dances in them. Many's the time I have sashayed to the left and swung my partner in a set where two grandparents were dancing with their grand- children.

And we are sociable. Not in the summer when outsiders mostly see us. Too much to do then. We take four months off from socia- bility for the exciting crescendo and the peaceable decrescendo of farming and gardening and canning or summer-boarder operations. Nobody expects to see anybody else, except in passing, in the sum- mer. "How have you all been?" we ask a neighbor we happen to meet, almost as though he or we had been away.

But come November, every Vermont group has a common meet- ing place, a Grange Hall, a plain old community house, church par- lors, some big room with a kitchen attached which your group pays no fee for. You meet and you eat, and you talk about everything— family affairs, town affairs, state offices, national and international relations; you dance, you play cards (those who like to), you sew. Even the people who come from the outside to live in Vermont share in this group life. When they want to come they're welcome. They're let alone if they don't feel like it. Since every party is everybody's party, there is no obligation to "return the hospitality." Take it or leave it is the lighthearted Vermont way of managing sociability. But the weightiest, deepest reason for your coming up to visit Ver- mont and share in our "traditions" is that *they are your traditions too.* You find here (with all kinds of individual exceptions, of course) life lived according to the basic ideas of the pre-industrial, pre-big- capitalistic-business, revolutionary young men who wrote the Dec- laration of Independence and the Bill of Rights.

Are you wondering why I have said nothing so far about Vermont cities? One reason is that their downtown business-center Main Streets look strikingly like those dotted all over the U.S.A., along every touring highway. Another reason, more important, is that, ex- cept for this standardized veneer, generally no deeper than a plate- glass show window, the people in them are not very different from Vermonters anywhere. There aren't enough cities in the state, and there aren't enough people in any one of them, to establish any no- ticeable big-town folkways in politics, customs, ideals.

Vermont has just three centers of population with more than ten thousand people. These three, lumped together (and actually they are miles apart), come to about 65,000 people. Their total is equal only to one moderate-sized U.S. human beehive such as Johnstown, Pennsylvania or Decatur, Illinois. Adding all other centers (whatever you want to call them—small cities, incorporated villages, towns, hamlets) from just below 10,000 down to 2500, we get another block of some 64,000 people. This means that of our total population, about a third live close enough to their neighbors to have somebody hear them when they shout out of a window.

Be that as it may, we Vermonters consider our "cities" big enough for our purposes. For the other two thirds of us, these clusters of buildings provide post offices, stores, churches, high schools, music teachers, courthouses and lawyers' offices, banks, newspapers, radio stations, business blocks (a few) which house insurance agents, dentists and doctors, and state, county and town officials.

It is, naturally, in these towns that our Vermont institutions of learning are located. There are quite a lot of them, for such a rustic state—colleges at Middlebury, Poultney, Rutland, Bennington, Northfield, Plainfield, Montpelier, Winooski, a good practical state agricultural school at Randolph Center and a State Agricultural Department with extension service at Burlington. There are normal colleges for training our teachers, business colleges, not to speak of a sure-enough university, with graduate schools, at Burlington.

Naturally, given the way the U.S.A. has developed, it is in our cities and towns, such as they are, that our industrial production is mostly centered. For there are factories in Vermont, many more than you might guess from the small number and low population of cities. They are widely scattered up and down the state, providing jobs which take care of many of those who don't find work on the farms or in the professions.

Our industrial production is varied, as it is in most Northern states, ranging from an output of woolen and cotton textiles, to woodworking establishments, to miscellaneous manufacturing, to lumber, paper and paper products, and knit goods. Of course lots more, too long a list to set down. You can see that serving ski and summer tourists (although we are very glad of the chance to do it) is not the only way Vermonters have of making a living. Yet, driving through the state in your car, you hardly ever see a traditional "factory town" recognizable as such. As like as not, elms and lawns and old lilac bushes and green shutters characterize houses lived in by factory workers.

Lifelong acquaintance with the state makes me guess that a good number of these industrial establishments are factories which demand much more skill, character, intelligence than just the ability to stand on an assembly line.

Springfield, Vermont, is a notable example of this kind of manufacturing. The factories there, clustered around the river, produce finely accurate steel instruments of precision and the like. Springfield needs accurately skilled workers, and continually encourages the high-school boys and girls of the region to learn those skills. For many miles around, every village, hamlet and many a farm sends workers daily to the Springfield manufacturing plants. These men and women bring back good industrial wages to their own communities, where they often own their own homes, not infrequently because they were born there and inherited the house. So little has industrialization disturbed Vermont personal and communal stability. My own town has two factories in it, plastics and chairs, to which cars stream every morning, bringing workers from thirty miles around.

In my list of the life elements of our more-or-less cities, I should mention those Vermonters whose families came from overseas more recently than the original 18th Century settlers. We have plenty of "foreign" blood in Vermont, most of it in the larger settlements. In Burlington, our biggest city, you hear French spoken familiarly on the streets. They have churches where the sermon is in French, and names over shops are often Gallic. Why not? It is only three hours by train to Montreal. Burlington people, Perkinses and Gallipeaux together, occasionally go to Montreal for concerts or to buy sweaters.

There are also plenty of Irish names among the city government officials. That goes without saying in New England. They all work together to make Burlington what it is, a city of factories, a shopping, banking and business center and, because of the rapid growth of the University of Vermont, an increasingly gracious college town.

Barre's prosperity has been a slow-motion Vermont kind of affair, based on the high-grade granite which underlies all that region. Vermonters are by tradition woodworkers, not stonecutters. Hence Barre was the magnet for many non-Vermont-stock families. Scots came in by the hundreds. There is an elaborate statue in honor of Robert

Burns in Barre. Is there in any other American city of the size of
Barre a monument commemorating not a rich man who gave the
money for the local hospital or library, nor yet anybody in a military
uniform, but a poet? I wonder. Nobody but the Barre Scots would
have achieved it in Vermont. They even have bagpipers up there.

Polish people came to Barre, too, and the Italians, natural-born
stoneworkers. Poletti, the former lieutenant-governor of New York
State, was born and brought up in Barre. He is a Vermont Italian
of the kind brought to Vermont by granite and marble, just as our
slate industry has brought choral-singing Welsh people. Of them it
is said, "Did you ever hear Poultney people sing a hymn? They take
the roof right off the church."

In the business city of Rutland, also, there are plenty of Italians
and Poles and Finns and French. So many of the inhabitants of
nearby Proctor, the marble town, are from Carrara, marble-quarry
center of Italy, that the saying goes, "Everybody in Proctor knows
Carrara gossip, and everybody in Carrara knows what's going on in
Proctor and Rutland."

My godfather was one kind of Vermonter, often seen, one who
went elsewhere and made a fortune. He was a highly paid big-city
corporation lawyer. But he never could keep away from Vermont.
He used to say, "Vermont is a hundred years ago. It ought to be
kept as a national park where modern Americans could come to see
how their great-grandfathers lived."

He died years ago. I often wish he were alive, so that I could
talk over with him a dimly glimmering idea I have that tourists who
now come to Vermont may not only see people living as their great-
grandparents lived but also, perhaps, in some respects, as their great-
grandchildren may live.

Modern society, everywhere, is undoubtedly bowing out the very
rich man, as the 19th Century bowed out the birthright aristocrat.
Social fibers which had clung around him will be bruised for a while.
Vermont never depended on, or crystallized around, great wealth.
There will be no empty place here. You can see here what ordinary
American life is like, without rich people.

What I have been describing is a classless society. Nowadays that
phrase carries a formidable political connotation. Not here. Through
a century and a half Vermont has remained classless and also pas-

sionately, fanatically anti-totalitarian. Perhaps because it never had any aristocrats or capitalists to liquidate.

Then there is the size of population. Till very recently Vermont had been laughed at because its population stood still. All my life long, my own home town (Arlington, population 1418) has stayed very close to the number shown in the census taken shortly after the American Revolution. Here is an aspect of life in which Vermont, with its small, stable, stationary and solvent population, unexpectedly looks more like the future than the past. The sight of it may provide you with some reassurance that Americanism will survive without constantly increasing numbers of Americans.

Much of what we call "Vermontism" is nothing but "old-Americanism" surviving in an out-of-the-main-current community, which has not been so beaten upon as communities elsewhere by the storms of modern life. For good and for not so good, it has kept its old personality, just because it has not been driven to become different by industrial prosperity. Maybe this is the reason why, as you drive over the state line, somebody in your car is apt to murmur, "There seems, somehow, to be a difference in the air."

You have come to a place not remarkable, pretty bare compared to what you are used to, but with something of the tension-relaxing old-shoe comfort of getting back home.

# Massachusetts

## by HENRY MORTON ROBINSON

Among persons who have heard of Massachusetts, there exists almost no agreement as to its geographical location, mode of support or reason for being. Americans living south of the Mason-Dixon line will tell you that the Bay State lies somewhere between Ipswich and Labrador. Lending-library readers claim that Massachusetts—far from being a sovereign state—is a proprietary fief hewn out of Mr. J. P. Marquand's imagination. Others regard it as a historic shrine, or a kind of National Park, maintained at public expense for the benefit of tourists. My post-card invitation to a hand-picked group of executives, "Define Massachusetts in any terms that you care to dictate," drew a mixed bag of replies: "Hallowed ground," "Appendix to Yesterday," "Cradle of Christian Science," and "A Body of Culture surrounded by Antique Shops."

Taken singly or together these viewpoints fail to convey even a pallid idea of the Bay State's unique charm or abiding mystery. No writer, living or dead, has ever succeeded in fusing all the elements of the Massachusetts story into a luminous, coherent whole. Not that attempts haven't been made. Seldom has a citizenry leaped so eagerly to the challenge of authorship, or recorded in such loving detail their native state. Every nook and cranberry, every brook and cornice in the 8000 square miles of Massachusetts has been immortalized—or at least photographed—in such works as *We Chose Co-*

*hasset, Yours Truro, Sandwich Now and Then,* and *Buyways of Old Byfield.* Collectors of old pewter will be delighted by the *fabulae* of Mr. Cleveland Amory; visiting gourmets will relish the optimistic forecasts of Mr. Duncan Hines. Microfilm copies of the *Boston Transcript* may be inspected at the Boston Public Library, and back numbers of the *Atlantic Monthly* are available the moment they hit the newsstands.

The warning, ALL RIGHTS RESERVED, on the title pages of these publications unfortunately places them beyond my poor power to pad or extract. My only recourse, then, is to resurrect the sheaf of moist-with-feeling notes collected during my travels up and down, around and about the Commonwealth at various intervals during the past fifty-six years.

I should warn you in advance that these personalized impressions are not intended to be a definitive treatment of Massachusetts. We must wait for Mr. John Gunther's brisk wrap-up before striking a final balance here. Call this, then, an interim report, and watch out for the tremolo in my voice as I begin by summoning up remembrance of things past.

My preparations for writing this eye-on-the-object, I-as-the-subject memoir began on September 7, 1898, when I was born scarcely an anchor chain's distance from the gilded dome of the Capitol on the "water side"—that is, the Charles River slope—of Beacon Hill. Two weeks later I was baptized by a rubicund curate named Father William O'Connell, who went on to become a wearer of the Red Hat and a fairly recognizable character in my novel *The Cardinal.* At the age of six months, mewling in my mother's arms, I was kissed by John L. Sullivan, the Boston Strong-Breath, and immediately sank into a profound slumber from which I awoke to find myself searching for Indian arrowheads on the outskirts of Malden, a suburb five miles north of Boston.

With no more conscious awareness than a tadpole in a pleasant pond, I began to feel quite early that Massachusetts was a special act of creation, set apart and above all others. History was something built into the bricks of Faneuil Hall, Bunker Hill Monument and the Old North Church; the very air was a laureate ozone breathed by benevolent poets. I grew up on level terms of intimacy with such neighbors as Miles Standish, Paul Revere, Lydia Pinkham, Lucius Beebe, Noah and Daniel Webster (for a long time I thought they

were brothers), Oliver Wendell Holmes, Frank Merriwell, Henry
David Thoreau and Bill Carrigan—the latter being a Red Sox catcher
who had sworn a mighty oath to block Ty Cobb at the plate. Carrigan's heroism left indelible scars on his shins—and my nervous system. To this day my first after-coffee question is: "How did the Red
Sox come out?" If they've won, the thorn's dew-pearled; if they lose,
I fall upon the thorns of life and bleed with Carrigan once more.

I wouldn't swap a single hour of my boyhood in Massachusetts for
the combined adventures of Tom Sawyer, Penrod Schofield and J.
Alfred Prufrock, a trio of insufferable prigs who have bewrayed
American youth these many years. How beggarly, how provincial,
their experiences compared with mine. While they scrounged
around for catfish and hominy grits, I was hooking fat cod in Massachusetts Bay and demolishing steaks at Locke-Ober's—then, as now,
one of the finest restaurants on the continent. To them, *Walden* was
merely the name of a book; to me, it was a swimming hole fringed
with checkerberries. Where Tom Sawyer had nothing better to admire than a whitewashed fence, I could feast my eyes on Abbey's
gold-and-scarlet murals in the Boston Public Library. Prufrock's
overwhelming question: "Dare I disturb the Universe?" never troubled my days. I joyously accepted the Universe and assumed that it
would return the compliment by accepting me.

Throbbing with political ambitions, I heard John F. ("Honey-
Boy") Fitzgerald, perennial Mayor of Boston, sway the electorate
with baritone renditions of *Sweet Adeline*. (We're going to hear more
about Johnny Fitz later, so keep his name in mind.) Another vocalist
of the period was Geraldine Farrar, a neighboring Melrose girl,
whose *Carmen* shook more than the chandeliers in the new Boston
Opera House. Somewhere about this time, I was permitted to give
a public performance on my Oliver Ditson "Strad" at the New England Conservatory of Music. After the concert, Professor Winternitz,
in charge of the violin section, gently advised me to become a
prodigy in some other branch of the arts.

On my tenth birthday—memorable because my father presented
me with a silver Waltham watch—I fell in with fast company. It was
considered fashionable in those days to keep a rig at the Victoria
Stables in Allston and go for a spin along the Fenway three or four
afternoons a week. On the afternoon in question I helped my father
hitch our pretty mare, Helen W., to a rubber-tired buggy, and half
an hour later we were warming her up along the measured mile

reserved for gentleman riders. A roan gelding drew alongside; its owner held up five fingers. My father upped the challenge another five, and the race was on. Helen W. laid back her ears and won going away. I could scarcely believe my Waltham! She did that mile in 2.39—considerably faster than an automobile can travel over that same traffic-congested mile today. Helen W. got an extra quart of oats that evening and I polished off another steak at Locke-Ober's. *Ah, le temps retrouvé!*

In winter I played hockey on Spot Pond; in summer I dug clams on the Duxbury flats, poled rafts across the salt marshes to Plymouth, and ventured on the first of those dory voyages across Massachusetts Bay which later took me to Provincetown, Marblehead and Gloucester, bailing for dear life as white water broke over my dory's prow. The nameless inventor of the dory, doubtless a Bay State fisherman, should have a monument erected to his memory; in my biased opinion, it is the most seaworthy small boat ever constructed by man. Or put it this way: A dory will take you any place that you dare to go, and instruct you meanwhile in the art of dead reckoning, the science of meteorology and the tricks of self-preservation—all of which are parts of a Massachusetts education.

The key word here is "meteorology," which brings us by supple transition to the subject of Massachusetts weather. Ill-conditioned strangers emphasize its worst features: the bone-chilling gales whirling inland from the North Atlantic, the Ides-of-March slush, and August's sweltering heat. Viewed at short range, the climate of Massachusetts *can* be disagreeable, but over the long pull one comes to regard it as the paradigm for all other climates. By comparison, the weather elsewhere seems monotonous—tepid and unchallenging or, at the other extreme, too brutal.

In Massachusetts as nowhere else, the seasons fall into place with measured precision. Snow usually falls shortly after Thanksgiving and is accompanied by an electric cold which brings an invigorating rush of adrenalin to the bloodstream. On a December night, the stars over Massachusetts don't glow—they *glitter* with a hard crystalline ray which has its earthly counterpart in the diamond snow. This snow of which I speak so lyrically remains on the ground until a late March sun converts it first to slush and afterward to mud. (Need I point out here the reason for Massachusetts' leadership in the manufacture of rubber footgear?) The slush is finally sluiced away by

spring rains; April laughs its vernal laughter, and May enters coolly
across a carpet of arbutus.

But wait, the best is yet in store. It was a Massachusetts poet who
asked: "What is so rare as a day in June?" then capped his own
quotation with lines that can be found in any good anthology. In
July one can hear the timothy growing; a month later it is cut down
for hay. On perhaps a dozen summer days the thermometer may
register in the high 90's, but relief is always nearby in numberless
inland ponds and coastal beaches.

The fine weather continues throughout September and, save for
red chevrons on the maple bough, one might fancy that June were
coming in. In October the year's last aster waits the year's first frost,
and it is during this waiting period that the North Temperate Zone
displays its finest product: football weather. Six or seven weekend
games culminate in the annual classic between Harvard and Yale.
Then, flurries of snow appear again, and the quartet of seasons repeats itself *da capo al fine*.

When coal, iron, oil—and even good farm dirt—were being handed
around, Massachusetts was hiding under a glacier, which probably
accounts for the poverty of its soil and the inexhaustible wealth of
its scenery. There is grander topography, of course; Mt. Greylock,
the loftiest peak in Massachusetts, could scarcely gain a foothold
among the foothills of the Rockies, and Chicopee Falls is somewhat
less impressive than Niagara. But nowhere in the United States does
the eye encounter a landscape more various and contrasting than
in the postage-stamp cosmos of Massachusetts.

The shore line, nearly two thousand miles long, is traditionally
stern and rockbound in places—Cape Ann, for instance; yet for the
most part, it is jigsawed into tiny coves and inlets which alternate
with marshy estuaries and long stretches of fine-sanded beaches sloping so gently seaward that one can bathe at any tide of day without
fear of undertow.

Motoring inland, the scenery unfolds in an ever-changing pattern
of weathered loveliness. Surprise lurks around every corner in the
road, which not only curves but also dips and climbs as if determined to avoid the flat tedium of Iowa or the monotony of Texas.
There are thirteen hundred lakes and ponds in Massachusetts, each
fringed with birch, willow, lily pads, and often enough tourist cabins.
No one has ever bothered to count the numberless brooks, or trace

their meandering courses through meadows and under wooden bridges; these brooks will accompany you for a mile or so in a purling roadside *obbligato*, then are seen and heard no more. Meanwhile you have passed a boulder-strewn field, an orchard laden with russet apples, or entered a chancel of aromatic pines. Resisting temptations to picnic in a fern-carpeted glade, you push on to the Connecticut Valley where the terrain levels off into tobacco fields and prosperous farms. West of Springfield, the altitude steadily rises and the incomparable scenery of the Berkshires begins.

At any point in your passage across the state, you are likely to encounter the cool white spire of a Congregational meetinghouse with its tiny plot of lichened burial stones. If your parents were American-born, some of your ancestors may be sleeping under these stones, for no matter what license plates your car bears, the chances are that your family got its New World start in Massachusetts.

A word, please, about the original settlers of the Bay State. By one of the luckiest coincidences in history, they were equipped by character (and purpose) to match, then master, an environment that would have broken the spirit of a softer race. Merely to survive they had to be ingenious, and their ingenuity swung like a pendulum between catchpenny opportunism and theological hairsplitting. They were skillful in the use of edged tools—whether that tool were a jackknife (whittling, like American history, began in Massachusetts), a quill pen pared down for "close figuring," or a mind sharpened upon the whetstone of Calvinism.

These settlers, and their descendants, lived in small houses, went to sea in small boats, worshiped in small churches, founded small colleges, worked in small factories, and made small articles of commerce—shoes, clocks, glassware, locks—each superior to anything else on the market. Emerson's maxim concerning "the better mousetrap" was based on first-hand observation of his neighbors; and when Thoreau needed a couple of dollars (enough to keep him through the winter) he turned his craftsman hand to the making of fine pencils.

The present inhabitants of the state—slightly more than five million in number—bear certain marked resemblances to the hardy Massachusetts originals. They still engage in the manufacture of small articles, dwell in small homes, worship in small churches, send their children to small colleges and have an intense love of local self-government. Inevitably, however, both the racial make-up and population pattern of the state have altered greatly. Strong admixtures of Irish, French-Canadian, Italian and Polish elements have now cross-fertilized, and enriched thereby, the native stock. Half of these people are concentrated within a twenty-five-mile radius of Boston.

You must not expect me to become ecstatic about our cities; some of them are fairly ugly. Yet others—I think particularly of Northampton on the Connecticut River, and Pittsfield near the western border of the state—combine the authentic New England flavor with a liberal gloss of industrial prosperity. I'm always refreshed by a visit to Northampton, where my two daughters attended Smith College; but because of Pittsfield's elm-shaded streets, broad lawns, substantial homes, the bustle of its business center (and more particularly because I've paid premiums for years to one of its leading insurance companies) I'm inclined to rank it first among the municipal "proud spots" of Massachusetts.

Any attempt to "do" Massachusetts—in the sense that one "does" the Norman cathedrals—would bring on an aggravated case of diplopia *cum* vertigo. The course of wisdom lies in selecting a limited number of objectives—each rewarding in itself and representing a typical aspect of the Bay State. But since it would be easier to catch the east wind with a butterfly net than snare Massachusetts in a few paragraphs, I phoned the Boston *Herald* and asked my old friend, Bill Cunningham, for advice as to where the deadfalls should be set.

For many years Bill has conducted the best column in New England and knows everything that can be known about the Bay State. Without even glancing into the bag, he can tell you the winner of the next fight in the Boston Garden, what the boys in Research Row are cooking up in electronics, and who's knifing who in City Hall. To give you a sample of Bill's quality: one summer I asked him where the Red Sox would finish in the pennant race. "Fourth," said Bill—and that's the way it came out. (O, that everything in life were as certain as Bill Cunningham's predictions!)

As we sat in the Ritz bar, I tested him with more difficult material. "For a light once-over of Massachusetts," I asked, "what points of interest, other than Plymouth Rock and Longfellow's Home, would you recommend to a well-heeled, reasonably literate and highly mobile audience?"

Quicker than you could say S. S. Pierce (pronounced "Perce" up here), Bill batted out twenty suggestions, which I promptly inserted into my portable electronic computer, moved the decimal point over a couple of notches, compared the results with my own findings, and came up with a card punched as follows: Old Sturbridge, Provincetown, the Arnold Arboretum, Tanglewood and (wouldn't you know?) Boston & Environs. Neither Mr. Cunningham nor myself are prepared to shoulder responsibility for these choices. Disgruntled letters from Old Grads of Andover, Groton, Deerfield, and other handsomely situated academies; curators of twenty-seven splendid museums; press agents for the Brockton Fair and Berkshire dance colonies; female poets who weave votive offerings around Emily Dickinson's shrine at Amherst; photographers with perfectly stunning shots of the Quabbin Reservoir and wee salt-box houses in Nantucket —all this correspondence should be addressed to the Dead Letter Office.

No one (and this means residents of Massachusetts as well as summer visitors) can visualize just what a Colonial village looked like until he has seen Old Sturbridge, approximately halfway between Springfield and Worcester just off Route 20. Old Sturbridge is the Yankee equivalent of Virginia's Williamsburg—but with this difference: Williamsburg represents a splendid reconstruction of an actual town, while Old Sturbridge is a piece of pure invention, a re-creation of a rural community as it might have appeared say, in the year 1790, built to actual scale with a fidelity unequaled, I think, elsewhere in the world.

Here are some fifty-one buildings—homes, shops, mills, barns and a general store—moved piecemeal from all parts of New England and carefully re-erected around an oblong village green. At one end of the Common stands the crisp white Meeting House (Baptist in this case); at the opposite end is the Mansion House, built in 1796 by General Salem Towne, the most substantial citizen of Charlton. Commoner folk dwelt in unpainted houses, the front doors flush with the ground and the simple furnishings—blackened pots, hand-hewn settles, rush-bottomed chairs and pewter porringers—visible through tiny-paned windows.

There is a tavern, of course, a replica of those hospitable inns which offered bodily comfort to the traveler and a rum-flavored forum for local oracles. In front of the tavern stand the pillory and stocks—instruments of public atonement so important in Colonial literature and penology. Although guiltless of any crime, scarlet or even mauve, I thrust my head into the wooden collar of the pillory and felt, at the distance of two centuries, its shaming ignominy. When my transgressions are discovered, please put me in a quiet cell far removed from the jeers of my neighbors.

A whole civilization came alive as I stepped inside the Sturbridge General Store. By comparison, today's supermarket offers a meager line of goods. From wooden pegs hung the intricate gear of leather and brass (generically known as harness) that transmitted Colonial horsepower *via* collar, hames and breeching to the wagon or plough. There on the shelves were the percales, ginghams and calicoes that fascinated my distaff ancestry, and an array of buggy whips, ax helves, sledges, wooden jacks and horseshoes. I bought horehound drops that didn't taste quite as I had remembered them, and a rope of twist tobacco which proved why snuff—also on sale—was so popular among the gentry.

Some notion of the moral qualities expected of a rising young man of the period may be gained from an ad, dated 1793, tacked to the door.

> Wanted: An apprentice to attend store—a lad about 15 years old —honest, healthy, obliging and naturally diligent; who can write and cypher and is full willing not to assume the Buck or Man of Pleasure till he is out of his apprenticeship, as the person that wants him expects he will attend to business. For terms &c enquire of the printers.

For three centuries a feud has existed between Provincetown and Plymouth; both claim the honor of being the original landing place of the Pilgrims, and although I'm a Plymouth partisan myself it's only fair to admit that Provincetown has marshaled an impressive array of documents and memorials. The most imposing of these is the Pilgrim Monument, 252 feet in height, bearing an inscription written by the late Charles W. Eliot, president emeritus of Harvard University.

I happened to be present at the dedication of the Pilgrim Monument on August 5, 1910, and a more unscheduled presence would be hard to imagine. Accompanied by two other twelve-year-old Vikings I had shoved out of Green Harbor on a predawn tide for the express purpose of robbing some choice lobster pots about three miles offshore. Now hauling up a lobster pot is a winch-sized job; in the process of boating a heavy trap we snapped off the centerboard of our dory, a catastrophe comparable to the *Queen Mary's* loss of her keel. A stiff offshore breeze drove us twenty-two miles straight into the fishhook pocket of Provincetown harbor; seeing the crowd at the base of the Monument, I thought that a committee had gathered to hail our safe passage. Not until I saw President Taft among the crowd did I realize that a landing more historic than mine was being commemorated.

In 1910, Provincetown was a sparsely populated village of rickety wharves and "Portygee" fishermen. Eugene O'Neill and Edna St. Vincent Millay hadn't yet added the luster of their names; and Harry Kemp, now the accredited laureate of the dunes, was scribbling verses in Greenwich Village. At that time one couldn't buy a post card or souvenir ash tray; the only merchandise on sale was cordage and fish nets, and the only mode of approach (other than by dory) was a narrow-gauge railroad that puffed interminably from Harwichport. The isolation of the place is illustrated by the case of the man who elected lifelong exile in Provincetown rather than live with his wife in Truro, some eight miles distant.

Today, although Provincetown struggles to maintain the fish-net simplicity of that earlier epoch, it has been taken over by "trippers" who arrive at noon by excursion boat from Boston and motorcars from every part of the United States. This daily influx is augmented by phalanges of Bohemians representing the seven moribund arts, and reaches a high-water mark during the summer months. When I was last there I found myself in a tide rip of tourists heavy with brummagem booty—hand-painted clamshells, periwinkle beads, glassware of dubious origin and pastels signed by the artist himself. The village of rickety wharves has become a neon-lighted midway flanked by motels, hamburger stands and gas stations.

Nothing in the foregoing paragraph should be interpreted as a slander against the natural beauties of Cape Cod or the unspoiled charm of such villages as Nauset, Eastham and other oceanside settlements which have managed to avoid the blight of summer mobs. Some of the finest smallboat harbors in the world are to be found on the southern coast of the Cape; among these, my personal choice is little-known Osterville. Approaching this snug anchorage by a winding road, I found myself crossing the Great Marshes, melancholy, though not somber, through a veil of gray rain. So Massasoit or any other pre-Colonial Indian must have seen these marshes and grieved at the prospect of losing them to the invaders, who first arrived in sailing ships but now come in twin-screw diesel yachts bringing plenty of wampum in their mahogany holds.

This wampum from all tourist sources now amounts to nearly a half-billion dollars annually. The care and feeding of out-of-state visitors ranks third among Massachusetts sources of revenue.

The Arnold Arboretum, controlled by Harvard University, is a 265-acre tract situated in Jamaica Plain and open to visitors throughout the year. Don't miss this nonstop show played by an everchanging cast of six thousand different specimens of flowers, shrubs and trees. The flowering season begins in late March with the blooming of exotic witch hazels, soon followed by alder and birch catkins heavy with pollen. Around the third week in April, Oriental cherry trees take over with a display of deep-pink blossoms, while Crabapple Sunday and Lilac Sunday, like ecclesiastic festivals, follow each other in blossomy procession. These weekend performances attract audiences of fifty thousand or more, and easily outdraw the attendance at a Red Sox double-header, which is about as high as one can go in estimating a Massachusetts crowd. On their appointed date in the horticultural calendar the torch azaleas flame into a red so brilliant that the air above them seems to be on fire. Mid-June sees the collection of shrub roses take the center of the stage, followed by the fragrant mock orange. As summer deepens into July, the viburnum is berried over with red fruit which ripens throughout August. Birds migrating to warmer climes pause in their passage for a day of feasting.

My personal interest reaches its peak when the mountain laurel (*Kalmia latifolia*) lies massed, pink-blossomed and glossy-leaved, at the base of Hemlock Hill. I have a special fondness for laurel, traceable in part to sentiment, yet mixed, unsentimentally enough, with bread-and-butter considerations. *Kalmia latifolia* gave my father his start in business; as a young man of eighteen, he plunged into the woods of Northern Massachusetts, gathered a wagonful of wild laurel, sold it in the Boston flower market, and thus founded the business which still bears his name. When I was old enough to enter the woods, I spent whole summers gathering this hardy growth in the most inaccessible parts of my native state. During my travels, sometimes on horseback but mostly on shank's mare, I climbed the slopes of Mt. Greylock, followed the Appalachian Trail in Western Massachusetts, and found not only laurel but, infinitely more valuable, the taproots of an inner tranquillity to which I often return, in memory at least, for renewal and courage.

Tanglewood is located between Lenox and Stockbridge in Western Massachusetts. More formally known as The Berkshire Music Center, it attracts hundreds of students and thousands of music lovers to its annual summer sessions. Tanglewood was established in 1937 by the Boston Symphony Orchestra as a training ground for promising young musicians; under the distinguished leadership of the late Serge Koussevitzky and Charles Münch it has become the American equivalent of Bayreuth.

For six midsummer weeks the Berkshire glade vibrates like a harp string. Merely to identify the sounds made by the various instruments —bassoons, oboes, horns, trumpets, trombones, bass fiddles, violas, flutes and timpani—as they rise singly or in unison from every part of the forest, is in itself a musical education. Public Open Rehearsals, held every Saturday morning, enable the lay visitor to watch and hear a Stravinsky *divertimento* or a Bach suite being whipped or cajoled (according to the maestro's temperament) into presentable form.

Anyone who presumes to write about Boston runs the risk of being branded a literary poacher. You see, the city has been sequestrated as a kind of game preserve by the author of *H. M. Pulham, Esq.* Anecdotal rights are fiefed out (in a manor of speaking) to Mr. Cleveland Amory, and thus Boston has become a strictly posted property with seignorial dues payable at the end of every royalty period.

I have no wish to disturb this highly profitable arrangement between two fellow authors—but look, I saw the place first. May I not be permitted (just this once) to mention Beacon Street, Commonwealth Avenue and Scollay Square without risking a plagiarism suit? I'll take the chance anyway. To paraphrase Van Wyck Brooks' remark about Bronson Alcott: "Who can expel a man from the Garden of Eden that exists behind his own brow?"

My favorite view of this personal Eden is the 180-degree panorama of Boston as seen from a twelfth-story window in the Ritz Carlton Hotel. The foreground of this nostalgic scene hasn't changed for fifty years. Directly below my eyes is a willow-fringed lake, its waters cloven by the prow of that enchanted vessel, the Swan Boat, familiar to good little boys and girls whose parents take them holidaying in the Public Gardens—as mine took me, and as I, in turn, took my own children. To the left are the Versailles-like flower beds; from their midst rises the equestrian statue of George Washington, heroic bronze gathering a patina of ever-deepening green. At the extreme left, Beacon Street climbs upward past a façade of fine Bulfinch houses, some of them jeweled with occasional panes of amethystine glass. My gaze, continuing to rise, encounters the dome of the State House, originally coppered by the ubiquitous Paul Revere.

In summer the foliage of specimen trees on the Common obscures the battlefield where young Henry Adams and his Brahmin schoolmates clashed with the "muckers" (sons of Irish immigrants) in snowball fights. When winter turns these trees into bare ruined choirs, the discerning eye can pick out the spire of the Park Street Church where Henry Ward Beecher preached hell-and-damnation sermons that still reek of brimstone every time you open their printed versions. Opposite the Boylston Street exit of the subway—the first to be built in the United States—the eye encounters two almost equally ancient landmarks: the once exclusive Touraine, and the Colonial Theatre.

All this, or something very much like it, has been going on forever. The changeless prospect gives one a sense of permanence—character, if you will—not to be found in any other American city. This sense of permanence will be undisturbed so long as you remain in your Ritz eyrie; the real test occurs when you descend, Leica in one hand, guidebook in the other, to the level of sidewalk mortals and start off jauntily for a tour of the city.

The late, greatly lamented Bernard DeVoto once advised: "The best way to see Boston is on foot." Excellent advice, I'd say; the only danger being that most people get lost. Boston is a model city— modeled that is, after the Cretan labyrinth with cowpath complications. As one who has trod this maze of narrow streets and still narrower alleys until they are as familiar as his own signature, let me lead you to a few well-remembered, and worth-remembering, scenes.

Stand with me on the steps of the Boston Public Library and gaze eastward across the wide, comparatively uncluttered plaza of Copley Square. You are looking at Trinity Church, a massive cruciform structure of Dedham granite, symbolizing (for me at least) the unbroken continuity between Renaissance architecture and its noble adaptation by Henry Hobson Richardson to a plot of New England real estate. On our right is the Sheraton Plaza . . .

But no, forgive me, I cannot wear the uniform of a Blue Line

Guide. I must wander off by myself, secretly grieving at the shabby blight that has fallen upon buildings once fresh with promise. The old Georgian Café, where Vernon and Irene Castle introduced the Castle Walk, is now a sea-food restaurant. The closed doors of the Opera House are plastered with ancient cinema posters. The mean streets in the North End become more desolate with the passing years; the long-ago fashionable Faubourg of the West End has deteriorated into a jungle of rooming houses, and not even Commonwealth Avenue has escaped the spreading rash of TO LET placards.

These symptoms of decay are more than offset by a terrific expansion in the suburban area. Successive migrations, first to Dorchester and Brookline, later to Milton, Winchester, Dover and Lexington, have created a flourishing metropolitan area outside of Boston proper. If these cities and a half-hundred like them could be induced to merge into a single municipality, Boston with a population of 2,500,000 would be the fourth largest city in the United States. (At present it's tenth.) Well, *tempers fidgit*, as James Joyce says, and who knows; a quarter of a century hence Boston may regain its former high rank in the census tabulation.

Meanwhile, I like the place just as it is. I like the benches beside the placid Charles, where I can watch one of the oldest rivers on the continent flow seaward past the oldest university in the United States. I like the sauerbraten in Jake Wirth's, and the bargain-stalls in Goodspeed's Book Store. I like the bustle of the Italian district; the fine shops along Marlboro Street and the seemly hush of the Boston Athenaeum. I like Paul Brooks to invite me to lunch at the Botolph Club, where I can hear urbane conversation and enjoy clam chowder uncontaminated by tomatoes. I like the purple haze of the Blue Hills as seen from my brother Charles' lawn in Milton; and I like to bake under a July sun along the first-base line in Fenway Park with my boyhood friend Lieutenant Governor Robert F. Murphy. Most particularly I like Louisburg Square with its prim-fronted bow-windowed houses facing each other across a central green enclosed by an iron fence with no gate. I do not, however, like Scollay Square, and the next few lines should tell you why.

Few remember more vividly than I the events which took place in Scollay Square on the evening of September 10, 1919, when the Boston Police Force went on strike. Within an hour after the police laid down their badges, the life and property of some half million persons were threatened by a reign of terror. Hordes of bullying rascals swarmed up from the North and South Ends; flying squadrons of petty thieves pilfered small shops, assaulted pedestrians and played dice in the middle of Court Square.

Shocked by these indignities, I immediately tendered my services to the mayor as a volunteer policeman. In the Joy Street station a grizzled police captain named Goff handed me a loaded .32-caliber revolver and asked me if I knew how to use it. As a former Navy instructor in small arms, I said "Yes." "Don't let them get behind you," he warned, then dispatched me to Scollay Square, the vortex of the riot.

Here I met the People, 20,000 of them, milling about in their raw unbolted state, throwing their nightcaps in the air, and acting like all mobs since and before Caesar. I had been directed to keep the trolley tracks clear; with some faint notion that my orders should be followed, I managed to get one trolley car through that human puddle; then the tidal wave of mob-rage broke. A cobblestone whizzed out of the crowd and traveled in a lethal arc toward my head; the cobblestone was intercepted by the cheekbone of a hunchback who was flailing me with his huge fists. The hunchback slumped unconscious, and the mob leaped for vengeance upon the Volunteer.

"Kill the bastard," they cried, stripping me of my coat and shirt. They knocked me down upon the cobblestones; they covered me with a filth of mud and language. As I lay on the stones, being kicked to death, I drew my revolver, and in language I'd rather not repeat—

*Well, why not repeat it?*

My exact words were: "I'll kill the next son of a bitch that touches me." And I meant it. The crowd opened like a fan and I stood with my back to a subway kiosk for sixteen mortal hours. I saw another volunteer make the fatal mistake of running away. The mob trampled him like a roach, and no bronze plaque marks the spot of the second Boston Massacre.

Violence, whether physical or intellectual, has always been the norm in Massachusetts; Henry Adams, most thoughtful of her sons, failed in his lifelong effort to discover harmony (education, he called it) in the scuffle of opposites—political, economic, religious and racial —which gives the state its dynamic character. Properly read, the *Book of Massachusetts* is a saga of fierce contradictions, loud on every page with the voices of tea spillers and Tories, patriots and six-per-centers, poet-idealists and bigot-reformers. Yes, the schism in the soul of Massachusetts is deep, but her tissues like those of Leviathan are mysteriously self-repairing. If the Bay State provides a study in contrasts, it may also be regarded as a triumph of adaptation.

Striking evidence of this adaptive process may be found in the personalities of the state's two U. S. Senators. Glance briefly at their lineage and achievements, then ask, "What hath evolution wrought?"

For three centuries the name Saltonstall has been a synonym for all that betokens tradition, social leadership and strongly entrenched wealth. The senior Senator from Massachusetts is a descendant of Sir Richard Saltonstall, who in 1630 sailed into Boston Harbor on the *Arbella* and proceeded to found Watertown, the first inland settlement of Massachusetts. The senior Senator is a former governor of Massachusetts, a Republican, a Unitarian, a member of the Somerset Club, a graduate of Harvard College and, if I may permit myself the luxury of a *non sequitur,* an outstanding public servant.

John F. Kennedy, Democrat, Roman Catholic, and also a Harvard graduate, is a grandson of that "Honey-Boy" Fitzgerald, whose repertory began and ended with *Sweet Adeline.* Johnny Fitz, as he was called by his loyal American-Irish constituents, could be mayor of Boston any time at all, at all, but higher he could not go. The Somerset Club, arbiter of who is or isn't a proper Bostonian, rolled out the wicked blackballs whenever his name came up for admission, and the close-packed phalanx of State Street investment brokers, "hard-shelled Protestants" and Republicans west of Boston seconded the motion by rebuffing "Honey-Boy's" gubernatorial aspirations.

The Fitzgerald story might have ended with Johnny Fitz's retirement to Hull, where I frequently saw him wandering rather aimlessly about his modest estate. But just about this time, one of "Honey-Boy's" daughters married a brilliant young man, Joseph Patrick Kennedy by name, and this J. P. Kennedy went on to become very rich—richer, probably, than any Saltonstall. Kennedy became in the space of two decades a bank president, an investment broker, Chairman of the S.E.C., and wound up—much to the consternation of the Somerset Club—as Ambassador to the Court of St. James's.

A phenomenal one-generation climb, as you'll agree. But his son, John F. Kennedy, has outstripped both his father and grandfather in a career of distinguished public service.

The moral of my tale—if indeed there be a moral—is this: in two generations the people of Massachusetts have closed the gulf that formerly yawned, deep as the Continental Abyss, between the Brahmin few and the immigrant-sprung many. The *rapprochement* existing between two such highly civilized human beings as Senators Saltonstall and Kennedy does not mean, of course, that the millennium has arrived in Massachusetts. Conflicts still rend the state; many barnacles must yet be scraped from her hull. But the collective impulse is definitely forward. My own feelings, which happily agree with those of less biased observers, tell me that Massachusetts is entering upon a second flowering more vigorous than its first.

The state may never again generate cultural energies exactly similar to those which emanated a century ago from Boston, Concord and Cambridge. Yet something deeper than personal optimism causes me to believe that this sixth-smallest, sixth-richest, much-visited state will continue to be "learning's altar," a magnet for capital, the Log, Ledger and Pentateuch of North Temperate Civilization—and, not too incidentally, one of the loveliest scenic cameos ever carved by Nature's hand.

# Rhode Island

## by CHRISTOPHER LAFARGE

I found myself talking about Providence, Rhode Island, with a man from Kansas City, Missouri.

Armed with considerable curiosity and a letter of introduction, he had lunched with me, and afterwards I had taken him to the cabin I use as a workshop, on the shore of Buckey Pond, in South County, Rhode Island. This man, whom I shall call the Stranger, had the intention of settling in Providence, moving his jewelry business and his family there from Kansas City; and he had asked me to tell him about Providence.

I inquired how much he knew about the city.

"I've just spent three days there," he said, "and I don't understand it. It doesn't add up according to my standards. From a business point of view I figure I can do well there, but what I want to know is, what's the city like to live in?"

"If you're prepared to conform rigidly to the doctrines of tolerance, individualism and conservatism—in other words, to follow strictly a pattern of nonconformity—you ought to be able to be happy in Providence," I said.

"That sounds pretty contradictory," said the Stranger.

"Maybe it is," I said. "But that's Providence. The city is full of inconsistencies and contradictions. That's part of its particular quality and charm."

"Is it?" he said. "For instance?"

Instead of answering his question, I asked what sort of impression the city had made on him.

"It didn't make a very good first impression," he answered. "But what struck me most was the wild country before you get to the city. Looked so deserted."

"That's one of the odd things about it," I said. "There's Providence, the second largest New England city, and the capital of the smallest state in the Union—with, incidentally, the longest name. . . ."

"Longest?" he interrupted.

"The State of Rhode Island and Providence Plantations," I said. "Almost 90 per cent of the state's population lives within a fifteen-mile radius of the downtown area of the city. So you have the curious fact that Rhode Island has huge areas so wild and sparsely settled that they look almost as they did a hundred and fifty years ago—and this in a state with the densest population in the Union; 712 people per square mile."

"Well," he said, "you land right in the middle of the population when you get off the train!"

"Did you see the State Capitol?" I asked.

"I got a good look at that from the train. That's a mighty handsome building. I can't say as much for the depot you land in, that Union Station."

"No," I said. "It's old and plain—though they used to serve the best clam chowder you ever sat down to. One of the sad things is the way the station and its elevated tracks block off the view of the capitol. One of America's most famous architects, Charles McKim, designed the capitol. A curious thing about it is the figure on top of its dome. It's not a statue of a famous Rhode Islander like Roger Williams, or General Nathanael Greene, or Canonicus, the Indian chief, or Benedict Arnold, or . . ."

"Benedict Arnold?" the Stranger said. "Why should anyone put his statue on a dome?"

"He was the excellent first Governor of Rhode Island," I said. "A different man; 17th Century. It's a tough break for him that his name was worn so differently later on."

"Who's the statue of?"

"The Independent Man," I said. "But he's more often referred to—and more accurately—as 'The Individual Man.' That's what you always come back to in Providence. Individualism. It costs a lot."

"It always does," said the Stranger. "Particularly nowadays. You wonder if it's worth it sometimes."

"It's worth it if you think it is," I said. "Providence thinks so. It began with it and it hangs on to it. It hangs on to a great many things that other cities have discarded. Some are good and some are bad."

"I don't get the picture, then," said the Stranger. "I came here because I was told Providence was an industrial city. I'm in the jewelry business, and it's the most important jewelry-manufacturing city in the country. It didn't get to be that by lack of progress, did it? Because I was interested, I asked questions and I found that there's nearly every kind of manufacture and industry you can think of. It's been rich and I guess it still is. What I don't understand is how a city can get to be like that and yet have a main street like Westminster Street."

"What struck you about it?"

"It's the contrasts that are so sudden," he went on. "When you get out of the Union Station you land in Exchange Place. There you see the only skyscraper in the city, the Industrial Trust Building. It's big and it's modern, but it's alone in its glory, and it certainly doesn't go very well with that ugly old City Hall at the other end. And right back of the Industrial Trust is that funny little tunnel they call The Arcade. It looks old."

"It is," I said. "It was built in 1828."

"You wouldn't think it could have survived in the middle of a business district," he said. "It may be good to look at but I can't see how it can claim enough usefulness to warrant survival."

"They like it," I said. "That's the reason."

"Anyway, after I got settled in at the Biltmore Hotel—that's a fine hotel, too—I took a walk through the shopping district. It seems to center on Westminster Street. Boy! I was brought up on the theory that the quickest way you could size up a town was to case its shopping district and see what sort of shops you found. Well, the busiest block on Westminster Street held three five-and-dime stores—and the streets of the shopping district are so narrow that the traffic can hardly move in them."

"That's true," I said. "But there's another shopping district, with good shops, small ones, up on Wayland Square, on the hill of the East Side."

"That may be," he said, "but I didn't find it. And another thing. I walked along South Main Street looking for an address, and the

building there that's numbered 50 stands between those numbered
72 and 86."

"That's right," I said. "That's the office of John Nicholas Brown.
You've probably heard of him. When he was little the papers used to
call him the richest baby in the world. Even with that handicap he
has become a fine citizen. His office was numbered 50 before the
other buildings were put up and the state passed a special law giving
it the right to keep its old number."

"Are there many more things like that?"

"Everything's like that," I said, "including the whole Brown family
that John Nicholas comes from. There's little about Providence that
hasn't a contradiction attached to it except the fact that the city isn't
like any other city—not even like any other in New England. I mean
in all ways—history, industry, wealth, social life, customs and manners, architecture and even politics."

"Can you give me some examples?"

I took a deep breath. "Make yourself comfortable," I said. "I love
to talk about Providence."

The Stranger lit a cigar.

"Begin with the history," he said.

"All right," I said. "There were five people who really founded the
state between 1636 and 1645, and all of them were kicked out of
Massachusetts. Individualists, too early in the game for the Bay State.
The first was Roger Williams. He got thrown out of Massachusetts in
1635 because they thought his religious preaching was seditious. He
settled in Providence and he gave the place that name in commemo-
ration of 'God's providence to him in his distress.' But what was unusual about Williams was that he instituted the doctrine of religious
tolerance so effectively that it continues with vitality today. When the
earliest settlers drew up a covenant to live under, it stated specifically that it bound its subscribers 'only in civil things.'"

"Who were the other four?"

"John Clarke and William Coddington, Anne Hutchinson and
Samuel Gorton. These people had been pushed around so much that
they set up a government that was against pushing around. They let
in a Jewish congregation in 1658. They let in the Quakers in 1657—
over the howls of protest of Massachusetts. Even as late as 1842,
Rhode Island had to refuse to co-operate with other states in ex-
pelling Quakerism."

"Were these people particularly religious?" the Stranger asked.

"Yes. Williams and a man called Ezekiel Holyman founded the Baptist Church soon after, and later Williams became what he called a Seeker."

"I don't know what a Seeker is," he said.

"Someone who accepted no organized doctrine but continued to search for the good in all doctrines."

"But do you class that as an inconsistency?"

"Only in the sense that it helped to set the pattern—still strong—of the ability of man to be a nonconformist there," I said. "All the inconsistencies followed—they still follow—that pattern. For instance, Rhode Island got rid of all religious bars to suffrage by 1783, but it didn't begin to remove the restriction of property ownership until Thomas Wilson Dorr staged his rebellion in 1842. It was abortive as a rebellion, but it was ultimately effective."

"Rebellion?" he asked. "Anyone get hurt?"

"The casualties were one cow and the wounding of the usual innocent bystander," I said. "But here is some more of the same sort of thing. The state eliminated slavery in 1784—you can still see the old slaves' graveyards in the state—yet it continued to make money by running slaves to the South. It had enough patriotic privateers turned pirate to hang twenty-six of them in 1723. It passed its own Act of Independence on May 4, 1776—two full months before the more famous July 4, so it can justly claim to be the oldest independent state in the union. Yet it nearly didn't join the union afterwards. It was little and it had been pushed around so much by its two bigger neighbors, Massachusetts and Connecticut, that it distrusted the whole idea of a federal union. It did finally join in May, 1790—but by a vote of only 34 to 32."

"Rhode Islanders sound as if they were tough people to push around," the Stranger said.

"They still are," I said. "We talked of the Capitol building in Providence. It was finished in 1900, and in that year this tiny state finally settled on Providence as its only capital. Before that it had five capitals, so that no district could push any other around."

"Five capitals!" he exclaimed. "Where were they?"

"Newport, South Kingstown, Bristol, East Greenwich and Providence," I said. "They were used in rotation. But I remember that my father told me most nostalgically of the final session of the legislature at Newport, quite as though something valuable had been lost. Centralization to him, as well as to masses of other Rhode Islanders, living and dead, must have seemed to make more difficult the free growth of the individual—the Individual Man who stands on the dome, as it were—and to limit his opportunities to practice nonconformity."

"You say they don't like change," said the Stranger, "but Providence couldn't always have been an industrial city."

"No," I said. "It made itself into a prosperous city with a remarkably large group of wealthy citizens by agriculture, with slaves, to begin with. And they raised horses—the famous Narragansett pacers. When all that declined, they took to commerce on the high seas, with profitable side lines in slaves and rum. Although it's thirty miles from city to ocean, Providence is a natural harbor, well sheltered, lying at the head of Narragansett Bay. Then when wars and railroads made shipping less than highly profitable, the city began a successful industrial growth, starting with the milling of textiles and going on to that great diversity of industry and manufacture you mentioned yourself. At that point, like every other city, it enlarged and changed its population."

"You see a lot of different sorts," he said. "I kept meeting people with Irish and French and Italian names."

"Yes," I said. "The foreign-born and their first-generation children are about 65 per cent of the population now. You mentioned the three largest groups, but there are also English, Germans, Swedes, Hungarians, Syrians, Greeks, Poles, Czechs, Portuguese, and Yugoslavs."

"How have they assimilated?" he asked.

"Very well," I said. "The Italians perhaps the best of the lot. They've produced many fine citizens. They've even fallen in with the doctrine of individualism. And in spite of a mixed population, Providence hasn't got a corrupt government, really. But it has some funny quirks to it. The state government is Republican in control and the city is unchangeably Democratic. In fact, it is said of city politics that to be backed by the G.O.P. is to receive the kiss of death."

"But they get Democratic governors and senators," he said.

"Yes," I said. "But look. There's the perennial deadlock on representational reform in government and, in particular, in the state senate. The Democrats, who have been in the ascendant for many years, keep trying to call a constitutional convention. It's the only way by which they can ever get control of the senate. The senate remains firmly Republican because senators are elected by an antiquated system which gives each town, regardless of size, equal representation.

A Republican town like Exeter, with only a few hundred voters, thereby elects a Republican senator—but Newport, for instance, also can elect only one. As there are a great many rural Republican towns you get what is in effect a 'rotten borough' system. A constitutional convention requires the sanction of the Senate which of course refuses. This long deadlock was almost broken in 1923, but the explosion of a stink bomb—an odd weapon for a conservative opposition—knocked out five senators, and the subsequent self-exile to Massachusetts—of all places—of twenty-one Republican senators prevented a quorum from assembling and neatly blocked the reform. It failed again in 1950. Perhaps it will require another Thomas Dorr to break the deadlock at the expense of another innocent bystander and cow."

The Stranger laughed and he said, "Well, you get funny business in politics everywhere. I'll take it easy till I get it all figured out."

"In the meantime," I said, "you've got to find a place to live with your family."

"What are the choices?" he asked.

"Depends on how you like to live and how much you want to spend. There are pretty violent contrasts. You have the sort of crowded sections you find on Federal Hill to the west of the Capitol, where the Italians congregate. Except for the physical appearance of the architecture—mostly shabby and wooden—the place is more foreign than American in atmosphere. The inhabitants call it 'The Hill'—which has its humor because the East Side, the social side of Providence, also refers to itself as 'The Hill.' Just depends on which hill you're climbing up to—or coming down from.

"If you want to live in Providence, you'll probably live in a house. There are very few apartments. The house will probably sit on a small plot of ground with a garden for flowers. Or you can live in the country and commute."

"I don't like commuting," he said. "I'd like to live in a really pleasant section of the city."

"That narrows your choice, then," I said. "It probably means the East Side—the other 'Hill.' That's the part that has so many of the beautiful old houses—and the streets with the delightful names, such as Benevolent, Hope, Benefit, Faith, and Friendship."

"Do the inhabitants live up to those names?"

I laughed and said, "About as well as any community. Have you seen that part of the city?"

"No," he said.

"You should go," I said, "and take your wife. Do it simply as tourists, it's well worth it. The famous houses are well listed in the WPA Guide for Rhode Island, but I'll tell you a few of my favorites that you shouldn't miss. Visit the First Baptist Meeting House, built in 1775, and the John Brown House on Power Street, which houses the magnificent collection of local material of the Rhode Island Historical Society. President John Quincy Adams said of the John Brown House that it was the most magnificent and elegant mansion he had seen in this country. From my own observation I'm inclined to agree with him. Both these buildings were designed by an extraordinary man named Joseph Brown, who was accomplished as an astronomer, merchant, philosopher and architect, and was one of four astonishing brothers who founded a fortune and a precedent so well that, in Providence to this day, there are members of the family who are still wealthy, intelligent and useful citizens. I spoke before of his descendant, John Nicholas Brown.

"You should also see the Nightingale house on Benefit Street, built about 1792, and the Crawford Allen house of 1820 on Benevolent Street. There are plenty of beautiful old buildings in the East of the United States, but there are none more lovely, or built with greater grace or sophistication than those in Providence."

"Does anyone still live in these houses?" the Stranger asked me.

"Oh, yes," I said. "In some of them. Lots of the houses are still lived in by descendants of their builders. If you could work it, you'd be interested to get inside some of those East Side houses. They might surprise you too. Mrs. Bruce Merriman's house, for example, is famous for the superb Chinese decorations in its unique ballroom by the late Harry Sleeper, in particular the ancient Chinese wallpaper. Then there's the lovely Edward Carrington House which belonged to a prominent shipping family and is now owned by the Rhode Island School of Design. About the only thing these houses have in common is excellence of taste—and that's traditional to Providence. Add the fact that in Providence there is absolutely no one 'fashionable' church, and you see what I mean by individualism and diversity."

"Your East Side, then," said the Stranger, "doesn't have the inconsistency you spoke of."

"Yes, it does," I said. "It consists in this: walk from the center of its grace and charm and, no matter which direction you choose, it declines architecturally into dreary wooden slums, or geographically into the open sewer of the Providence River. The contrast is striking and depressing, and I'm afraid it's quite as typical of Providence as any other single characteristic. Sometimes the act of preservation of what you have leads to atrophy."

"What causes that, in so rich a city?" he asked.

"Maybe it's because Providence is a city where the bulk of the wealth, which is very considerable, is held by an infinitesimal minority of the citizens—who have struck a cool and workable bargain with the politically dominant majority; where intelligent planning and reform, for roads, airports, housing developments (Providence is successfully busy at all of these), can coexist with the fact that the city did not inaugurate its own rubbish-collection service until 1950.

"Tolerance, the freedom of the individual to be nonconformist— indeed the necessity to be so—these remain. But they have bred over the years a splitting off of wealth from the responsibilities and the risks of government.

"This is not to say that there is no vitality left in Providence. There is plenty of it. But no city group can flourish where most of its money is tied up in the sterility of the custodian account—the 'it's-so-safe-I-don't-have-to-think-or-take-any-responsibility' attitude. People like Mr. Royal Little keep fighting against this, and they're now being listened to."

"Well," said the Stranger, "that's all very interesting, but I don't think you're talking about my kind of person. What do people like me and my family do for recreation?"

"Again, it depends on what you're looking for," I said. "You can go sailing and fishing in the waters of Narragansett Bay. You can occupy your spare time pleasantly at Roger Williams Park, which is an uncommonly good one, with so many trees that there's hardly room for any more.

"Providence has a mild climate—except when hurricanes lambaste it the way they did in 1938 and 1944—and it's neither very cold in winter nor very hot in summer. But it can be hot enough so that you will want to take your family somewhere for a swim in salt water. That presents somewhat of a problem unless you are sufficiently well off to afford a summer place in the southern part of the state. Those who have money enough own or rent houses near Newport or Narragansett, and some of them, of course, belong to the very expensive clubs like Bailey's Beach or the Dunes Club. But it's a sad fact that the upper reaches of Narragansett Bay—that is to say, about the first twenty miles south of Providence—are polluted enough to make bathing disagreeable. The average inhabitant of Providence, therefore, must either buck the tremendous week-end traffic in his own car, or take a bus down to the magnificent beaches of Narragansett and Scarborough, almost thirty miles away—and there are no finer beaches, nor better salt-water bathing in the world.

"There's a good deal of music. The Boston Symphony Orchestra plays a series of Tuesday evening concerts and is supported and attended slightly more religiously than any of the churches. I think that orchestra has been playing in Providence for close to sixty years. The Rhode Island Philharmonic, under Francis Madeira, is particularly interesting because it is a full symphony orchestra using both professionals and amateurs. There are various groups of string quartettes that do chamber music, the Monday Morning Musical Club (which doesn't meet on Monday mornings), and the Chaminade Club.

"The Providence Public Library is a really first-class institution. Or you might be able to buy one of the 1009 membership shares in the Providence Athenaeum. This charming little library was founded in 1800 but it merged with an older one which had been founded in the 18th Century, and thus the contents of the library go back almost 200 years. It contains an interesting collection of books on travel, voyages, history, and a very complete line of detective stories."

"That sounds like a pretty complete cultural layout," said the Stranger.

"Yes," I said, "but maybe I should repeat to you Albert Jay Nock's observation about Providence. He said that he had never seen a city endowed with so superb a machinery of culture and without any visible, general effect of it through the city itself."

"But I understand Providence has its own colleges," the Stranger said. "How about them?"

"It's well supplied," I said. "It has Brown University, which is the seventh-oldest college in the United States and was chartered first in 1764 as Rhode Island College. It moved to Providence in 1770 and took the name of the Brown family in 1804. It's an excellent university with a lovely campus and some fine old buildings. An enormous proportion of those who can be called influential in Providence are graduates of Brown; yet it's a curious fact that the university as such has very little connection with the life of the city—even though it is situated in the middle of it. Pembroke College is the female counterpart of Brown. There are also the Rhode Island College of Education, a normal school, Providence College, which is Dominican-Catholic, and the Rhode Island School of Design. This last was helped by many gifts, notably from the Metcalf family, and began literally as a school of design, but is now an active and fully accredited college. If you have a son of college age, you should be able to satisfy his needs without his leaving Providence."

"I read a little about that in the papers," said the Stranger. "I can't remember whether it was in the Providence *Journal* or the *Evening Bulletin.* And speaking of that, how is it that a city the size of Providence has only those two papers?"

"I don't know," I said. "But what's even more extraordinary is that both of them are the property of the same Metcalf family I just spoke of. Both of them are really excellent in their reportage of local and foreign news, and both are notable for their editorials—but what beats me is that, although both are Republican and are thus, in Providence, on the conservative side of the fence, they can excoriate a Republican senator for isolationism and praise a Democratic mayor for his outstanding eleven-year record in the restoration of a sound financial system. Maybe this is one of the things that made you feel Providence didn't add up?"

"I hadn't thought of that specifically," said the Stranger. "It was just that the whole place sort of baffled me. I'm beginning to think it's because of these inconsistencies and contradictions you tell about."

"I've told you almost enough," I said. "But I'll add just one or two more observations. Maybe they will help you to understand Providence.

"First, I'll tell you about a brilliant individual of the older generation, whom I shall call Mr. X. Mr. X has a mind thoroughly educated in the best sense of the word. He retains, in the fashion of Macaulay, practically anything which he has ever read in the course of his long life—and he is a constant reader of catholic taste. He comes from one of the old Providence families and he has been (until recently) head of an old, established, and once very prosperous Providence concern. He owns one of the fine houses of Providence and he has another outside of the city. He subscribes, for himself, his friends, and in particular for his employees, to the doctrine of punctuality and hard work.

"This gentleman—I am using the term advisedly—almost wrecked the business he owned, by refusing to modernize his methods. This business has been heavily indebted for years, but it has been kept alive by its creditors because there was always hope that a younger relative, a man of ability and imagination, would ultimately be able to wrest control from Mr. X. During this prolonged process, before the relative *did* succeed, Mr. X continued to live as handsomely as he had always lived and to withdraw from the business, regardless of its condition, such sums as he needed to continue his pleasant process of living. And all that time, he remained one of the most interesting and distinguished minds of his city.

"Yet even when the concern, by sheer necessity, had passed into the management of the younger man, Mr. X continued to arrive with punctuality at the office—a blessing of dubious value, since he was likely to send out to buy expensive cigars with the concern's petty cash.

"I know of almost no other American community where such an individual, operating openly and with a sort of rugged acerbity and contempt for opinion, could continue to be tolerated and even somewhat admired.

"The last observation I shall make is this one. There are lots of charitable enterprises in Providence, but there's one that's really unique. It's called the Providence Female Charitable Society, and it was founded during the Civil War to sew for the wives and widows of soldiers. From this not unusual beginning it developed into a society where each member made it her personal concern to help privately, with comfort, or with money, some woman who needed help but was of a class that could not—or because of pride, would not—be helped by public charities. Aid from their funds is never accounted for except to the Directress or the Treasurer. What's done is done by the individual for the individual, in such a fashion that no regimentation is possible nor can interfere with the graciousness of its method.

"I have told you these stories because they sum up for me much of the quality of Providence: its stiffly maintained individuality; its civilized, tolerant, flexible backwardness; its juxtapositions of opposites in beauty and ugliness, progress and reaction, intelligence and mediocrity.

"If you decide to live in Providence, it may take five or even ten years before they really accept you. Once you have been accepted you will find many things and places and people to respect, to admire, and to love. But don't try to conform—be yourself if it kills you. You may even become enough of a Providencian to look down your nose at the rest of New England."

"All right," said the Stranger. "I think I'll give it a whack. Sounds as if the place was full of quality."

"It is," I said. "It's stiff with it."

# Connecticut

## by ARTHUR BARTLETT

The Indian word *Quinnehtukqut* meant: "Beside the long tidal river." The state of Connecticut, as now constituted, is well served by rivers—7600 miles of them; but the one from which it takes its name, along which it was originally settled, and which is still its central axis, is the Connecticut. "The Great River," the early settlers called it. Perhaps this was partly because the Indian word was too much of a mouthful, but it was also an honest evaluation. After the New England hurricane of 1938, a descendant of those early settlers expressed a like view. Surveying his fishing boat securely wedged between two trees in his back yard, where the wind and the gigantic tidal wave had deposited it, he remarked in melancholy admiration: "Ain't many rivers could do that."

It is indeed a Great River, the longest in New England. Up at the Canadian border, where it rises, it is just a trickle, but it picks up force and volume all the way down its 360-mile course between New Hampshire and Vermont, through Massachusetts, and then through Connecticut to Long Island Sound. Dropping some 1600 feet en route, it provides the water power on which are based many of New England's cities—Bellows Falls, Brattleboro, Turners Falls, Greenfield, Holyoke, Springfield, Windsor Locks, Hartford, Middletown. These are important cities in the economic life of New England, and the Great River made them so.

Yet by the time the river crosses the Connecticut state line—and it is with the river and its valley from that point on that this writer is primarily concerned—it is, for the most part, a practical Yankee river, little given to the exhibitionism of swirls and rapids. For some five miles, above Hartford, it does churn up what the settlers called the "white water" of Enfield Rapids, but for the rest of its course through the state it offers no more serious menace to navigation than currents and tides and an occasional sand bar through which a channel must be kept dredged. Ever since Adriaen Block, a Dutch seafarer, discovered it in 1614, and sailed up as far as the "white water," the river has been a busy waterway.

For well over two centuries, sailing ships came in and out, and as towns grew up in the river valley, sailors from these towns went all over the world in ships built along its banks. After the steamboat era came, every town from the mouth of the river up to Hartford had its dock; and such vessels as the *Oliver Ellsworth,* the *Water Witch* and the *City of Hartford* successively cut down the length of time it took to make the run to and from New York—only a few of them bursting their boilers in the attempt. Today the commercial vessels moving up and down the river are mostly barges and tankers; but in summer white sails again stand out against the green shores, and little skiffs with outboard motors share the water with ocean-going power yachts, as a generation of pleasure sailors makes the river a playground.

The broad central valley through which the river flows for two thirds of its course through Connecticut is the heart of the state, a rich, busy, self-sufficient middle ground between an extended New York suburbia to the west and a hilly hinterland to the east. Some of the state's greatest industrial cities are here—though one hardly thinks of them as river towns; and the center of population of the state is only slightly to the southwest of the valley. Here, too, are the state's richest agricultural lands. The valley is the most important tobacco-growing area in the North, and the tobacco raised in half a dozen of its towns is the state's third greatest crop in cash value; while in total value of all farm products sold, Hartford County, which is the upper half of the valley, is the twenty-fourth ranking county in the nation. Even culture seems to flourish along what is sometimes called the River of Colleges, though at least four of the institutions which justify the name are above the Connecticut state line—Dartmouth in New Hampshire and Amherst, Smith and Mt. Holyoke in

Massachusetts—and the famous College Highway veers westward from the river at Northampton to emerge, eventually, at New Haven, the seat of Yale. Yet Yale itself was originally founded in the valley, at Saybrook, and Trinity at Hartford and Wesleyan at Middletown still have their being in the valley.

At Middletown the river takes an eastward swing, cutting through hill country to Long Island Sound. Thus its shoreline varies from green fields and meadows to wooded slopes, sandy beaches and sheer ledges, and brought from Timothy Dwight over a century ago the boastful opinion: "No other tract within the United States can be compared to it with respect to those objects which arrest the eye of painter and poet."

Mr. Dwight could hardly have seen, at that time, all that the United States has to offer, and, as a Connecticut Yankee, he may have been prejudiced; but in recent years this valley has arrested so many eyes—of painters, poets and many more—that country towns have been changed into suburban communities, farms into country estates, barns into summer theaters, lodge halls into art museums, hayfields into airports, and steamboat docks into yacht stations. Pratt's Village Smithy in Essex, which, until old Jim Pratt died a few years ago, had been a blacksmith shop for more than 250 years and was said to have been handed down from father to son longer than any other business in the United States, has since been converted, first into headquarters for a group of industrial-product planners, transplanted from New York, then into an antique shop. An old cranberry bog in Deep River has been dredged out to make a private harbor in front of the home of a wealthy new resident. So it goes.

Old Yankee families, with their roots in an earlier civilization of farming, shipbuilding and going to sea, still dominate the town meetings of most of the smaller towns, and much of the business and industry of the valley, but their control is being increasingly challenged by the newcomers. Two or three years ago the legislature held a hearing on a bill to permit certain zoning restrictions in one area where many newcomers had established homes. "Artists, writers and retired rich people," an old-timer scornfully called them, in opposing the bill, which was subsequently defeated. This is a very incomplete cataloguing, however, of the many new kinds of people who have moved into the valley in recent years, and whose ideas often tend to conflict with those of conservative Connecticut Yankees. "We're glad to have them buy property and improve it," said the opponent of

change. "That's good for the tax list. But we don't like to have new
people telling us how we can use our own property."

All this is in the pattern of the valley's history. In 1633, some Dutch-
men from Manhattan Island tacked a sign on a tree at the mouth of
the river. It bore the Dutch coat of arms, signifying, in modern terms:
"Private Property. No Trespassing." A couple of years later, a party
of English settlers pitched camp in the very shadow of the tree, tearing the sign down unceremoniously. Where it had been, one of the
Englishmen carved a crude comment on Dutch pretensions to exclusive possession: a grinning face with the tongue stuck out de-
risively.

Ever since the Indians watched Adriaen Block sailing up the river
in 1614, old-timers have been learning that when new people discover this covetable valley it is likely to mean a change in the way of
life within it. The Indians were delighted to sell land to the white
men for red calico and rum. They thought—not unlike some of their
successors of more recent date—that it was a fine thing to have new
neighbors move in to trade with them. By the time it had dawned on
them that their own institutions were being overwhelmed, all they
could do was to move to extinction as bloodily as possible.

The Dutch were quicker—but not quick enough—to realize the consequences of sharing the valley with new people. At first, thinking
English help would be valuable to them in developing it, they had
sent word to the Pilgrims at Plymouth that it was "a fine place for
both plantation and trade." Their "No Trespassing" sign retracted
this invitation when they concluded that the English might try to
squeeze them out. The English moved in anyway, and did just that.
The Dutch held on for a few years with a fortified trading post at
Hartford, but finally gave up. The English, by that time, had well-
established settlements at Windsor, Wethersfield, Hartford and Saybrook, and were spreading out all through the valley.

Even the Plymouth Pilgrims, the first Englishmen to start a settlement in the valley—or anywhere in Connecticut, for that matter—
had to learn the lesson the hard way. Having explored the valley
and been impressed by it, the Pilgrims invited the Puritans of Massachusetts Bay to join them in sending settlers. The Bay people, not
having seen the place, declined, and the Pilgrims went ahead with
their own expedition. Settling at Windsor, their party erected a house
which had been built in sections and brought along on their boat—
undoubtedly the first prefabricated house ever built in America. In

the meantime, however, the Bay people had done some exploring of their own, and had changed their minds about the desirability of the valley. The Pilgrim settlers had hardly expanded beyond their one prefabricated house when an outnumbering detachment of Puritans arrived and insisted on taking over Windsor and running it their way. The Pilgrims argued their prior rights, but it finally became obvious that they were wasting their breath, and they sold out to their Bay brethren, bemoaning their "unkindness."

The Old Yankees of the valley today are therefore mostly descendants of Massachusetts Puritans, who kept things firmly in their own hands and remained overwhelmingly in the majority for two hundred years or so. Back in the early 1800's, Elbridge Gerry, Jr., son of the Massachusetts statesman, crossed the valley on horseback, on his way to Washington, and left in his diary a pen picture of Connecticut Yankees which has never found its way into chamber of commerce literature. "With a very few exceptions," wrote Gerry, "they are rude and surly, and partake of the manner of bears. Always unwilling to oblige, when at any trouble, and the most inquisitive and officious of any people I know." Of course all this was many years ago, and no doubt young Gerry was a captious youth. It seems highly unlikely that Connecticut Yankees ever differed very much from other Yankees in the characteristics of which countless writers have sung—some singing sweet, some sour. Nevertheless, they have always been unmistakably Yankee, and they are today.

Just before World War I, an old gentleman named Mather—a name prominent in valley towns ever since divines of that formidable breed came with the early settlers—delivered a sort of valedictory address to his neighbors in the town of Deep River. He recalled that in his youth he had never seen anyone in the village who was not native born, that the "hired help" sat in complete equality at the family table, that the village store was the country club, and that everybody went to prayer meeting on Saturday night to get in the proper mood for observance of the Sabbath. "My years are about numbered," he concluded, "and my solicitude is that this town shall retain the tone the founders gave it."

It was a pious but futile hope. During his very lifetime, the valley had felt the inevitable effects of another influx of new people, European immigrants, mostly, who came during the era of industrialization. The first to come in any considerable numbers were Irish, but in the years just before and after the turn of the century even larger contingents of Italians and Poles moved in, along with occasional groups of others. Their threat to the previous way of life was not so much in any militant determination to take things over as in the evolutionary forces of economic and social change which they represented. Hartford, a town of only about 5000 in the early 19th Century, grew rapidly into a great industrial city. Middletown underwent a similar though less expansive metamorphosis.

To the west of the river, but still in the broad valley belt, in places where there had been little but farms and woodland, such new industrial cities as Meriden and New Britain grew up. Many of the smaller towns, like Mr. Mather's Deep River, also acquired new industries—and new people to man them. Today the families of these later arrivals from Europe outnumber the Old Yankees even in many of the small towns, while in the cities they are heavily in the majority. Though most of them came originally to work in factories, they have branched out into many other lines of activity. The change in the pattern of community life is never more apparent than on Sunday mornings, when the white-steepled Congregational meetinghouses, which dominate most of the valley towns architecturally, hold services for mere handfuls by comparison with the newer, cross-crowned Catholic churches.

Yet the small towns retain a definite Yankee flavor, which gives the valley its main character. The beautiful old colonial houses of Windsor and Wethersfield, for instance, face typical New England village greens; and Wethersfield takes a chuckling pride in the sagacity of an earlier generation which equipped the meetinghouse with a three-faced clock, saving the cost of a fourth face because it would serve only the burying ground. "All the old characters are gone," one Old Yankee mourned recently, as he braced himself against the counter of a general store in one of the valley's crossroads villages. The other loungers in the store looked at each other and grinned. The old relic, with his drooping mustache, his rubber boots, his wool shirt and his critical outlook on a changing civilization, was apparently unaware that he was a living refutation of his complaint. At the Chester and Hamburg fairs, yokes of oxen still engage in pulling contests, and, though tractors have long since become the major source of farm power, a few Old Yankees still hitch up the oxen for plowing.

In the spring, shad nets appear all along the river, from Higganum (from an Indian word for fishing place) to Saybrook, as they have for nearly three centuries, and Yankee fishermen peddle by day the

fish they have taken by night. Connecticut River shad have long been
hailed by many connoisseurs—and by astute Connecticut Yankees
with an eye to markets—as the best in the world. Admittedly, the
shad that goes up the Connecticut to spawn is the same shad—*Alosa
sapidissima*—that goes up the Hudson, the Chesapeake and various
other rivers, but some magic of Nature assumedly favors the Connecticut branch of the family with a superior flavor and texture—a superiority, many Old Yankee shad addicts insist, that is wasted on
those finicky moderns who have their shad boned before cooking it.
Old-timers can remember when shad were so plentiful in the spring
that they sold at ten cents each, and eating places like the Pease
House at Saybrook—still a famous shore-dinner resort—made a spe-
cialty of shad dinners which included all the shad a customer could
eat. The shad run is smaller nowadays, but everybody still eats shad
in season, and hundreds of thousands of pounds are shipped every
year to New York and other markets. If the run is comparatively
heavy, some surplus buck shad, even in these days of locker plants
and home freezers, are still thriftily "put down" in brine, while
smoked shad is one of the valley's notable delicacies.

A business directory of Essex, which is fairly typical, would include
such names as Ferranti, Czepiel, Kelly, Greenberg, MacWhinney
and Alexaitis along with such others as Doane, Lord, Burdick, Bush-
nell, Pratt and Prann, but the bankers are still likely to be named
Bailey or Barnes, and such families as the Comstocks and the
Wrights still live in the big Victorian houses and own the principal
factories.

It is frequently said in the Connecticut Valley, as in many other
parts of New England, that it takes at least twenty-five years for a
newcomer to be accepted. This is an arbitrary and inexact rule of
thumb. The actual length of time varies, depending on the newcomer's background, personality, manners and way of life. Most of
the foreign families that moved into the valley during the era of industrialization won acceptance, or at least toleration, remarkably
fast, considering their strangeness. As one veteran Yankee merchant
explains: "They worked hard, paid their bills and minded their own
business." Nothing could have commended them more to Yankee
favor. By now most of these families have grown up with the Yankees, have been to school with them, and in some cases have intermarried with them, and they are no longer considered foreigners,
except in the rarefied sense that only an Old Yankee is a bona-fide
native.

Many of the more recent immigrants into the valley, though of old
American stock, fit less readily into a simple, workaday pattern of
life, and tend to set up new societies of their own. Their acceptance
by the old society is accordingly less readily achieved. Artists are an
obvious example. In the 1890's, an artist named Clark G. Voorhees,
bicycling through Connecticut, made his own personal discovery of
the valley and was so pleased with it that he bought an old house by
the river and settled down. A year or so later, another artist, Henry
W. Ranger, came along, was similarly impressed, and prevailed upon
an Old Yankee maiden lady, Miss Florence Griswold, to take him
and some of his friends into her ancient colonial house in Old Lyme
as boarders.

This was the beginning of Old Lyme as an artists' colony: it soon
became the largest in the East. Artists began buying old houses and
farms, and today they own much of Old Lyme. Many of the most
famous artists of the century have lived and worked there, and their
work has made Old Lyme itself famous.

Only a moderate proportion of the valley's newer residents are
"artists, writers and retired rich people." Other kinds of people, following other interests, have also settled here, and they have worked
changes in the old communities. Essex, for instance, with its fine harbor just a few miles up the river from the Sound, was a famous shipbuilding port in the old days. In recent years it has become one of
the most popular yachting centers along the North Atlantic coast,
and a considerable number of its newer residents are yachtsmen. One
of them, Chester Bowles, who built his house on Hayden's Point some
years ago—partly, at least, because it gave him anchorage at his very
front door—later went into politics.

Elsewhere in the valley towns, businesses and small industries have
been started by new people, most of whom, like the artists, have
been attracted by the rusticism and the Old Yankee character of
the valley—which, of course, they are somewhat diluting by their
presence.

Many of the younger and more modern-minded Yankees fraternize
with them, and welcome them into the Rotary Clubs, the chambers
of commerce and even into politics; but the more unreconstructed
Old Yankees find it difficult to give their full approval to the kind of
people who value a farm primarily on the basis of its view, the number of Dutch ovens and the width of the floor boards.

The Yankee ideal was left on record in the Mather valedictory address to Deep River. Captain Al Pratt, a schooner captain, had decided to quit the sea, Mr. Mather related, and had therefore bought a place to live. After much discussion around the potbellied stove in the store, one of his neighbors gave the final verdict:

"It's just the place Captain Al wants—four or five acres of ground, a stunwall around it, a story-and-a-half house, can keep a cow and a pig and what on airth more does a man want?"

Most valley towns have summer residents, though only a few are full-fledged resort towns. East Haddam, where Nathan Hale taught school, and where occasional subterranean rumblings known as the "Moodus Noises" have mystified people since Indian days, has a dozen or more big camps, hotels and boardinghouses, which cater to vacationists. Along the shore of the Sound, on either side of the mouth of the river, are beach colonies. One is Fenwick, named for George Fenwick, a leader of the early colonists, whose wife lies buried nearby. (Also nearby is the original site of Yale College, now marked only by a boulder in a field.) Katharine Hepburn has a summer home at Fenwick. As a Hartford girl, Miss Hepburn is, of course, an Old Yankee, and most of her Fenwick neighbors are well-to-do Hartfordians; but the majority of summer residents through the rest of the valley are New Yorkers, who may be considered a seasonal reinforcement of the other new people.

One summer recently, the *New Era*, a weekly newspaper circulating in the lower valley towns, published a gracious little editorial welcoming the summer folks back for the season. Being engaged, at the time, in a series of post-card opinion polls, the paper queried a sampling of its readers as to whether they enjoyed the valley more in the summer, when the summer residents were there, or in the winter, when they were not. A majority promptly voted for the winter. The editor was frankly surprised.

"Oh, well," said one Old Yankee, "he's only been around these parts himself a dozen years or so, or he wouldn't have asked the question. He said a lot of nice things about the summer folks, and he took it for granted that everybody would agree with him. Well, I expect most people did. Most of the summer folks are fine people—and what's more, they put money in our pockets by coming here. We wouldn't have 'em *not* come. But—well, when they come, the place is different, that's all."

It was ever so along the Great River.

# PART II *The Mid Atlantic States*

# New York

## by CARL CARMER

The happiest entry into New York State, my grandfather used to say, is to be born there. The only disadvantage, he would add, is that you will not realize your enviable lot until you have grown old enough to travel and see how much less fortunate the natives of other regions are. Since he wore the long white beard of a patriarch and unfailingly served buckwheat pancakes and maple sirup for breakfast, I received his every word as gospel. Indeed, my boyish pride in New York was fortified on each of my frequent visits to his home in Dryden, in the center of the state, especially when he reminded me, as he did invariably, that my very birth might have occurred uncomfortably, high on a Tomkins County hill, had not his team of white-faced, York-State-bred Morgans made a record dash to the Cortland hospital.

If a life is begun by a hopscotch jump into a state's middle, it is natural that the early years of it be spent in concentric circles. The Genesee Valley, my mother's former home, was the first perimeter. My earliest memory is of a cobblestone inn beside the waters of Conesus, a minor digit of the Finger Lakes about twenty-five miles south of the city of Rochester. I was wakened in a second-floor bedroom and carried to a balcony outside a window. Below me, horses switched nervously under blue-jacketed riders, and long-eared dogs, brown-spotted on white, padded about eagerly snuffling the ground.

Such images lie far back in an adult's life; clouds surround them, then open for only a split second of sun. I would be a man before I knew that these riders of the Genesee Valley Hunt had 18th Century prototypes, that the Wadsworth family, who organized the Hunt in post-Revolutionary times, had chosen the blue-and-buff of Continental uniforms for their jackets rather than the conventional "hunting pink," which former riflemen of Washington's army might mistake for the garb of a British lobster-back. It was upon a latter-day unit of this same hunt that I looked down from the inn balcony.

My State is bright with glinting waters. That first glimpse of Conesus Lake was only a happy sample. Before too long I discovered that the winding Genesee River, pastoral in most of its reaches, raced so far below high bluffs at Mount Morris and at Letchworth Park that few dared stand at the edge of the Palisades to watch its white-water rapids and foaming cascades. At Rochester, the river was roofed over and went boiling under Main Street stores to make its long drop to the jagged rocks below. The waves of Ontario welcomed it a few miles farther north, making a wide blue ribbon border for the land.

I also discovered Niagara Falls, from the high wet spot where the Niagara thundered down past the Cave of the Winds and raced into the whirlpool beyond. My father and I once embarked on the little steamer *Maid-of-the-Mist*, whence we could see ahead of us the rushing mass of water leap from the high, sharp ledges and crash into the pool below, lifting clouds of spray which glittered into rainbows under the bright sun. "Why did you come here for your honeymoon?" my father asked of a couple standing beside us. "Because," said the bride, "it's the most wonderful place in all the world for a honeymoon," and I wondered why my dignified parent chuckled occasionally throughout the rest of the day. The mid-century elegance of the Cataract House impressed me, and I was awed when the desk clerk took an old register from the safe behind him and showed me the signature, "A. Lincoln."

And I discovered the bubbling springs that dot the countryside—springs that burn with a blue flame when ignited, like those in the Bristol Hills and in the little town of Cuba; waters that spurt hot from the depths of the earth and bring healing to men, like those at Sharon and Clifton and Lebanon; and others containing yellow sulphur of such repellent taste and smell that God-fearing folk agree it *must* be good for what ails them. Rambling, many-verandaed hotels grew up where people "took the waters"—not only at the famous spas in Saratoga and Ballston but even in little towns like Dryden where the taste of the springs was peculiarly abhorrent. My grandfather could recall when there was a cotillion almost every Saturday night in Dryden, and folks dressed fit-to-kill "promenaded" while the orchestra rested on the high balcony above the shining ballroom floor. Most of the guests were ladies, so there was always a need for extra gentlemen, and many a farm boy, if he had a clean shirt and a blue suit, received a little flowered card from the hotel management inviting him to foot it with the smart set.

In the red and gold of mid-October, 1825, came the opening of the great Erie Canal, with a boat parade that began at Buffalo and ended in New York Harbor. Governor Clinton's man-made river proved its worth by paying for itself promptly. It also scattered along its length the quick-grown settlements with the nautical names—Lockport, Middleport, Eagle Harbor, Brockport, Adams Basin, Spencerport, Weedsport, Port Byron—to compete with the older towns, those that had been given scholarly names years before by a lover of the classics—Syracuse, Ilion, Rome, Utica, Pompey, Homer, Marathon.

When I was seven we moved from the Genesee Valley to a canal town first named Newport but rechristened Albion, between Rochester and Niagara Falls. First I mourned the high hills we had left behind, then blessed the day we did. I learned to swim in a swift-running culvert that tapped the Erie to run a gristmill. I practiced jumping to the decks of the slow canal boats at one bridge and climbing back at the next. In the town's grimy newspaper office, whence a man of authority could spit through an open window into mid-channel, I heard tell of a day when a break in the canal bank left the water level so low that an Albion housewife, scooping out a washtubful, grounded all boats west of Rochester. And a certain carpenter, nearly seven foot tall and bearded like God—or Moses—sometimes came by to tell how he carried the Stars and Stripes through battle after battle in the Civil War and was never hit.

There was always work for a boy in Western New York State in the days that followed the turn of the century. Farmers had retired after a lucky run of five good harvests, industrialists had invested in the Suspension Bridge at Niagara Falls, speculators had risked a few hundred on Eastman Kodak stock at ten dollars a share, against the advice of their elders. ("It's only a passing fad.")

With their new wealth they had built big, rectangular, cupola-crowned houses far back from the wooden sidewalks, and hired boys to mow the level green lawns on Saturdays.

North toward the lake was more work, in the apple country—Baldwins, they keep well in the cellar; Greenings, nothing can beat 'em for pies; Pound Sweets, if you like 'em that way; Maiden Blush, pretty as they sound; Seek-no-furthers, they mean what they say; Northern Spies, best flavor in the world. Through the autumn days, pickers rode the swaying ladders, and when they emptied their pick-bags into the barrels there was a hollow thundering against the staves. All night long the pickers tossed restlessly, as if their ladders were still bouncing on the resilient boughs.

Sometimes we bicycled nine miles to Oak Orchard, on Ontario's sandy shore. Our object was swimming and sunburn, but there were rewards en route. The road led through the "Land of the Cobblestone Houses," dwellings with local fieldstones, rounded and smoothed by the waves of Ontario, set into the mortar walls. Some are reddish because their walls hold only disks of a local rust-colored sandstone; others are striped in alternate red and white rows or have the stones slanted in herringbone patterns or set alternately deep and shallow to give a dappled shadow effect. Finding enough stones took as long as three years, even with neighborhood "gathering bees" which ended in feasting and dancing.

Oak Orchard today holds a more solemn mood than when I ped-aled the country miles to its refreshing beach. The covered bridge that sang echoing welcome when a team trotted through and also offered deep shade to canoeing couples—("Paddle from under quick when a wagon comes, those floorboards don't sprinkle talcum pow-der")—has now been replaced by sullen steel and concrete. The Victorian dwellings no longer look upon green lawns. Wind-blown whitecaps have dug under the banks on which they were founded, and the gabled structures seem to waver in precarious balance as if they were about to dive into the rolling surf.

Other communities on the southern shore of Ontario have a gayer and more lasting look. Follow the coastline east to Sodus Bay and you will see stable, commodious summer residences sporting whim-sical labels ("Our Social Security"), and boathouses sheltering fast sleep-in cruisers and faster speedboats. And westward, in the neighborhood of Buffalo, lakeside communities are numerous and crowded, and there are still others on the southern shores of smaller, more treacherous Lake Erie. And inland, along the slim streaks of blue water called the Finger Lakes, towns that until recently took their water-vacation advantages as personal blessings, have realized that people will travel long distances to enjoy cool breezes, fishing, sailing, water skiing, swimming, yacht-club life.

The most irresistible of all lures to vacationing Yorkers is culture. In summer months the whole area teems with it. New Englanders were the chief settlers, and an inherited Yankee conscience makes their descendants so uneasy over idling during their vacations that they demand intellectual "improvement." How strongly this attitude persists can be seen on the shores of one of the state's westernmost small lakes, Chautauqua, where the famous Chautauqua Institution has been functioning since Victorian times.

Life changes somewhat once you have entered the gates of the Chautauqua Institution. Its taboos are simple—no automobiles, no cats, no alcoholic beverages. You may live in one of the old cottages that shoulder each other along the brick-paved, leaf-shadowed streets—which were built long before the first horseless buggy and are too narrow for two-way motor traffic—or in a hotel, possibly in the dignified Athenaeum, the last American tavern, so far as I know, to abandon the custom of serving cornmeal mush and milk for supper every Sunday night.

You soon discover that the taboos at Chautauqua are balanced by intellectual and spiritual blessings. The loud-speaker in the sunken Amphitheatre, center of the most important activities, carries morning hymns and the sermon of a distinguished prelate. In the intervals between events the bells of the carillon down by the lake tumble appropriate tunes into the quiet air, and the morning program continues with an economist, a sociologist or an explorer at the Amphitheatre microphone. Comes then the cacophony of an orchestra (made up mostly of artists from the New York Philharmonic) tuning up to run through the evening's concert.

In the meantime, the distinguished artist who is head of the Art Center has sought a dell where light streams from the north upon the canvases of his elderly pupils; the Chautauqua Repertory Theatre rehearses a comedy (there are few demands for heavier fare); the writers giving courses in the Writers' Workshop strive mightily

to tell the ambitious amateurs ("I've always thought I could write")
how to compose and sell their works.

To facilitate adult improvement, the clubs of Chautauqua are remarkably active. The Bird and Tree (it exiled the cats) now works
continuously at beautifying the grounds. The Woman's Club is active
in good works. The W.C.T.U. (it has tried, not always with success,
to keep the liquor out) still wields a powerful influence. One Amphitheatre speaker, according to local folklore, tried to recommend
an occasional cocktail to his white-haired audience and was ushered
from the platform to the gate, where his suitcase awaited him,
packed by an efficient member of the W.C.T.U. The Literary and
Scientific Circle, oldest book club in the United States, has been pre-
scribing reading to its thousands of members for more than three
quarters of a century. Those who complete its four-year course are
graduated at Chautauqua each year on Recognition Day with ceremonies that are impressive if somewhat sentimental and dated by
now.

Far to the east of Chautauqua, a little over an hour's ride southwest of Albany and inaccessible except by automobile, lovely old
Cooperstown curves about the southern end of Otsego Lake, known
as Glimmerglass in the *Leatherstocking* novels of James Fenimore
Cooper, whose father founded the town. No gate or fence guards
the treasures of this cluster of historic houses, quiet and luxurious
hotels and three museums, but the small population is used to seeing
automobiles from all over the Union pour into Main Street, park for
an hour or two, and move on.

The Baseball Museum, a modest red-brick building, is not easily
identifiable, but a Cooperstonian can spot a pilgrim unfailingly and
issue directions almost before he is asked. The cars are crowded,
and they have baggage tied on top, and there's pretty sure to be a
boy inside. Once past the ticket office, the family scatters. Mother
and the girls look at the paintings and the old programs, and soon
tire. Grandpa finds a photograph of Christy Mathewson, who
pitched a game he saw in the old days. Father sentimentalizes over
Lou Gehrig's uniform, and sonny dashes from the cleated shoes of
Babe Ruth to the ball Mickey Mantle socked over the center-field
fence in Washington.

Not all the baseball enthusiasts visit the other two educational
showplaces of Cooperstown. One is the Farmers' Museum, which

houses fascinating relics of rural New York before the Civil War and also serves as the last resting place of the Cardiff Giant. Yorkers love the story of this stone man who was carved in Iowa and buried in 1869 behind Stub Newell's barn in Cardiff, a midstate village not far from Syracuse. The figure's "discovery" led to controversy and controversy to fortune for Stub and for David Hannum and the rest of the conspirators who plotted the magnificent hoax. Many a noted scientist lost his reputation by claiming the "grand old sleeper" to be the petrified body of a man who lived when giants walked the earth. Even today the curious wait in long queues to look upon his passive form, and since an admission is charged, he is still making money for his custodians.

Most rewarding of Cooperstown treasures is Fenimore House, once an elaborate private residence, now a treasure house of Americana. Here you will see early paintings, both skilled and primitive, that show the nation as it looked long ago; the remarkable life masks, made by J. H. I. Browere, of the great men of America's beginnings (some of them the only true likenesses we have); furniture made by Shakers, whose prohibitions of ornament led to clean lines and exquisite curves. For two weeks each summer, in the auditorium of this building and in make-do assembly rooms nearby, large groups attend the New York State Historical Association's Seminars on American Culture. One titled The Frugal American Housewife, in which they baked bread in "beehive" ovens, made butter in wooden churns and wove homespun on ancient looms has proved so popular it has been often repeated.

Yorkers approve all this so strongly that the state is fairly peppered with exhibitions of their pioneering past, yet they squirm a little when reminded of all their ancestors who were stricken with moon madness. Consider the Shakers, who whirled, danced, marched in the "square order" or the "quick manner," and spoke strange gibberish when endowed with "the gift of tongues." Their sturdy dwellings had two doors—one leading to the men's dormitory and the other to the women's—because they believed that only when all sexual practices ceased would the Kingdom of the Lord arrive. They increased their numbers only by conversion and by adoption of orphans. They believed all adornments wicked, wore plain costumes, and made furniture and utensils so beautiful in functional simplicity that they are cherished by a grateful posterity. "Hands to work and hearts to God" was their creed—and through the streets of their villages, neat and quiet, drifted the odors of their herb gardens.

Eventually the Shakers moved into Ohio, where a section of Cleveland still remembers them with its name, Shaker Heights. The last of those who remained in New York died only a few years ago, held in warm affection by other Yorkers, who hope that in Shaker heaven the Sisters are wearing the promised gowns "of twelve different colours," with colored handkerchiefs about their necks, blue silk gloves, silver shoes and bonnets "of silver colour trimmed with white ribbon," and that they are marching in the square order and the quick manner with Shaker gentlemen dressed in sky-blue jackets with gold buttons, "beautiful fine trousers, as white as snow" and adorned with shining stars and sky-blue glass buttons, neck scarves of white silk bordered with gold, flawlessly white shoes and fine fur hats of a silver color.

While the Shakers were moving toward Ohio, a ten-year-old boy named Joseph Smith left Vermont with his mother and came to the bustling York State town of Palmyra. Twelve years later, on a September midnight, he climbed to the summit of a nearby drumlin and found, or claimed he found, a book of golden pages. This was the Book of Mormon, which he translated with the aid of diamond-lensed spectacles that were lying beside it. Then he organized the Church of Jesus Christ of the Latter Day Saints, which considers the words of Mormon an authentic complement of the Christian Bible. While Shakerism died because it denounced propagation of the race, the Mormon faith succeeded, aided partly by an early tenet (discontinued in the 1890's) which encouraged polygamy. Today the disciples of Joseph Smith and his successor, Brigham Young, number more than a million and a half.

In 1847 another prophet came out of Vermont, this time to Oneida and with another idea regarding human continuance. Exiled by his Yankee neighbors, John Humphrey Noyes, Dartmouth graduate, arrived with his disciples to put into practice his theories on Perfect Living. Noyes believed that spiritual and physical love were parts of a unified quality, and that all Perfectionists must love one another equally well. Monogamous love he denounced as wickedness and sin.

If any man or any woman in the colony desired to mate, it was necessary only to ask the Central Committee's permission—usually granted if the prospective partner agreed; and thanks to a contraceptive technique called "male continence," only four out of fifty-eight births at Oneida were unintended. When the object of mating was parenthood, the Central Committee held a solemn meeting to discuss the health, background and temperaments of both parties. The children were raised in a separate house as wards of the entire community, and parents were advised to show no preference for their own offspring. Pierrepont Noyes, one of the founder's nine children, each by a different mother, has delightfully described the life of the youngsters in his book *My Father's House, an Oneida Boyhood.*

The Oneida Community's eugenic theories died out in 1880. One reason was that the younger people objected to the sexual proposals they received from their elders. Another was the disapproval of many neighbors, who proclaimed the colony a hotbed of sin. But not to this day has there been so meticulous an experiment in breeding humans. Researches indicate that the Oneida Community's children had physical and mental endowments far above the average in their vicinity, though fifty-four examples of planned births would seem to be too few to justify grand generalizations.

Now that the boy remembered in earlier paragraphs has long been a man, I am glad to live no farther from the surroundings of my youth than the width of the state. Here in eastern New York, the towns that are nearest me are older than the towns of my boyhood, and the land more thickly settled. Crowds flow daily back and forth in this area, as inevitably as the tidal waters of the Hudson River. Morning takes them southward to New York City, the many-towered metropolis that most of them regard as alien territory. Evening brings them back to the river-town stations, where queues of automobiles await them, each piloted by a pitying wife bent on reacclimating her husband to restful greenery and the contentments of family life.

There is, however, a wavering boundary beyond which the crowds move north to their work. The line falls across the Hudson at a point where the Catskill Mountains lift blue summits into the sky of its western banks. North and west of this line lies a cherished land called upstate.

The Catskills are the most gregarious and hospitable of American mountains. Neither high nor steep, they suggest no climbing ropes, no spiked shoes. Each spring they welcome thousands of happy companions to the almost countless hostelries hidden within their comfortable folds. A cheerful uproar prevails, provided partly by the hotel guests, who are mostly from New York City, and partly by the hotel managements, which offer lavish entertainments. Professional entertainers, theatrical troupes, dance orchestras, famous basketball teams, tennis players, golfers travel the profitable trail known as the Borscht Circuit. Once happily described by Arthur Kober's comedy, *Having Wonderful Time,* this vacationland is crowded with people who are openly enthusiastic about people. An air of carnival rises from these hills that were named for squalling wildcats. Rip Van Winkle would find a long sleep difficult here today!

Ride north along the Hudson, beside the Catskills, then leave its shores at Rip Van Winkle Bridge and make west for Cairo, a country town proclaimed cosmopolitan by its pizzerias, cafés, beer halls, delicatessens. Roads join in a star here. One goes north to more Catskill caravansaries. Another, branching south, leads to the hill-circled hamlet of Purling, where the Old Heidelberg and the Bavarian Manor invite to dark elegance and darker beer. Take the northwest route numbered 145, the Sharon Road, to the old village of Leeds, and at midtown you will see a building labeled Jerry Shea's Irish Center. Roll on a few miles and suddenly Ireland has confiscated the hillsides. Here, in fittingly named Greene County, stand the Emerald Isle, the Shannon View, the Shamrock House. Here the O'Neills, the Weldons, the Hagans, the Kearneys, the Mooneys, the Donellys are hosts to families whose old-country names are their best references. Turn in for an Irish stew at Erin's Melody, caper a bit at Blarney's Star Casino and go to early Mass next morning at the tiny chapel of St. Mary's.

"New York State has everything" is a familiar boast among New Yorkers, and sometimes they add, "even two kinds of mountains." North of the Catskills lie rolling hills and the river plain of the east-flowing Mohawk, and beyond that lies rising land again—the foothills of the Adirondacks. Steeper and higher than the Catskills, the tree-lined slopes of the Adirondacks offer silence, the companionship of nature, the shade of balsam, spruce and hemlock, and hidden lakes where the only sounds are those of fish jumping and the whisper of wind riffling the water.

While the Adirondacks are not high compared with Western mountains, more than two score of their countless peaks rise above the four-thousand-foot level. The highest, to which the Adirondack

Indians gave the name of Tahawus (the cloud splitter), is over five thousand feet and provides on its steep sides not only a level nook for Lake Tear-of-the-Clouds, where the Hudson rises, but also an iron mine.

The "uphisted lands," as lumberjacks call this country, fill most of the northeast corner of the state. The towns of Lake Placid and Saranac Lake are in the busiest vacation areas, with palacelike clubs and inns and sophisticated shops where people can spend money when they are bored with other diversions. But such places are far from characteristic. Simple log dwellings, even log inns, are not infrequent in the Adirondacks. In many towns, by mid-August, stores are displaying checkered mackinaws, wool shirts, red-flannel underwear, lumberjack peaveys and snowshoes. "Summer up here," said one native mountaineer, "lasts about twenty minutes and *that* seems to come around noon dinner."

Three roads leave Albany, the York State capital, in an east-west course across the rolling hills and river flats that separate the Catskills from the Adirondacks. The northernmost is the Schenectady-Utica-Syracuse turnpike, which runs along the north bank of the historic Mohawk. The southernmost is the Cherry Valley Pike, one of the world's most beautiful highways, which sweeps up and down mile-long hills as if it were the track of a magnificent outsized roller coaster. Between the two, at least part of the way, runs the new Thruway, the comfortable speedway that unhappily bypasses the fine old towns and buildings and the restaurants that serve the distinctive foods and wines of the region.

This is the upstate area. Only the inhabitants, legend claims, can define its boundaries, and they are not given to exactitude in matters of geography. The late Samuel Hopkins Adams, the distinguished author who lived all his years in the area, once said, "Upstate is west of Albany," and considered the subject closed. Upstaters sniff scornfully at New York City's society-page headlines that say, "Upstate Wedding at Peekskill-on-Hudson." They look upon the island of Manhattan as a subject city-state which very properly pays heavy tribute to Albany. As for that other island, called Long, they regard its people as a salt-water breed more closely akin to New England Yankees than to people dwelling beside pure, fresh lake waters.

Some writers claim that the upstater can be distinguished by his physical, mental and social attributes. Not so lean as the New England Yankee (he is too well fed), his manner indicates that he will never stoop to dieting for the sake of vanity. He is hearty and friendly, and his conversation is intelligent and sometimes penetrating except on the subject of fine arts, which he regards as unmanly or at best a lot of foolishness, even if he is a college graduate. ("My wife does the reading for the family.")

Refusal to conform is a cardinal sin to the upstater. He will not let himself be called pretentious by his neighbors. He avoids fancy clothing, nor does he want his wife to be conspicuously dressed. He may go all out in business or in sports without fear of ridicule, but in other areas his self-expression is hampered because he may fail and be laughed at or else succeed and be regarded as one who has tried to set himself above his fellows. Once I heard an upstater admit to a group of friends that he felt that he had done "a pretty good job" on a project. The remark caused a shocked silence.

While the upstater is greatly moved by the subject of food, his tastes run generally to meat, mashed potatoes with gravy, green vegetables and pie. Generous helpings are as likely to win his praise as skilled preparation. Visitors sometimes wail that they cannot find rare beef in the restaurants. ("I'll have rare roast beef," said one. "There isn't any," said the waiter, "and it isn't rare.") Few places serve French or Spanish dishes, and a *spécialité de la maison* is not usually offered. The chief influences on upstate restaurants are Italian, German and tearoom.

Upstate cities follow a pattern too. Through the old part of town runs the chief residential thoroughfare. Here, in lawn-girt rows, stand the sprawling dark Victorian piles built by the old families who made their money early—the tribes referred to, with some awe, as Old Amsterdam, Old Herkimer, Old Rome. Inevitably, some of the elegant mansions have been converted to funeral homes and others have been sold to enterprising immigrant families—and their colorful alterations of conservative façades sometimes startle their neighbors. On the side streets, near this major aisle of aristocracy, stand the expensive new residences of the well-to-do come-latelies whose ranking is less sacrosanct. And on the "other side" of town, in thousands of homes varying little in design, live the employees of the big industries.

Of the smaller upstate cities, many are identified with a single industry. Troy, upriver about ten miles from Albany, is widely recognized as the source of shirts and collars. Schenectady is associated

with electric appliances, Gloversville and Johnstown with gloves,
Rome with copper, Endicott with business machines, Johnson City
with shoes, Little Falls and Herkimer with dairy products, Jamestown with furniture—and so on. All of these vary little from the usual
upstate pattern. Three, however, differ very markedly.

The first is Albany. No one who has ever seen wide State Street
rise from the Hudson River docks to the Capitol building is likely
to forget the sight. It is a sweeping and majestic approach to ornate
nothingness—to the three-acre, $25,000,000 gingerbread castle in
whose façade the period influences come and go as raggedly as do
political influences within. But politics aside—and architecture, too,
for most of Albany's other streets are lined with dull look-alike houses
of dark red brick or brownstone—Albany has one surpassing distinction. This is Keeler's, the best year-round city restaurant in all upstate, an eating house that feeds sophisticated Manhattanites, rural
politicians, foreign diplomats whose palates can be weaned from
exotic dishes—and all come away singing the praises of the food. Upstate contains only two other like establishments, and both are in
small towns—the Krebs in Skaneateles and Halloway House in East
Bloomfield.

The second atypical city is Syracuse, now a center for electronics
products and a boom town so overextended that it has hired city-
planning experts to ease its growing pains. Syracuse University, city-
sized itself and surrounded by the seething town, has retreated skyward—with its 15,000 students—from the slopes where it began to
the summit of Mount Olympus, where its newest dormitories look
out over the vast reaches, tumbling hills and water-streaked valleys
of upstate.

Third is Geneva, the most distinctive of upstate cities. Nowhere
else in the Northeast are such gracious city houses standing like
Godey's *Lady's Book* matrons in a close row, presenting faces of
unquestionable fashion toward the street. Behind them, on sunny
days, long narrow Seneca Lake accentuates the white of sails with
the blue of water. A genteel provincialism flavors both the houses
and their occupants, so that Geneva is something like South Carolina's Charleston, complete with Church of England touches and an
"old Geneva" Shintoism of its own.

The two largest upstate cities are Rochester and Buffalo, and the
smaller of these, Rochester, is the better organized and the more

homogeneous. Although a few miles separate it from Lake Ontario, it has profited from Great Lakes commerce for more than a hundred and fifty years and now seems stabilized on a high level of genial and genteel conformity. Samuel Hopkins Adams, who was brought up there, pronounced Rochester (from his eyrie on Owasco Lake about sixty-five miles away) as nearly perfect as a city may become. Others are not so sure—like the young executive who told me this: "The city hasn't changed. Yesterday I was summoned to an immediate staff meeting. I showed up wearing a yellow shirt under my jacket. I didn't mind that I was the only one in a colored shirt, but I *did* mind that every mother's son there mentioned it."

Downtown Rochester looks more like an enlarged village than a planned city, despite an ill-inspired yellow-brick department store standing like a medieval cathedral at the top of the mall. It is a town of beautiful shade trees and comfortable homes, and in spring its many parks are green and white and purple pleasure-grounds when more than five hundred species of lilacs perfume the whole area and canoes drift in a sun-tinted haze on the river.

Rochester remains the Kodak City, of course, and George Eastman lavished more than $30,000,000 on making it a city of culture. His dream was to provide an art center where his fellow citizens could enjoy fine paintings and great symphonies. Yet little has come of the dream, and Rochester continues on its way, satisfied and comfortable.

At Buffalo, the port may not be denied. Long ships, the ore-bearing "whale-backs," dock in the shadow of towering grain elevators. The lake winds roar into the wide streets. Nights are peppered with the yellow glares of steel furnaces. Delaware Avenue—"Old Buffalo" —is losing face as trade crowds in where society elegants once lived. Impromptu quartettes send *Zwei Herzen im Drei-Viertel Takt* out through the swinging doors of malt-scented German restaurants. And thousands of weathered houses shelter one of the largest Polish populations in the world—a group not to be inhibited by a drab environment. The proof is to see them on a Sunday, walking to their churches with the bulbous spires, or to be a guest at one of their wedding festivals, which run to three full days of gaiety.

Buffalo has a freer "feel" about it than any other York State city. Possibly the wild gusts from the lake, the port atmosphere, the heartiness and *Gemütlichkeit* of the music-loving Germans, the humor and excitability of the Poles are responsible for this. Possibly, too, the English spoken here may be a clue. It abounds in the flat *a* sounds and protracted *r*'s used by the town's Midwestern neighbors, and this would make Buffalo the place where the Midwest begins.

The affection and admiration in which Yorkers hold their state is of a distinctive nature. The breezy enthusiasms of Texans, the lush poesy of Californians and Floridians, the dry assumptions of Down East Yankees are not emulated by natives of my state. Their feeling is articulated by a small voice deep within themselves. The language that a region speaks to its inhabitants is not easily translatable. To a child who discovers all new things in an ecstasy of wonder it is not at first understandable. But to an adult Yorker, who knows that the time of becoming one with the soil inexorably advances, the voice of his own landscape is clear.

Yorkers hear this voice and sometimes, on appropriate occasions illumined by wood fires or by stars, they talk about it. They are, they say modestly, a common-sense people, realistic, thrifty, healthy minded, humorous and easygoing, the very antithesis of mystics. Nevertheless, in those unguarded moments, the honest Yorker will confess that he sometimes feels a "something unnatural" that comes from his natural surroundings. Whether most of his days are spent in the sharp Adirondack clarity of Keene Valley, or among the misty vineyards that line one of the Finger Lakes, or beside the level orchards on blue Ontario's plain, or in the forest shadows where stand the cabins of the Cattauraugus Reservation Indians, this is true.

Your Yorker will point out that, from the time the tribes of the Iroquois Confederacy realized that the Onondagas were more psychic than other Indians, and chose them as the keepers of the eternal fires through whose informing flames the messages of the Creator are translated, men have known that the land which is now upstate holds a peculiar enchantment. He will add that Shakers, Perfectionists, Mormons were only three of more than a dozen religious sects that have burgeoned on the forty-mile-wide east-west strip where beings from another world have spoken to his fellow Yorkers. And to clinch his argument he will assert that drumbeats punctuate the windless air above the Finger Lakes on certain magic days, though no living person has ever beheld the instrument or its player. He will say, truthfully, that he has himself heard the lonesome drum and he will laugh at the science departments of the many col-

leges roundabout which have considered the phenomenon and pro-
pounded several learned explanations, no two alike.

Scoff at him and he will tell you *sotto voce* that, while most of his
neighbors have their feet on the ground, like himself, he knows some
who appear as sane now as their grandfathers did before they joined
the Oneida Community, but who might at any time surprise him—
and themselves—by surrendering to mystic influences which never
cease to hover in the otherwise salubrious upstate air.

In no other region, I believe, is there a more comprehensive rap-
port between inhabitant and environment. To its people, rivers and
lakes mean boundaries, water traffic, irrigation, pure drinking water,
and an intangible something more. Mountains, and valleys between,
mean vacation lands and tourism, bottom lands mean fertile soil and
rich harvests, cities mean vast industries and wide employment, but
all these blessings have an added indefinable and mysterious quality that banishes monotony from York State life.

# New Jersey

## by CARL L. BIEMILLER

### THE NORTH

Few places in the United States are as susceptible to snap judgments as the eleven counties which make up Northern New Jersey. Most people get their first view of North Jersey from the windows of a Pennsylvania Railroad car leaving New York, and a grim view it is. They see a montage of dreary, brackish marsh where tall rushes cover the lower courses of the Hackensack and Passaic Rivers and where the sun glints feebly on the luminescent ooze of mud flats. Pig farms dapple the meadows, vast factories line the polluted rivers, and the skyline is crisscrossed by skeletal radio towers and high-altitude express highways. Fifteen minutes later, the southbound traveler is whisked into a belt of cities—Newark, Elizabeth, Linden, Rahway, New Brunswick—all characterized by a merged blur of factories. At this point, the train rider gives up on North Jersey, and goes back to his newspaper. Yet if he looks up five minutes later he will be astonished to see a pretty, softly rolling countryside beautified by green farms, stands of second-growth oak and pine and patches of brown popple. He may even see a white-tailed deer inquisitively poking its head through the scrub—and this less than half an hour from Manhattan. Northern New Jersey is like that; it is a quick-change artist defying quick analysis.

Now take, for the other side, a motorist driving north toward New

York through the rich and gentle valley farm lands of Hunterdon, Somerset and Morris Counties, or through the aged and forested mountain slopes of Warren and Sussex Counties. Rolling through this countryside, our motorist will decide that this is one part of the East which must be truly loved by its residents, and one which, at the same time, has kept in touch with its historic past.

These neat villages, spacious village greens and tree-shaded walks can have changed but little in two hundred years, and in some sections the place names sound as if they had come right out of medieval England or from the tribal incantations of the Lenni-Lenape, the Delaware Indians who once held the commonwealth. Here, says our motorist, is a sweet bit of country.

Yet no sooner has he made his pronouncement than he finds himself snatched up in a vast complex of concrete-and-steel ramps, high-speed highways, no-speed traffic jams and multilevel bridges. The countryside has vanished, replaced by looming factories, stop lights and vast dumps, where the air is smog-laden with chemical fumes and strange industrial odors. By the time the embittered motorist reaches one of the tunnels or bridges leading into New York he is through with Northern New Jersey. The place, he decides, makes no sense.

He is at least partly right. And if he comes to know more about upper Jersey, he will discover even more startling paradoxes. To wit:

The northernmost counties—Bergen, Essex, Union, Passaic, Hudson and part of Middlesex—contain one of the greatest industrial concentrations in the world; yet here, among the smokestacks, live a good half of the entire population of New Jersey.

Here is a whole section of a state living in the shadow of the world's biggest city. It might be supposed that these north-county residents would have a raging sense of inferiority. Yet North Jerseymen are gusty, independent, inventive, and immensely proud of their own communities. They have built Newark, the biggest and richest city in their state, in plain and defiant view of the colossus across the Hudson.

North Jersey is a commuters' land, a farmers' land, a millworkers' land and a fox-hunters' land. It has produced great prize fighters and great inventors. Its greatest poet is a suburban doctor. It has given birth to engineering impossibilities, medical marvels, agricultural innovations and the movies. It has some entrancing vacation resorts and even a few great country landholdings.

In the hill and valley lands around Somerville, Bedminster, Bernardsville and Morristown are baronial remnants of a lush past that have survived changing times and mounting taxes. They remain as a wistful rear guard fighting for the last real luxury money can buy—simple privacy.

Just how long the classical countryside will remain rural is a matter of much speculation today. A recent census revealed that many of the northern counties have gained new citizens in fantastic numbers. And some of the suburbs which lie within the long shadow of Manhattan have doubled in size.

The growth of the suburbs is understandable. Many New Jersey citizens have good reasons for wanting to move away from the part of their state which is adjacent to New York Harbor, Newark Bay and Raritan Bay. This area holds one of the world's greatest concentrations of industrial capacity. It is a center of electrical machinery-and-equipment production, of chemicals, paints, steel fabrication, food products, textiles, aircraft and automobiles, clocks, instruments, jewelry, drugs and petroleum products. The musk of a motorized nation lies heavy upon it, and the cities within the industrial belt are far from scenic. Railroads bisect them. Trucks pound and crowd their streets. They are immensely productive cities, however, with a neon-lighted vigor, yet most of them are shedding citizens to the suburbs which surround them.

Life within these suburbs is standard suburbia. Montclair, the Oranges, Englewood, Plainfield, Teaneck, Morristown, Summit, Maplewood, Bloomfield, Chatham, Dunellen, Tenafly, and a hundred others belong to the "sundowners." "Sundown citizens" are Jerseymen during evenings and week ends. They decimate whole towns each morning to catch buses or trains to city office or factory. They are earnest breadwinners who travel astronomical miles going nowhere in particular and coming home again to sleep.

The shuttle-minded Jerseyman who commutes to New York daily takes his miracles for granted. Not so the first-time visitor to the North Jersey metropolitan area. The bridges and tunnels across the Hudson are authentic wonders and are appreciated as such. They are operated by the Port of New York Authority, a self-supporting, bi-state agency, without tax burden upon either state. Oldest of the submarine crossings is the Holland Tunnel built at a cost of $50,000,-000, named for its first chief engineer, Clifford M. Holland, and opened to the public in 1927. It links 12th Street, Jersey City, with

Canal Street, New York, and collects approximately 15,000,000 car tolls each year. Newest of the great tunnels is the six-lane, triple-tube Lincoln Tunnel which burrows beneath the river to join Weehawken with midtown Manhattan at 39th Street.

The most glamorous river crossing, however, is the George Washington Bridge. This soaring two-level span links Fort Lee with 178th Street and New York's Riverside Drive and Henry Hudson Parkway. Drivers of the vehicles which pay more than 15,000,000 tolls each year to cross upon this eight-lane highway have a tendency to move a bit slower than usual simply to absorb the view. Here is the sweep of the Hudson River at its finest, with the ruler-straight shadows of the span and the cobweb tracery of the suspension cables blurring the water surface 260 feet below.

Not all North Jerseymen, of course, fall into such simple categories as the gentry, the suburbanites and the city dwellers. The state has produced its full quota of great names. Certainly there is no schoolboy in Northern New Jersey so dull-witted as not to know the name and the saga of Thomas Alva Edison, the "Wizard of Menlo Park," the confidant of presidents, the greatest inventor (*Pravda* notwithstanding) of his time, and the father, incidentally, of a later governor of New Jersey, Charles Edison.

Edison's patents were listed by the hundreds. He was the father of the stock ticker, the mimeograph machine, the grandsire of modern radio. He came close enough to television to warrant an assist. The companies that he founded within the electrical industry became the giant of General Electric and its many subsidiary corporations today. If any man were to try to assay the relative importance of his inventions in their impact upon life in the United States, he would have a herculean job of judgment upon his hands. Perhaps his best known invention was the electric-light bulb, the first practical incandescent lamp which came out of his laboratories in 1879. The Pennsylvania Railroad ran special trains to see its public demonstration at Menlo Park.

However, two years before the electric-light bulb and immediately following his invention of the phonograph, the inventor sought to create "eyes" to go with his mechanical "voice." Assisted by W. K. L. Dickson, a young Englishman, Edison came up with the Kinetoscope, a device that gave pictures the illusion of motion. Almost simultaneously, Hannibal Goodwin, a Newark minister, created a "film" base to take the place of glass plates in cameras. Edison's Kinetoscope, literally a "peep show" device, built a demand for film. By the time his improved Vitascope hit the market, causing the "nickelodeons" to mushroom throughout the East, the North of Jersey was cradling the infant motion-picture industry in no uncertain terms.

Edwin S. Porter, a former Edison employee turned producer, created the industry's pioneer classic. He borrowed a train from the Lackawanna Railroad and took a company on location at Paterson, where a Passaic River bridge was commandeered for a scene in which a man was "thrown from a moving train." Later he moved into the "wilds" of Essex County for some daring horseback sequences. The result was *The Great Train Robbery* with "Broncho Billy" Anderson—the first action-filled movie melodrama.

There are middle-aged Jerseymen who vividly recall the pioneer thrillers made along the scenic Palisades which form the Jersey bank of the Hudson. Fort Lee's Coytesville section was the Hollywood of the East then. The Barrymores lived there: Mr. and Mrs. Maurice, sons Lionel and John, and daughter Ethel. So did the Bennetts: Mr. and Mrs. Richard, and daughter Constance. Early studios erected buildings for such players as Mary Pickford, Theda Bara, Marie Dressler, John Bunny, Charlie Chaplin, "Fatty" Arbuckle, Lon Chaney and Alice Brady, most of whom commuted to New York when the day's grimacing was done. Pearl White's Palisades cliff hanging in the *Perils of Pauline* brought the later term "cliff hangers" into being to describe movie serials.

Edison's invention of the moving picture and the area's pioneer development of the movie-art form is possibly New Jersey's greatest contribution to American culture. But the State has not entirely ignored the individual arts. William Carlos Williams, poet, doctor, and a native of Rutherford, has won a whole cluster of poetry awards while pursuing a very busy and successful practice as a pediatrician. And in Bergen County, in the twenties, Upton Sinclair founded an art colony known as Helicon Hall.

Sinclair and his group of beautiful dreamers took over a huge and dilapidated mansion along the Palisades and opened it to some 300 applicants who came to create. The colonists lacked necessities, but they were long on the intellectual conversations of the times. Some were long on talent too—the late Sinclair Lewis, for instance, who passed briefly through Helicon Hall. The old mansion finally burned to the ground, its only remnant a law suit filed by the colonists for lost manuscripts.

The region's creativeness is mostly professional. The research laboratories scattered throughout North Jersey represent about one tenth of the entire nation's probing into the scientific world of the future. Estimates of the annual research outlay within this region run to several hundred million.

Yet the one research and educational institution closest to the hearts of Jerseymen is no commercial enterprise. It is gray, quiet Rutgers University on the banks of the Raritan River where it winds through New Brunswick. Chartered in 1766 as Queen's College, Rutgers is the eighth-oldest college in the United States. It was selected by the state legislature as a land-grant institution in 1864 and formally designated as the State University of New Jersey in 1945.

It was Rutgers' College of Agriculture which, not long ago, gave Dr. Selman Waksman's now famous antibiotic, streptomycin, to the world and moved mankind another step ahead in the conquest of disease.

Waksman's work is not so well known as other Rutgers contributions, of lesser importance, to American civilization, such as the game of football and its associated declaration which has become a cliché for phony heroism: "I'd die for dear old Rutgers." The first American game of intercollegiate football was played at New Brunswick between Rutgers and its southern neighbor, Princeton, in 1869. Rutgers won that first game, a feat it only sparingly repeats during their now-traditional rivalry.

The character of North Jersey is shaped by factors other than its people and its institutions. Some of the area, for instance, is made lovely by a simple geologic formation known as the Highlands, which is part of the Appalachian foothills. The extreme northwest corner of the state in Warren and Sussex Counties is Appalachian Valley country, with the flat, crested ridge of Kittatinny Mountain overlooking it for more than thirty miles. This reach of ground stretches from the most northerly tip of the state, south to the Delaware Water Gap, where the Delaware River has sliced through rock to form a tourist attraction that annually lures thousands of visitors. More than half of this land is owned by the state and forms the scenic sweep of Stokes State Forest and High Point Park.

High Point, of course, gets its name because its 1823-foot elevation is higher than anything else in Jersey with the possible exception of the state budget. It is a wildlife sanctuary as nearly primitive in character as modern man can comfortably stand, and a camper's delight in the summer. Hikers know it for the section of the Appalachian Trail which enters the park at the New York border and runs south to Stokes Forest. Once a grant from the English king to Lord Rutherford, the land that is now High Point Park was donated to the state in 1923.

The view from High Point is an unbroken one, scanning adjacent Pennsylvania and New York. Enthusiasts claim that from its summit it is possible to see some twenty or more villages, as well as the Alleghenies of Pennsylvania and the Catskills of New York.

It is in the hill country of Northwest Jersey that much of metropolitan and suburban New Jersey plays. Some eighty lakes shimmer in Sussex County. There are forty-one more in Passaic County, including the Pompton Lakes area, ten miles northwest of Paterson, where for years the nation's better prize fighters have conditioned themselves for major bouts. Largest of all the cabin- and resort-lined lakes of the North is Hopatcong, whose forty miles of shoreline ramble from Morris County into Sussex. The coves formed by its indentations make more shoreline than one might expect in a lake that is only nine miles long, but this is a condition that pleases the hundreds of cabin owners. The tiny coves provide green privacy.

Hopatcong in the summer is a recreational mural in tree green and lake blue, a panorama of rafts, floats, canoes and swimmers. It is a giant fresco of small sails, power boats, and grubby boys picking fishing worms out of cans; of moonlight and dance music; of rocking chairs, lighted cigars and cold beer. There are smaller, more exclusive lake colonies in the North, but the recreational pattern, give or take a few tonier facilities, is about the same. Approximately 250,000 vacationists pour into the region annually, many of them "lake families" who have been coming into these playlands since the turn of the century.

It would be wrong to imply that a major proportion of Jersey pleasure seekers spill into the mountain and lake country. As many more go to favored spots along the 120 miles of ocean beaches which stretch the entire length of Jersey.

Many Jerseymen find recreation in other, non-athletic ways. There are probably more amateur historians, antiquarians, folklorists and genealogists in the North of Jersey than in any other American sector, including New England. To them the Jersey hinterlands are one immensely fertile Yesterday. It is not enough to say that preoccupation with the past is a common characteristic. A waspish dowager explained this during a Humus Committee meeting at a local garden club. "My dear," she said. "There are no natives in this community. We are all descendants."

There are, for instance, eighty-five chapters of Daughters of the American Revolution operative within the state, in addition to auxiliary chapters of Sons of, Children of, and other organizations recalling historical data. Only in Jersey would the doughty Daughters be considered a johnny-come-lately group as compared to the Order of Founders and Patriots of America which commemorates "the *founders* of the country as *distinct* from the colonists who reaped the benefit of earlier work and hardships."

The Garden State was properly called "the cockpit of the Revolution." From the time the embattled colonists deposed the last royal governor, William Franklin, to the time George Washington delivered his farewell address to his troops at Rocky Hill outside Princeton, in 1783, Jersey saw the bulk of a rebellious nation's military traffic. More than one hundred battles and skirmishes were fought on the state's soil, most of them in the hinterland of the North, and all of them vital in some manner to control of the all-important Hudson and Delaware River valleys. The campaigning, marked by highway signs, embodied in preserved and restored sites and perpetuated by native fervor for historical gatherings, will never die.

There are places in the North today where so much of the past is physically present that it is possible to believe with a minimum of imagination that Washington and his men never left the state. Morristown, a community of some 17,000 residents and the county seat of Morris County, is such a place. Tourists driving over U. S. Route 202, which runs a diagonal course across Jersey from Lambertville on the Delaware to Suffern in New York State, inevitably dawdle through its tree-lined streets and move cautiously around the Green, which has been the parklike heart of its business center for two centuries. It is not a place for hurry. Even the bustle of its commercial area is a decorous bustle, a mingling of shoppers aware of opportunities to chat.

At one time more millionaires lived within a mile of its environs than in any other similar area in the world, and these were turn-of-the-century millionaires who never knew an income tax. The estates of the Wall Street barons and early industrial leaders have long since moved to the somewhat less-traveled areas around Bedminster and Bernardsville a few miles away, yet Morristown still owns a substantial air of well-being. There is no one to maintain a hundred servants as did the long-gone Otto Kahn, but there is still the foxhunting. Polo, played before World War I at the Whippany River Club, is a middle-aged memory, but genteel dog raising endures in the grand tradition. The one-day show sponsored by Mrs. Marcellus Hartley Dodge at Giralda Farms each May is the best of its type in the country.

Such civic mementos as the $400,000 mansion built by former A. T. & T. president Theodore N. Vail, which now serves as the community's Municipal Building, remind its people of a plush era; but Morristown's affection belongs to a much earlier past, to the days when the Whippany River powered the pre-Revolution iron forges, and the rich ore of West Morris County supplied a hundred mines, forges, furnaces and rolling mills. The county was not only the arsenal of the Continental troops during the Revolution, it was also a major battleground and rest camp, the essence of the Revolution. It saw troop desertions, foraging atrocities and mutiny. It is probably the richest single-source spot of Revolutionary history and lore in the nation. Citizen Tom Paine wrote his crisis papers there. "The times that try men's souls" are impressively recalled by the 1000-acre Morristown National Historical Park established by the Federal Government in 1933, the first of its type created in the United States. Thousands of tourists enter its expanse each year to walk the Colonial camp ground of Jocky Hollow, where, in 1781, the mutiny of the Pennsylvania Line nearly destroyed the Continental war effort, and where Captain Adam Bettin, killed resisting his own men, still lies beneath the "Bettin Oak." The visitors troop across Fort Nonsense, an earthwork boondoggle built, allegedly, to keep Washington's soldiers busy, and see the house that Washington and his wife occupied.

The trim town about the Green is far from being the only gateway to the Jersey past. North of Morristown, where the giant Wanaque Reservoir lies in the folded hills, and the quiet Ramapo River winds through its shaded valley, lies a country seemingly untouched by the metropolitan regions so near in miles, so distant in time.

There is no peace to match a dusk in July along the South Branch of the Raritan River, between Flemington and Washington, when the fireflies are busy in the cornfields and the perfume of new-cut alfalfa hangs on the sloping knolls and the cicadas are drilling holes in the sundown haze, prophesying heat for the morrow. There is no tranquillity to excel a mid-morning in January on the oldest road in America, the Old Mine Road near Montague, with the sun so bright on a fresh fall of snow that the shadows of the hills and trees are black, and the river itself is a vivid green slash on a white blanket. Yet a long tradition of violence, raiding and murder taints the pastoral of the state.

The classic criminal case of modern America was a product of rural Jersey. It happened March 1, 1932, near Hopewell in Mercer County. It was the Lindbergh kidnap case, which reached its climax in the drowsy little town of Flemington in 1935 when Bruno Richard Hauptmann was sentenced to die in the electric chair. The case rocked the political structure of New Jersey, reverberated over the entire country. The story of how 20-month-old Charles Lindbergh, Jr., then the only son of his distinguished parents, was stolen from his crib and found dead on a forest trail is now a national drama.

Jersey folks still remember the roads leading into Flemington blocked, at trial time, by a parade of vehicles which extended across the state. It was a morbid caravan which moved, sometimes as slowly as three miles an hour, and which produced traffic jams that half the State Police was unable to disengage. Applications for trial tickets came from U. S. Senators, Hollywood stars, society luminaries, concert singers and reformers. Reporters covering Flemington sent more than a million words of copy from the scene each day.

The Lindbergh case is matched by only one other in the annals of American crime, and that too was a rural-Jersey murder mystery which to this day remains officially unsolved. It broke in September, 1922, but its impact was so great that it still makes Sunday-supplement copy. No case ever held such bizarre elements or so strange a cast of characters as that which began when the Rev. Edward Wheeler Hall and Mrs. James Mills, one of his choir singers, were found shot and slashed to death on a farm near New Brunswick. Its preliminary investigations turned up dalliant church workers, a Hindu "swami," and a gross proprietor of a nearby farm who was for evermore to be known as "the pig woman."

Not until four years after the original investigations did the Hall-Mills case reach trial. The accused were wealthy Mrs. Hall herself, widow of the slain clergyman, and her brothers. The trial opened in

Somerville, in November, 1926, and a month later Mrs. Hall and her brothers were acquitted.

Such hectic events, of course, do not occur frequently but it would be wrong to assume that any part of North Jersey is entirely calm today. As one Newark bookmaker said when Senator Estes Kefauver's Senate Investigating Committee on organized crime sent agents into the area that lies in the shadow of New York's skyscrapers: "Everything's hassle and risk these days."

But Northern New Jersey has been experiencing hassle and risk for nearly three centuries and thriving on it. The contradictory, quick-changing, vital region remains inured to surprises. They are part of the fascination of its future. At present, North Jersey is trying something new—a re-evaluation of its two, sharply distinctive ways of life. The cities are spreading into the suburbs and the factories are moving into the farmlands. Nervous assembly-line living in the smoky cities and crowded suburbs in the shadow of Manhattan is slowly going out of style, and may some day be as old-fashioned as the baronial way of life on the great estates. There is a new awareness among North Jersey citizens of the beauties and assets of their countryside and perhaps even a longing for the simpler days of the rich New Jersey past.

## THE COAST

The most concentrated playtime strand in the United States is a more or less continuous slash of white beach which extends from Sandy Hook, an Army post which rams a fortified finger into New York's Lower Bay, to Cape May. For 125 miles the waters of the Atlantic Ocean are merely a form of liquid money during the months of high summer, and as such are appreciated by the hospitable residents of New Jersey washed by its tides.

Along this coast, dominated by the famous resort towns of Long Branch, Asbury Park, Atlantic City, Wildwood and Cape May, the summer seashore vacation in the United States originated and flowered. Along this coast, each summer, the greatest number of hot-weather holiday rovers in the United States happily congregates.

Cape May is probably the oldest seaside resort in the United States. The Lenni-Lenape Indians were using the cape as a recreation spot before Henry Hudson sailed by the point in 1609 en route to Sandy Hook. Aristocratic Philadelphians, bored with the war years of the

Revolution, sailed Delaware Bay and found recreational pleasure at a fishing village on the same cape before President George Washington took his oath of office. As early as 1788 a boardinghouse at Long Branch on the northern sector of the coast hung out its shingle to attract visitors.

The wild and comparatively isolated coast of Jersey has always been a haven for fishermen, nature lovers, people seeking rest cures, fugitives, and for adventurers who couldn't abide the disciplines of city life. It still is.

Each spring the winter-gray waters of the Atlantic subside into creaming blue swells, which gently lave the Jersey coast as if sorry they spent the winter months eroding chunks out of the beach front. The lead-hued sand dries white and gleaming beneath the high-climbing vernal sun; and from Sandy Hook to Cape May, the shore looks scrubbed. All the days are blue and white and somehow highly tonic.

The sedges of the salt marshes, and the rushes along the fiddler-drilled bay banks wage green war against the brittle browns of winter. On the wilder beaches of the lesser developed resorts the bay-berry bushes sprout leaves and the branches of the beach plums darken with new shoots.

Red-winged blackbirds dart in the meadows. Sandpipers run their skimming gait along the surf, and the black-polled terns fly incredible formations at wave-crest heights. The graceful American egrets fish in the thousands of drainage sloughs in the meadows, the ditches which first began the fight against the Jersey mosquito. Poles of the Jersey Central Power and Light Company and the Atlantic City Electric Company get clumsy adornment as the ospreys rebalance their top-heavy nests.

On 10,000 pilings, pierheads, rickety wharves and fancy docks, the slovenly, lumbering herring gulls bleat, "Put on the blond feathers, kids, the summer folks are coming."

From early June to October, 50,000,000 vacationers move from the cities of the East to the Jersey coast.

Officials of the New Jersey Resort Association—who think nothing of counting each visitor four or five times—estimate that these pleasure seekers spend over a billion dollars each season in the more than fifty-five large, small and eternally hopeful resort communities which line the shore.

The magnitude of this bonanza points up the fact that the genus "guest" is to the resident of the Jersey coast what the reindeer is to the Laplander, his comfort and sustenance. For the big business of the strand is pleasure, and with the possible exception of Ocean Grove (a Methodist resort on the northern reach of the beaches which on Sunday prohibits bathing and stretches chains across its main streets to stop all traffic), few of the coastal towns ever forget it.

Atlantic City, the colossus of the strand, never stops entertaining. This party metropolis, sixty-two miles from Philadelphia and 125 miles from New York by virtually any means of transportation (including one recorded balloon trip in 1906), is not a beautiful resort in the sense that lusher, more verdantly scenic resorts are beautiful. Not all of the luxury hotels along the beach front—including Chalfonte-Haddon Hall, the 1000-room hostel which ranks as the biggest and among the best on the strand—are sleek models of contemporary architecture. No one, however, can deny that they are impressive. And when all of the scenically pampered resorts have run their course up and down the scale of public popularity, this daffy dowager of a town will still be entertaining more guests than any other single resort area in the land. Atlantic City has been harassed by the sea, thumped by national depression, and literally annexed by the military during World War II. Nothing has dampened its monumental vitality or curbed its ebullience.

The 60,000 permanent residents of this gusty town welcome 15,000,000 guests each year, right around the calendar. As Atlantic City goes, so goes the entire Jersey coast. People come to Atlantic City because the town offers a wonderfully infectious brand of foolery, assembly-line entertainment, and a general air of expansiveness not to be found in other places prior to the fourth highball. It is an expansiveness that does not belong to any one segment of society, a democratic euphoria which is just as lifting to the courting couple down for the evening as it is to the retired millionaire registered for the season at the Traymore.

There is no more direct proof that the Jersey coast developed the summer seaside vacation than the mass amusement innovations produced by its biggest resort. The boardwalk, for instance, is an internationally known promenade and an integral part of most seaside resorts. Atlantic City created the original in 1870, at the joint behest of Jacob Keim, a hotel operator who tired of having guests track up his establishment with sandy feet, and Alexander Boardman, a railroad conductor with a hypochondriac's dislike of wet shoes. The resort's boardwalk, sixty feet wide and eight miles long, is a bright-light rialto today where you may buy anything from an ice-cream cone to a $10,000 piece of Ming pottery.

On a midsummer week end, with the sea breaking within sight of the strollers and the beaches filled with bathers, it is a timber highway worth going miles to see. But at night, crowded rail to rail with nearly a half million people and with its incredible bursts of neon emitting silent screams of color, it is a living lane of light that casts a radiance far out over the ocean.

The boardwalk is not the only Atlantic City contribution to summertime. The town fostered the invention of the rolling chair (modern versions are mechanized), salt-water taffy, the picture post card, and what might be termed the first "packaged entertainment" in the form of the amusement pier.

The best example of the last-mentioned today is George Abou Hamid's Steel Pier, a sturdy platform structure mounted on pilings which extends 2000 feet to sea. It has four movie theaters, a dance floor and assorted features ranging from a zoo to Danny Kaye—all for one admission price. In the fifty-four years of Steel Pier's existence some 90,000,000 persons have paid to goggle its variety acts—from the high-diving Hawaiian who one night conked a porpoise on the way down from his 150-foot perch to "John the Baptist," a diving horse who made a lesser leap for thirty years without contact with fish. Steel Pier has offered gorillas, movie horses, flagpole sitters and crooners by the score.

Performers have been paid as high as $50,000 for a single week's appearance, and have earned every nickel of it.

Not all of the town's ingenuity has been directed toward the laughing side of resort pleasures. Atlantic City's past shows a shrewd cognizance of such summertime fundamentals as safety for the millions who use its broad beach. As early as 1855, when the municipality appointed a "constable of the surf" for $117 a year, the lifeguard became a clearly discernible specimen along the strand. Wherever he may function, today's lifeguard, tanned shoulders and peeled nose, is an evolutionary product of the Jersey coast.

Atlantic City is the only real year-round resort along the coast, although Asbury Park is a valid pretender. Winter visitors, for the most part, are convention delegates (by the thousands), sinus sufferers who find balm in the clean salt air, tired executives who haunt hotel

sun decks and watch the hypnotic sea, and the usual night-out people
who drive from nearby cities for a shore dinner at Hackney's Restaurant, a walk on the boards, and a night-club evening.

To remain a twelve-month host, the resort discovered long ago
that constant promotion effort is a virtue, and that the best type of
resort promotion is feminine either in appeal or content. The annual
Palm Sunday and Easter parades are among the biggest fashion
shows in the East.

Best known of all the resort's annual events, however, is the Miss
America Pageant. In its early days the Pageant was an out-and-out
callipygian display, but today it is one of the authentically beautiful,
handsomely staged shows of the year. The Pageant, born in the mind
of newspaperman Herb Test, in 1921, was the pioneer event which
subsequently spread the now-familiar beauty-contest idea from the
Jersey shore to every whistle stop in the nation. Pageant officials
estimate that there are 25,000 such competitions held annually in the
United States, and that since Margaret Gorman, of Washington,
D.C., was crowned in 1921, some 500,000 "queens" of everything
from cheese to oranges have been selected throughout the country.
Further, the "queen" movement in our increasingly matriarchal society shows no signs of abatement. Asbury Park, for instance, has
been featuring a *Mrs.* America contest for the past few years.

Gone are the days when the girls competed and were judged by
such loose standards as "loveliness, charm and pulchritude." Since
1944, the judges have been coping with the quality known as "talent."
Further, it is authentic talent spread over a wide range. By the
Saturday night of the official coronation of a new queen in Convention Hall, the judges, and the huge audiences that have paid high
for the privilege have usually heard some better-than-good voices.
They have seen some intense, if yet unpolished, bits of acting, some
creative dancing, and lesser aptitudes ranging from cartooning to
water-skiing demonstrations to "chantootsie" versions of hardy peren-
nials like the *Lullaby of Broadway* and *Daddy's Little Girl.*

Despite the nationally known reputations of such resorts as Atlantic City and Asbury Park, and the still warm turn-of-the-century
memories of Long Branch and Cape May, many of the fifty-odd shore
municipalities are almost one merged entity today.

Municipal distinctions are not as varied as the enthusiasts of individual shore towns might suppose. In fact, there are no really exclusive Jersey resorts, although there are a few minor beach colonies which would like to assume such a cachet.

The huge, landscape-pampered mansions around Rumson in North Jersey and those which line the Ocean Drive through nearby Deal bespeak wealth, as do the scattered, quiet estates which are still sprinkled through the pinelands bordering the strand; but many of the most impressive are valiant remnants of older glories. Bay Head and Mantoloking proclaim reasonably moneyed substantiality mostly in terms of the huge, weather-silvered homes which tower over the dunes. There are luxury hotels and lavish structures from one end of the entire 125-mile surf line to another.

But, by and large, the Jersey coast belongs to the middle-class millions that throng to it from the great metropolitan feeder cities —hard-working, family people.

Naturally, the mink-and-sable set is noticeable among them, but hardly for the tinsel flamboyance which characterizes wintertime along the Florida Gold Coast. The Cadillacs at the Atlantic City Race Track and at Monmouth Park are black, not lavender. The party urge is normally expressed in yacht-club dancing, garden teas and restrained dinner parties at some luxury hotel or surf club. Comfort, rather than excitement, is the keynote of the substantial summer people. Expressed in terms of sloppy game-fishing garb, rumpled golf apparel and denim gardening gear, this comfort disguises if not quite hides the wearers' bank accounts. A genuine air of democracy blows, sweet as the salt breezes, along the Jersey strand, a condition stated succinctly by a retired banker: "There are no wallet pockets in a pair of bathing trunks."

Variations in vacation tastes, and minor geographic distinctions, account for most of the differences between Jersey resorts.

Game fishermen, for instance, flock to Brielle, where the Manasquan Inlet leads offshore to a deep, known as the "mudhole"; here, in season, they troll for school tuna, bluefish, bonita and infrequent marlin.

All the resorts have their individual problems; but from the time the first tourist sat a sundown rocking chair, his head haloed by a nimbus of mosquitos, they all have shared one major concern: that mysterious, capricious element known as "the condition of the beach." Dat Ole Debbil Sea can be a villain as well as a friend. Within a single decade the state has spent almost $7,000,000 on various save-the-sands measures, most of which has been matched, dollar for dollar, by the collective communities involved. And, though there are no exact figures, informed guesses say that private property owners and solvent towns have spent millions more. But, as the horse players at Monmouth Park and Atlantic City race tracks are frequently heard to remark, "Nobody comes here to worry."

There is still virgin beach along the coast, some of it as unspoiled as it was when the shoal reefs of the midcoast were known as "the graveyard of the Atlantic." Perhaps the wildest of all such areas is Island Beach, a nine-mile-long, 2200-acre strip of Barnegat Peninsula, a paradise for marine birds, a haven for dune deer and rabbits, and a wonderful garden where beach heather blooms yellow and the green of cedar and holly seems black against the glaring sands.

The best of the shore's facilities remain the ones nature produced eons ago—beaches and the bays whose "windward-leeward" reaches are dappled with sails each summer. There are still natives shaped by the beaches and bays whose lives remain indigenous to them, but it's pretty hard to tell the year-round residents from the summer people these days. Single-hour access to the big cities over fine highways works both ways.

Once in a while a lucky visitor meets a rawhide-tough old-timer whose life typifies its undefiled saltwater habitat. Not too many years ago the little creeks and the tiny coves held many of them. They lived in snuggish shanty boats at peace with a chunk stove that was winter-red with driftwood. They blessed their walls with cardboard calendars which did double duty as wall caulking, and waited out the time they shared with the sea. Now and again, for tobacco money, they'd remember a minor fish hole for a summer vistor, or confide a favored duck slough to a high-school kid bright with a new shotgun and the memory of a hasty summer promise. They owned an elemental quiet and were jealous of it. They've gone now, but the bays are still building rugged men, and the best of them, in this opinion, are sailors.

There are thousands of power craft operating along the Jersey coast and thousands more sailboats; but the craft best known to the greatest number of people are the rowboats which blanket the back bays with fishermen on a Sunday afternoon or the party boats which chug offshore with rails packed shoulder to shoulder with bottom fishermen.

The railroad which connected Long Branch to New York in 1874, and Monmouth Park race track, opened in 1870, brought social and saloon society from Manhattan.

President Ulysses S. Grant made The Branch a summer home and so did President Garfield, who died here in 1881, after a vain attempt to recover from an assassin's bullet.

Presidents Hayes and Harrison stayed at the old Elberon Hotel and, later, Woodrow Wilson lived at Shadow Lawn, on the west side of the resort. But even presidential patronage could not curb the gusty high jinks which gave The Branch its golden reputation. Lillie Langtry kept a private railroad car on a siding adjoining the home of her current gentleman friend for an entire summer. Diamond Jim Brady bought an electric coupé brightly lighted inside for the benefit of the admiring crowds who watched him and Lillian Russell pass the length of Blue Drive.

While the northern sector of the coast bloomed and blazed with the fulsome antics of the Gay Nineties, the southernmost tip of the strand was entering its second century as a resort, more quietly, more restrained, infinitely more social, as if the Cape itself knew that there were more descendants of the Mayflower colony living in Cape May County than remained in Plymouth, Massachusetts.

The Cape was settled early. Fourteen years after Hudson sailed up the coast in 1609, Captain Cornelius Jacobus Mey arrived in Delaware Bay in the *Good Tidings,* to give the Cape his name and establish settlements. In 1801, Postmaster Ellis Hughes advertised in a Philadelphia newspaper that he had "prepared himself for entertaining company who use sea bathing" and that he was "accommodated with extensive houseroom, with fish, oysters, crabs and good liquors."

Hughes' "extensive houseroom," with coed sleeping quarters divided by a sheet, became the Hotel Atlantic. Stephen Decatur, weary of fighting Barbary pirates, came to it for sixteen years, fought weakfish, croakers and crabs from gentler decks instead. The year after Hughes' advertisement, boats ran regularly from Philadelphia to Cape May. Congress Hall, the same Congress whose painted brick L and impressive, wooden pillars attract visitors today, was erected in 1816. By 1850, Cape May was the leading summer resort in the country, and by 1867, when the West Jersey Railroad linked it with Philadelphia, it had no close rivals, not even New York's Saratoga, which was, in the genteel parlance of the Cape, "a rather fast place."

Cape May lies below the Mason-Dixon line, and much of its custom came from the same place. Antebellum society leaders from Richmond, Washington and Baltimore, as well as Philadelphia, shared its pleasures. To this day there are still soft accents in a few of the hotels where tradition is respected, like the wistfully passé Chalfonte, a gingerbread scrollwork, wooden-frame remnant of the Cape's Southern hospitality.

Hot breads still grace its tables, its cocktails are bourbon and branch water, and on gala occasions it is not uncommon to find the flag of the Confederacy whipping in the sea breeze.

The Cape also knew its presidential sun lovers. Presidents Lincoln, Grant, Pierce, Buchanan and Harrison were among those regally entertained in its hotels. Merchant John Wanamaker summered there as did editor Horace Greeley who, after admonishing young men to head West, climbed a train and went south-by-east.

The grandeur of the Cape as a resort began to fade as early as 1900. Many of its cottagers, however, and many of the guests who have made it part of their lives for succeeding generations prefer its gradual retreat into history.

They love it for its old shade, its historic homes, its narrow, picturesque streets which, even today, seem reminiscent of a New England fishing village. Compared to much of the Jersey shore, Cape May is not bustling beyond ordinary politeness to attract visitors in herd numbers. Its hotels are full enough, the remains of its once broad beaches are adequate; in midsummer it is just properly crowded—no more. After all, there are just so many things nice people can do well, and the Cape does them—fine plays presented by the Cape Theater, one of the oldest and best of the "straw-hat circuit," sailing at the Yacht Club, and the interminable round of parties and teas and dances which distinguish this brine-scented variation of Philadelphia's Main Line.

Cape May's future as a resort lies somewhere between two statements overheard on a porch of the Lafayette Hotel not long ago; one, made by a placid woman wearing a form-fitting rocking chair; the other, rapped out by a young officer from the nearby Coast Guard base. "In two hundred years of history, one should learn perspective," said the first. "Let's go over to Wildwood and see how fast the night goes," remarked the second, "I'm tired of relaxed drinking."

Chances are that the resort towns strung along the 125 miles of Jersey coast will go right on entertaining; the fish will bite, the sails will fill, the breakers will continue to babble along the sand. If it takes new vacation innovations to remain the most popular recreational area in the country, the rollicking, carefree coast will provide.

# Pennsylvania

## by CONRAD RICHTER

To the very young boy, the word Pennsylvania meant the world. He saw the red-brick house that he and his brothers were born in, and the house was Pennsylvania. He looked at the blue-green mountain walls rimming his home town, and the mountains were Pennsylvania. He waded in the Old Lutheran Church run. His mother told him that the run flowed into Swatara Creek, which flowed into the Susquehanna River, which flowed more than two hundred winding miles from the northern to the southern border of the Commonwealth, and it was Pennsylvania all the way. Fifteen, fifty and seventy miles to the east, she said, three other rivers carried Pennsylvania water, the Schuylkill, the Lehigh and the Delaware. A hundred miles or more over the Alleghenies to the west you could find greater rivers, the Youghiogheny, the Monongahela, the Allegheny and the Ohio, one pouring into the other, and all this was still Pennsylvania.

As that boy who was I grew, he had to concede that Pennsylvania didn't constitute the whole known world, but at least it led the rest. Hadn't the Liberty Bell rung here for all mankind to hear? Wasn't the Declaration of Independence first read within its boundaries? Weren't the Stars and Stripes supposed to have been first sewn here? The First Congress of the Republic had taken place on its sacred soil, not to mention Braddock's Defeat, the Wyoming Massacre, the winter at Valley Forge and the Battle of Gettysburg. William Penn, the Quaker who treated the Indians according to Scripture, had founded the province much as Moses had the Holy Land, with a sense of divine guidance and brotherly love that made Pennsylvanians a chosen people. As the nation expanded, the sons and daughters of Pennsylvania had gone forth like the disciples in the Gospels and had colonized many of the newer states. One of the Pennsylvania Lincolns had migrated from Berks County, and a descendant in Springfield, Illinois, had become perhaps the most famous of all Americans. Daniel Boone and other Pennsylvanians had taken the Pennsylvania-German rifle south, where it became known as the Kentucky rifle. They took the Conestoga wagon west, where it became known as the prairie schooner, and they carried Pennsylvania pioneer words and phrases both south and west, implanting them in what became Southern, Southwestern and Western speech.

More concessions to the world had to be made as I grew older, but ever while traveling around with horse and buggy and on foot with my preacher father, my understanding of and feeling for my native state grew. Most of my family had been here a long time. From childhood I had heard how my double-great-grandfather—a country blacksmith, squire and member of Congress from Pennsylvania for four terms around the time of Jefferson—would tell stories to the litigants on both sides of a case brought before him until he had them in a good humor and willing to settle their dispute without a hearing; how my great-grandfather, a store and hotel keeper and officer in the War of 1812, later sheltered escaping slaves, and how one of them, Black Hetty, had stayed and lived to nurse me as a baby; and how my grandfather, a passionate gardener, and horseman, whose name is still legend around our home town, preached for nearly fifty years in his one charge, baptized more than six thousand people, and drew such a crowd at his funeral that three sermons had to be preached simultaneously, one in the roped-off street.

But what moved me most deeply about Pennsylvania as a boy, and still does today, is her ancient symbol of freedom, the mountains; not a few isolated ranges, as in some states, but a whole province swarming with them, often one against the other with only narrow valleys between. The sight of their backs raised to the sky, sometimes humped or flared, green and lush in summer, brown, hairy and wild in winter, seldom failed to stir me. I liked to study them and learn the lay of their land, how some ran parallel for twenty or even fifty miles and then turned or joined or threw out spurs to form coves and pinnacles or plateaus; how their aspect changed when seen from different angles; how the benches lay like smaller ridges, often with intervening forest swamps or wild hemlock hollows that the old mountain trails and early roads invariably followed; and how water from one mountain tasted sweeter and purer than that from another.

This wilderness of Pennsylvania, much of it still in woods, which aroused my devotion years ago as it does that of a legion of hunters, fishermen and tourists today, is what excited the imagination of the immigrants from Britain and Germany some two hundred years before. Pennsylvania meant Penn's Woods, and that's what set off the fire in men's breasts, the promise of freedom and free land, virgin woods and more virgin woods, mountains and more mountains. Between the mountains were uncounted valleys, small and large, hidden and open, red and yellow shale valleys, black bottom valleys and white limestone valleys, all rank with timber that attested to the richness of the soil. Meat was for the taking, house and barn timber for the cutting, and land for the clearing, well watered for man and stock.

The Indians had other ideas about the woods, which they had reason to believe belonged to them. My great-aunt Esther had told me about Indians; about her namesake, queen of the Senecas; about the massacres near our home town; and about the Severlings who lived near the covered bridge. Hadn't I noticed the Indian blood in their high cheekbones and coarse black hair? More than a hundred years before, a Severling had taken an Indian girl to wife, and so had a Coover, which was why the Coovers still walked straight as pines, usually with gun and dog, and why they lived as they did, resisting white men's ways.

If you knew the Coovers, you knew why the Indians, after William Penn the Just was gone, had fought his descendants and the other colonists tooth and nail, with arrow and fire, lead and scalping knife. They had tried to contain the white intruders first south of one mountain and then south of another. North and northwestward the conflict ran. The gory border advanced and receded across Pennsylvania's mountains through the long French and Indian wars.

Today you can cross these bloodstained mountains with no danger to your hair. Beyond Philadelphia, traveling northwestward along the path of the early white men, you see at first the low Welsh

Mountains, little more than hills. Then, across the garden spots of Lancaster County, you reach the long broken line of South Mountain, where the fabulous Cornwall iron is mined. Beyond lies the fertile Kittatinny Valley, and north of that, from almost any point on a clear day, you can see a wall of mountain hundreds of miles long. This is the Blue Ridge, called hereabouts the Blue Mountain. From the south it looks like a solitary ridge, but once you cross it you find yourself in a prodigality of mountains, long and slender with narrow valleys between. The crests seem to rise higher as you go on, some of them jumping rivers and changing their names, some stopping short while new ones of great length start farther on.

Finally you reach the still-higher Alleghenies, in the north-central area of the state, and see the orderly northeast-to-southwest pattern break up in violent confusion, the ridges running in any direction they choose. When you are no longer in the mountains, you are probably no longer in Pennsylvania.

Pennsylvania's nickname, the Keystone State, has less meaning in the greatly enlarged Union of today. A more apt name might be the Liberty State, not only because it played a leading part in the achievement of independence but for the tremendously varied mixture of its people and regions, in this resembling the character of the nation. The northwestern section, for example, including Erie, belongs in viewpoint and topography more to the Midwest, while the eastern border, including New Hope, the Poconos and Stroudsburg, is by nature a seasonal suburb of New York City. The state is much too vast and diversified to be portrayed fully here, so this report will set down only that Pennsylvania and its people seen and felt by one observer, boy and man.

You will find the Pennsylvania Dutch in the valleys. Like certain species of plants that grow on a particular kind of rock and nowhere else, they flourish in limestone country. If sometimes a Pennsylvania Dutchman is found tilling other soil, it's because there isn't enough limestone to go around. He and his fellows, for the most part, occupy a broad belt running across the state south of the Blue Mountain. Occasional limestone valleys occur in the mountains farther north, where pockets and sometimes an entire county of these people may be found.

Like the French provincials in Canada and the Spanish Americans in the Southwest, the Pennsylvania Dutch keep alive their own language. It's called a dialect but is really more of a German patois, incomprehensible to visitors. And though they settled here two hundred years ago, their English still carries a peculiar accent and turn of phrase that can stop an outsider in his tracks. The accent varies in different sections; some of the thickest accents may be found in the Hegins Valley in Dauphin County and between Kutztown and Allentown in Berks and Lehigh counties. Nor can the idiom be imitated easily. *Papa Is All* was meant to be a play about the Pennsylvania Dutch, but the title betrays the outlander's heavy hand. Pepper and salt and even vacation may be all, but papa and mamma, never.

Being Pennsylvania Dutch myself, I know how hard it is to get rid of the local (pronounced "logal") speech. Children whose parents have little trace of it, pick it up in school and at play, to be called Dutch the rest of their lives. Native men and women who have lived elsewhere for many years, even college professors of English, find to their dismay that certain inflections cling like birthmarks to betray them, along with telltale phrases such as "come here once," "sprinkle down the clothes," "it will be late till we get home," and referring to one's hair in the plural.

The word "dumb," in the sense of stupid, was in my boyhood purely Pennsylvania Dutch, and our teachers disparaged its use. Similar words used widely in the Pennsylvania Dutch belt by English-speaking people, and which may some day contribute to the American language, are: strubbly, used to describe disheveled, unkempt or rumpled hair; to grex, which means to complain or grunt complainingly; doppick for awkward; spritz for splash and spray; wunnerfitzick for inquisitive; and blutz for jolt and bruise. These words undoubtedly persist because they impart a shade of meaning which the nearest English synonym fails to convey, and also, perhaps chiefly, for their comic expressiveness.

The Pennsylvania Dutch like to laugh. Buildings are erected and automobile engines repaired amid frequent sallies and laughter such as I have heard nowhere else in America. An English traveler of nearly two hundred years ago left a record of the Pennsylvania Dutch custom of standing outside their churches to joke until it was time for the service to start—then coming out and resuming when it was over. Sometimes they laugh over trifles, out of pure animal spirits. Or they may see another meaning unintelligible to outsiders, as in the classic story about the Pennsylvania Dutch woman who came into a store; the clerk asked what he could do for her, and she said, "Oh, I don't want nothing. I just came in to go out."

There is, of course, one class of Pennsylvania Dutch jokes the outsider can understand and laugh at—those at the expense of the natives. These may be such banal and familiar ones as the sign on the door reading, "If the bell don't make, bump," or the remark of a child watching a freight train go by—"Ain't, Mom, when the little red house comes, then it's all?" For every one of these, however, the observing resident of the southern counties knows a dozen that seldom reach print. The woman who cleans our house said triumphantly after killing a snake, "Well, that's one more copperhead less," a statement that shines with succinctness if not with logic.

Tom Lyter, of Ono, tells the story of the widow who was called on by a man who wanted to see her husband.

"You can't see him. He's dead," she said.

"Dead?" the man exclaimed. "Why, when did he die?"

"Well," she said, "if he'd a lived till Thursday he'd be dead two weeks."

Paul Strickler, of Lebanon, relates how he went with a countryman to look for his lost dog, Wasser.

"Now you go up one side of the crick," the man said. "I'll go up the other. You know, he may come back both sides."

If such stories strike you as funny, you have an affinity for Pennsylvania Dutch humor. I have heard these, and many like them, told in my living room until a half score of people, all of them with a dash or more of native blood, shouted with laughter.

On the serious side, the Pennsylvania Dutch have been accused of leaning toward powwowing and hexerei. This is true enough, particularly in the recent past. My grandfather could powwow and was regularly called on to practice his art. He tried to persuade my mother to let me hold a worm in my hand while I was being baptized. This was supposed to give me the power, but my mother, whose maiden name was Henry, declined. As for hex stories, I have heard them all my life, many at firsthand, some told by men and women whose veracity in other matters was unquestioned. I remember as a boy the half-scared sensation of walking past the house of an alleged hex in my home town, and there were others in the surrounding countryside. Some of these reputed hexes, like their counterparts in New England, had a hard time among their fellows, although the

Pennsylvania Dutch, the first to talk against slavery in America, did not hang their witches.

The traveler may think he sees evidence of hexerei in Pennsylvania Dutch barn signs, which an enterprising Yankee by name of Wallace Nutting told the public were witches' feet. Actually, these are harmless symbols of sun and rain and crop fertility. More than that, they are simply ornaments, of which the Pennsylvania Dutch are very fond. Their early baptism and marriage certificates, their furniture and many other articles are decorated with brightly colored designs of tulips, doves, parrots, roosters, vines and like motifs. They love color, especially red, as attested by their big bank barns and by their houses, often of brick and frequently painted over to make the brick redder.

Pennsylvania Dutch houses are "crazy clean"; porches and cellar steps are regularly scrubbed; sidewalks, gutters and sometimes the street are scrupulously swept; even farms and fields look neat as toy yards under Christmas trees. And the food is something to be remembered in Gath. . . . The tables of the Pennsylvania Dutch groan with good things to eat, particularly when visitors, no matter how humble, are being entertained. The legend that seven sweets and seven sours are served is something of a fantasy, but there are always plenty of both. If there are many guests at dinner, the fare will probably include chicken accompanied by beef or ham, hard-boiled eggs in red-beet juice, as well as vegetables, relishes, fruits and several kinds of pie and cake. Notable Pennsylvania Dutch dishes, for some of which I still grow hungry in far places, are dandelion greens, chowchow, chicken corn soup, pannhaas (a kind of richer scrapple made from country "butchering"), Lebanon bologna, smoked sausage (generally half beef, half pork and cured in an old-fashioned smokehouse), snitz and knepp, fastnachts, pretzels, and shoofly pie with deep goo.

Just off the Pennsylvania Dutch belt lies the metropolis of Philadelphia, exiled inland and yet one of the titanic ports of the world, rich as Croesus and yet quiet and unobtrusive as the Quakers, the municipality of brotherly love and humility and also of the haughty tradition, now almost vanished, that no lady or gentleman would live north of Market Street. A modern center of music and publishing, medicine, manufacturing and refining, it still has streets where time has stood still. Crammed with historic spots, tombs, churches and buildings, as well as with libraries, museums and colleges, Philadelphia's list of firsts tops the nation.

But to me and my fellow townsmen, a hundred miles away, all this was simply "the city." "Are you going to the city today?" we'd say.

North of the Pennsylvania Dutch country, and interlaced by it, lies the rugged hard-coal region. I was born on the southern edge of the anthracite country, and one of my earliest memories is the sound of heavy boots marching up the street to one of the miners' trains that left long before dawn. By afternoon the same trains returned, crowded with homecoming miners like blackface minstrels in overalls, dinner buckets slung over their shoulders, the men dropping off the train before it stopped and breaking into a dogtrot toward home and washtub.

A few years later, we moved to a hard-coal town at the foot of what was known as Fighting Hill, where women during the Great Strike had torn each other's hair in the street. I picked slate in a breaker, swam in a sulphur creek and heard the pioneer union leader, John Mitchell, speak in my home street. My brothers and I found it a kind of storybook country: the man-made mountains of coal dirt down which children of the patch coasted on staves; the "batching" shanties of miners who tramped back and forth to their distant farms on weekends, over forest trails and usually several mountains; the dangerous uncharted air holes in the mountains, where the unwary walker might fall to oblivion; the great sooty collieries; the terrifying mine slopes that dropped into dripping blackness; the endless underground gangways by which miners could come out miles from where they went in; the older, robbed and abandoned workings flooded by water and eternal night; the mules that never saw the light of day; the mine rats born a thousand feet underground that lived on mules' feed; and above all, the brave men who went down into the sunless pits to work and joke while the ghosts of dead men hovered beside them.

Today the hard-coal region has changed. The old-time labor abuses have given way to reform. The price of coal has risen so high that, even in hard-coal mining towns, many oil burners are in use. Other ways of earning a living have been necessarily found. The drab and sordid look of some of the coal towns has changed. Houses that never knew any coating but soot are often painted today, and the white gleam of electric washers and refrigerators may be glimpsed through the rudest cabin doors. But it's still the hard-coal region, the only one of its kind in the country. The picturesque onion steeples of the Greek and Russian Orthodox churches continue to mark the towns. The men and women of the patch, no matter what their ancestry, speak English with an accent that is Welsh in origin. And veteran miners still carry the telltale sign of their calling, a fine sky-blue marking where coal dirt has tattooed them beneath the skin and won't wash off.

The younger generation hasn't wholly rejected the calling. Not long ago, in a supply store near home, I saw a pair of youths come in to buy explosives. It seemed incredible that such smooth-faced lads could be miners. They looked little more than sixteen. They wore miners' caps, and their faces and hands were black. I guessed that they were bootlegging coal on "company" property in some neglected mountain spot, that they had only an old oil drum for a cage and bucket and the engine of some ancient wrecked car for hoist power, that the rope was probably unsafe, the shaft untimbered and the workings uninspected. But they walked into that store like seasoned miners, and their eyes looked out at you with an old-time pride in their calling, something almost vanished from the American scene.

Across the Susquehanna and the Alleghenies, on the western side of the state for the most part, lie the soft-coal fields. My restless father soon moved us here, and I learned to live in a town surrounded by mining patches called camps, where for block after block no blade of grass grew, where the peculiar incense of soft-coal smoke and of burning mine dumps was the familiar home-town atmosphere. The same mixture of nationalities prevailed here as in the hard-coal region, including the Pennsylvania Dutch. Magyar handlebar mustaches moved proudly down the street. Foreign priests muffled in greatcoats with astrakhan collars became friends of my father, and garlic scented the trolley cars and moving-picture houses.

Anecdotes from the two coal fields are nearly interchangeable. In a hard-coal town with a heavy Slav population, Jim Haas tells of a miner named Stosh Chernitsky. At a wedding flowing with cheer in Miners' Hall, Chernitsky fell out of a second-story window and broke some bones. Some of his friends visited him at the hospital.

"How did I get up there, anyway?" the patient asked them.

"You wanted to fly out one window and back through another, like a bird."

"Why did you let me do it?"

"Let you do it?" his friends said. "We even bet ten dollars you'd make it!"

In a play given at the opera house in Shenandoah, a local coal miner was one of the supers. His only part was to be shot and fall dead on the stage. His appreciative miner friends clapped his act, so he got to his feet and dropped dead again as an encore.

Unlike the hard-coal region, the bituminous country has more native products than coal. Flaming coke ovens light up the countryside at night. In my boyhood they flickered on my eyelids when I tried to sleep, as did the flare of blast furnaces in Johnstown later on. More than one evening, from my boardinghouse on the hill, I watched the night-long pageant in the steel yards below, the cars and buckets of melted ore handled like soup, the castings of red-hot metal carried on cars and transmission lines until finally the great hammers pounded and the sparks flew like red-gold fireflies.

A still-better-known Western Pennsylvania product is oil. The derricks run a little farther north than the coal tipples, but in a number of counties both may be seen. The founding of the world oil industry took place here. Oil from this area was peddled as early as the 1700's, but it was not until Colonel Drake drilled his famous well in 1859 that oil-field fever developed, to run like a wild contagion over most of the world. Here, more than a hundred years ago, $1,500,000 was paid for a single farm. The original Coal Oil Johnny was not John D. Rockefeller, Sr., but John W. Steele, a fabulous man who took a company of black-face minstrels along with him for his amusement and bought hotels to lodge them on overnight stops. Wild Ben Hogan had a sign outside his saloon, "The Wickedest Man in the World," and Gib Morgan told his famous stories of the "whickles," a cross between the canary and the bumblebee, and of the "rubber rock" that bounced drills off the richest oil basin in the world.

The giant heart and umbilicus of Western Pennsylvania's soft-coal, iron, oil and gas fields is Pittsburgh, whose mammoth sprawling limbs I knew first as a sixteen-year-old clerk in one of the monster Westinghouse plants; then, later, as a reporter on the now-vanished *Dispatch*. Yet so rapid and immense have the changes been that when I go back I find myself a stranger in a strange land of towers, towering bridges and the cyclopean steel and aluminum hives of commerce and culture.

Of the entire state, the northern-central region was my favorite, an area roughly defined by the railroad that once served it—the old Northern Central. Shaped like a tree, the broad trunk has its roots at Harrisburg, then rises and spreads northeast above the hard-coal region and west above the soft-coal fields. Here, in large, prosperous valleys as well as in smaller ones shut off from the rest of the world, I found people of the old-time pioneer stock, people who had a flavor of individuality and woodsmoke going back hundreds of years. From them I learned the art of leisure and of enjoyment in storytelling, the luxurious extravagance of sitting and talking an afternoon away under a chestnut-shingled roof or a live walnut tree.

In all life, nothing is quite so pleasant to the soul as forgetting the banalities of politics and the artificialities of book learning to lose oneself in an older and realer world concerned with such things as the sagacity of horses and oxen, the natural cunning of wolves, the loyalty of dogs, the value of tanning with hemlock and rock-oak bark, the matchless fur of the mink, marten and fisher, on which no frost would stick and which no cold could penetrate. Many of these people had seen the pine marten, a creature faster than any squirrel on a tree. The extinct passenger pigeons, which they called red breasts, were still a commonplace in their conversation—their long tails and swift flight, how one would make a man a meal, and the way they talked among themselves—"Just like us folks atalkin' together."

The hours here went by for me in pagan deliciousness. These people spoke the meaty old English, Irish and Scotch idiom. They "might as well die with the chills as the fever." Something small was "about as big as a piece of soap after a hard day's washing." Their hounds "blowed like a horn," and they would "sooner see a buck's tail any day than a tavern sign." This was the stock whose great-grandfathers' brothers went south and west taking with them their salty expressions and the time and inclination to figure out new ones. They said things like, "Them folks spend all they have for something to eat and never have a drop of whisky in the house."

In northern-central Pennsylvania, the Pennsylvania Dutch cooking fused with that of the Scotch-Irish and the French to create the best fare I ever tasted. I remember superlative homemade bread and rolls, raw-fried potatoes steamed under a pan lid to a delicacy unknown elsewhere, and home-cured ham so delectable that, after the first taste, a boy I knew would cover his portion with potatoes and pass his plate for a second helping while it was still to be had.

One of the finest cooks I ever knew lived in Lycoming County, a tall, thin, blond woman, half Irish, half Pennsylvania Dutch, who refused to sit with her guests but hovered constantly behind them in a manner that betrayed a nervous pride in her creations.

"Take some of these here potato buns," she would say. "Why, you folks aren't eating! Have some more of them there corn fritters." This, I learned, was ever a sign of special excellence in what she had prepared. But when she said, for example, "My cherry pie didn't get so good today. The store didn't have my regular flour and I had to get along the best I could. But maybe you can eat it"—when she said that, it was the ultimate accolade of humility for something that would melt in your mouth and leave a void that nothing in the future would ever fill.

Her grandmother had had the same hand of genius. She measured nothing, trusting all to her art and the Lord. Her personal salute to a crowning dish, spoken in a ruder and rougher age, was, "It didn't get good today. It's not fit for a hog to eat." Her family, friends, her kin, the hired man and sundry diners were accustomed to such self-immolation and knew what to expect. But a new preacher in his ignorance said bluntly, "If it's not fit for a hog to eat, I don't want any of it," and this practically crucified the woman, who couldn't praise the special dish without praising herself and couldn't endure the thought of her crowning piece of art going untasted and unappreciated by her reverend guest.

There remains one region of the state, the area referred to as the Northern Tier of Counties. The name always cast a spell on my imagination, particularly since we had lived in the shadow of the magic North Mountain, whose formidable battlements stood over the parsonage we occupied in the Muncy Hills.

Every time the buggy crested a hill, my father or I, who often went with him, could see the dark brooding wall, and once, from some poor backwoods parishioner's house where we were spending the night, I had a glimpse of the twinkling lights of Eagles Mere, the rich man's playground on the summit of the unattainable mountain, a never-to-be-forgotten symbol of luxury and ease far above the rude tick of straw and cornhusk on which my father and I were lying.

When I grew older and penetrated beyond North Mountain, I

found the most uniformly high country in the state. As in parts of the region just below it, life in the Northern Tier hadn't greatly changed over the generations. Only the people were different, New England people who had drifted down through New York State, bringing along their taste for gambrel-roof barns, for green tea, sage in sausage, strawberries on biscuits, for New England boiled dinners and New England baked beans. They still read York State rather than Pennsylvania newspapers, and their towns are reminiscent of New England, with wide streets, houses set well back from the sidewalks, with beautiful trees and a common in the center of town.

The legendary lumbering empire of Pennsylvania, once the greatest producer in the Union, sprawled and still sprawls over this and the north-central regions. Here was the famous Black Forest of the New World. As a boy I knew pine and hemlock ravines where the sun never reached the ground, each a natural cathedral which I entered with awe for the work of the Creator and yet with uneasiness lest it be the lair of the devil. But these "dark woods," as they were called locally, paled beside the Black Forest on the west branch of the Susquehanna, which covered hundreds of square miles and some of the most rugged terrain in the Commonwealth.

The Black Forest was the home of the pine marten and silence. The hemlocks were the bearded giants that Longfellow wrote about in *Evangeline,* the white pines such a fabulous stand that they furnished lumber to much of the world of their day, white, strong and yet easily worked; such lumber as no longer exists. An old axman and raftsman of the Black Forest, whose face bore evidence of "loggers' smallpox," the scars left by the spikes of an opponent's boots, told me the white pines stood so close that trees which ran a hundred feet without a knot, and contained up to six thousand board feet of lumber each, often had no more branches than you could pick up in your hands.

Not all the logs were sawed into lumber. The Black Forest furnished masts to the seven seas—spars, they were called in the woods —some a hundred and twenty feet long and nearly two feet in diameter at the small end. The logs were lashed in rafts two and three hundred feet long, and floated down the Susquehanna's spring flood in a wild ride in which the oarsman pilot was king of the river. The masts were shipped to Liverpool, the logs sawed at hundreds of mills scattered down the river to the Chesapeake Bay, and the raftsmen rewarded with four kinds of whisky, Squirrel, Fighting, Sleeping and

Loggers' Delight. The first made you want to climb trees. The last was said to be grain alcohol that had been aged in a barrel with four pounds of fine-cut tobacco to the gallon.

Pennsylvania houses, made more or less from Pennsylvania lumber, vary with their region. One kind that I learned to admire is the old unpainted wooden house, sometimes modest, sometimes of prouder proportions, still to be found in remote valleys of the state.

They were built when white pine was more plentiful than white lead and linseed oil, and now age and weather have stained the clapboards and timbers to a deep shade of brown which, to me at least, furnishes the countryside with an unusual contrast, in summer intensifying the bright colors of the flower garden outside it, in winter enriching the sense of bright life and human warmth within.

Once Pennsylvania had also a wealth of lovely colonial brick houses with fine doorways, windows and chimneys. A few that have escaped the growth of business may still be seen in Carlisle, Bedford, Harrisburg, Philadelphia and other cities and towns. Some noble country houses, erected mostly by Frenchmen in the 1700's, are to be found in the Oley Valley in Berks County. Indeed all through the Southern Pennsylvania countryside, scattered in unexpected and sometimes not easily accessible places, often on minor roads, one comes upon solid old brick and limestone houses built with integrity, their wood carved by loving hands. A modern practice among couples is to beat the countryside for such a find, and then restore it to its original dignity.

The Indian was only one of a long line of Pennsylvania peoples who believed passionately in liberty. Ole Bull, the greatest violinist of his day, founded in Potter County what he called "a new Norway consecrated to liberty, baptized with independence." He brought in eight hundred Norwegian settlers and fiddled all over the world to support the project, which eventually failed. Another refuge, this for victims of the French Revolution, was established by the followers of Marie Antoinette on the North Branch of the Susquehanna. It was being prepared as asylum for the queen herself before tragedy overtook her. Off the beaten path even now, it must then have been an almost inaccessible spot in the American wilderness of the 1700's. Yet it was visited by Louis Philippe, afterward King of France, the Prince de Talleyrand, the Duke de la Rochefoucauld and many others.

Some of the freedom seekers in Pennsylvania came to establish a kind of early communism with its inevitable dictator. One of these was George Rapp of the Harmony Society, founder of Economy, a communal town on the Ohio River. He is most famous for his edict forbidding intercourse between the sexes.

Most of these refuges and utopias have vanished, but one that remains is a showplace today—the Cloisters at Ephrata. Established more than two hundred years ago by a community of Dunkers, it is still a place where the visitor must lower his head in humility to enter the tiny cells, each furnished with a rude bench-cot made purposely short to prevent stretching out in slothful slumber. The passageways are narrow and winding, and the whole effect distills such a medieval atmosphere that it is easy to picture the brothers and sisters moving about in their white friars' robes, woolen in winter and linen in summer, pursuing their daily tasks of baking, printing, hymn-singing and praying; living on vegetables, using goblets, plates, forks, spoons, candlesticks and pillows all of wood. They declined to bear arms, but opened their doors to the wounded at Brandywine during the Revolution. Harder to recapture is the quality of their music—of their thousand and more original compositions which are now lost. The scores were written in many parts, and the choir sounded like an immense organ producing tones that visitors of those days claimed never to have heard before.

On the other hand, the music of the Moravians, a religious society in Bethlehem and Nazareth, was never lost but continues and grows in fame from year to year. Originally a communal colony, it has adapted itself wisely to modern times without losing its religious character. A friend tells me he is constantly impressed by the peace and serenity of Moravian faces. They appear to see beyond the veil. Today, more than two hundred years after the society was founded, their spring festival of Bach music has become famous and draws visitors from all over the world.

Of all the societies which sought religious freedom in Pennsylvania, probably the best known are the Quakers, the "peculiar people," whose Friends Service Committee and Relief Fund, as well as their sympathy for and understanding of other peoples, have won them praise abroad and at home. They stand so high in public confidence that non-Quakers contribute the bulk of the money for their philanthropies, and I know of several Friends today who deny them-

**NEW JERSEY** This beach scene, on the coast between Avalon and Stone Harbor, is one of wind-ruffled dunes and lonely loveliness.

**NEW YORK** (*center spread*) The Thousand Islands lie like scattered emeralds on the blue St. Lawrence.

**DELAWARE** An outdoor tea party enjoyed by costumed ladies at the Colonial J. Dansforth Bush home in New Castle.

selves almost to the point of poverty to provide food and clothing for distant destitute people they will never see.

Of all Pennsylvania's tremendous wealth, this spiritual background of refuge and freedom is the greatest of its treasures and goes to the very heart of the nation. Early business deals were sometimes transacted in an unworldly and even poetic spirit. Several religious congregations in Pennsylvania, notably one at Manheim and another near Myerstown, were originally deeded land on which to build their churches for the express sum of one rose to be paid annually to the donor. Similar sentiment sometimes went into commercial transactions. The early owners of the rich Cornwall iron mines made a grant to supply ore free to their small neighboring Robesonia furnace "as long as grass grows green and water flows down hill."

To most native sons, Pennsylvania is the greatest state in the Union. If you come from another, it's your misfortune, not necessarily fatal but too bad. Pennsylvanians are also great travelers, eager to go and eager to get back. They become easily infected with homesickness. A prodigious amount of native food is sent to sons in exile—and not only food. Each spring my father used to mail a shoebox full of arbutus to an old friend who had moved away but pined to see and smell it again. I have heard more than one Pennsylvanian say on his return from a trip, "I've driven six or seven thousand miles and seen a lot of country, but nothing half so pretty as what we've got right here."

# Delaware

## by JAMES WARNER BELLAH

To understand the Delaware character you will have to know my great-great-uncle, and that will be difficult, for he was born in 1816 and died in 1899—and we have no forwarding address. I never knew the Honorable Edward Tatnall Bellah myself, but he fascinates me. He made his own brandy from his own apples grown for that sole purpose on his own lands outside Brandywine Village, appropriately enough. In his long career as a banker and public servant, he refused ever to take an oath or make a sworn statement. "Such specious approaches to the truth," he wrote, "are the terminal resorts of liars."

His telephone number in Wilmington was 9. He unscrewed the bell at four-thirty in the afternoon and did not let it ring thereafter until half past ten the next morning. "I will not have my home invaded by any means whatever, until a card is first sent in."

By considered choice he left no will. "No heir shall hate my dead hand. Let them hate the courts' live ones instead."

In the mornings, on his way to his seat in the House of Representatives in Dover or to his director's chair in the Union Bank in Wilmington, he would greet his friends on first meeting, but thereafter throughout the day he would cut them cold. "I have made my courtesies. What purpose can be served by hollow repetition?"

But of most lasting memory, this pertinent monument to Uncle Edward: when a deed is searched by the older legal gentry of Wilmington to this day, and Edward Tatnall Bellah's ownership is found of record—no further search is necessary. If he owned the land, *he damned well owned it.*

Uncle Edward was the ultimate native Delawarean. Know the mold—and you will understand the people of the state. Hardheaded with money. Courteous, to minimum requirements, with no urban frills. Completely self-sufficient in private living. Fine judges of good food and drink—in the castles of their own homes, which accounts for the indifferent public eating places throughout the state to this day. Honest at heart—but watch yourself carefully in all business transactions, for Delawareans are, of ancient times, close traders. Comfortably cynical in all basic philosophy. And utterly unchangeable, come hell, high water, the Du Pont overlordship or thermonuclear reaction.

We speak of three small counties, New Castle, Kent and Sussex, on the Delaware River and the Atlantic seaboard, for that is all the state has ever had; or, as was once most uncharitably said, of *two* counties at high tide and three at low, for the loftiest elevation the state attains is a towering 440 feet above sea level at Centerville, north of Wilmington. One hundred and ten miles long, Delaware is only nine miles wide at its narrowest and thirty-five at its widest. But from its earliest beginnings, it has raised a product for which there is no synthesis in chemistry. No substitute. No foreshortened manufacturing process to this day. That basic product is men, and because of their record Delaware has always been called the Diamond State. That is no glib slogan from a latter-day chamber of commerce. It is a treasured heritage from Thomas Jefferson, who coined the glittering term.

Few outsiders have known Delaware (beyond Wilmington) for three centuries past, for like the Eastern Shore of Maryland, it has always lain off the beaten track of north-south travel. But in the last few years the Memorial Bridge from New Jersey and Maryland's Chesapeake Bay Bridge have made it a major link in the motor route from Maine to Florida. This has opened to the world an almost virginal territory of precious colonial architecture, a visible history of our deep past still alive today, under the bounced echo of jet planes —and a world of honest bucolic living, and of fishing and hunting close to home that for years, except to native Delawareans, has remained almost completely unknown.

The land of Delaware is so flat that, from Wilmington for the almost hundred miles south to the Maryland border, the bubble in a spirit level hardly twitches as you go from township to township. But only a geographical snob would object to this flatness, for there are fifty fresh-water lakes spotted through it, with an excellent run of large-mouth bass in season, and there is the long Atlantic coast-line of Sussex County with succulent clams for the raking in un-limited numbers.

The fishing of Delaware, known to the work fleets for generations, is rapidly becoming a newly discovered paradise within everyone's range of fish and pocketbook, from sea trout, ling and porgies, through shad, herring and sturgeon to the offshore drum, marlin and dolphin—with Bowers, Mispillion Light, Lewes, Indian River and Rehoboth the main centers of facility and accommodation.

Quail, reed and railbird—duck if the season is kind—possum and mourning dove can give you excellent gun days in Kent and Sussex counties—as can deer. For over a generation, the deer disappeared almost completely from the state, then a few years ago they multi-plied so prolifically that a brief open season was proclaimed and the freezer chests filled with venison. A Wilmington friend once said to me: "It hardly seems believable but there were a few wild buffalo in Delaware quite a few years after they disappeared for-ever from Texas and the Western plains. I have never seen one, nor do I hope to now—but I have talked to men who have, and if a buffalo is shot in Delaware before I die, I'd like a steak, because my mouth still waters from Bret Harte's description of what they do for a man's inner being."

This primeval approach to Delaware seems the natural one, even though the state is the central ganglion of the world's largest indus-trial chemical empire. In spite of Du Pont, the colonial character of Delaware still exists throughout its length and breadth, with con-tinuous outcroppings of beauty and texture that surprise even native Delawareans—and because of Du Pont roads every corner of the state is accessible.

The Green and the Strand of the ancient town of New Castle re-main much the same today as they were when Delaware's James A. Bayard and the other commissioners took sailing ship there to nego-tiate the Treaty of Ghent.

The pirates Kidd and Teach once skulked the Delaware inlets, and if part of their treasure be not still sequestered somewhere near, then a broached galleon of the Main must lie fathoms deep off the

Sussex shore, for not so many years ago, after a savage Atlantic storm, Spanish coins were picked up on the resort beaches of Bethany and Rehoboth.

On a Saturday evening along Dover's Loockerman Street, you will see bearded Mennonites with their bonneted wives and long-skirted little girls, marketing for the week.

Until a 1915 fire, you could still see bloodstains on an upper stair of gracious Belmont Hall in Smyrna—one of the finest examples of colonial family homes in America. The blood of a Continental sentry, who was shot on the roof walk by a Britisher, and crawled down to give the alarm more than a century and a half ago.

The Green and State Street in Dover are still buttressed by the ancient houses that saw Caesar Rodney tighten cinch to ride to Philadelphia with the crucial deciding vote for colonial independence. Had Delaware *not* voted, the Declaration would have died for want of unanimous support. To this day, only one member of the House of Representatives goes to Washington with Delaware's two senators (the population being less than Rhode Island's) but the state takes precedence over all of the other forty-nine, for it was the first to ratify the Constitution.

One stray enemy plane coming in low from the Pennsylvania border, and jettisoning its stick of bombs before crashing on the outskirts of Wilmington (for somehow a Delawarean would shoot it down), could obliterate one of the most closely knit industrial targets the United States offers. This target is set up almost in a straight line along the Delaware River, from northeast of Wilmington to a few miles southwest, where the bomb run would end logically on the Chrysler Plant near Newark, a few miles from the Maryland line. On the way, in two minutes' close attention, a meticulous bombardier could take out the steel mill of the Colorado Fuel and Iron Company, the plant of Allied Chemical and Dye Corporation, the Du Pont pigments installation at Edge Moor, and the Delaware Power and Light Company. Slight rudder pressure would bring him over the Pusey and Jones shipyards, the Du Pont and Nemours buildings at Wilmington—the Pentagons of the Du Pont empire—Du Pont's experimental station and the experimental station of the Hercules Powder Company. Kicking left again a smidgen, he could add the New Castle Rayon Plant to the destruction, the central research laboratories of Atlas Powder and the American Brake Shoe Company's manganese-steel division. A lucrative bag.

Wilmington has been a mill town since colonial times, because of the water power of the Brandywine. When Washington was President, 400,000 bushels of wheat were ground there every year for years, and Joseph Tatnall of the Tatnall Mills would haul thirty thousand dollars cash from his Quaker small clothes to pay Edward Lloyd of Wye, Maryland, for his standing wheat. (The receipts are still extant at Wye House.) Wilmington has grown steadily in the mill-working tradition, until today thrity-seven out of every 100 working residents are factory laborers. Better than one third of the producing population.

That is not the nation's largest percentage for manufacturing centers, but because Wilmington has a population of only 115,000 concentrated in sixteen square miles, the mark of the belted wheel is inevitable. For years one has come into the city on the Pennsylvania, through slums, junkyards and fish markets. One progresses then through narrow, traffic-jammed streets of tiny wall-to-wall houses toward the few open spaces left in town, where 19th Century middle-class money has added a tower or a cupola to the walls and moated them with "yards." Beyond is the Kennett Pike, where the sprawling du Pont estates stretch full north to the Pennsylvania border and across it in virtually feudal grandeur, with the names of old France on their gateposts. The whole social gamut therefore is Wilmington's —from grinding poverty in the Negro, poor-white and foreign-born sections, through the suffocating country-club midstage—to wealth of astronomical proportions.

One searches in vain in Wilmington history for a past of silk-ruffed and surcoated frimpery, or of gaiety of living such as Annapolis, Baltimore and Philadelphia knew in their time. Although the home of comparative wealth since the earliest days of its shipping history and the mills on the Brandywine, this was fundamentally a Quaker town, subdued by the Quaker approach to the serious and somber business of the journey through this vale of tears.

Wilmington is also a literal town. A woman you have just met will, over a warm Martini, ask you if your father-in-law owns his house in Wawaset—or rents it. But sooner or later a cousin will straighten it all out: "She asked you because she really wanted to know. Her great-grandfather and yours were both caught in the failure of Springer, Morley and Gause. You have much in common."

In Wilmington, let there be a suspicion of the bar sinister in a family, no matter how far back, and the word is passed from mother to daughter so that the shadow still lies across the bloodline to this day —and the next. Let your grandfather have been born on the wrong side of the railroad tracks—fairly easy in three-railroaded Wilmington—and it makes scant difference whether you go to Harvard, join the Wilmington Country Club, live in Wawaset and send your offspring to Friends or Tower Hill School (where they are sure to meet young du Ponts)—there will be those who remember that your ancestors are not buried in Brandywine Cemetery, and there are certain weddings you will never be invited to attend.

But far more important to an essentially Quaker tradition, let there ever have been bankruptcy or financial chicanery of a less heinous nature in a family, and no matter how many generations succeed— the change they make for a dollar is always very carefully counted in Wilmington.

If all of this were a chip-on-the-shoulder attitude, it would be insufferable. But it isn't. Among native Wilmingtonians, it's a family attitude and as they are all members of the same old family, in effect, any objections, appeals, reclaimers will be taken up in family council. Outsiders excluded.

Yet in spite of its deep commercial tradition—rooted in firms like J. E. Rhoads and Sons, founded by John Rhoads in 1702 and the oldest manufactory in America that still does business under the family name, and the Charles Warner Company, founded in 1794, the oldest commercial concern in America still controlled by the founding family—Wilmington was the home of that great American painter, Howard Pyle, who executed his most important canvases with mill smoke in his nostrils. In his tradition, Stanley M. Arthurs, the muralist, spent most of his productive lifetime in Pyle's old studio, still extant. Robert Shaw picked out his fine water-color detail in his house on Penny Hill. Andrew Wyeth, the landscapist, works not far from Wilmington at the present time, as do Gale Hoskins and the amazing Ed Loper, who paints the tortured soul of his transplanted race with terrible, constrained understanding. Scott Fitzgerald once wrote in a rented house on Wilmington's Delaware River, and Victor Thaddeus, whose definitive critique of Voltaire is a modern classic, still lives just outside of town.

So much has been written about Du Pont and the du Ponts, by carpingly critical, coldly objective and servilely subsidized pens, that almost anything goes, but it shouldn't, for the whole saga is a magnificent American story that echoes now the world around.

For a century they made explosives. For a century "The Company" was a closed family project. The original Eleuthère Irénée du Pont, who built the first mill on the Brandywine in 1802, was an apprentice of the great chemist Lavoisier at the French government powder works at Essone. His son Henry went to West Point for the finest engineering courses offered in this country. The next generation went to the University of Pennsylvania for chemistry, and after Massachusetts Institute of Technology was founded in 1861, subsequent offspring studied there. From the very nature of their business, technical educations were prerequisite, because powder making is a volatile affair and knowledge is the basic life insurance.

When the company was founded, the original Irénée drew a salary of $1800 a year. The capitalization was $36,000. By 1809, the profits had averaged only $7268.94 a year. The War of 1812 increased the Du Pont gross receipts, of course, but in his lifetime Irénée never knew real security or complete freedom from debt—only hard and grueling work and an eternal scramble to meet his obligations.

It is a myth that the du Ponts have always been American rich. They have not. It is a close but plausible bet that as late as 1900 no individual du Pont was yet a millionaire. For there are two factors in making powder. You can build an expensive plant over many months—and lose it in half a blinding second. Du Pont did, several times, and started again. And there are two factors in making powder for wars. You can't expand plant fast enough to meet their beginning needs. And you are left fully expanded—with plummeting demand—when they end.

In a century, Du Pont faced these conditions five times—with the War of 1812, the Mexican War, the Crimean War, the Civil War and the Spanish-American War. However, in that same century, the peacetime market for powder steadily expanded. The vast stumping, dredging, tunneling, building and mining of a growing country required industrial powder. Du Pont furnished it. Through Henry du Pont's gunpowder trust, by manufacturers' agreement initially, and then by slick deals for actual Du Pont ownership of competing companies, they came close to supplying *all* of it—and at their own price. If a competitor undercut, he was soon working for Du Pont or he wasn't working. (Such tooth-and-claw methods were so usual at that time that business itself was like the vast flocks of black sheep in

Connemara: if you see a white one, you wonder what its mother
has done.)

In 1907 the Department of Justice took notice and the Government charged the Company had violated the Sherman Anti-Trust
Act. The suit showed Du Pont to be either a public benefactor or an
industrial monster. Morally, it was never quite decided which, so
that you may still take your choice. Du Pont was, however, definitely
Big Business by then—although not yet the ultimate giant—the colossus that was to inspire in present times a second anti-trust suit, the
hugest in history, and defend itself handsomely, winning against the
Government after a five-year battle in the courts.

World War I had to be fought first. By official British admission
Du Pont explosives saved the British Empire on the battlefields of
France, and Du Pont explosives tilted the balance of victory in favor
of the American manpower effort. Capitalization of the Company in
1915 was $60,000,000. After the Armistice of 1918 Du Pont had
$90,000,000 of surplus funds in its treasury. The basic Company pol-
icy required continuous reinvestment. The fine hand of John Jacob
Raskob, who had originally left a $45-a-month job to start with Du
Pont as a secretary, found the medium. $49,000,000 was put into
Durant's General Motors and Du Pont took financial control.

There is no sanity in going further with figures. Everybody in this
world, directly or indirectly, pays Du Pont for something—from the
stenographer who buys her nylons for 98 cents a pair to the coolie in
Kuala Lumpur who makes his family's sandals from a worn synthetic
auto tire he has bought for five Straits cents.

What manner of people are these du Ponts of Delaware, whose
collective holdings dominate a larger portion of industry than do
those of the Rockefellers, Mellons, Morgans or any other family combine in the United States, including oil-soaked Texas, or any other
part of the globe? Forty-five of their individual names appear in the
Wilmington telephone book, but without specific census, it can
conservatively be said that well over a hundred individuals now
comprise the immediate family—those who directly by birth or for-
tuitously by marriage share the dividends through the medium of
Christiana Securities, which is the super holding company for the
family's interests. Of this far-flung and prolific clan only a scant half-
dozen "of the name" are now active employees of the Company or its
subsidiaries. Possibly another half-dozen men of distaff connection

are also in active employment, including the president, Crawford Greenewalt.

I have known several du Ponts. One ranks high among the world's most charming hostesses—an incisive mind denying the moated walls of great wealth and living eternally in the reality of the world. One is an insufferable travesty of Chaucer's Eglentyne, eternally prefacing a complete absence of any sound opinion with "As a Dewopawn." One is the victim of sadistic family possessiveness to a point of shuddering almost visibly at the sound of the name. And one, with an excellent war record behind him, works hard at the family trade as his forebears did before him. Some are known intimately and as well in Wilmington as any run-of-the-mill neighbors in any small town. Some are towering swells, only heard of from distant places. Some people in Wilmington whisper the name in awed reverence. One prominent Wilmingtonian who bore it as a middle name never even used the initials.

In the light of Du Pont's complete dominance of present-day Delaware, it is interesting to note how the wheel will turn, given time. How one side of the tracks becomes the other. Who rides the horse who used to walk.

The emigrant du Ponts, if not snubbed by Wilmington, were completely ignored. They were suspect because they borrowed money in Philadelphia, and because they did not live in Wilmington but kept to themselves in a small stone house (successor to their original log cabin) close by their first mill on the Brandywine, and in closely adjacent houses as the family grew.

They were further frowned upon by early Wilmington because not infrequently their mill blew up and destroyed property as well as life and limb. Once, in 1854, three of their powder wagons disintegrated right in town, atomizing the twelve horses, the three drivers and several staid Wilmingtonians passing by.

But be it said for the heroic older breed that the first man into a mill fire that threatened an annihilating blast was always a du Pont, the man who led the rescue party after a blast was always a du Pont, and at least two du Ponts in their time have gone to glory in a holocaust of their mills and several have died indirectly from results, including one du Pont woman. For they were powder-men for almost a century, sweat-stained and charcoal-grimed, living close by their mills, toiling in them personally, giving of their souls to the business.

For this reason, Wilmington's attitude never bothered them much. When they wanted the State of Delaware, they stretched forth a firm hand from the Brandywine and took it. They have never let go.

They took it in 1861, when Major General Henry du Pont, the West Pointer in command of all Delaware militia, changed it from a potential Southern state to a Northern state in a matter of half an hour. Delaware was then a Democratic state and slave owning. In 1860 less than one third of the state's vote supported Lincoln. With war clouds hovering, and with threats of rebellion against the pro-Union minority mounting, General Henry wired the Federal commander in Baltimore, General John A. Dix, for troops. They came at once. Delaware did not secede. She furnished subsequently 13,651 men to the Union—one eighth of her population—and met every Federal tax assessment throughout four years of war.

From that day to this, Delaware has fought and bucked, hated, reviled, admired and fawned upon, ignored and courted the du Ponts, but in the end, it has invariably bowed to Du Pont's benevolent paternalism. Du Pont roads belt Delaware from end to end. Du Pont practical interest in its school system raised the state from thirtieth place in literacy to close to the top. Du Pont endowments to institutions for the sick, handicapped and aged lowered the state's mortality figures drastically. Adding in its lifelong record of fair labor practices, sick and retirement benefits and, in recent years, ownership-participation policies, the Du Pont Company has raised the standard of living directly or indirectly in all three counties.

But the price has been stiff. It is whispered that no candidate of either party running for office in Delaware has a Chinaman's chance of election unless Du Pont approves. (The term is used collectively to indicate a way of life.) That no one is elected to membership in the Wilmington Club, the Vicmead Hunt or the Wilmington Country Club unless, again collectively, Du Pont approves. That nothing is printed in the Du Pont-owned Wilmington papers unless Du Pont approves.

Speaking noncollectively, some Delaware du Ponts live with imposing formality. Some answer their own doorbells. Some dwell in a hundred rooms. Some in three and a kitchenette. At least one has committed suicide. One held the Congressional Medal of Honor. One enclosed his 300 acres of home park with a ten-foot wall topped with jagged inset glass "to keep all the skunks in Delaware out"— as he put it—"most of them named du Pont." Two were United States senators. One has been married four times (you must be married five times to be an *officer* of that club). One, for whom du Pont Circle is named in Washington, broke the Atlantic naval power of the Confederacy from the deck of his flagship. One beat a nasty paternity suit in the Wilmington courts. One built the Equitable Building in New York. One tried to sue half the female population of Wilmington for libel. One is a ranking tennis champion. One married an Irish barmaid between boats at Queenstown—and never came home. One used to march in uniform in the Wilmington Police Band tooting a French horn. One even married a Hyde Park Roosevelt, for all the du Ponts' Republican tradition, and there is the logical place to leave them—if in Delaware you ever can.

North of Wilmington, there is the Henry Francis du Pont Winterthur Museum, which when it was his home, was admittedly the most expensively furnished in America.

You may not barge in and ask to be shown through the museum. If you wish to see it, you must write and receive a card of admission by mail. You go through in groups of four. The number of groups for each day is limited and requests are granted in the order of their receipt. There is an admission charge and ladies must deposit their handbags before entering.

There are about eighty period rooms on seven floors, and they cover in the most minute detail the entire spread of American living from 1640 to the early 19th Century—down to newspapers, magazines and books of the various periods. There is Martha Washington's cake plate, a book of Cotton Mather's sermons, John Hancock's bedspread, William Penn's bed curtains, several ale tankards made by Paul Revere. Whole rooms, façades, staircases, hallways and porticoes were moved bodily from their original locales, set up at Winterthur and then furnished to the last detail.

Winterthur was no rich man's hobby, pursued impersonally through agents. "H.F." was his own ultimate purchaser, his own agent, his own scout, and still exercises the over-all directorial hand through his curator. For years he has operated his own line of trucks to take his treasures to and from seasonal reupholsterings and necessary repairs. He maintains a staff of furniture repairmen and fabric workers in New York for this purpose. It all started with his rather meticulous bent for embellishing his own home. From that it has grown into a $20,000,000 semi-public museum and one of the ultimate shrines of Americana in the entire country.

Delaware in a manner of speaking was a stepchild of the Colonies (but never of the Union) who from her earliest days took care of herself in her own forthright way. The state takes its name from one Thomas West, who, raised to the peerage as Lord de la Warr, was a onetime Royal Governor of Virginia, and under whom the area that is now Delaware became a part of Virginia in 1609. But at seven o'clock on the evening of August 28, 1609, one Henry Hudson, shipmaster in the employ of the Dutch East India Company, let go the *Half Moon's* anchor in lower Delaware Bay, about a mile offshore of the present resort of Bethany Beach. On the strength of that anchoring, two things transpired—a Dutch colony of thirty-three souls was established at Zwaanendael (so called from the wild swans) in 1631, near the latter-day town of Lewes; and New York got a North River on the *west* side of Manhattan—a geographical misplacement which has never seemed to bother New Yorkers one bit.

Eighteen months later the Indians had massacred all but one Dutchman and laid waste the stockade and stores. Nothing remains today except the Zwaanendael House in Lewes, built as a museum and library in 1931 and modeled after a wing of the Town Hall at Hoorn in Holland. It is a must for the traveler, as it is the sole repository of reliquary Dutch culture in America south of New York.

The phrase "south of New York" gives the key to the river enigma. From Henry Hudson's time onward, until the more modern times of great-circle navigation—the direct route from Europe was a departure from the Portuguese coast to the Canaries, passing to the eastward of the Bahamas and to the westward of Bermuda. Your landfall was therefore the bay shores of either the southern river (the Delaware) or the northern river (the Hudson).

Swedes settled in Delaware in 1638 and their colony remained under the Swedish flag for seventeen years until the Dutch took over for nine years again and the British from the Dutch for one hundred and twelve years until the colonists declared their independence from Britain. William Penn, to whom the Duke of York originally indentured the Three Lower Counties for 10,000 years, for a fee of one rose a year, held the upper hand there only about long enough to grant them their demanded autonomy.

History in Delaware, as in Scotland and Ireland, is a close-knit family affair. Touch a man in any of the three counties and you touch my brother. Kinship is ubiquitous and ramified. Cooches still live at Cooch's Bridge where Cornwallis' Hessians tarried five days—where

the Stars and Stripes were first flown in combat. Simplers and Mc-
Cabes still live in Selbyville. Tatnalls teach school or work in banks,
close by their old houses near Wilmington that knew the spur chink
of Washington, Lafayette and "Dandy" Wayne. Ridgelys still sleep
in their ancestral beds at Dover. Judge Richard S. Rodney's law offices overlook Caesar Rodney's equestrian statue in Rodney Square,
Wilmington. A Prettyman still keeps store in Milford—another in Wilmington. The name of Bayard is of some continuing political significance in the land. Bancrofts are abroad in the state to this day,
as are Deputys, Buckalews, Irons, Gilpins, Comegys, Richardsons,
Brinkleys—and Warners.

The pillory as an apparatus for punishment was not officially done
away with in Delaware until 1905. You may still lay yourself open to
strokes of the lash in Delaware for wife beating, burglary, attempted
poisoning and horse stealing—a real enough threat to keep racketeers
well beyond the state's borders. For rape in Delaware, you will be
imprisoned for life, but only if you employ the best trial lawyer in
the state and the jury recommends clemency. Otherwise, you die for
the transgression.

I never cross the Christina River (the "Christeen" still to the native tongue) to head for the southern part of the state but I see the
flying curls of gallant Nancy Hanson once again. (Her hair *must* have
been red.) After Brandywine Battle, Nancy so befuddled a British
officer with blandishment and coquetry that he unwittingly got her a
carriage and two long redingotes to cover the uniforms of two Continental officers in imminent danger of their lives. But the ruse was
discovered and a dozen British dragoons came galloping in pursuit,
with pistols blazing. The Americans had to return the fire—and family
tradition has it that the comely Nancy did some very fancy shooting
herself in close support. One officer was Colonel Tilton. Had the escape not been successful these pages would not have been penned,
for the other was my namesake and progenitor, Captain James Bel-
lach of Caesar Rodney's Regiment. In which there is no simpering
pride but quite an open boast, for, as it is said, ancestry is important
not only in Dover but all over Delaware.

The Christina River which borders the southern reaches of Wilmington divides the two cultures of the state—the starkly industrial
city and the agricultural lower counties.

A detour to the right on the way south brings one into the town of

Newark (accent on the final syllable) wherein Wilmington's industrial overflow encroaches on the academic precincts of the University
of Delaware. A state university, Delaware however ranks very high
among all state universities in the number of alumni who go on to
graduate work—a large percentage in chemistry and engineering—
due to practical Du Pont stimulus.

Beyond Newark lie the five tracks of Delaware Park, home of the
Delaware Steeplechase and Race Association. A total of fourteen
fixture stakes are raced for annually here, ten flat and four between
flags, and the track owners do not take a cent of profit. Whatever is
made above expenses and taxes is invested in improvement of the
installation, so that it is one of the finest tracks in the United States.

A detour to the left on the way south brings one into the ancient
town of New Castle, the state's first capital and a town still authentic in its colonial atmosphere. The sprawling modern area encroaches
upon the old in a dynamic continuity of history. The spot where
William Penn first set foot on the continent, in 1682, is less than a
mile from the Bellanca Aircraft Company.

In May of each year, the residents of New Castle open a score
or more of the old houses to the public, with guides and hostesses
in colonial dress. The George Read house in the Strand is one of the
finest examples extant of American Georgian. The Court House
dates, in part, to 1682. Packet Alley at dark still whispers with the
ghosts of other years—when the boats from Philadelphia connected
with the cars of the old Frenchtown railroad to the Chesapeake Bay,
one of the first steam railroads in America. The ticket office, about
the size of a telephone booth, is still preserved.

Immanuel Episcopal Church in New Castle, with parish records
that date to 1689, together with Old Swedes Church in Wilmington,
start a chain of significant church buildings that runs southward
through the state. Near Odessa, there is old Drawyers Presbyterian
Church—one of the earliest in America—built in 1773 on the site of a
wooden church built in 1711. At Frederica, there is Barratt's Chapel,
known as the "Cradle of Methodism in America." At Broad Creek,
there is Christ Episcopal Church, built in 1771, with the original interior woodwork still preserved. And in Dover, the present capital,
there is Christ Episcopal Church, dating from 1734, in the cemetery
of which are buried Caesar Rodney, the Signer, and those two
derring-do officers Miss Nancy Hanson snatched from British nooses
so many years ago in Revolutionary Wilmington.

Dover was laid out in 1717, and the old Green at moonrise still gives one the illusion of powdered wigs and crinolines, even though, as in New Castle, the new town grows directly from the old in present leaps and bounds that bid fair to make Dover one of the most important Air Force bases in the United States. The ancient houses are still lived in, in great part by the descendants of the builders, and the old buildings are still used—the State House since 1722. There is no museum flavor, no dead aspect of history as something done with, to be kept apart from life in mothballs. It is all one in both Dover and New Castle, the whole American scene from the beginning, irrevocably intertwined from silver-handled dragoon pistols to Nikes.

They still call in hats and gloves in Dover and drop cards—as they do in Wilmington, but, one thinks, in Wilmington merely to see how you live. When the telephone wires went underground in Dover, the company was required to trench them down the middle of the streets, as side trenching would have damaged the roots of the ancient elms and sycamores—and the complete disruption of traffic was a small price to pay for shade. Possibly ten thousand corporations have their home offices in Dover, for Delaware corporate law is facile and convenient. Lawyers prosper there on this account—in fact almost everyone but the postmen and the police force is a member of the bar. You will note that I have not included the fire department? Purposely. It is volunteer and, at strength, composed of one hundred male citizens. Using the most modern equipment, it is still a gentleman's club. The engine house has billiard tables and card rooms. Its lounge is comfortably appointed in overstuffed chairs and divans, with tapestried walls and curtains of heavy velvet. But Dover has never burned down yet.

Sussex and Kent counties still hold to a certain Southern flavor of living to this day. If you want a tire changed, you may not get it changed, and the reason will be as valid as it would be in the Georgia hinterland. "Cain't, suh. Ain' got no tar arns." In these two southern counties the spoken word is softer than in Wilmington, and life is taken more slowly. There is more time for living—which is to say shooting, fishing, politics and conversation—and ancestry is more an accepted condition than a belligerent major premise, as it is in Wilmington.

Kent and Sussex are largely agricultural, for their climate allows a growing season of about 185 days—a condition that challenges everyone to part-time farming at least. Farms run to between 125 and 150 acres and the most important farm product is broilers, better than 60,000,000 being marketed each year, although 10,000 Southern Delaware acres are planted in fruit trees and 40,000 in truck crops.

A Chicken Festival is held in Harrington each June, with recipe prizes offered to "Chicken Cooks, U. S. A." If you are under the impression that you have eaten chicken in its quintessential succulence, you are sadly mistaken—unless you have been to Harrington, the chicken ganglion of the known world. A "Delawine broiled chicken" done in white wine and apple jelly has brought a first prize—but old-line Delawareans of Sussex and Kent counties are of the considered opinion that no matter how you try to "fancy the bird up" you cannot beat plain old Delaware fricasseed chicken.

At Rehoboth and Bethany beaches there are simple and delightful shore resorts of unpretentious hotels and family cottages. Their flavor is reminiscent of the old Newport, in the days when old New Yorkers went there for the climate—not for the Vanderbilts and the flamboyant horde that followed in their train.

The late Ben Albertson, of Lewes, once refused to sell me a musket that Abraham Lincoln was supposed to have carried as a captain in the Black Hawk War. Said he couldn't in all honesty, because he wasn't sure whether it had been carried by Abe or just by one of the other men in Abe's company. Said he'd still work on it and when he found out for sure, I could have it—because he wasn't particularly a Lincoln man himself. I never got it, for Ben was still working on it when he died.

The British Captain Beresford once tried to dust up Lewes during the War of 1812. He got the dusting himself instead at the hands of the citizenry and left for Bermuda without his fresh water. They had no ammunition, so they picked up the British cannonballs and fired them back. Casualties in Lewes: two chickens and a broken leg.

Delaware has a stubborn, continuing record of producing fighting men that dates well back into the colonial Indian wars. Always with a comparatively small population, she has invariably sent to the colors as large or larger a percentage of troops than any other state in the Union, whenever sovereignty was in jeopardy. The Delaware regiment, which, with the gallant Marylanders, fought the bitter rearguard action at Long Island and saved Washington's army from threatened debacle, carried Delaware fighting cocks with them. A

means, one supposes, of eking out their scant and uncertain pay by
betting. The best of these game cocks were descended from a traditional blue hen. From her, the Delaware troops were nicknamed the
Blue Hen's Chickens. Since that day, the Blue Hen's Chickens have
been stubbornly present on every American battlefield. Little men
for the most part, but grown tall by circumstances.

Among them, some giants walked as well, nor does the breed
die. Delaware's James A. Bayard stands apart in the select company
of bygone statesmen—among the Clays, Websters and Calhouns.

So then what have we really? A small but fiercely prideful state
with the faint cavalier and bond-servant shadow of Virginia upon its
beginnings, a kinship with Maryland's delightful Eastern Shore, the
ponderous heritage of Penn's hardheaded Roundheads—a touch of
the Dutch, a lacing of Scandinavian, a broad overlay of Scotch, Irish
and English, and a self-determined independence of thought and
political entity that has given Delaware character and its people individuality for almost three centuries. And still does, in three small
counties a hundred and ten miles in over-all length, by nine miles
wide at its narrowest and thirty-five at its widest.

So possibly you have come to know my Uncle Edward.

# Wisconsin

## by MARK SCHORER

In Wisconsin, history always seems very near; it is so much a part of daily life that it is never quite remarkable. It has not yet been entombed in monuments, and thus it cannot be resurrected because it has not been buried. It is not something that you come and look at casually; it is something that you live. History is like a green shade in which the little towns of Wisconsin slumber.

Look closely at any town. Look at any lake or river town, for these are the characteristic towns—Sauk City, for example, which lies in a slow bend of the Wisconsin River almost in the center of the southern half of the state. It takes its name from the Indians who abandoned this, their ancient prairie, hardly more than a hundred years ago. Across the river stretch the green rounded hills where they fought their last real battle with the white men, and where village boys still find arrowheads. One hill rises to a sharp and jagged point, where granite rocks are piled like broken statuary. In local myth, this is known as Black Hawk Lookout, after the chief who led his fleeing, stumbling, starving people through this prairie valley.

With the defeat of Black Hawk in 1832, the Wisconsin territory was opened to enterprise, and a bright, wild spirit arrived in Sauk City. He was Agoston Haraszthy, a Hungarian political refugee who came to Wisconsin after reading in Marryat's American travel diary that this was the finest portion of North America. Haraszthy was a tall man, very dark, with a great black mustache and beard, an expert horseman and hunter who charged through the wilderness and across the prairie, wearing a bright green shirt and a red silk sash. A romantic idealist of nearly frantic energies, he established almost singlehanded the enterprises which gave Sauk City its first social pattern.

The main street of the town follows the undulant line of the river where, soon after Haraszthy arrived, lumber rafts drew up in rude processional.

Not far from the edge of the water, between a market and a neon-lighted bar, there is a kind of grass-grown pit. The bar was once a saloon where drunken lumbermen roistered, and the pit was a dugout, branch-and-bough covered, which sheltered first settlers through a long winter. (The term "Badger State" comes down from early miners and others who, like the animal, burrowed in the ground when the icy winter closed in.) The pit is there today, a neglected feature of the street.

In Sauk City you will find a pleasant park of pine and oak, with a large, square, wooden hall in its center, an edifice austerely angular and gray, and behind it a crested, circular bandstand suggestive of communal frivolity. This is the property of the *Freie Gemeinde,* the Freethinkers' Congregation. Organized as The Humanist Society by Agoston Haraszthy in 1842, it was the direct expression of his restless cosmopolitanism and of the liberal views which characterized European revolutionary movements in the 19th century. Largely through this group, Sauk City became known abroad as the atheist's heaven. To the Freethinkers' hall came such famous theorists as Carl Schurz, such notorious atheists as Robert Ingersoll. Liberal professors from the University still come out from Madison to address the members on philosophical and political issues. And even if this group has grown smaller and somewhat staid with the years, even if Reason, which once smiled with such bright promise, has been dusted over by a hundred years of village habit, such occasional intellectual gatherings are as natural to these people as the dances through which they whirl on festival occasions, or the large town picnics in the park, around the bandstand, on the Fourth of July.

In a hundred years Sauk City has grown to only a little more than a thousand people, and in that time its life has become the same as American small-town life everywhere—the neon, the motorcycles roaring through the streets on dead Sundays, the ugly unplanned buildings, the well-kept, dull houses and the neat vegetable gardens behind them, the national highway whose trucks and cars usurp its main street in the summer, and that same street desolate and raw and piled high with snow after stormy winter days.

Yet at night, after the farmers have driven back to their prosperous farms, after the shopkeepers have put out their electric signs, after the townspeople have gone to bed and the small yellow lights flicker out at last, and the town lies asleep on the great breast of the whispering prairie, the presence of the primordial land makes itself felt. The tragic shadow of Black Hawk and the pathos no less than the courage of the pioneers are still in the air as the darkness settles heavily in the empty streets. The little pioneering community of a hundred years ago is not very far back.

This is the character and the quality of a thousand Wisconsin towns.

The name Wisconsin is popularly thought to mean "a gathering of waters." Wisconsin is, indeed, a kind of peninsula: three of its four sides, notched and undulating, are determined by natural waterways —Great Lakes to the east and north, rivers to the north and west. The state is everywhere shot through with rivers, streams and lakes —there are over 8500 counted lakes, 10,000 miles of trout streams— and it is actually bisected from Lake Michigan to the Mississippi by the Fox and Wisconsin rivers.

The peninsular character of the state suggests nearly every economic activity which has developed within it, beginning with Jean Nicolet, the first white man to step upon this ground. He was searching for the mythical northwest waterway to China, and landed near Green Bay in 1634, in the name of the governor of New France. He wore ritual robes to meet expected mandarins, but soon was shooting pistols from both hands when, instead, naked red men appeared. Today Green Bay is a harbor city, snug in the sharp angle of two coast lines dotted with thriving fishing villages.

By way of the Fox-Wisconsin riverway, we cross to the western boundary of the state in the wake of early missionaries like Marquette, and early inland explorers like Jolliet, and of numberless, nameless French and British fur traders. Into Lake Winnebago and out, into the smaller Puckaway and out, past busy mill towns, past somnolent river villages which have grown up on the site of the shacks and cabins of forgotten *coureurs de bois* and company agents, we come to Portage, where the rivers link by a canal, and where the old Indian Agency House reminds us of the bygone importance of this pleasant leafy village.

The Wisconsin River flows through the richest farmland in the state, where wooded valley gives way to rolling hills, and hills to folding prairie. At Spring Green, Taliesin, the Frank Lloyd Wright home, seems to lift itself from the very body of the hills to look down upon the blue river with its yellow sand bars and its green oval islands. Taliesin is a Welsh word meaning "shining brow," and the name suggests the perfect harmony between the house's roofs and the lines of the ridges on which it is built. Here the aging architect, after a life of marked unconventionality and stormy personal tragedies, lived peacefully amid his students, transmitting through the Taliesin Fellowship some of the genius which distinguished his professional career.

Below Spring Green, the Wisconsin River winds through bluffy country, country haunted by the ghost of Whisky Jack. Whisky Jack is a brother of Paul Bunyan and Mike Fink, but of purely local habitation. Born out of the hard life of the river raftsmen, the most reckless, adventurous, dissolute and humorous tribe on the American frontier, Whisky Jack was their mythological ideal. He was a giant in strength and size; he could pick up a grounded raft and set it back in deep water, and he could consume raw liquor—always the test of stature in American folklore—in monstrous quantities without disaster. Yet at least one tale shows this Achilles to have had his heel. Jack believed that when a man had drunk whisky, he was no match for a snake. When he met a huge blue racer in the woods, there was nothing to do but run for it: he ran, swam the river, ran again and swam again, ran and swam, and finally took to leaping from bank to bank, but the snake swam and leaped behind him, until, having covered half the state, Jack was rescued by his fellows, who beat the thirty-two-foot snake to death with cant hooks.

Today this heroic clown is shrunken to the stature of "river rats" who drift through makeshift lives in the lower Wisconsin, in shacks or patchwork boats, living off the fat catfish and other unrespected creatures that thrive in the muddy bottoms. Through this neglected neighborhood, the Wisconsin flows at last into the wooded flood plain to join the Mississippi.

Prairie du Chien, north of the flood plain, is sleepy modern testimony of historical activity. One of the oldest of Wisconsin towns, it was once nearly the most important, the distant sister of Green Bay. Here the agent of the Astor interests, the American Fur Company, gathered in the pelts which Indian trappers shipped from all over the state, and built himself a lordly house, the Villa Louis. The town itself sleeps now in a kind of slow dream of a past that is still too real to escape, too near; and thus most of the Mississippi towns sleep. They are picturesque towns, set in bluffs, many of them terraced to the contours of the bluffs, and all facing out across the wide river to the Minnesota plains. They seem to gaze with dusty melancholy to the westward expanses where the economic forces—the fur trade, lumber, then wheat—which once gave them their life, have vanished.

Northward, the character of the land changes again, as the amplitude and vast placidity of prairie farmland give way to the darker, dramatic landscape of timber. Here in the northwest, the rivers fan out in a great hand—the Chippewa alone has seven important tributaries—and the number of lakes increases, until, in both the northwest and the northeast portions of the state, one has the impression that there is more water than land.

It was inevitable that this entire area should become renowned for sport. Surely it is difficult to think of many other states in the Union where sport is in so large a measure a natural and nearly daily activity of the natives. For every Chicago or Milwaukee amateur who comes here to hunt or fish, for every vacationer who comes to ski or swim, there are a hundred local inhabitants who hunt and fish, ski and swim as naturally as they eat or sleep.

To the ordinary small-town and country people of Wisconsin, who do not take citified vacations, every day provides some out-of-doors pleasure. The bobsled and team which hauls sacks of grain or lumber by day pulls a country singing party through the frosty night, and the hayrick is taken out of the field to consolidate high-school romance on a river lane under the harvest moon. At the end of a summer day, the small-town shopkeeper will row his wife up the river or across the lake, hardly listening to the whippoorwills and frogs. In winter, every spry soul in the village will skate or iceboat on the same river or lake, impervious then to the blue-and-silver splendor of snow and ice which is a daily possession. Infants learn to swim, little girls to fish, and future ski champions begin as small boys on the hill behind the house, using barrel staves that they have smoothed with broken glass.

In the north central and northeast portions, especially, recreation has become a considerable industry. Here every resort inducement is exploited to the full, and in the summer the land is full of strangers. But the winters come early, and they are long, and then—hotels boarded up, cottages half buried in great drifts of snow—the qualities of a more primitive life reassert themselves. Nearly everywhere, at any time, even at the height of the season, there is a curious mingling of the atmosphere of the raw, tough community of the past with that of the modern resort, sometimes the very sophisticated resort.

To the northwest, where commercial exploitation is much less extensive, hardier men pursue their pleasure and their work, in any season, under the most rugged of circumstances. Life is still nearly as primitive as it was when these small communities were lumber towns: a sawmill and a general store, a saloon and a few shacks. This is still the frontier, inhabited by modern frontiersmen. Wolves and bear roam these forests, deer are a commonplace, and the solitary trappers and woodsmen who live deep in the wilderness are almost exact replicas of the earliest *coureurs de bois*, even to their bright wool shirts and fur caps.

Old lumbermen, who can remember when most of the state was covered with virgin timber, live ghost-ridden lives in the haunts of their youthful prowess, and the dream of Paul Bunyan hangs on. Near Wausau, in the north center of the state, the great man is said to be buried under Rib Mountain, while the sons of the wealthier families, who affect the lumberjack's dress and borrow his lingo, ski over him on the best trails in Wisconsin. The sons of the old lumbermen, employed in the woods with a modernly equipped crew or engaged in the production of wood by-products, live easier lives, yet the sight of them absorbed in that most treacherous of physical contests, logrolling, suggests that they delight in maintaining the tradition of their mythical ancestor.

There are whole communities which, even when they will it, cannot shake off their inheritance. It was proverbial among lumbermen in the old days that the four toughest places in the world were Cumberland, Hayward, Hurley and Hell, and that the first three were tougher than the last. Cumberland has managed to reform its lumber-camp morality. In its wild days, a new marshal, to stay in town, had to beat up the strongest saloonkeeper; today, Cumberland boasts more peacefully of its rutabagas, and as a climax to its annual festival, it crowns as Rutabaga King the man who can eat the largest amount of mash. Hayward, too, has mended its manners, and today it is a successful vacation town and enjoys a considerable reputation for its wrought iron, a modern inheritance from logging-camp blacksmiths who preserved a European skill.

Hurley has had a harder time. A phenomenal boom town in the 1880's, it developed a nearly allegorical reputation for viciousness. Edna Ferber's novel *Come and Get It* pictures authentically the rowdy drunkenness and robbery and murder which systematically went on in Hurley's innumerable wooden saloons. When the lumber market collapsed, the population of Hurley shrank, but not its reputation. Prohibition gave it occasion to reassert its historic rowdy role, and throughout the '20's and into the '30's, with over half a hundred speakeasies, it became a haven of gangsters and rumrunners—the one wholly wide-open town in Wisconsin.

Nearby, at a resort called Little Bohemia, John Dillinger and his mob hid out in 1934, and, leaving the molls, shot their way free when the place was surrounded by G-men. The bullet holes in the lodge are shown today in a spirit of local pride. For a time, Dillinger's father operated a small roadside stand where, for twenty-five cents, tourists could inspect the personal possessions of his son and other Chicago notables.

Hurley is exceptional, yet not wholly so. Most of these northern towns have something stark about them, even something rather brutal. They were the products and the victims of the lumber interests, an enterprise too ruthless to allow for geniality or social grace.

The Wisconsin timber industry, controlled by a group of "robber barons" in the old pattern of American avarice, lordly feudal beings who made the law their servant, was like a monster which devoured itself. Alexander, Ross, Spooner, Stephenson, Sawyer, Weyerhaeuser —these are names to conjure with in the development of the state. They are no less the names which repel the Wisconsin citizen today, as his eye sweeps across bleak, cut-over areas and is forced to contemplate the ruthlessness with which these men stripped the forest or, by their neglect, let it burn.

In 1870, five sixths of the state was still covered with virgin forest; forty rapacious years later, there was hardly a stick of it. Fire traveled with the cutters. Almost every northern county has suffered at least one great conflagration. In 1871, a fire which began near the village of Peshtigo spread over six counties, burning a swath forty miles long and ten miles wide within four hours, wiping out entire settlements and killing 1200 people.

The impression of ruin is not, to be sure, persistent. If there are towns today which seem to squat hopelessly in the midst of desolation, there are many more where the surrounding forests seem to crowd down into the very streets. In large measure, this luxuriance is due to state legislation, which belatedly—but then with great progressive brilliance—taught the lesson that timber is a crop. In a spectacular program of conservation, begun under the influence of Charles Van Hise, a social-minded man and one of the greatest of university presidents, the state allowed enormous tax reductions on land that was being reforested. County reforestation projects are tax free, and these, with state and Federal park areas, now comprise almost half the land in Northern Wisconsin.

The spirit of public interest which motivates this program is expressed by the tags which are tied on the thousands of Christmas trees taken each year from the Chequamegon National Forest; these read: "This tree brings a Christmas message from the great outdoors. Its cutting was not destructive but gave needed room for neighboring trees to grow faster and better. It was cut under the supervision of the United States Forest Service from a crowded stand——"

Reforestation is implemented today by an excellent fire-control service, and this, in turn, by intelligent fish-and-game laws.

The lumber industry today is largely concerned with the manufacture of wood products, especially pulp and paper, and this wise economic pursuit is, characteristically, encouraged by the state, and through the magnificent facilities of the Forest Products Laboratory. This is a Federal institution that is appropriately located in the back yard of the University, which aids it and prides itself on its own great commercial and agricultural research. The forest will return to the forest.

The modern dairy farm, in its setting of wooded, rolling land, is the most familiar symbol of Southern Wisconsin. The neat white house, the tidy fences, the enormous red or white barn, the solid, prosperous-looking silo and the cattle standing knee-deep in a stream or pond, or lying in the shade of a cluster of oak in the middle of a meadow—this is the prevailing pastoral image.

The Wisconsin farmer is apt to be a very modern man, as informed about agricultural hygiene or crop rotation as he is about machinery. If he is not himself a University graduate, at least one of his sons is, and the sons return to the farm with expert knowledge. Father and sons are the beneficiaries of the University Extension educational services, and every now and then one or another will go to Madison to attend the famous "short course" for farmers. There he is almost as likely to learn something about regional literature or regional art as he is to pick up the latest information on Bang's disease.

Given even a minimum of co-operation between man and Nature, the chances of agricultural success in Wisconsin are greater than in most states. The very names of the towns suggest the lavish potentialities of earth—Spring Green, Richland Center, Black Earth. Thousands of farms have their own small lake, their own rippling brook, and it is difficult to find one which does not have at least a pond. The prairie that is flat in Iowa and Minnesota rolls richly over domed hills in Wisconsin, and everywhere it is marked by corn or wheat fields flush with a thicket of oak or pine. The landscape begrudges man nothing and almost never plagues him with monotony.

This natural prodigality has found its way from the Wisconsin landscape into the Wisconsin character. The friendly mingling, at a village market or a county fair, is symbolical. There one is likely to see a village banker closing the arrangements for a loan to a shopkeeper, as the two of them pour down a social mug of beer. Or one can hear a farmer, between panting breaths as he rests from mauling a test-your-strength machine, name his fee to a neighbor for putting his stallion at stud. Or two men, pitching balls at rag dolls on a rack, will break off their easy discussion of the indiscretions of a neighbor's girl to take up the lease of pasture rights which one is interested in obtaining from the other.

Fairs in Wisconsin have always been a choice place for political speeches, formal and informal, serving almost as the rural equivalent of the Boston Common, or Union Square in New York, or Hyde Park in London. A common sight at a county fair is some village character haranguing a small crowd on his favorite subject, whether it be Utopian socialism or the sober co-operative movement or a fanatical atheism.

The state fair is not in essence different from the humbler county fair or the tiniest village festival. Behind each of them is the modern farm, and behind the farm is feudal Europe. The midway, with all its gaudy color and noisy rides and sharp-practicing "outsiders," is much like a European village street in carnival mood and infested by mountebanks. The contests of skill and strength, even though their prizes are plaster Kewpie dolls and cheap electric clocks, have their simpler archetypes, and the tug of war for men, the potato or the hobble race for women, the greasy pig or pole for boys are still commonplace. The Central European grandfather who brought his cow or his vegetables to town in the hope of a sale is present still in the scientific grandson who brings his best bull to the county seat in the hope of winning a blue ribbon, or in his wife, whose preserves or pies may get her name into the weekly newspaper. The difference is most eloquently represented in the displays of modern farm equipment.

In many Wisconsin communities, the fair has not yet disassociated itself from European practices. At Sparta, it is held not at a "fairgrounds," but in the streets of the city, and prize cattle are displayed in the courthouse square. The tiny village of Hales Corners, in the southeastern corner of the state, undergoes a metamorphosis on the first Monday of every month, when a fair instituted a hundred years ago by gypsy horse traders usurps the town, and every possible kind of household ware, garden produce and farm animal fill the crowded street. At Watertown, farther inland, a similar event takes place every month, but what was once an ordinary German cattle market now specializes in little pigs and fat, force-fed geese. Abbotsford, in the center of the state, holds a monthly village auction, where anyone can offer anything for sale, and where games and contests share the public interest in bargain prices for a barrel of apples or a bedstead.

Wisconsin's past-in-present character shows clearly in the way its European immigrant groups preserve their national identity. The main groups can be mapped roughly—using climate as a guide—with the Finns and early Poles in the northern timberland, where the winters are sometimes appallingly severe; the Norwegians and Swedes in a loose belt below them, where timber shades to grain; the Swiss and Germans in the milder corn and dairy and orchard regions of the central and southwestern prairie; and the southern Europeans and late-coming Poles in the industrial lake cities to the southeast.

In the 1830's, Cornish miners settled in Mineral Point, and the town was first known as Shake Rag, after its main street. Here the miners built a row of limestone houses precisely as they would have built them in Cornwall, and from their doorsteps their wives called the men home from the hillside mines at mealtime by waving dish-rags. The houses stand occupied today—low cottages of roughly hewn stone, built close together and nearly flush with the street, gleaming pale yellow in the sun—and the town is known as a place where one can buy saffron bread, curdled-cream desserts, and, above all, pasties. The pasty consists of a rather tough pie crust made large and round, then folded over a combination of onions, potatoes, meat and ruta-baga turnips, in a sort of half moon, and baked. The Cornish people of Mineral Point are so stubbornly proud of this national dish that once, when a printer mistakenly set the word "pastries" for "pasties" in a pamphlet advertising a local inn, he was asked to destroy his entire edition.

On Door Peninsula, there is a farming community named Brussels; it was settled by Belgians in the mid-fifties and has lost little of its first flavor. Children learn to weave the complicated maypole dance, the six-week Flemish harvest festival is still celebrated, and on such occasions national costumes are worn with a happy lack of self-con-sciousness. Genoa, on the western boundary of the state, was popu-lated almost entirely by fishermen from the city whose name they brought with them, and the community retains its Italian character. A number of towns in Waukesha County, notably Wales, were settled by groups of Welshmen who were friends and neighbors in the home country, and these people have maintained with a particular fervor not only their domestic and religious ways but the Welsh traditions of poetry and song. Poles settled at Stevens Point, transporting nearly whole their European way of life and preserving much of it into the heart of the 20th century.

In the north, there are the Finns, who likewise brought their man-ners with them. In these lonely areas, Finnish millmen still visit the *sauna*, or wooden bathhouse, on Saturday nights. They sit on benches that line the wall, cooking themselves in steam made by pouring cold water on hot stones. Then they whip one another with branches to stimulate blood flow, and finally they dash outside to roll and tumble and sprawl, naked and shouting, in the great snow drifts.

A more serious Finnish contribution is the co-operative movement, which they imported and developed in nearly every community they entered or established. While the Grange influence, which had native beginnings in the post-Civil War years and has always been strong in

Wisconsin, served as an encouragement, it was no doubt the strong co-operative impulse of the Finns and Scandinavians which created so many active local systems. The city of Superior, where these two groups have always been the most important, has been called "the consumer co-operative center of the United States."

Most tenacious of all are the Swiss-Germans and the Norwegians. In towns like Stoughton and Westby, Norwegian is as commonly spoken as English, Norwegian holidays and feast days are faithfully observed, and food is almost exclusively Norwegian. At Mt. Horeb, which is about evenly divided between Swiss and Norwegians, a game called *Le Hornuss*, which is Swiss for "hornet," has been popular for a half century. It is a kind of elaborate hockey, involving three rubber disks—the buzzing hornets—instead of a puck. One team drives the disks across the field with willow branches, while the other tries to stop them with wooden shields. "Can you take it?" the offense shouts in the dialect of Bern, and, in the same dialect, the defense cries back, "Just try us!"

In the same neighborhood is an establishment called Little Norway, or *Nissedahle*. This is a sentimentalist's dream of a Norwegian valley village, fabricated by the late Isak Dahle, the Chicago business-man who bought the 160 acres on which Little Norway is situated. In 1926 he hired workmen to revise the landscape according to a Norwegian post-card model. His carpenters built a number of small, oak structures with sod roofs and brilliantly painted ginger-bread trimming. Norwegian artisans furnished them with examples of native craftsmanship, and Dahle added his own modest collection of Norwegian furniture, bric-a-brac and silver. Today it is a kind of dollhouse stockade, and the admission fee strengthens the impression that this quaint establishment is some kind of concession at an exposition.

An animated contrast to Little Norway is the community life of a town like near-by Monroe. Monroe, with a large Swiss element, is the center of the Wisconsin cheese industry. It proclaims an annual Cheese Day, has been known to conduct cheese-smelling contests, reeks of limburger on the right breeze, and is not at all averse to publicity. Yet, quite without self-consciousness, its yodeling societies retain the vocal style and skill of their Alpine forebears, and at its Saturday-night dances young men and women mix the traditional folk patterns of Switzerland with jazz. This is no halfhearted attempt to revive a dead past; the past is as vigorous in the life of the community as is the mysterious thing which most of us think of as the present.

Nowhere in Wisconsin is this fact clearer than in New Glarus, a slightly younger Swiss settlement. The site was discovered by *Schweitzers* who were looking for a spot which duplicated as exactly as possible the physical features of the home canton of Glarus. It was settled exclusively by the 100-odd immigrants from this single community, and the present population of about a thousand is largely composed of their descendants. For some years they raised wheat; but the market was fickle, and their soil did not yield an ideal crop. Forced back to what they knew best—dairying—they had such extraordinary success that New Glarus became a kind of ideal dairying community, its settlers wise in the ways of an ancient agricultural tradition and at the same time eager to refresh that tradition with new knowledge.

Nevertheless, while prosperous cheese factories began to spring up around the town, its people preserved an even older homeland industry—lace making. Its farmers pursue the newest methods of dairying and its shops stock the most modern equipment, yet its church continues each year to celebrate the two-day festival of Kilbi, which commemorates the dedication of the Reformed Church in old Glarus centuries ago.

New Glarus represents in quite beautiful miniature the outstanding characteristic of Wisconsin life—a candid love of the past, which preserves the patterns of an ancient European culture; and a lively interest in the present, which expresses itself in some of the most progressive attitudes in America.

In the cities of Wisconsin, old national ties are dispersed and very often dissipated, and the appearance of modern America goes much deeper than the surface. Wisconsin cities are not, in general, distinguishable from small cities anywhere in the United States.

Manitowoc is an example, or Milwaukee, or any of the Lake Michigan ports, which are the chief Wisconsin cities. Manitowoc, first settled because of easy access to water power and transportation, moved through the several stages of farm town, lumber camp, fishing village, ship-construction center and modern industrial city all in just over a hundred years. Today its heavy industry plays a major role in the economic life of Wisconsin; its industrial products have many times the value of its agricultural products.

Yet the accumulated atmosphere of such a city—its persisting mill-town rawness, the farmers in the streets on Saturday night, the old merchant sailors in its water-front saloons—invokes at any moment the whole of its past, even the frontier on which it grew and the European shadow out of which it came.

Milwaukee points up the contrast better, perhaps, than any other city. On almost any busy street the smell of *Apfeltorten* or *Sauerbraten* is mingled with exhaust fumes, and homesick zither strains from the open door of a tavern blend with the imperious blast of a taxi horn outside.

The city combines an insatiable appetite for beer, or for *Gemütlichkeit*, with a passion for art and music, or for political justice. It has a taste for sausages and socialism, for the worst German middle-class vulgarities along with the most enlightened liberal aspirations.

Yet for a sense of the true character of the state as a whole, for the best understanding of what is called the "Wisconsin Idea," one looks to towns like Ephraim, which began as a Moravian settlement with communal ownership of property, or to Sauk City with its Humanist Society, or the hamlet of St. Nazianz, which for twenty years successfully maintained an experiment in Christian communism. Or one looks to Ripon, originally a socialist community, which saw the birth of the Republican Party in 1854, when a coalition of angry Whigs, antislavery Democrats and Free Soilers met to revolt against the extension of slavery under the Kansas-Nebraska Act. Or one looks to the near-by village of Valders, where Thorstein Veblen was born— Veblen, distinguished social economist later dismissed from the University of Chicago for his unconventional private life; or to Watertown, the home of Carl Schurz, a great political theorist who became Lincoln's Minister to Spain. Or one looks to Portage, the birthplace of Frederick Jackson Turner, the famous historian of the American frontier; and of Zona Gale, brilliant liberal spirit in Wisconsin social activity for thirty years, and acid etcher, in her best fiction, of its sometimes petty, sometimes cruel provinciality.

Above all, one looks to the farmland of Primrose Township in Dane County, where, in 1855, Robert La Follette was born and where he lived until he was eighteen. "Old Bob" had the qualities of a lesser Lincoln. Raised in the humblest rural circumstances, he never lost the common touch, as he never lost sight of his one basic principle that democracy rests on a real representation of the popular will. Like Lincoln, he was famous as an orator before he was a political success. His was an old-fashioned kind of oratory, prodigal with rhetoric, full of gesture, nearly fanatic in its intensity, capable of intolerably boring protraction. Unlike Lincoln's speeches, La Follette's do not read well—they depended for their vitality on the style of the man himself, on the physical presence of a personality.

Like Lincoln, again, La Follette held very small office before he held large office, and he had, at times, the same kind of dry humor. When he was asked why he had run for the unprofitable office of district attorney in Dane County, he answered, "For the money," and the humor lay in the fact that this was largely true, for he was penniless. When he at last won the gubernatorial election in 1900, his wife, Belle Case, who was his moral and intellectual prop and an object of positive reverence to the people of Wisconsin, said, "I have been prouder of him when he has suffered defeat." She admired his stanch truculence, even in failure, more than his human grace.

Like Lincoln's personality, La Follette's elicited either loathing or love; there was nothing between these extremes. When, as a young man, he won a Midwest university oratorical contest, his fellow students pulled him home from the railroad station in a triumphal surrey, but not many decades later, when he made his antiwar filibuster in the Senate, students burned him in effigy on the Lower Campus, and in the general hysteria he was denounced for his pacifism in a round-robin statement signed by 399 faculty members. On occasion he was called insane and degenerate, or a chronic drunkard, and sometimes even liberals were convinced that the success of the Progressive movement in Wisconsin meant La Follette was a "crook." Lincoln Steffens thought so until his famous investigation persuaded him that La Follette actually embodied his own ideal of a politician whose aim was truly to represent the will of the people.

What Robert La Follette conspicuously lacked was the broad generosity of Lincoln's character, the enormously relaxed will, that total absence of egotism which puts Lincoln among the very greatest men. Without that, La Follette is left in the second rank of greatness. Yet he had something in place of Lincoln's melancholy resignation and brooding love; he had a kind of dramatic life within himself, a frenzy of faith and self-confidence, an unshakable stubbornness and noisiness of conviction, an inexhaustible reserve of energy which was like fire.

These qualities, taken together, were the perfect expression of the vital unrest and excitement which were fermenting in the intellectual life of Wisconsin at the start of this century. La Follette did not make history so much as he made himself its spearhead.

He came up in politics through the Republican Party, which had dominated the state since the early 1870's and was in turn dominated by the all-powerful lumber and railroad monopolies.

From the beginning, La Follette appealed to the people directly, over the heads of the bosses. When he became a real threat, Philetus Sawyer, the Republican leader, offered him an indiscreet bribe—which brought on the inevitable break with the Party. From then on, until the formation of the Progressive Party itself in 1934, the Republicans were split in two—"stalwarts" and "progressives." It required a six-year battle before La Follette's first election to the governorship in 1900, but antimonopoly legislation followed quickly after that, chiefly in revised railroad taxation and through the newly instituted direct primary.

In his campaign against the railroads, no single event was more important than that of "Scofield's cow." In 1897 it was revealed that Governor Scofield had shipped free of charge, on frank number 2169, from the northern part of the state to Madison in the south, a variety of personal possessions, including a sewing machine, a buggy pole, a barrel of potatoes (small) and a cow (crated). Scofield had not violated the law, but the goods he had shipped dramatized, in a comic way, the privilege he had abused. A storm of public indignation and satire blew up. The cow's picture was printed in the newspapers, and she became, for the people of Wisconsin, the folk symbol of corrupt privilege. Whenever La Follette mentioned "Scofield's cow" he brought down his house in wild laughter.

La Follette embodied the triumph of the "Wisconsin Idea," and in a way, the forces which made it up came to an end with the death of the man, as if his public life had exactly measured the vital extension of an idea in time.

When, on a memorable hot June Sunday in 1925, thousands and thousands of men and women and children from all over the state passed his open bier under the dome of the statehouse in a daylong procession, they were mourning not only the death of a beloved man but a death in their lives as citizens, and the close of an era.

The "Wisconsin Idea" may be defined as the laboratory method in politics. It regards institutions as flexible and government as experimental. It insists that a healthy political life requires that politicians accept the advice of nonpolitical experts. Thus it draws into politics the best available intellectual power and the most experienced minds.

To the older La Follette's administration, the advice of such economics experts as Richard T. Ely and John R. Commons, of such experts in education and public welfare as President Van Hise, and of such specialists in the theory of public administration as Charles McCarthy—all from the University—was nothing less than integral. Commons, for example, was mainly responsible for the writing of Wisconsin's civil-service law, which remains a model in the United States. Together, men such as these were responsible for the long-range planning which went on under La Follette, as the "Wisconsin Idea" developed a systematic program to make the democratic state positively democratic, to keep the public welfare always, and in every detail, in the ascendancy. Much of this program was derived from the most liberal elements in 19th-century German politics, and its appeal to the people of Wisconsin was clearly that it fulfilled here social ambitions which had been frustrated there. It was, in a way, the "best" of Europe, and it came to independent life in Wisconsin.

All this seems less extraordinary today, now that most of the social legislation which Wisconsin first achieved has been written into Federal law and into the law of many states. But in 1912, when Charles McCarthy coined the phrase "Wisconsin Idea" and defined its program in a book of that name, all this was new. When he conceived the idea that a state-university professor has an obligation to counsel a representative in Congress or a governor no less than a farmer, and that the major obligation of the University itself is to serve the state, he was formulating the principles of social idealism which gave Wisconsin in the first quarter of this century its special public quality, and, in effect, created the greatness of its University.

Madison, the capital, dramatizes the "Idea" perfectly. All around it the Wisconsin country rolls in, as it were, to its beautiful center, which is surrounded by three lakes. In the town itself, all streets, by a kind of inverse radiation, lead to the Capitol. This stands on a hill in the heart of the city, facing down a half-mile of straight and open

street—State Street—to the University, which, again, is built on a hill.
It is as if all the life of the state were being drawn into the statehouse
and the University, to flow back out into the state, enlightened and
fulfilled.

The "Wisconsin Idea" represents the double strand of practicality
and idealism which is woven so deep in the state's character. All
through Wisconsin history, its people's feeling toward Europe has
been one of nostalgia combined with a deep fear and suspicion. If
"grass roots" can throw up great popular leaders like the elder La
Follette, they can also foster the most depressed kind of insularity.
The antiwar attitude of the elder La Follette and the later attitude
of Robert La Follette, Jr., toward President Roosevelt's "twelve obsolete destroyers" were based on the same principle that always
guided both father and son: let the people know and let the people
choose. Yet many Wisconsin people responded to this position not
from allegiance to democratic principle but from a profound provincialism.

No La Follette now occupies public office. The excitement and
the vitality of Wisconsin intellectual life of twenty-five years ago are
gone. The University still serves the state, but in humbler ways than
Charles McCarthy planned—not in ideas so much as in agricultural
and economic skills. Something has changed since 1894, when Prof.
Richard Ely was, in effect, on trial before the board of regents for
economic heresy, and the regents declared, "Whatever may be the
limitations which trammel inquiry elsewhere, we believe the great
state University of Wisconsin should ever encourage that continual
and fearless sifting and winnowing by which alone the truth can be
found."

Educational reaction scored a significant triumph over the Experimental College of Alexander Meiklejohn. This was an attempt to set
up, within the over-mechanized framework of a vast university, informal methods of study and teaching in place of recitations and the
lecture system and, instead of "subjects," the study of entire civili-
zations. Two hundred students, bright and rather bohemian young
men, were selected for the experiment and at once became known
as "the guinea pigs." With them came a brilliant faculty—chiefly men
who had been sympathetic to Doctor Meiklejohn at Amherst, where
he had previously been relieved of the presidency.

The Experimental College, founded in 1928 was one of the first proposals of a new president, Glenn Frank, and it represented the ambitious plans which he had made for his administration. Glenn Frank was not, however, an able administrator, and by 1932, when the experiment was assessed, he had so lost prestige with his faculty, the regents and the people of the state, that the development of Meiklejohn's ideas was doomed to be cut off. The orthodox educational theorists in the University were happy to wield their axes on this monster which had made them so uneasy. Frank did not come to its defense, and in 1933 the experiment was pronounced a failure —and discontinued.

The provincial tendency was revealed more entertainingly in the famous "rocking-chair case." One night the Dean of Women telephoned the Dean of Men to inform him that coeducation was being carried too far by a student couple in a certain private apartment. It was the male dean's duty, she felt, to interfere. The Dean of Men, according to the story which swept the community, went to the indicated apartment and pounded on the door. When the young man would not admit him, the Dean sat down in a rocking chair in the hall and waited until the victims emerged to face expulsion.

The affair reached its peak when the poet William Ellery Leonard, a faculty member, denounced the deans in plain words. The colorful teacher, himself the subject of many scandals, accused the deans of an indecent invasion of sacred human rights. The newspapers loved him for the fuss. Glenn Frank vacillated, and the affair came to a close when he exonerated the Dean of Men and dismissed the Dean of Women. Her comment on Frank's attitude was, "You can't nail a custard pie to the wall."

The problem of academic freedom became acute in the Frank administration. In 1935, the legislature conducted an investigation of subversive political activities in the University, with the implication that President Frank—who, at the time of his death in 1940, was national chairman of the Republican Party program committee—encouraged communism among the faculty and students. This was, of course, nonsense, yet it led to the end of his university career. Whatever his deficiencies, the cause of academic freedom and the reputation of the University were in no way enhanced when Governor Philip La Follette, who was by then Frank's political enemy, forced his resignation.

Something has gone. The State of Wisconsin, like the University, seems today to have slipped into a period of intellectual contraction. Some things, of course, cannot go. The various and brilliant landscape remains, and all that it offers. Old social habits remain. Laws remain. Yet the world moves on, and if social habits and laws merely remain and do not grow, they become old-fashioned.

It is time, perhaps, to look back to certain events in Wisconsin as closed, to certain attitudes as dead. The past, which has always kept itself so alive in the present, may just now be solidifying. If this is true, Wisconsin stands today at the end of its first great period.

# Illinois

## by CLYDE BRION DAVIS

On a map the state of Illinois is bounded on the west by the Mississippi River and on the east by Indiana and the sycamore-fringed Wabash, but actually, it refuses to be limited by mere geography. It has a faculty for stretching out, and far; so you might say that Illinois is bounded on the west by a ranch house near some such place as Chinook, Montana, and on the east by the Museum of Modern Art on West Fifty-third Street, New York City. You might also say that although the geographical center of the United States is 500 miles to the west, Illinois is the axis of the nation, the hub and vortex of all the wonderful and eccentric hullabaloo that comprises our sweet land of liberty; and it's even possible that this off-center center may account for some of the wabble and vibration in our body politic.

For Illinois is perhaps the most American of all the states. It's the U.S.A. in a capsule. Here our virtues and our faults are most exaggerated and magnified. Here somehow the heroes seem more heroic, the villains more villainous, the buffoons more comic. Here violence is more unrestrained, and the capacity for greatness is as limitless as the sweep of the unending cornfields.

With its great, teeming, beautiful, ugly metropolis on Lake Michigan, Illinois is the economic, agricultural, industrial and cultural heart of America. All roads—steel, concrete and aerial—lead to Chicago. It's the dynamic nucleus of a rich and vital land, the mag-

net which draws not only millions of cattle from the western plains
but talented youth from the valleys of the Mississippi, Missouri, Ohio
and Arkansas in search of fame and fortune. The mark of Chicago is
on towns and homes that are a thousand miles from the Loop, and
on most of the vigorously original American literature written in the
20th Century.

The state of Illinois is a manufacturer, a processor, a distributor
and a hog butcher, and one of the great farmers of the world. Central
Illinois is the soybean capital of the world, but it is corn that aston-
ishes the summertime traveler. And well it might, for the cornfields
of central Illinois are incredible. Mile after mile and county after
county of tall, rustling corn, corn, corn, interspersed by big barns,
neat farmhouses and rows of cylindrical steel storage bins. The eager
black loam of the flat or gently undulating prairie is planted early
in May, and in a few weeks of rain and hot weather the corn is taller
than a basketball player.

Pull off the highway on a warm, humid night where the road is a
mere aisle through a forest of corn, and above the clash and rattle
of the shard-like leaves in the constant wind you'll hear a curious
brittle popping on every side, a staccato popping like distant fire-
crackers. That is the corn growing, audibly and enthusiastically. But,
unless your sense of direction is exceptionally good, don't wander
off between the corn rows or they may not find you until husking
time.

As states go, Illinois is not exceptionally large, ranking twenty-
fourth in the nation, measuring about four hundred miles from north
to south and averaging maybe two hundred miles wide. If Illinois
were in Europe it probably would be supporting a population of forty
millions or so—when not being invaded by a foreign army. However,
nobody is invading Illinois these days except young hopefuls seeking
their fortunes and visiting politicians seeking votes.

Yet an invasion should be fairly easy, for the state, and especially
its greatest city, is the hub of America—the center of a giant web of
railroads, highways and waterways. It was the waterways that first
established Illinois and Chicago as the continental axis—for rivers
and lakes were the initial highways for the canoes and bateaux of
Indian and voyageur. Friendly Indians showed the white man the
seven-mile portage from the Chicago to the Des Plaines River, which
led to the Illinois River and thence to the Mississippi. The route

worked just as well in the opposite direction for those who had come down the Ohio River and up the Mississippi and Illinois to navigate the Great Lakes and the St. Lawrence.

Railroads followed the waterways, turning Chicago into such a bewildering maze of intersecting tracks with seventeen hundred passenger trains entering and leaving seven stations daily—plus heaven only knows how many freight trains—that it's quite understandable how an occasional boxcar gets lost in the shuffle and wanders around the Chicago yards for days. The wonder is that whole passenger trains don't do the same thing.

Easterners naturally regard Illinois as a Western state. And while that seems ridiculous to people in the Pacific and Rocky Mountain regions, the Easterners have a point. Communities like Tombstone, Arizona, and Dodge City, Kansas, bask in their tradition of violence and proudly direct tourists to their "Boot Hills" where rest many early-day characters who died with their boots on. Actually there has been more real Wild West gun-fighting—and gang fighting—over a longer period of time in Illinois than in any state west of the Mississippi.

One incident of many was the Fort Dearborn massacre of 1812, in which sixty-three men, women and children were slaughtered by the Indian allies of the British, for which the late Mayor William Hale (Big Bill) Thompson of Chicago held the late King George V (1865–1936) personally responsible. This indictment was considered too narrow by the late Colonel Robert Rutherford McCormick, proprietor of the Chicago *Tribune* ("the world's greatest newspaper"), to whom all British, including Queen Elizabeth II, Sir Winston Churchill and the Archbishop of Canterbury, were Redcoats. In his newspaper and in addresses before his Chicago Theater of the Air, Colonel McCormick always cherished an active distrust of all Britishers. And Mayor Thompson disliked the English so much that he even pushed a bill through the state legislature making the official tongue of Illinois "the American language."

It would take volumes to recount the spectacular wild western violence of Illinois, but the case of Elijah Lovejoy has a place in any Illinois chronicle because he was a moderate Abolitionist and Illinois was officially an antislave state. Lovejoy, a young clergyman, was publisher of the Alton *Observer*. On Independence Day, 1837, he wrote a Fourth of July editorial which said, "Even the very flag of freedom that waves over our heads is formed from materials cultivated by slaves, on a soil moistened by their blood, drawn from their backs by the whip of the republican task master."

Alton was in free Illinois all right, but there was plenty of Southern thought in that river town. That night a mob broke into the *Observer* office and destroyed the press. Lovejoy's friends bought a new one, but on September 21 a masked mob smashed it to pieces and threw the wreckage into the river. Even then Lovejoy and his backers were not whipped. They raised more money and ordered another press. When it arrived Lovejoy and a dozen friends who were guarding it were attacked by a mob which set the building afire and put an end to Lovejoy's editorials by riddling him with bullets.

Alton is now a city of great manufacturing plants—steel fabrication, oil refining, copper, bronze, dynamite and the Owens-Illinois Glass Company, the biggest bottle plant in the world. It's a hilly country rising from the river bluffs and the principal highways wind this way and that way through the city with hard-working policemen at busy intersections trying desperately to keep the traffic moving. Outside of town, if you get off the main highways you may find yourself on a narrow, horse-and-buggy road of old red brick rambling through the trees, and if it's a hot, muggy night the millions of lightning bugs will make you dizzy.

If you're going South on this muggy night you'll see a strange glow in the sky that does not come from burning barns or oil wells but from big, self-sufficient St. Louis, Missouri, across the river, and from East St. Louis, Illinois, on the eastern flood plain.

East St. Louis is the home of meat packing houses, stockyards, iron foundries, oil refineries and rubber plants. It used to be a quite tough town. But they say now that it has tamed down enough so the old bass-singing canary birds are up to a medium baritone.

About one hundred and fifty miles up the Mississippi from East St. Louis is the strange old town of Nauvoo, once the Zion of Mormonism and the largest city in Illinois—an autonomous state within a state where Joseph Smith's Nauvoo Legion caused some uneasiness because it was bigger and better-trained than the Illinois state militia. Driving up, the most plausible route is U.S. 67, which passes through Jacksonville and Beardstown.

Jacksonville might be called a typical city in America's Midwest heartland. It's neither too large and bustling nor too small and sleepy, but there's a nice balance between industry and agriculture to form a pleasant, well-behaved community. Like many Illinois towns, Jack-

sonville is built around a central square. The city, named for Andrew
Jackson, has three distinctions: The Eli Bridge Company, which
manufactures no bridges but claims to be the only factory on earth
making Ferris wheels; a residential intersection with a church on
each of four corners; and the fact that it was the boyhood home of
"the Great Commoner," William Jennings Bryan, who was graduated
from the State College there.

Forty-three miles on is Beardstown, where a gangling lawyer
named Abraham Lincoln won acquittal on a charge of murder for a
young ruffian named Duff Armstrong by impeaching the prosecu-
tion's star witness with an almanac. That, of course, was the famous
dark-of-the-moon case.

The Keokuk dam stretches across the Mississippi from Hamilton,
Illinois, to Keokuk, Iowa, spreading the river out to a width of perhaps two miles. From the dam it's a beautiful twelve-mile drive
winding up the east shore of this great river to historic Nauvoo. And
the first thing you notice about Mulholland Street in modern Nauvoo
is the number of "clubs"—a situation usually indicative of severe local
restrictions. Modern Nauvoo is known for blue cheese and wine.
Each September a grape festival is held, including a ceremony borrowed from Roquefort, France, called the wedding of the wine and
cheese.

The prophet Joseph Smith said the name Nauvoo was given him
by the Angel Moroni and is Hebrew for "Beautiful Place." Some Hebrew scholars have questioned that, but if it comes to deciding between a scholar's word and an angel's, who wouldn't take the angel's?
"Nauvoo" probably is the lost Hebrew gerund or subjunctive or something for Naturally Beautiful Spot Being Enhanced by Saintly Men.

Led by Joseph Smith and a revelation, a troop of Latter Day Saints
fled persecution in Missouri and bought five thousand acres around
the tiny settlement of Commerce City, Illinois. They changed the
name in accordance with Prophet Smith's revelation and began
building a new Zion in 1840. So many Mormon converts from the
eastern United States and Europe migrated to Nauvoo that the population of the town five years later was 20,000.

All the Mormon property in Nauvoo—the impressive mansion of
Joseph Smith, the part-log, part-frame homestead, just across the
street, he occupied while the big house was abuilding, a large brick
hotel and thousands of residences—now is owned by the Reorganized

Church of Jesus Christ of Latter Day Saints which has headquarters in Independence, Missouri.

There's a sign on the old hotel building saying the Nauvoo House was begun in 1841 and completed in 1869. Then it reads, "It served as the last home of Emma, Joseph Smith's *only* wife. She died in this building in 1879." That "only" is underlined on the sign.

About twenty-five miles away, in Carthage, Illinois, the historic Carthage jail is owned and maintained by the Utah branch of the church. There's a sign on this two-story building of smooth limestone reading, "No smoking. Please remove hats. This is a shrine of the Church of Latter Day Saints." In this old jail Joseph and Hyrum Smith were killed by a mob in 1844.

The two had been arrested after a detachment of the Nauvoo army, under orders from Joseph Smith, had wrecked the office of a newspaper which had attacked his leadership. They were not locked in cells but were given quarters in a second-floor bedroom of the jail. It was there the mob found them.

A volley was fired through the door to their room, and Hyrum fell mortally wounded. Joseph went to the side window with a thought, probably, of leaping to the ground twenty feet below. But the door flew open as the bolt was shot off and Joseph was struck by three bullets.

The caretaker of the jail introduced himself as Elder Matthews of Logan, Utah. Elder Matthews told me, "Joseph cried out, 'Oh, my Lord, my God!' and fell out of the window, landing next to the old well down there." On the floor of the bedroom is a brown stain protected by a glass frame, and this stain, Elder Matthews said reverently, is the sacred blood of brother Hyrum.

No one ever was prosecuted for the murders.

With the slaying of Joseph and Hyrum, Brigham Young, who openly advocated polygamy, took command at Nauvoo and began preparations for the great exodus to a new Zion in the West. Nauvoo became a virtual ghost city, the victim of incendiaries and other vandals.

Up the winding Mississippi a hundred miles or so are the manufacturing cities of Moline, Rock Island and (across the river) Davenport, Iowa.

Moline is especially important historically because a young Vermonter named John Deere established himself there, drawn by the magnet of Illinois, as so very many men of talent, vision and great ideas have been drawn to America's heartland. It was in Moline that Deere perfected his steel plow that made agricultural conquest of the prairie possible. The tough prairie sod had resisted attempts to cultivate it with the old iron and wood plows, but Deere's invention helped to turn the Midwestern prairies into the breadbasket of America and make Moline the farm-machinery capital of the nation.

Eighty-five miles farther up the river, in the junior mountains of Jo Daviess County, is the sleepy town of Galena, known now as the spot where in April of 1860 a stoop-shouldered, middle-aged little man came to clerk for his younger brothers in a leather-goods store after whisky had ruined an Army career. He had failed as a farmer, real-estate agent and tanyard employee, and he was to fail again as clerk. But a year from then he was teaching close-order drill to the Jo Daviess Guards, and five years from then he was to accept the surrender of Robert E. Lee at Appomattox.

There's a sense of age and drowsiness to Galena, with its cobbled streets and houses clinging to the steep hillsides. It is a very old town for the Midwest, and so was spared what has been called the General Grant architecture of the 1870's and 80's, even though it was the general's home town. There are five churches in Galena that are more than a hundred years old, four typically New England in style, the fifth early English Gothic.

Galena is in the northwestern corner of Illinois, close to the Wisconsin border. Swinging south and east, you drive through the famous prairies of Illinois—mile after mile of black loam, gently undulating or as flat as western Kansas or the Texas Panhandle.

A Decatur man told me of riding on the train with a friend from Providence, Rhode Island, who was used to the hill farms and small fields of New England. The friend stared silently from the window as the streamliner whipped past waving corn for the better part of an hour and then he finally turned to the Decatur man and blinked his eyes and said huskily, "What in *hell* can they do with all that corn?"

And that was a good question. What can they do with the five hundred million bushels of corn that are produced annually in Illinois? And what, also, can they do with three hundred million bushels of soybeans, which has become the state's number-two crop?

Of course, human beings consume most of the corn in one way or another. It is fed to stock and poultry and then we eat it as ham and eggs and butter and cheese and ice cream and pork chops and beef-steak. A not inconsiderable amount is also consumed in the form of bourbon whisky. But the only human use I knew for soybeans was the Chinese sauce you douse on chop suey.

Around the corn belt, however, there are a number of processing plants for corn and soybeans, and in Decatur I dropped in on one of the largest, the A. E. Staley Manufacturing Company, to find out the less obvious uses of these crops.

The things made from corn include, of course, cornstarch, laundry starch and corn sirup. And the starches are used by the cotton and synthetic textile industry in sizing fabrics. Paper manufacturers use even more. Cornstarch and dextrin are the binders in aspirin and other pills. Starch is used in smelting minerals, and the reason commercial ice cream doesn't taste like that grandma used to whip up for Sunday dinner is this same good old cornstarch.

Cornstarch and sirup are used in the rubber industry, in cigarettes, in tanning leather, making spark plugs, dynamite and candy. And the "steep water" after corn is soaked for processing is the source of yeast and penicillin.

The once lowly soybean is now America's largest source of vegetable oil, while the meal that's left is used not only in livestock and poultry feed but also in the manufacture of human foods, including pancake flour, spaghetti, sausage, canned soups and peanut butter. And, to round up the subject, soybean oil is also an ingredient of paints, printing ink, linoleum, antiknock gasoline, pharmaceutical products, TNT, candy, mayonnaise and cooking oil.

Decatur is one of the fastest-growing cities in the Midwest. You can scarcely recognize the place after an absence of a couple of years. But Decatur and Macon County were part of the prairie-ringed Sangamon River wilderness when the magnet that is Illinois drew a thin, moody Kentuckian across the Wabash from his boyhood home in Indiana.

The twenty-one-year-old Abe Lincoln drifted into Decatur in 1830 and for a year made a living splitting rails with his cousin John Hanks. Thirty years later this same John Hanks, perhaps prompted by Ward Lamon or Jesse Fell or David Davis, carted a load of fence rails to the famous Wigwam Convention in Chicago and led a parade of Lincoln enthusiasts, each with a rail on his shoulder, to help stampede the convention for the Rail-Splitter. If you wonder where they found timber to split into rails on the treeless prairie, dense forests grew along the Sangamon and other Illinois rivers, and there still is plenty of scrub timber there.

All of Illinois claims Abraham Lincoln for its own and the automobile license plates cry out "Land of Lincoln," but Decatur stands at the southeast corner of the real Lincoln country. Over this whole area—up to Bloomington, over to Peoria, down to Petersburg and the restored log village of New Salem and Springfield—one is never allowed to forget that the Great Emancipator called this home. There are Lincoln theaters, Lincoln hotels, Lincoln parking lots, Lincoln streets and the city of Lincoln. In more than a few restaurants the sad face of Old Abe peers up at you from your dinner plate.

There are so many bronze plaques bearing the Gettysburg Address on public and commercial buildings that one wonders if some enterprising foundry didn't peddle them over the Lincoln country. Once in a while a plaque will contain the Farewell Address or Second Inaugural. And there are other custom jobs which announce that here on such and such a date Lincoln and Stephen A. Douglas engaged in one of their debates.

The town of Bloomington adjoins the town of Normal, the home of Jesse Fell, one of the great characters of Illinois history, who established the normal school that gave Normal its name, and who persuaded Lincoln to write the autobiography which Fell published to acquaint the nation with facts about the tall Rail-Splitter before the 1860 national convention. It was Jesse Fell, with his law partner Judge David Davis, Ward Lamon and Leonard Swett who engineered the nomination of the little-known Lincoln over the distinguished William Henry Seward.

Jesse Fell met Abraham Lincoln early and saw a man of destiny. He conceived the idea of the debates with Douglas, was a leader in forming the Republican Party in Illinois and he put Lincoln's name before the 1858 state convention for United States Senator. Jesse Fell was a self-effacing man of great vision, of great generosity and great creative energy who would never accept public office for himself.

Lincoln first saw New Salem when twenty-two and his flatboat stuck on the mill dam, giving him opportunity to show his mechanical ingenuity in getting it off. It was in this attenuated log village on the hill above the Sangamon River that he clerked in the store, became postmaster, wrestled with Jack Armstrong, borrowed Jack Kelso's

books, studied under Mentor Graham and allegedly fell in love with
Anne Rutledge. But it was a deserted village and falling to ruin by
the time he penned the Emancipation Proclamation.

Now the state of Illinois has done a remarkable job of restoration
and the village stands as a sort of national shrine in New Salem State
Park. Furniture and utensils stand or lie as if the inhabitants had just
walked out from the cabins, mill, store and tavern, but there also is a
curious sense of dusty desiccation about New Salem comparable to
the ancient cliff dwellings of the Southwest. You feel that New Salem
has been a ghost town drying out in the sun for half a millennium.

There is none of that aura of dry antiquity about Lincoln's home
in Springfield, though. You really feel as if Abe and Mary and the
boys had just stepped out and will be back in an hour or so. You can
picture his lanky form on the haircloth sofa or working at his desk.
The well-built, two-story frame house is obviously the home of a
fairly prosperous professional man. Stick in a couple of bathrooms
and modernize the kitchen and it would be that today.

The Lincoln Tomb State Memorial in Springfield's Oak Ridge
Cemetery is, of course, a tourist mecca. Mrs. Lincoln and three of
their four children also are buried there.

The ancient state capitol, which has been the Sangamon County
Court House since 1887 when the "new" Capitol was completed,
stands in the old Town Square between Washington and Adams
Streets. It was in this building that Lincoln served as a state legislator
and pleaded cases before the State Supreme Court.

Springfield itself is one of the most attractive state capitals in
America, especially along tree-lined Second Street where the Capitol
Building, Centennial Building, Supreme Court and State Armory are
grouped behind broad lawns.

There's a 4000-acre artificial lake in beautiful Springfield Park
where regattas of national importance to sailboat enthusiasts are held
annually.

Fifty miles above New Salem but still in the Lincoln country is
Peoria, the second city in Illinois—although Peoria feels the hot
breath of Rockford on its neck. Peoria first was an Indian village
where the Illinois River widens out to lake proportions, then a
French settlement called *Au Pe* for the Peoria Indians, and is now
a sizable manufacturing city known for bourbon whisky and cater-
pillar tractors.

There's a story about a Springfield man whose brother-in-law was an enthusiastic addict of Peoria's principal product. One evening the Springfield man said, "Come on, Joe, let's go for a ride," and they went up to Peoria where they could look down upon the acres and acres of lights of the Hiram Walker and National Distillers and Century Distilling corn-whisky factories, and he said, "Now, look, Joe, you can see you haven't got a chance of drinking all the bourbon they can make." And Joe shook his head sadly. "Gosh," he said, "maybe you're right." Then he brightened. "But, brother, you got to admit I've got 'em working nights."

On the Court House lawn (where Lincoln and Douglas debated) there's one of the most elaborate Civil War monuments I ever saw. It's a high shaft topped by an angry eagle and surrounding the shaft are fourteen bronze figures including a tall, robed gal (one breast bare, of course) in the act of writing, "We write on page of granite what they wrought on field of battle," and the thirteen other people are contorted Peoria soldiers, dead, dying or fighting desperately. One is a young drummer boy with his drumsticks sheathed, firing a large horse pistol right at you.

Roller-coaster addicts never have seen anything until they roll down a steep hill in a barrel or ride the Rock Island Jet Rocket between Peoria and Chicago. It's a beautiful train and how it does travel. A visit to the dining car is a real adventure in eating. Not only is the food good but the service is downright astonishing.

So to Chicago—the second largest city in America. Of course someone has said that Chicago isn't a city at all, but merely a collection of wards. But it looks like a city to me. And—although this may be heresy—I think the "Hog Butcher for the World" is a *beautiful* city, especially around the Loop and Michigan Avenue and Lake Shore Drive. And everywhere it's a city with personality and down-to-earth vigor.

Oh, you can find "arty" things in Chicago, and you pay for them. But mostly Chicago is blunt and real and beautiful. For example, there's a saloon on Addison Street with the most honest sign you ever saw on a saloon. It reads Good and Bad Whisky.

Of course there's a custom among esthetes to poke sneers at Chicago, even among some esthetes who got their start in Chicago. And, while Rudyard Kipling was not exactly an esthete, he wrote of Chicago, "Having seen it, I urgently desire never to see it again. It is inhabited by savages." Well, I doubt that many Chicago people cried themselves to sleep over that.

It has often been said that the great fire of 1871 was a blessing in disguise to Chicago, that the city had grown too fast and the disaster gave opportunity to rebuild. But Chicago rebuilt pretty fast, too, and a short drive through some of the older North Side residential districts reveals every type of architecture known to man, separately and in weird combination.

The only municipal structure to survive the fire is the well-loved old yellow stone water tower which rises about a hundred and eighty-six feet above North Michigan Avenue. Oscar Wilde, a true esthete, called the water tower "a castellated monstrosity with pepper pots stuck all over it." But they're not pepper pots at all. They're turrets from which the defenders of Chicago can shoot their crossbows and pour boiling oil upon the attackers.

With forty-one railroads homing into Chicago, making it the world's greatest railroad center, it was inevitable that the city should become the livestock and meat-packing capital of America, with the greatest stockyards in the world and headquarters for Armour, Swift, Wilson and other packing houses. G. F. Swift was the Chicago pioneer in meat packing soon after the great fire and, with the new refrigerator car, practically no more Western livestock was shipped east of Chicago. Easterners ate Chicago meat.

For most women of the Midwest who get to Chicago occasionally, the city means Marshall Field's, for Marshall Field & Company is one of the three largest department stores in America, and in some respects the greatest. The first Marshall Field was a Massachusetts farm boy who responded to the pull of the Illinois magnet in 1856 and went to work for a Chicago dry-goods firm. He slept in the store and saved half of his $400 a year salary. Eight years later he was a partner with Potter Palmer in the firm of Field, Palmer and Leiter.

Young Field believed in the "personal touch" and he kept a notebook on the preferences of women customers. He was an originator of the theory that the customer is always right, and the theory paid off. At forty-seven the dignified Marshall Field was one of the richest men in America, and his store was a national institution. In 1893 he established the Field Museum of Natural History, at the southeast extension of Grant Park, and the Field Museum has become one of the nation's greatest scientific assets.

For people of rural America who don't get to Chicago, however, the Midwest metropolis means Sears, Roebuck or Montgomery Ward. In 1872 Montgomery Ward, a young salesman for Marshall

Field, pioneered the mail-order business in Chicago with a capital of $2400 and a one-page catalogue.

Richard W. Sears, a twenty-three-year-old railroad telegrapher, started in business in 1886 when he bought a consignment of cheap watches and sold them up and down the railroad. Then he bought more watchcases and watchworks and hired a tall, thin watch repairer named Alvah Roebuck to assemble them. Presently Sears and Roebuck were in partnership, selling general merchandise by mail and doing quite well despite the antipathy of small-town merchants and newspapers. Ed Howe, the "Sage of Potato Hill," famous editor of the Atchison, Kansas, *Globe,* declared mail-order buying actually was treason to one's community and a greater sin than adultery.

It has been estimated that out of every $100 spent for general merchandise in America today five dollars goes to Sears, Roebuck.

The Chicago World's Fair—meaning the 1893 World's Columbian Fair and Exposition—opened the Midwest to late 19th Century culture and, with railroads offering special excursion rates, brought millions of visitors from every state in the Union and from virtually every country on the globe. Residents of bleak Far-Western communities were dazzled by the beauty of the Great White Plaster City that stood between Jackson and Washington parks; they rode the gigantic Ferris wheel and were properly frightened; they viewed with awe the exhibits and art treasures of all the European nations, the Liberty Bell, the replica of a United States battleship, the wonders of science and agriculture—and they never got over it. Neither have many of their home towns, even after sixty-three years. The late Frank Lloyd Wright said this romantic borrowing from undigested ancient culture, architecturally speaking, was a "national calamity."

The same furious drive and energy which made Chicago the merchandising and railroad capital of America seems somehow to have made it our capital of violence; at least it had that reputation for many years. It was the bootleg era that brought Chicago and Illinois nationwide notoriety. The first of the bootleg-period bosses to be mowed down was Jim Colosimo. His successor, John Torrio, is known now chiefly because he served as agent for the old Illinois magnet in drawing to Chicago a New York gunman called Scarface Al Brown, who later went by his real name, Al Capone. Capone had an early reputation in Chicago for being lazy, not very bright but plenty tough. He retained that last reputation over the years and, like so many others drawn to America's heartland, gained fame and fortune.

On November 10, 1924, a supposedly gentle florist named Dion O'Banion was shot to death amidst his posies. The truth came out at O'Banion's elaborate funeral; he was a former safecracker turned gang leader. At that time it was alleged that fifty dollars would buy a murder in the North Clark Street region. It was in a garage at 2122 North Clark that seven men were lined up on Valentine's Day, 1929, and shot down by a gang wearing police uniforms. That would have been a three-hundred-and-fifty-dollar job.

Chicago may have been the cradle of gang warfare in the United States but the same kind of super-American energy made it the cradle of the most forthright writing in American literature. H. L. Mencken once said that all but two contemporary writers of note sprang "from the Middle Empire that has Chicago for its capital." He mentioned in particular Theodore Dreiser, Sherwood Anderson, Willa Cather and Booth Tarkington.

Hulking, brooding Dreiser was drawn inevitably to Chicago from his native Terre Haute, Indiana, and did newspaper work and wandered the night streets, lonely, lustful and bitter. Dreiser left Chicago for New York, but the influence of Chicago never left him. He was a great bear that wrote like a man—with bearlike clumsiness and bearlike strength. The magnet of Illinois drew the house painter and wanderer, Sherwood Anderson, from Camden, Ohio, and while employed in a Chicago advertising agency he met Dreiser, Carl Sandburg, Floyd Dell, Ben Hecht and others of the Chicago literary colony. Of course Chicago and Illinois ride through Sandburg's greatest works.

Sandburg was born in Galesburg, the son of a poor Scandinavian immigrant, and was tremendously influenced by Abraham Lincoln. He worked as a farm hand, milk-wagon driver and restaurant dishwasher. He served in the Spanish-American War, did newspaper work, and blossomed as a first-rank poet in 1915 with *Chicago Poems* celebrating "the hog butcher for the world." And he's still writing his big, burly, sometimes brawling and often magnificent verse.

Edgar Lee Masters was a lawyer and the son of a lawyer in the Lincoln country. Writing—poetry and prose—was an avocation for him, but his *Spoon River Anthology* broke upon America as a startling innovation in poetry. Both Sandburg and Masters were helped considerably by Harriet Monroe, a dedicated Chicago woman who nurtured talent from 1912 until her death in 1936 in her struggling little magazine *Poetry*. She also gave her poetry prize to a troubled soul in Springfield named Vachel Lindsay whose brain throbbed with jungle rhythms until he pulled the switch in 1931.

Chicago seems forever to be alive with literary talent and even genius. There was young Ernest Hemingway, born in metropolitan Chicago, who became a sort of protégé of Sherwood Anderson before achieving a style that his master never could approach. There was James T. Farrell, who wrote with brutal honesty of adolescence on the South Side; and Ben Hecht, the "Pagliacci of the Fire Escapes," who gained fame in 1923 with his *1001 Afternoons in Chicago* and who in collaboration with the late Charles MacArthur wrote *The Front Page* and probably caused several thousand cub reporters to be fired for trying to act like a Hecht-MacArthur character. And there was Eugene Field, who worked on the *Daily News*; Finley Peter Dunne, who brought *Mr. Dooley* to life in the *Times-Herald*; there was George Ade and his *Fables in Slang*; and the fabulous Ring Lardner, who wrote some of the best short stories in the language.

Talented youngsters not only from the great midland empire but from all over America are drawn by the magnet that is Illinois to its many institutions of higher learning. Chicago has two major ones —Northwestern University at Evanston and the University of Chicago. And, while Northwestern has a student body of about 18,000 as compared with Chicago's some 7000, Chicago has the reputation of shooting the loudest fireworks.

In a way this is strange, for the University of Chicago was founded in 1890 with gifts of thirty-five million dollars from John D. Rockefeller, chiefly to train Baptist missionaries, though this idea became minimized over the years. The fireworks really started popping at the University in 1929 when the old Illinois magnet drew a thirty-year-old Yale bachelor of arts named Robert Maynard Hutchins to Chicago with a "new plan" for education. Young President Hutchins was progressive. And he had a flair for publicity.

First he abolished compulsory class attendance, which met with student approval, and followed that with a program to give students a comprehensive background of the arts and sciences during the first two years of college, specialized work coming later. In 1939 President Hutchins abolished the football team. Then, with young Professor of the Philosophy of Law Mortimer Jerome Adler (later author of *How to Read a Book*) he presented a plan for education which consisted of reading one hundred selected books. Read the hundred and you're educated.

Other educators gave the University of Chicago plans and programs a mixed reception. Some newspapers, notably Colonel McCormick's *Tribune*, were positively hostile, but Hutchins stayed on as president of Chicago until 1945.

Chicago is uniquely Chicago. Almost anything you say about it may be partly true, but nothing the shrewdest analyst or most intuitive poet can say will be more than partly true, for Chicago is too big and too varied and too squalid and too magnificent to fit into a pigeonhole, or a million pigeonholes.

About sixty miles south of Chicago is the old city of Kankakee where the stone walls and buildings of the original French-Canadian settlers still stand, and seventy-five miles farther are the twin cities of Urbana and Champaign with the great University of Illinois and Memorial Stadium where back in the 1920's Red Grange, the "Galloping Ghost," made football history.

South of Decatur you begin to run into the old coal region, and there is the town of Pana which once seemed on the point of death after mining dwindled. Now it is prosperous, and because of roses, of all things. Five major growers ship roses all over the country. Why roses in a coal town? Well, one man liked roses and started a greenhouse; others followed.

Wind in Illinois is not limited to the Chicago region. Driving toward Vandalia, a former state capital, I ran into a curious phenomenon: a rain squall forced the rain to run *up* the sloping windshield. And at a Vandalia filling station a traveler declared the wind had lifted the front wheels of his car off the pavement several times. He seemed perturbed about it.

As a matter of fact a *still* summer day seems ominous in Illinois. The sky is pallid. The trees droop. Then in the afternoon great cumulo-nimbus clouds pile up in the southwest and march forward, and the birds get anxious and fly this way and that. And presently the wind comes back with a rush, an advance guard to the cavalry charge of rain and the mad flash, crash and boom of a Mississippi Valley thunderstorm.

Such a storm is an appropriate accompaniment to entrance into Williamson County in the hills of Little Egypt. For "Bloody Williamson County" over the longest period of time has been the wildest, toughest, gun-fightingest county in the United States, when you count the feud killings after the Civil War, the mine strike riots, the massacres, the Ku Klux Klan operations, the gang wars and plain private murders reaching into the second half of the 20th Century. When you think of violence, you have to think of Williamson County first.

Marion is the county seat. But the old coal mining town of Herrin was the blood-letting center and the scene of the 1922 massacre, which can't be surpassed for cold-blooded brutality. The Herrin massacre took place on the morning of June 22, 1922. Attempting to operate with nonunion labor, the Herrin strip mine of the Southern Illinois Coal Company was besieged by striking union men. There had been considerable gunfire and company guards had killed three strikers before a group of guards and strikebreakers agreed to surrender on the promise of safe conduct out of the county. But as these twenty men were being escorted out of Herrin they picked up a hooting, jeering following that finally got completely out of hand. Men, women and children began throwing stones and beating the marching prisoners. By the time the parade reached the Herrin cemetery east of town, all twenty prisoners had been murdered. A number of trials were held on charges of murder. But no one was convicted.

Prohibition sat lightly on the hills of Williamson County until the advent of the Ku Klux Klan and S. Glenn Young. He was a 140-pound thug from Kansas who wore riding breeches and two pearl-handled forty-fives. He was a brawling braggart who ruled Williamson County as a dictator, mostly without official authority, from 1923 to the time of his death in 1925 in a Herrin cigar-store gun fight.

In the spring of 1923 hooded and robed platoons of the Ku Klux Klan began marching into Protestant churches of Williamson County and making cash contributions to the ministers in the name of "Christian one-hundred-per-cent Americanism." On November 1, 1923, the Klan hired Young to take charge of its "law-enforcement" program and, incredible as it may seem, Young got five hundred members of the Klan deputized as Federal prohibition agents.

Finally, even the state "Grand Dragon" of the Klan, aghast at Williamson County activities, had Young officially expelled from membership. The expulsion meant nothing. Young continued his swaggering two-gun course as leader and hero of the Klan in Williamson County. On January 24, 1925, Deputy Sheriff Ora Thomas, a pale, quiet former bootlegger and gunman, entered a Herrin cigar store to quiet an argument. Inside were several men including Young and two bodyguards. When the gun smoke cleared, Thomas was dead. But so were Young and his bodyguards.

Despite his expulsion from the Klan, Young was buried in the Herrin cemetery in the purple robes of a kleagle. Hundreds of robed Klansmen marched behind the hearse followed by five hundred cars and oceans of flowers. Five Protestant ministers delivered eulogies.

Though the Klan wars virtually ended, rival gang fights and killings continued for the next twenty-five years. The most bitter rivals were the tough Shelton brothers—Carl, Earl, Bernie, and Roy—against the equally tough bank robber, bootlegger and gunman Charlie Birger. At the Herrin police department they say things have been quiet for several years. "All the gangsters are either dead now or have got out of the country."

There is very little coal mining in Williamson County now. But Herrin appears fairly busy with new industry and has a very nice residential district.

South of Herrin and Marion the black Illinois soil often is supplanted by yellow clay hills and swamps with cypress growing from the dark water. And cotton fields make their appearance. It is the deep South except for one thing: a young filling station attendant at Goreville said no Negroes are allowed in the town or immediate vicinity. Six miles south of Goreville is a dreary-looking village with unpainted and sagging wooden awnings over the sidewalk and its extraordinary name is Buncombe. Thirty miles or so beyond, you come to the Ohio River where the Ohio joins the Mississippi and there at Cairo is the end of Illinois.

Cairo (pronounced like the corn sirup) is a busy and noisy city. The region is a haven for Canadian geese, and consequently for goose hunters. Cairo's tourist attraction is Magnolia Manor, the great house built of imported brick in 1869 by the merchant Charles A. Galigher, whose social life was climaxed in 1880 when that little bearded man from upstate Galena was entertained there. They still have the bed in which General and Mrs. Grant slept. Cairo also is known as the town that Huckleberry Finn and Jim passed in the fog, to their sorrow.

Politics is really *politics* in Illinois, and the fainthearted or unwary had better hunt another arena. Even before the days of Abe Lincoln and Steve Douglas it was a tradition that the suave pleasantries of an Illinois politician should be labeled *caveat emptor* to warn against the rugged dose of dynamite under that honeyed cover.

The frontier law of no-holds-barred was in effect with the sinewy boys of old New Salem, and it never has been repealed. In Illinois where they speak the "American language" (with a few casual borrowings from early Saxon) you must be your own bodyguard whether you're in politics, on the Chicago Board of Trade, teaching modern poetry in one of the many colleges or merely driving along one of the excellent highways.

As I said a moment ago, Illinois is the U.S.A. in capsule form— though it's certainly a king-size capsule. It's a distillate of America, the volatile core of Americanism after the lighter substances have been whirled off in the centrifuge of our hurly-burly life.

Thus Illinois is a concentrate of the best of America and the worst of America. Handle with care. Keep away from open flame. Put on the top shelf out of the children's reach.

In other words, the United States of America is a magnificent and astonishing land, spectacularly rich, powerful, generous, God-fearing, lawless, bumbling, emotional, silly and wise. And so, naturally, is Illinois, the heart of America.

Only more so.

# $\mathcal{M}$*ichigan*

## by BRUCE CATTON

Michigan is perhaps the strangest state in the Union, a place where the past, the present and the future are all tied up together in a hard knot. It is the 20th Century incarnate, and if you look closely you can also see the twenty-first coming in; but it is also the 19th Century, the backward glance and the authentic feel and taste of a day that is gone forever. It killed the past and it is the past; it is the skyscraper, the mass-production line and the frantic rush into what the machine will some day make of all of us, and at the same time it is golden sand, blue water, green pine trees on empty hills, and a wind that comes down from the cold spaces, scented with the forests that were butchered by hard-handed men in checked flannel shirts and floppy pants. It is the North Country wedded to the force that destroyed it.

You enter Michigan, mostly, by way of Detroit, which is something special. It is a profound weight on the land; an enormous city, with great skyscrapers taking the light from Canada, automobile factories and used-car lots scattered across the flat prairies, enough business strewn along the Detroit River to make a Russian's eyes pop; and in the old days, which lasted until World War II, you came into Detroit, usually, by steamboat, which was an experience in itself. The boats came up from the Lake Erie ports, Cleveland and Buffalo and Sandusky, and they gave a theatrical touch to the whole business. Lake Erie is beautiful and shallow and treacherous, with a capacity for whipping up unexpected storms that would bother any mariner who ever lived, although mostly it is pleasant enough; and the old side-wheelers came paddling down its length, usually in the middle of the night—it was nice sleeping, in a snug stateroom on one of those boats, with an air-conditioned wind coming in at the open porthole, and the wash of the paddle wheels beating a quiet rhythm in the darkness—and in the morning the boat came up the Detroit River, and the factories and pumping stations on the bank suddenly made you realize that man had taken over Nature and was trying to make something out of it. Then, a little after breakfast time, the boat docked along the Detroit water front, and no city in America offered a more thrilling or exciting entrance.

The boats are mostly gone, and this is really Detroit's fault. Detroit did not exactly invent the automobile, but it picked the thing up when it was nothing better than a costly and unreliable toy for the rich and made it a necessity for everybody in America, and the automobile—getting slightly out of hand—killed the Great Lakes passenger boats, except for a few cruise ships. You come into Detroit nowadays in your own car, or perhaps by train, and the old impact is gone. The place dawns on you gradually now; it used to hit you between the eyes, with the early light slanting in from beyond Ontario. But even now Detroit clamors at you, arrogantly, with all the confidence that comes to men who know they are really in charge of things and who don't mind enjoying the feeling, and there is something overwhelming about it all.

For here is a foretaste of what the machine is doing to us. Here men picked up the Industrial Revolution and swung it; this place, with its infinite genius for making any sort of contrivance men have ever dreamed of, and making it more cheaply and better than anyone else, is the doorway to the future. Everything goes in a rush, everybody is busy—and the place is big and sprawling and grimy and pulsing with life. Here is where we are going, make no mistake about it, and the big financial centers down East can say what they like and be hanged. Detroit sets the pace because this is where the muscle and the knowledge are; and if you don't think the future belongs to America, you should come here and breathe the air for a while.

Detroit makes its bow to the past, of course. It has such a place as Greenfield Village, in Dearborn, and here the past that Detroit killed forever—the past of wayside inns, one-man machine shops,

quiet country villages snuggling by the route of stagecoaches, and
rural dancers moving to the wheezy tunes scraped out by self-
taught fiddlers—is preserved like a fly in amber, and it is very much
worth visiting. But this, after all, is only a gesture. Detroit has been
taking us away from that for half a century, and if it shows you
Greenfield Village it also shows you the machine-age pace which
turned everything Dearborn has on exhibit into museum pieces.
Dearborn houses both this fragment of the past and also the Ford
Motor Company, which did as much as any one organism could do
to put the past in its place.

Detroit's streets come in like the spokes of a wheel, the other half
of the wheel having been cut off by the Detroit River. Because the
pace has been uneven there are vast skyscrapers standing beside
parking lots, with rummy old brick buildings from the Civil War era
snuggling up against twenty-story hotels and elongated office buildings; burlesque theaters and sleazy secondhand-book stores rub el-
bows with the most up-to-date, chromium-and-cutstone buildings
that America can build, and the river drifts by, down in front, bearing the iron ore and coal and petroleum on which modern America is
built; and whether you like it or not you can feel the hard pulse of
America beating up and down these automobile-clogged streets.

Some years ago a civic-minded booster dreamed up the phrase,
"dynamic Detroit," to express the essence of this city. He hit it off
perfectly. Detroit *is* dynamic. Here is where they call the tune, and
it is not a tune the Greenfield Village fiddlers ever quite managed
to express.

But Detroit, after all, is not really Michigan. Its industrial empire
spraddles over a good part of the state, to be sure—with Flint, and
Pontiac, and Jackson and Lansing and Grand Rapids and all the
rest—but the tremendous industrial nexus centered here is only half
of the story. The other half is something very different—old times,
the breath of bygone days and memories that went out of date before the men who remembered them were old—and as a man born
out of his proper time I love this other Michigan a good deal more
than I love Detroit.

The map of the Lower Peninsula of Michigan is shaped like a fat
old-fashioned mitten—a left-hand mitten, placed palm down, with a
bulky thumb sticking out into the cold blue of Lake Huron. Detroit
is down in the lower right-hand margin, below where the thumb begins, and the great industrial network lies across the lower part of

the state: across the upper part of the wrist. But if you will take
the map, and draw a line from Bay City—at the bottom of the gap
between the bulbous thumb and the rest of the hand—straight west
across the state, you will have cut Michigan into its two distinctive
parts. Everything below the line is 20th Century; everything above
it is North Country—old, half empty, touched by the cold winds
that drift down from the Arctic, with trees and sand and crystal-
clear water and drowsy small towns as its distinguishing marks. It
is a country that will put its seal on you if you are not careful, because it offers a lonely beauty and an escape from almost everything
Detroit stands for.

The present falls away, when you go up into this part of the state.
Suppose you drive up from Detroit, along U. S. Route 10; it goes
through places like Flint and Saginaw and Midland, any one of
which would be world-famous if it were in some other country—and
then, suddenly, it takes you into the empty cut-over land, where ghost
towns cluster by the road, where the rivers flow cold and clear past
hills that furnished lumber for half the world a generation or two ago,
where cabins nestle down by quiet lakes and where the air drifts
straight through you as if nobody had ever soiled it with smoke or
grime or gas fumes. From here on north there are not so many farms,
the soil is very sandy, excellent for growing pine trees, not often so
good for growing anything else, and if it amuses you to count abandoned farms (unpainted shacks going peacefully to ruin amid fields
nobody has tilled for a quarter century or more) you can make quite
a list in an afternoon's drive. The road leads you out of ambition
into peace and contentment; the deceptive light of an eternal summer afternoon lies on the rolling country; the innumerable lakes
glitter brightly blue in the fading light, and when you stop your car
and listen you hear a blessed quiet.

This part of the state must have been quite a sight, a hundred years
ago. Over an area of better than 25,000 square miles there was a
magnificent forest—great pines, mostly, with a healthy sprinkling of
hardwoods like maples and beeches—like nothing you can find in
America today. From lake to lake and for 250 miles from north to
south there was an eternal green twilight, with open spaces where
the lakes and rivers were; twilight, with the wind forever making an
unobtrusive noise in the branches overhead, brown matted needles
and leaves underfoot—everything just about as it was shortly after the
last ice age.

There is one tiny fragment of it left. If you will go to the little town of Kalkaska, in the northwest part of the state's Lower Peninsula, and drive thirty miles or so to the east, you will reach Hartwick Pines State Park; and here, running down to the bank of the Au Sable River, is an eighty-five-acre tract of virgin timber, the last that remains, preserved for tourists. You leave your car by the park-administration building and suddenly you are in the middle of it, with trees rising 150 feet overhead, and a shaded coolness all about that is proof against the summer's worst heat wave. Walking through it is not unlike walking through a cathedral. It has that effect on people. It is even more moving in the dead of winter, with the big trees coming up out of a white silence that is all but absolute; the trouble is that then you have to use skis or snowshoes to get there.

Anyway, Michigan a century ago was one magnificent forest, and even as recently as the Civil War it had hardly been touched. But then the lumberjacks went to work, and they shaved the countryside the way a razor shaves a man's chin. Where there had been wilderness, boom lumber towns sprang up, with rickety railroad lines threading their way back into the hills. In the springtime, every stream was clogged with logs, with lumberjacks scampering across the treacherous shifting carpet with peavy and cant hook, mounds of sawdust rising beside the busy mills, and a mill town with 1200 inhabitants normally supported from twelve to twenty saloons. Michigan voted for prohibition before the Federal prohibition amendment went into effect in 1920, and anyone who remembers what those saloons did to small-town life can easily understand why. For a time Saginaw was the greatest lumber city in the world, then Muskegon had the title, and then some other place; fresh-cut boards were stacked in endless piles by the railroad sidings or the lake-side wharves . . . and then, all of a sudden, it was all over. The lumber was gone, the mills were dismantled, the booming cities and towns lapsed into drowsiness, store-fronts were boarded up—and the razor which had done all of this shaving had left a stubble of stumps like a frowsy three-day beard across thousands of square miles. Some towns died entirely, some almost died, and the endless whine of the gang saws became quiet forever.

All of which put its mark on a whole generation of people. Here was a region half the size of Ireland which, after only fifty years of history, suddenly found itself at a dead end. A society began to decay before it had matured. Towns dwindled and died before the eyes of the very men who had founded them. Boys who grew to manhood in these dying towns moved off to the city, leaving behind the old folks and the girls—half a century ago it was not so simple for an untrained girl to make a place for herself in a far-off city, and thousands upon thousands of these girls were condemned to lives of unwanted loneliness. They were strong and healthy and they had dreams and high hopes, and these came to very little because life had shoved them off into a side alley, since marriage was just about the only career a girl could hope for in those days. The human cost of a dying boom can be pretty high.

So they killed the infinite forest, once and for all. But there was still the land itself, rolling in vast gentle waves under a clear blue sky; there were the hundreds and hundreds of lakes, blue and cold and sparkling with imitation whitecaps; there was the great stretch of sand, putting a golden border on the water; there were the rivers, so clear you could count bits of gravel ten feet deep, so cold they turned your feet numb if you tried to wade; and there was the air, filtered by its eternal drift down from the ultimate edge of icy nowhere, fresh enough to revive a Peruvian mummy, odorous with the scent of jack pines.

All of this adds up to an earthly paradise for people from the hot cities who want to get away from asphalt and noise and muggy heat when they have a chance and touch base with Mother Nature; and today the tourist trade is the second industry in the entire state, topped only by the exalted automobile industry itself. This place where the wilderness used to be may indeed be the North Country, but it is only a hop-skip-and-jump from enormous centers of population. From Detroit or Chicago, it is a handy one-day drive to any spot in the Lower Peninsula, but at the end of the drive you feel that you have left the city and all of its works in another world.

So the old lumber area has had a rebirth, and the air of defeat and decline has vanished. This change has gone hand in hand with others. For one thing, the trees are coming back; huge state and national forests lie across vast stretches of empty land. In addition, there is a belt of cherry and peach orchards twenty miles wide and 200 miles long down the western side of the state. In spring, when the blossoms are out, the rolling hillsides near Lake Michigan offer a spectacle of breath-taking beauty, and many a town that used to live on its sawmills now lives on its cannery-and-packing plant. Every spring they have a big "cherry festival" at Traverse City—a bright,

bustling little city which has made full recovery from the death of
the lumber boom—and a pretty girl is named Cherry Queen; her
function, usually, in addition to posing for photographs, is to take a
cherry pie to Washington and present it to the President. This makes
a nice trip for the girl, nets the President a first-rate pie, and presumably makes everybody happy.

But under everything there is this strange, beautiful, lonely land
itself, this land of blue sky and clear water, where puff-ball clouds
drift lazily overhead, trailing pleasant shadows over water and forest and bright little towns as if nobody ever had to be in a hurry
about anything and time had come to a standstill just because what
is here and now is too pleasant to leave. This is good country to
come from and it is even better to go back to. It is a land of memories and also a land of escape: a place where you can be utterly
idle in more pleasant ways than any other place I know.

I was born in Michigan and I grew up there, and not long ago I
went back to see what it is like today. I came in through the industrial network in the lower-right hand corner of the state, and
after a while I was driving northwest on U. S. Route 10—a fine road
which goes for many miles at a stretch without touching a town,
and which cannot in any case touch a real, full-dress city because in
all of Michigan, north of that east-west line from Bay City, there is
not a single place with as many as 20,000 permanent residents.

Beyond Clare, which calls itself the gateway to the northland, I
turned right on M 115, which goes on past pleasant little lakes dotted
with summer cottages, past a sprinkling of drowsy farms, and past
uncounted miles of unused land. Yet a road, after all, takes you where
you yourself are going, and not where the road goes, and what you
see depends mostly on what's inside of you; and when you go back
to re-explore your own country you are likely to find memories and
dreams all mixed up with solid reality. I was heading for my own
particular corner of the state, where I spent my boyhood, because
I wanted to see what the years had done to it; and if in the end
I learned more about what the years had done to me—well, that is
what usually happens when you go on a pilgrimage.

My own land is mostly Benzie County, which has fewer inhabitants now than it had half a century ago but which has lost its old
backwoods isolation and is a homey, friendly sort of country. There
is a tiny town with the improbable name of Benzonia, which was

founded by some eager folk from Oberlin College just before the
Civil War when all of this land was new. The air was so clear and
good that they wanted a name that would tell about it, so they
dipped into their erudition and came up with a Latin-Greek hybrid
which means, roughly, fragrant air. They built a little college, and for
fifty years it struggled along, graduating eight or ten people a year;
then it was turned into a preparatory school, and my father was
principal of it when I was a boy, and just after World War I there
was no longer any need for this school because the state's high schools
had improved, and it quietly died. Nothing is left of it now except
a brick building which has been turned into a village community
house, but the little town drowses under the long sunlight, with a
special flavor that other little towns don't have, touched by the
memory of the old-timers who wanted to bring education to the lumber country.

Every man makes his own state—or maybe his state makes him;
it is hard to be certain about such things. But you grow up with
something on your mind, and it comes out of the place where you
were born and reared, and you never can get away from it no matter
where you go. And if you go back, long afterward, to the place you
knew when you were young, you see it through eyes that were specially conditioned; you cannot be objective about it; you try to write
about your background and find that you are really writing about
yourself.

I remember, some forty years ago, a January night when the thermometer registered five below and there was a brilliant full moon,
and I went to the front door, late at night, to lock up. I stood in the
doorway for a moment, looking out at the moonlit landscape, the
little grove of trees across the street and the three feet of snow that
covered everything. There is not in all America today anything quite
as still and quiet as a Michigan small town could be, late on a moon-
swept night, in January, in the days before World War I. Nobody in
all the earth was making a sound, nothing was moving, there was only
the white snow, the black trees, the blue shadows lying on the white-
ness, and the big moon in a cloudless sky; and to stand there and
look out at it was, inexplicably, to be in touch with the Infinite—
and, somehow, the Infinite was good, it was lonely but friendly, it
meant something you did not have to be afraid of if you understood
it. So Michigan means that to me—along with much else—and cold-
ness and loneliness and shattering loveliness go hand in hand, so that

while you will always be awed and abashed when you come up against the Infinite you do not really need to be afraid. And maybe that is a fairly good idea to get and take with you.

I can remember another night, in summertime, much earlier, when as a rather small boy my family took me across Lake Michigan on a steamboat from Milwaukee. It was dark and cool and windy, and we came out of the river and out past the breakwater, and the steamer began to rise and fall on the waves of the big lake. For a small child it was quite scary—nothing but water and the dark, with big waves coming in from nowhere and making foaming noises under the bow, and the Michigan shore seemed an unimaginable distance away and the dark sea ahead was what all adventurers have always seen when they pitted themselves against the great emptiness and its wonder and peril, and life itself is an enormous gamble played by people who are eager and frightened at the same time, with nothingness before and above and the chance of a dawn-swept land-fall in the morning lying there, insubstantial and improbable beyond the night, as the possible reward. That is really the truth of it, and that too is good to know.

I am well aware, of course, that, as the world's seas go, Lake Michigan is not really a very large body of water. To cross it by steamer is to spend no more than half a dozen hours afloat, and when the trip is over you have reached only the state of Michigan, which actually is as prosaic a bit of land as you can find. Yet the thoughts of a small boy can be lonely, frightening and touched with unfathomable wonder, and the borders of an unattainable land can glimmer, insubstantial but genuine, over the most matter-of-fact horizon. What you owe the land where you were born and reared is something you can never quite pin down; but if that land can stir dreams and fears and the hints of a completely illogical but convincing promise, you are that much ahead of the game. For what you think and feel when you are very small never quite leaves you, and if it always lures you on to something that the visible landscape does not quite make explicit you are immeasurably the gainer.

All of this means very little, probably, by any rational scheme of things. Yet somehow it is part of the color and the flavor which this strange, light-struck, improbable country gave to me when I was too young to know any better, and it has had its own queer effect on everything I have thought or done ever since. So I bring it in here, along with the pine trees and the cold winds and the everlasting golden sands, to try to explain why I like to go back to Michigan. I am probably trying to recapture something unattainable, but that does not matter; so long as the feel and the gleam of it still lie on the edge of my subconscious it is real, for me, and the only value in any dream consists in the fact that you have to keep pursuing it even though you know that you can never quite reach it. If the real Michigan keeps getting overlaid with the Michigan I thought I saw in the old days, I can only say that I am that much better off—for what I thought I saw then was worth a lifetime's quest.

There is plenty to see up here. Half a mile from this hilltop village is one of America's loveliest lakes—Crystal Lake, named with an utter literalness; it is so clear you can see the bottom where it is twenty feet deep—nine miles long by three miles wide, with wooded hills all around and a fringe of pleasant summer cottages along its sandy shores.

Crystal Lake itself will always be something special for me, because it symbolizes an emotion that goes beyond time and space. When I was very small the minister of the one church in my town of Benzonia took some months off, and—by dint of what patient frugality I do not know: the pastor of a country church at that time earned precious little money—made a trip to the Holy Land. When he returned he made his report, and of it I remember just one thing. The magical Sea of Galilee, he said, the sea where our Lord walked and taught and performed miracles, was just about the size and shape of our Crystal Lake. To be sure, the hills which bordered Galilee were dun-colored, barren of trees, a bleak and impoverished landscape; while our hills, green as the heart of a maple leaf, were ringed with clear water, set about with pleasant little towns, cool and pleasant, inviting people to linger on their long journey from one mystery to another. But the resemblance was there, and the lake in which I caught diminutive perch was very like the lake on which Peter tried to walk dry-shod; and for some reason my life is richer because a saintlike little pastor, half a century ago, saw Galilee through innocent eyes which could interpret any lake in terms of Michigan's pine trees and green open valleys. I have never been to Palestine, but somehow I have seen the Sea of Galilee, and the Word that was preached by that Near-Eastern sea has a special sound for me.

Over the range of hills at the western end of my Crystal Lake there is Lake Michigan itself, and where a little river cuts a channel through the high bluffs there is Frankfort, a summer-resort town and a busy little seaport as well. The Ann Arbor Railroad has its terminus here, with a fleet of car ferries that carry whole freight trains across Lake Michigan, and these big black steamers come and go at all hours of the day and night, 365 days a year. In the winter when the big lake is full of ice these boats often have quite a time of it, but they are sturdy icebreakers and they hack their way through regardless, although they sometimes make port with their upper works encased in ice.

From Frankfort you swing up toward Traverse City on route M 22, which cuts up across what is known as the Leelanau Peninsula. Once this was lumber country and now it is cherry country, but mostly it is a region for summer vacationers. Every little town has its lake (Glen Lake, which lies back of Sleeping Bear Point, is a show place) and there are other lakes with no towns at all, locked in by ice and snow for four or five months of the year.

Sleeping Bear Point is an enormous sand dune, five miles long by 500 feet high, jutting out into Lake Michigan. A road of sorts leads to the top, but your car would stall in the deep, fine sand, so you go to the town of Glen Haven and take passage in one of the special low-gear cars with oversized, half-inflated tires, which waddle through the sand as if they were made for it. On the crest there is nothing at all to see but this golden empty ridge and the great blue plain of Lake Michigan far below, with white surf curling on the beach at the foot of the bluff, yet it is one of the finest sights in the Middle West. There is no noise except the lake wind ruffling the spare trees: there is just nothing except a feeling of infinite space and brightness, and utter freedom from the smoke and the rush and the racket of ordinary 20th Century life.

The country north of Traverse City is high and open, with Lake Michigan nearly always in view off to the left, and the little towns and villages along the way reflect the past in a curious manner. First there was the lumber era, in which today's sleepy hamlet was a rip-roaring little city with a solid mile of sawmills along the water front. Then, when the lumber was gone, there was the early summer-resort trade: passenger boats coming up from Chicago or around from Detroit; imposing but flimsy frame hotels, all veranda and white pillars, overlooking every beach; Pullman cars unloading a new consignment of vacationers at the railroad depot every morning . . . and after a while the automobiles came and killed boat lines, passenger trains and most of the hotels, so that these towns which had made one readjustment had to make another. The result is odd. Every town contains echoes of those two vanished eras, and seems to be looking back regretfully to the past; and yet most of them are brighter and more hopeful than they ever were before, the old feeling of backwoods isolation is gone, the people who live here are having a better time of it than ever before and the general level of prosperity is higher and more stable. Yet the feeling of the past does linger, so that in this area which has hardly been settled more than a century there are haunting echoes of antiquity.

Your memory can play queer tricks on you. At Charlevoix I drove east, skirting the south shore of beautiful Lake Charlevoix to reach Boyne City. Boyne City was perhaps the last lumber boom town in the Lower Peninsula. We lived there, for a year or so, when I was about six years old, and it was a lively place then. There were four immense sawmills along the lake front, and a big "chemical plant"— I suppose it was a place where they extracted turpentine and other by-products from the pines—and there was even a blast furnace, although what it may have been doing there I have never been able to understand. Anyway, Boyne City was bustling and exciting, and our back yard ran down to the Boyne River, where the log drives came down in the spring. To my six-year-old eyes that river was immense; it was, I realized, probably smaller than the Mississippi, but it was fascinating, wide, turbulent, somehow menacing—a dangerous river which easily could (and, two or three times, very nearly did) drown a small boy who incautiously tried to play on its treacherous carpet of moving logs. So I returned to the old back yard and took another look at the river—and realized that either the river had shrunk or I had stretched considerably. The river is charming—gentle, crystal-clear, friendly, no more hostile than a brook. Along the lake front there is an uncommonly pleasant park, where the sawmills used to be. A rusted remnant of the old blast furnace still survives, but everything else seems to be gone; and this is not the exciting town where I used to live, it is just a bright, friendly little community where old memories are held in suspension in the sunlight.

Another of my favorite towns in this part of the state is Petoskey, where I was born. No man ever breaks completely away from his birthplace; you carry the mark of your home town with you. I remember it as a sleepy sort of place, built on a spectacular side hill that slants up steeply from the cold blue of Little Traverse Bay, with funny little tourist-bait shops at the bottom where Indian wares

and other trinkets were offered for sale to the "summer people."
These shops always smelled pleasantly of birch bark—there were
baskets, and toy canoes, and other contrivances—and to this day the
odor of birch bark takes me back to tiny stores which must have gone
out of existence a whole generation ago.

Petoskey has grown up to date and prosperous. It is no longer a
lumber center, and the great trains of flatcars piled high with pine
logs no longer go rumbling past what used to be the Grand Rapids
& Indiana depot, and the sprawling summer hotels I remember so
well are not there any more; but because the hill is so high and
because so much of the big lake lies open at the foot of the hill
Petoskey gives you what so much of this part of Michigan always
gives—the strange feeling that you are at an immense altitude, on
some sort of ridge where you can look down on half of the Middle
West and where the wind that never quite dies down has come to
you without touching anything at all along the way from wherever
it is that winds are born.

Even though it always speaks of the past, and seems to look back
toward it in a dreamy sort of way, most of this part of Michigan has
no particular history. But when you go north from Petoskey you
step far back into legend and the distant past. Things were going
on here when the eastern seaboard colonies were still young. La
Salle, Jolliet and Marquette were here nearly three centuries ago.
At Mackinaw City, at the very tip of Michigan's Lower Peninsula,
and an hour's easy drive from Petoskey, there is a lake-front park
with a rebuilt stockade which marks the site of one of early America's
most significant strong points—Fort Michilimackinac. Here, around
1681, missionaries and fur traders and French soldiers and a scattering of just plain adventurers built an outpost of French civilization in a spot which was more remote and isolated than any spot on
earth can be today.

After the French left Canada the British took over, and in 1763
Pontiac's painted warriors broke in, seized stockade and fort, and
massacred the British garrison. Then the fort was abandoned, to be
rebuilt on Mackinac Island, which lies in the center of the straits.
The Americans took it over after the Revolution, and the British re-
captured it in the War of 1812, and then it was returned to American
possession again. Now it stands empty, a tourists' show place, looking out at the unending procession of freighters that cruise slowly
past on their way to and from the lower lakes.

Mackinac Island is a delightful spot, and it is unusual in two ways. In the first place, although it is spelled Mackinac it is, for some incomprehensible reason, pronounced Mackinaw; and in the second place it is the one spot in the whole state of Michigan—one of the very few spots in all the United States—where you never see an automobile. Automobiles are not allowed on the island, and to come to this place, with its hotels and boardinghouses and curio shops lining the quiet streets, and the old-fashioned horse-drawn surreys leisurely wheeling their way in and out, is to step straight back into the Victorian era. To get about the island you walk, or ride behind a horse, or get on a bicycle. More so than any other place in the state, this is a refuge from the present.

Big changes are coming to Upper Michigan and the symbol of their approach is the stupendous five-mile-long bridge across the straits connecting the Lower and Upper Peninsula. The bridge cost around $100,000,000; it at last ties the two halves of the state firmly together. Before, you crossed the straits by one of a fleet of state-owned ferry boats.

Michigan's Upper Peninsula is an immense finger of land running 300 miles from west to east, with cold, steely-blue Lake Superior, the largest lake in the world, lying all along its northern flank. Eighty-five per cent of this area is forested and lumbering is still going on, the Marquette iron range still turns out iron ore, and some copper is still being mined; but comparatively speaking the Upper Peninsula is almost empty, with fewer than 300,000 inhabitants. If the northern half of the Lower Peninsula is North Country the Upper Peninsula is the same thing at treble strength. It is traversed by excellent concrete roads, and you can drive for two hours without seeing a town, or anything that looks like permanent human habitation. For mile after mile there is nothing except clear blue lakes, vast areas of cut-over timber, forests which look as if nobody had ever taken an ax into them, and outcroppings of bleak rock. With Lake Superior so close this country has its own built-in air-conditioning; there is a sharp edge to the air, a feeling of unlimited space and quiet and peace, and that strange quality of half-ominous, half-friendly loneliness is with you all of the time. Now that the bridge is finished, all of this will probably be watered down, but it can never be wholly destroyed. After all, up in this country there is nothing between you and the North Pole except a few thousand miles of totally empty land and water.

One of the interesting things to see up here is the canal at Sault Ste. Marie, whose big locks connect Lake Superior with the lower lakes. The Soo, as everybody calls it, is a lively little city during the eight months of the navigation season; it boasts that its canal handles more traffic than Panama and Suez combined. All day and all night the ships—enormous things, 500 and 600 feet in length—come majestically in from the upper lake, floating high above your head, sinking slowly as the water burbles out of the locks, and then gliding off for the great industrial region hundreds of miles to the south. In an average day, eighty or ninety of them will go through. Day and night, you are forever hearing the deep, haunting bass of their whistles—the inescapable, wholly characteristic and somehow deeply romantic noise of the Soo region. (Progress is taking a hand here, these immense boats are being equipped with air horns, which emit a blatting which carries a great deal farther than the traditional steam whistle but which is pure discord and nothing more.)

Driving west from the Soo, on the broad highway that leads to Marquette and the iron-range country, you pass Seney, a drowsy little country town so unobtrusive that you can go all the way through it before you realize you have reached it. It's quiet and orderly today, but half a century ago Seney was a hell-roaring lumber town, with a reputation for unrestrained misconduct that did not need to take second place to any Western cattle town or mining camp. There is a myth, formerly given wide circulation in the Sunday supplements, about a log stockade that once adorned the town. In it, according to one version, dance-hall girls were kept when not dancing; according to another, captive lumberjacks were immured here between spells in the backwoods. There is one odd thing about these fancy yarns of the high-wide-and-handsome days of the lumber towns; the sins which were committed in these places were never really attractive. It is very hard to glamorize a village rowdy, and the lumberjack tough mugs were at bottom village rowdies and nothing better. Seney's most notorious character, for instance, was a loafer who used to win free drinks in bars by biting the heads off frogs, mice and other vermin. He finally came to a well-merited end, according to the story, when he bit the head off a small owl which was the particular pet of a burly lumberjack, who promptly brought this unattractive character's career to a close by smiting him vigorously over the head with the handle of a peavy.

Marquette is the metropolis of the Upper Peninsula. It is a solid industrial town, with red ore from the great ridges behind it coming down to the docks in red hopper cars, and if it is not the most lovely city in the United States it occupies one of the nation's most beautiful sites. The south shore of Lake Superior curves in and out, along here, with deep bays and jutting, pine-crowned headlands; the old primeval rock breaks through the crust of the land to remind you that this is the backbone of the continent, where rocks so ancient they even lack fossils lie bare under the long summer sunlight, grim and lonely and desolate. Just at sunset, from east of Marquette, you can see the city with the opaque blue panel of Lake Superior silent in front of it and a flaming red sky behind it, lying in the evening stillness like a dream of the city that never was; it is transfigured, a strange light lies on its towers and parapets, and this place that for so long was a Mecca for Cornish miners (the roadside stands still peddle Cornish pasties instead of hot dogs, and very good they are too) becomes an unattainable no-place out of fable, dropping long dark shadows on a silent cold sea.

If you are well-advised, you will head west from Marquette for the copper country. Do it, if possible, early in October when the lonely road will take you through forests aflame with scarlet and gold and bronze, and a wild, doomed beauty that belongs beyond the farthest edge of the world lies on all the landscape; the touch of everlasting winter is in the air and yet for an hour or so the sunlight is still warm, and nothing you will ever see will move you more or linger with you longer. You come out, at last, onto the long spine of the Keweenaw Peninsula—an outcrop of rock and wild trees, reaching far up into Lake Superior, perhaps the oldest land in the new world. The copper mines which caused men to come here in the first place go deep under the lake—some of the shafts go down for more than a mile. You get the feeling of a land that has been passed by, a hard, forbidding and strangely charming bit of country that had a short hectic history and does not especially want any more; and all about is the cold steely blue of the greatest of lakes, and the picturesque little settlements that manage to be both friendly and forsaken at the same moment.

It would be possible, of course, to drive on, noting the points of interest in the Upper Peninsula, mentioning the more unusual towns—like Eagle Harbor, one of the most completely beautiful villages I ever expect to see, with two long headlands enclosing a quiet strip of water and the great angry lake piling destructive surging waves against the rocks outside—but my state is half reality and half the dim, enchanted memories of a long-lost boyhood, and anyway I did not live in the entire state of Michigan. I knew only selected parts of it, and these parts stay in my memory and call back unforgettable things which were born of the cold emptiness and the inviting, menacing beauty of this North Country.

They are Upper Michigan, the part that lies north of the automobile belt, the doomed, bewitched country which is surrendering to the Mackinac bridge and to the superhighway and which, ultimately, will undoubtedly become just another part of the sprawling, industrialized Middle West. But while today's light lasts it is still a land apart; there is a pleasantly melancholy flavor of a lost past to it, and although men murdered the forests with a passionate ferocity the forests somehow still live and put their strange touch on the countryside. There are cool shadows under the trees and a timeless peace lies on the cutover tracts and the fields where the young second growth is hiding the stumps.

It is a strange country: lonely enough, even in summer, and cold as the far side of the moon when winter comes, with the far-off hills rising pale blue from the frozen white landscape. It offers a chance to draw a deep breath, to turn around and look back at the traveled path, to stand on a high hill and be alone with the fresh air and the sunlight. It is wood and water, golden sand and blue lakes, emptiness and memories and the sort of isolation which it is hard for a city man to come by, these days. All in all, it is quite a state.

# Indiana

## by WILLIAM E. WILSON

We were riding—my uncle Clarence A. Cook and I—along a black-topped road from Indianapolis to Turkey Run State Park. It was early morning and there was hardly any traffic. Although the midsummer day had promised to be fair, the sky was now overcast, a solid, sullen gray, and the air that came through the car window was damp and heavy, almost tropical.

My uncle was driving—"to prove to my sisters-in-law," he said defiantly, "that I am not too old yet to make this trip by myself." He did not have to prove it to me. As I sat beside him, I was thinking that if I could be sure of inheriting his youthfulness of appearance, mind and spirit when I reached my seventies, I'd stop resenting the advance of years.

I knew a great many men and women like him in Indiana. There were the old friends of my father, who himself had lived to be almost seventy-nine, and there were also the chance acquaintances who were continually surprising me by proving to be older than they looked—like the man at the magazine counter in Lafayette who had told me proudly that he was born the day Lee surrendered, and a farmer on a bus out of Fort Wayne who said, "I'll be ninety-two tomorrow, but I can still handle a square meal—or anything else." There must be something in the atmosphere of Indiana as well as the tempo of living that makes for a vigorous longevity.

As we rolled along through Hendricks and Montgomery counties, my uncle kept up a lively comment on the countryside and its people. He was in especially good spirits, for the trip to Turkey Run was one that delighted him. He had been going there for brief holidays ever since it was the Lusk farm, back in 1916.

"All this land round here was once a swamp," my uncle said, as we approached the village of Lizton. "A man that worked for me years ago in Indianapolis came from here. We always kidded him— asked him to take his shoes off and show us his webbed feet."

Farther along, we passed some charred ruins, and my uncle told me a farmer there had lost most of his stock and his corn crop the year before. "But the corn crop will be good again this year," he added. "In fact, there's so much of it that the farmers don't know where they're going to store it."

I gazed out the window. The corn did look good, very tall and green and so thick that the slanting, crosswise pattern of the rows was hardly discernible. Farther north, in the heart of the great, flat corn belt that sweeps across the upper half of Indiana, the corn no doubt looked even better.

My uncle swerved the car expertly round a tractor-drawn hay-rake that was clattering and banging along the side of the road.

"In the Columbia Club the other day," he laughed, "they were telling about a farmer in Putnam County who was finally tracked down by the Federal income-tax people. He owed the United States nineteen hundred dollars. 'You mean I got to send a check to the Guvment?' the farmer said. 'Why, hell, man, the Guvment has always sent checks to me!'"

That was the kind of story members of the Columbia Club in Indianapolis had been telling ever since 1933. In fact, a crack about Cleveland's first administration is probably still good for a laugh in that Republican stronghold.

But at that moment I wasn't interested in the Columbia Club or corn crops or farmers; for in my pleasure in my uncle's companionship on this lonely Indiana road, I had come upon a riddle. Why, I was asking myself, did I always find it so refreshing to be back home again in Indiana?

Previously, on my annual visits to the state, I had supposed I was put at ease primarily by the familiar, rich, warm sound of Hoosier voices. In those days, I was coming "home" from the East, where

I had never learned to speak in the Harvard fashion. But this year, I had come "home" from the West—from Colorado—and had felt the spell of belonging in Indiana just as strong, although the difference in speech was barely noticeable.

True, the Hoosier's "r," like the bosoms of his farm girls, is more robustly developed than the Westerner's, and he has a half-Southern and yet not-Southern way of speaking softly and slowly that is unique. "How are *yew?*" he says; and if you listen closely, you will hear even the best educated of Hoosiers slipping into the pioneer's "whur" for "where" and "git" for "get." Moreover, what Indiana people do to the little word "it" is not duplicated anywhere else in the country. They make it stand up in their sentences like a silo on a low, flat, Hoosier horizon.

I noticed, too, the difference in climate, and that difference was certainly not in Indiana's favor. Indiana's climate, especially in summer, with the heavy, humid stuff that passes for atmosphere, is not designed to put anyone at ease. But after the first gasp or two, I actually relished the Indiana air. Although it clings to you like an impoverished second cousin, it at least has body and character. I even liked the stench of the heaven trees near the Indianapolis airport.

There was no doubt about it; I was a steadfast Hoosier still.

But why, I asked myself, does a Hoosier always remain a Hoosier, even after years of exile?

As we dipped down into Browns Valley, my uncle unwittingly gave me the first clue to an answer.

"A friend of a chap I went to college with lives round here somewhere," he said. "For years I've intended to look him up. Would you mind if we did it now?"

There was the answer—at least, a beginning of it—as plain and understandable as a Hoosier farmer's face.

From Hammond to Rising Sun, from Steuben County to Posey County, there are people whom a returning Hoosier can look up if he wants to take the time. And where there happen to be no such people, he can quickly establish a cordial relationship by announcing to any group of strangers the locality in which he originated. "Then you must know so-and-so," someone will be sure to say. Come to think of it, this is not a bad way to select one's friends in any part of the world. As Abe Martin says, "You kin git a purty fair line on new acquaintances by th' people they ask about."

"Indiana is like a big family," the president of Indiana University once remarked to me. "Being Hoosiers somehow makes us all kin. And that goes for our relatives who have left the family homestead as well as those who have remained in the state."

The family "homestead" of Indiana is actually two houses instead of one. Ask any Hoosier where he is from and the chances are that he will not say simply, "Indiana," but either "Northern Indiana" or "Southern Indiana," depending upon which side of the Old National Road he lives on. The Old National Road, owned by the state since 1839, enters Indiana from the east at Richmond, passes through Indianapolis, and leaves the state for the west at Terre Haute. For years, it was the finest road in the world. Today, as U.S. 40, it is still one of the best east-west thoroughfares. But its importance to Indiana is not the same as its importance to the tourists who traverse it in an endless two-way procession each year. In Indiana, the Old National Road is a kind of boundary.

North of the Old National Road, Indiana has long been populated by descendants of Yankees, New York Staters and immigrants from foreign lands. This is the more vigorous, the more progressive and aggressive, and the more prosperous half of the state. Folks get things done more quickly up here and, by some standards, better. They haven't as much time on their hands as folks in Southern Indiana, and if you stop to ask directions in Gary or South Bend, you may find the busy Hoosier won't walk more than two or three blocks out of his way to direct you.

South of the historic highway, Indiana has been inhabited even longer by descendants of Southerners, with a strong infusion of German and Irish in their blood. Southern Indiana is not so rich as the northern section of the state, but it has a more storied past and more varied scenery. Down here, the Hoosier is more leisurely and more gracious. Also more loquacious. Ask a man in Evansville or New Albany to direct you and he will probably close up his shop for half a day to accompany you to the right road. But he may talk so much while doing it that he will make you late for supper.

But Indiana is not a house divided against itself. Like the double cabins of the pioneers, it has a friendly dogtrot between the two parts. This neutral ground, where the North and the South meet, lies a few miles above and below the Old National Road; and because it blends the elements of the North and the South, it represents most typically what people think of when they hear the word "Hoosier."

(What that word Hoosier originally meant, by the way, has never been authoritatively established. Some say it is a corruption of the pioneer's greeting from his cabin window—"Who's thar?" Others say it was originally "husher," a giant of a man who could hush anybody in a fight. Still others have discovered a contractor named Samuel Hoosier at Louisville in 1825 who hired only Indiana labor and whose men were consequently called "Hoosier men.")

To get back to the two divisions, Northern Indiana is mostly flat land, rich in industry and agriculture. Chicago and the state of Michigan stand atop it, like the legs of a colossus. Ohio borders it on the east—all the way down to the Ohio River, in fact, but with less influence in the southern region. Illinois borders it on the west. In the thick, urban spread of northwest Indiana, it is impossible to tell where one leaves the Hoosier State and enters Illinois. In the South Bend area, eastward, Michigan's significance in trade and commerce is so great that South Benders call the region "Michiana." In Fort Wayne, in the northeast, one sometimes has the feeling that one has already crossed into Ohio. But the people up here are all Hoosiers, just the same, and they don't like being confused with Suckers, Michiganders and Buckeyes.

Traveling the main lines of the New York Central and Pennsylvania railroads through Northern Indiana, I did not feel a sense of homecoming until I got off the trains and talked with the people; for the towns and cities, in the Calumet region particularly, with their miles and miles of steel mills and other industrial plants bordering Lake Michigan, are strung together as tightly as beads in the Indian wampum that used to pass for currency in the neighborhood.

At the turn of the century, Gary, Indiana, was a desolate, uninhabited waste of sand. In the annual report of the United States Steel Corporation for 1905 appeared a statement by Judge Elbert H. Gary: "It has been decided to construct and put in operation a new plant to be located on the south shore of Lake Michigan in Calumet Township, Lake County, Indiana, and a large acreage of land has been purchased for that purpose." Soon afterward great hills of sand were being pulled down and the sloughs between them filled with silt sucked from the bottom of Lake Michigan. A river was picked up bodily and moved one hundred yards out of the way. A tunnel was driven two miles out under the lake for a water supply. By 1907, there was a crude town on the site, and the site itself was fifteen feet higher above sea level than it had been when the work commenced. Today it is one of the largest cities in the state.

Like Gary, every town and city in the north of Indiana makes something—or many things. Hammond is noted for the manufacture of soap. East Chicago, Indiana, is dominated by Cudahy's giant Dutch Girl. Whiting is headquarters of Standard Oil in Indiana. South Bend, which produces Studebaker cars, retains what is left of Indiana's prestige in the automobile industry—a Hoosier enterprise that once produced not only the Studebaker but also the Premier, National, Stutz, Cole, Marmon, Roosevelt, Duesenberg, Haynes, Apperson, Maxwell, Auburn, Cord, Elcar, Davis, McFarlan, Lexington, Reeves, Lambert, Imp, Revere, Zimmerman, Henderson, Marion, Empire, and Waverly Electric, names which are something for oldsters still to conjure with. But South Bend is also famous now for mint distilling and the football teams of Notre Dame University. In Elkhart, Conn musical instruments are manufactured. Fort Wayne, in the northeast, produces radio-phonograph and television equipment—Capehart-Farnsworth and Magnavox—and is the Indiana home of General Electric and International Harvester. South of it is Muncie, maker of bottles, jars and glasses.

It is unfortunate that this northern train view is the only Indiana many East-West travelers get to know; for from the Pullman windows it must seem little different from parts of Ohio and Illinois. It is no wonder that they ask how the Hoosier can be so staunchly lyrical in his local pride. If only these birds of passage would spend the night in South Bend during the football season, or in Gary during the basketball season, if only they would ride a few miles south and meet a few Indiana farmers when the corn is ripe. But they won't. They're in too big a hurry to get to Chicago or New York.

Or these travelers might delay for a week or a month to take a look at the summer resorts of Indiana, most of which are located in the north. Here, just below and to the east of Lake Michigan, are the famous Indiana Dunes, great wastes of singing sands. This northern landscape, beyond the cities' smokestacks, is also studded with lakes having such mellifluous names as Wawasee, Maxinkuckee, Winona, Shipshewanna, Manitou and Koontz.

I shall never forget how we looked forward to our annual two weeks in this magic northern land when I was a boy. Those were the

days of the leather-topped car and goggles and the linen duster. The
first hazard of the journey from the south was the Reelsville Hill,
but if the car surmounted that obstacle and its passengers survived a night in a country hotel, the second day of driving opened
up a new world—a world of tamarack and jack pine and blue water.

It was the blue water that impressed me most. Before my first
of such journeys, made when I was six, I could hardly believe my
father's descriptions of the lakes, for to me at that time all water
was brown, like the waters of the muddy Wabash and Ohio rivers.
I recall heralding the appearance of the first blue shimmering water
with shouts of ecstasy from the back seat of our Reo.

Steel, soap, automobiles, machinery, nationally respected football
teams and blue water they boast of up here in the north above the
Old National Road. And corn they grow, too, in abundance. But
steel is not this country's king, nor are automobiles, nor blue water,
nor even the "four horsemen and seven mules" of Knute Rockne's
invention. Nor, indeed, is corn. The king of Northern Indiana—of the
whole state, in fact, is a phlegmatic individual who troubles himself not at all over the vicissitudes of economics or the applause of
multitudes. He never strikes for higher wages or tries to build monopolies. He doesn't come out with a new model each year. He never
worries about new maneuvers that the coaches have devised in Texas
or California or Minnesota. And as for water, he much prefers it
brown. In fact, only the quality and quantity of Indiana corn interest him, for corn is his inseparable companion.

Concerning this stolid monarch, Logan Esarey has written most
eloquently: "We may sing the praises of all the heroes of Indiana
from La Salle or George Rogers Clark to the present, but the prosperity of our state . . . has depended on Mr. Hog. In fat years and
lean years . . . he has come up with his part, even though he does
grunt about it considerably. . . ."

A sharp contrast with the north is Southern Indiana. It is mostly
hilly land, rich in scenery and tradition. Kentucky bounds it on the
south, but the Ohio River is wide enough to prevent the Blue
Grass State from dominating the region as Chicago and Michigan
dominate the North. There is a constant and not always friendly feud
abrewing between Kentuckians and Southern Hoosiers. In the little
town of Newburgh on the Ohio, for instance, the fishermen of the
two states are often even on shooting terms with each other.

"I says to them fellers," a Newburgh fisherman told me, describing an encounter with Kentucky wardens who were inspecting his lines, "I says, 'I'm asettin' in my boat on Indiana water and I got a gun in my hands,' I says, 'and they ain't a judge nor jury in the whole state of Indiana would convict me if I happened to have a mind to pull the trigger.'"

When I was home on leave in Evansville during the war, my father illustrated to me not only the Southern Hoosiers' suspicion of Kentuckians but also their peculiar pride and sense of justice.

We were enjoying the pleasant Hoosier custom of sitting on the front porch after supper. From the back of the house, where my mother and sister were working, came the clatter of dishes and the low sound of voices. Up the street, a screened door slammed from time to time, and someone thereabouts was playing Hoagy Carmichael's *Stardust* on a piano. It was late summer, and the locusts in the oaks and maples across the way were droning an antiphonal chorus. Occasionally we heard a throaty blast from a towboat whistle down on the river and the shriek and moan of switch engines out in the C. & E. I. yards by the Dixie Bee Highway.

After a long silence, my father stirred in his place beside me in the swing and said, "You know, we're having a crime wave here in Evansville now."

I made no comment.

"It's these Kentuckians," he continued, "come up to work in our war plants, that are causing all the trouble."

"But, father," I said, "there's always been crime in Evansville."

"I know that, son. I've lived in Southern Indiana all my life, and I know Evansville has always had two or three murders a year. But until these Kentuckians came swarming in here across the river, nobody was ever murdered in this town by somebody he didn't know."

Even before the war, Southern Indiana had its industries. Evansville was the nation's biggest producer of refrigerators for a long time, and it once claimed the largest furniture factory in the world. When I was a boy there, the chorus of factory whistles on cold winter mornings was my favorite music, as I lay abed sniffing the fragrance of frying crullers coming up from my mother's kitchen and listening for her final and peremptory call to me to get up and dress for school.

In recent years, New Albany and Jeffersonville, too, have grown into thriving industrial centers. They now boast a shipyard, a U. S. Army quartermaster depot, and a Government ammunition plant so extensive that when a friend drove me past it at ninety-two miles an hour recently, it took us several minutes to go by. At Lawrenceburg, upriver, the whisky industry has practically rebuilt the town since the 1937 flood. Near Bedford and Bloomington, Indiana limestone is quarried, and Terre Haute is prosperous because of beer and bituminous coal.

But the commerce and industry of Southern Indiana, taken all together, don't begin to compare with the concentration of invested capital in the Gary-Hammond region in the north.

To reach Southern Indiana by rail from the east or west, one uses principally the Baltimore & Ohio and the Louisville & Nashville roads, although the New York Central and the Pennsylvania have main lines as far south as Terre Haute. From the windows of these trains, the view of Indiana is different from what one sees in the north. It is a land of thick forest growth in a tangle of rank, sub-tropical vines, of hills and hollows and, in winter, flooded bottom lands. To anyone who knows the state, there can be no confusion here as to whether the train is in Indiana, Ohio or Illinois.

But these big transcontinental trains cut across only a corner of Indiana. To have a full view of Hoosierland, north as well as south, one must travel on the Monon.

The Monon, which gets its name from an Indian word meaning "swift-running," is a Hoosier institution. Hoosiers used to say that you took the Monon only if you "wanted to go the worst way," but in recent years it has been streamlined and improved. The Monon now ventures into both Chicago and Louisville, but it is still Indiana's own railroad; in fact, no one is really at home in Indiana until he is able to listen without a smile to the brakeman's chant on a Monon local:

"Crawfordsville and Wabash College! Don't forget your valise and parcels!"

In Southern Indiana the farms are smaller and less productive than those in the north, but the farmhouses—some of them, at least—are more interesting in their architecture. I am remembering now the tall, two-story brick houses, set on knolls in groves of oak or hickory trees, their two front doors offering a double welcome and their front porches as ornate with jigsaw work as the deck of an old-time steamboat.

Behind them are the barn lots flanked by big red barns and a half-dozen leaning sheds, and beyond are man-made muddy ponds, where the stock are watered. The hills fling the fields about like colored banners and are dotted with clumps of trees and an occasional single persimmon under whose branches, in the fall, it is sweet to browse. True, the land in some places is almost completely impoverished by soil erosion; but what these rural Southern Hoosiers lack in profits they make up for in scenery.

As one of them in Pike County told me: "Most of the time I ain't very financial, mister, but I got something to look at when I'm tired." Only he said "tard."

Although the southern portion of the state has few summer resorts because of its excessive heat, there is one playground that is nationally famous. It is the French Lick Springs Hotel, once owned by Thomas Taggart and for years the "Tammany Hall of the Middle West," hidden away in the woods of the Orange County hills. It has seven stories, contains a thousand rooms and twenty-five acres of floor space, and looks like something imported from Atlantic City. Its vast dining room will seat several thousand convening Democrats or insurance men at one time. Surrounding the massive yellow-brick building are 4000 acres of well-trimmed lawn and gardens. And in the front yard are the tracks of the ubiquitous Monon.

Though Brown County is also in Southern Indiana, it belongs to the whole state—to the whole nation, in fact. Brown County characterizes Indiana, although it is a caricature too. Certainly it preserves the aspect and atmosphere of Western pioneer life in America better than any other place I know. I doubt whether many Americans can escape a stirring in their hearts as they travel through the county's settlements of Bean Blossom, Bear Wallow, Needmore and Gnaw Bone.

The countryside here is at its best in the fall, when the foliage is aflame with color and the melancholy haze of Indiana autumn blankets the hills. Persimmons lie rotting on the ground then, and walnuts are scattered through the woods for squirrels to gather and small boys to stain their hands with. Wagons loaded with golden pumpkins creak along the steep roads, and in the fields khaki-colored fodder stands in regimented shocks.

Sounds come softly but with a sharp clarity across the hills at this time of year, like words whispered in the night, and the air is perfumed with hickory smoke threading skyward from the chimneys of log cabins tucked in a hundred hollows.

Probably no one has given more fame and reality to Brown County than Kin Hubbard, creator of the legendary Abe Martin. Hubbard kept his Abe Martin feature alive in the Indianapolis *News* for more than twenty-five years, supplementing it with drawings of the characters involved and their Brown County background; and by so doing he populated Brown County. No one who has followed the doings of these rustic folks—or who follows them today in reprint, many years after Kin's death—can forget Lafe Bud, "traveling representative Red Seal Beer Makings," Tell Binkley, salesman of Florida country-club sites and stick-up insurance; Lemmie Peters, "whose graduation essay *We've Left the Bay and the Ocean Lies Before Us* electrified the community in 1913"; Uncle Ez Pash, "lifelong Democrat"; Miss Fawn Lippincutt, "elocutionist," or Honorable Ex-Editor Cale Fluhart.

The owner of an inn at Nashville in Brown County told me that one day a tourist asked him to direct her to the local five-and-ten.

"We don't have a five-and-ten here, ma'am," he explained to her.

"But you must have!" she protested. "That's where Mrs. Lafe Bud works—at the optometrist counter."

Across the street from the country store is the courthouse, a brick building with an outside iron stairway; and behind the courthouse is the log jail, built in 1837. As long as I can remember, it has been in the custody of an overalled ancient who begins his spiel as soon as a sight-seer appears within fifty yards.

Nashville would not be Nashville without the group of loafers who sit on the "Liars' Bench" on the courthouse lawn, ready at all times to assume studied poses for passing photographers. They add to the scenery and the local color and they inevitably remind me of Abe Martin's remark:

"Some fellers have a way of loafin' that makes 'em look indispensable."

About one sixth of Brown County is owned by the state, preserved in one of the most popular of Indiana's fourteen remarkable state parks. The rest is largely inhabited by painters and writers, who live in log cabins, both original and restored. In the dining room of one of the largest of these cabins, on a rise north of Nashville, hangs the only extant copy of the Nashville *Democrat* that announced the victory of Grover Cleveland and Indiana's own Thomas A. Hendricks in 1884.

"GLORY TO GOD!" reads the headline, in letters half a page high. "DEMOCRACY TRIUMPHANT!"

And the Columbia Club in Indianapolis only fifty miles away!

But that is Indiana. While it is not a house divided against itself, politically it is a house divided within itself. In politics, Hoosiers are not notably orginal or idealistic in their thinking, but they are practical, stubborn and always eloquent. Indiana's history is mainly a story of individuals and the loyalty they have inspired; it is not a story of social movements or struggles for causes. When a Hoosier tells you he is a Democrat or a Republican, it usually means that his father was one before him. Or it may mean that he has a friend in the party whom he would like to see in public office—or that he hankers for office himself.

Take the town of Vincennes, on the Wabash halfway between Terre Haute and Evansville. A great deal of Indiana's history is commemorated there, and this history gives you the Hoosier spirit in a microcosm. It is a story of people very much like the people who still inhabit the state—heroes, practical politicians, opportunists, people easily swayed by histrionics or sentiment, but individualists all.

The first inhabitants of Vincennes were French traders and, later, colonists. They came as early as 1700, possibly earlier. In 1763, they shifted their allegiance from France to England without a qualm. And when Father Pierre Gibault, Francis Vigo, and the Piankeshaw chief, Grand Door of the Wabash, helped George Rogers Clark take Vincennes from the British, the citizens and the soldiers who did that heroic job understood little of the principles involved in the American Revolution. They were merely rallying round men in whose good judgment and courage they had confidence.

William Henry Harrison was the next hero of Vincennes. He came more than a century later than the French, as the first governor after Indiana had become a territory. In a somewhat dubious battle at Tippecanoe, Harrison defeated the great Tecumseh's Shawnees while Tecumseh himself was absent in the South; but neither Harrison's men nor Tecumseh's fully realized that the destruction of local Indian unity at Tippecanoe meant the failure of the Indian cause in the whole Northwest.

The French were in Northern Indiana before they established the post of Vincennes. In fact, the first white man to set foot on Indiana soil was probably Robert Cavelier, Sieur de La Salle, who camped in 1679 near the present site of South Bend. But La Salle did not stay. Like so many Hoosiers today, he had the itching foot.

The only northern town that actually rivals Vincennes in antiquity is Fort Wayne. Here, where the St. Joseph and St. Mary's Rivers unite to form the Maumee, the Miami Indians maintained their headquarters in the distant past. Fort Wayne's history has been, first, one of white and Indian skirmishes and, later, one of steady growth as a major Indiana community. Today, like Vincennes, it preserves its past in markers and monuments rather than relics. Fort Wayne has always seemed to me one of the most modern and progressive and perhaps the most livable cities in the state.

After Clark's victory in the Revolution, the age of the flatboat came to Indiana; and after Harrison's triumph over Tecumseh came the steamboat. Most reminiscent of the steamboat's golden age today is the town of Madison on the Ohio. Many Hoosiers will agree with me, I think, that it is also Indiana's prettiest town.

I drove over to Madison one rainy Sunday recently to revisit some of the sites I had seen for the first time eleven years before, when I was collecting material for my Rivers of America book, *The Wabash.* I went through the James F. D. Lanier mansion, which commands a dramatic view of the Ohio through the pillars of its broad portico, and I saw again the Schofield Mansion and the Shrewsbury House. But I was grieved to discover that the Madison Hotel, designed by Francis Costigan, had disappeared and a chain store had taken its place.

Corydon, some fifteen miles north of the Ohio in Harrison County, is another of my favorite Indiana towns. Indiana's first capitol still stands there. Originally the county courthouse, it became the seat of the state's government in 1816 and remained so until 1825, when newly platted Indianapolis on the National Road took over the honor. Corydon today prefers to remember the battle that was fought at its outskirts in 1863—the only Civil War battle on Indiana soil— when John Hunt Morgan, with his 2500 Confederate raiders, crossed the Ohio River at Mauckport and swept northward. At Corydon, he was met by four hundred home guards, who stood him off for an hour.

In sleepy, quiet Corydon today, people still mention the name of

John Morgan somewhat breathlessly. A lad in a dry-goods store re-
cited to me the story of the battle by rote, as he had learned it from
his father or his grandfather. An old-timer on the courthouse lawn
paused in his whittling long enough to give me a mischievous wink
and say: "Know what my pap used to say when I asked him what he
did at the Battle of Corydon? Said, 'Why, boy, I ran like a bat out
of hell—jist like ever'body else!'"

It is typical of the Hoosiers that, during the Civil War, although
Indiana is geographically a Northern state, they were sharply divided in their sympathies; and especially in Southern Indiana there
was strong support for the Confederacy in spite of the fact that Abe
Lincoln had spent fourteen years of his youth in the state. Knowing
the stubborn perversity of the Hoosier spirit, I am almost tempted
to say it was true because of that fact. After all, Lincoln did leave
Indiana and move over into Illinois.

In Indiana, Lincoln became a giant in body, under the harsh discipline of pioneer life; he became an independent and idealistic
thinker, under the influence of his neighbors, who loaned him books,
and of his wonderful stepmother, Sarah Bush Lincoln, who saw him
through his growing pains. Every time I visit the Nancy Hanks Lincoln Memorial Park in Spencer County, I am deeply moved by
thoughts of those formative years of Abe's in my native state. But I
am always somewhat disappointed in the park itself. It is beautiful.
It is peaceful. It is noble. But it should be equally dedicated to the
memory of Sarah Bush Lincoln, and it should have a monument of
some kind honoring those two Hoosier qualities—ambition and neighborly helpfulness—that made Lincoln and so many other native and
adopted Indianans great.

Indiana people, with their Southern heritage, have a strong sense
of family loyalty as well as devotion to friends, and this may explain both the division within themselves and the united front they
present to the outside world. My paternal grandfather, who in his
youth drove a stagecoach between Princeton and New Harmony,
stopped once in the wilderness to dissuade a man from beating his
wife. He did not succeed. Instead, he emerged from the man's cabin
in a hurry and with two black eyes—one given to him by the husband and the other administered by the wife. Whenever I think about
Indiana history, I remember my grandfather's two black eyes.

In regard to family, I think I was for a time the luckiest kid in
the whole state. All my uncles and aunts on my father's side lived

in the historic little town of New Harmony on the Wabash, and they owned, among them, the only hotel in the village, its only picture show and its best soda fountain. When I went to New Harmony for the summer to visit my relatives, I was in a small boy's seventh heaven.

My aunts conscientiously took me to see the historic Rappite community houses, dating from 1815, and "Gabriel's footprints," which Father George Rapp said were left on the stone by an angel who came down out of the sky to advise him. They exposed me to lectures at the Workingmen's Institute and to the books in the town's remarkable library. But I must confess that what really meant most to me were old Lizzie's good cooking at the Tavern, the delicacies Cousin Clyde concocted at his soda fountain, and *The Perils of Pauline* at Uncle Gene's movie palace, where I was sometimes allowed to sit in the projection booth.

George Rapp's and Robert Owen's communistic experiments failed at New Harmony, and in the years since, that little town has had a curious history. For almost a century it dozed in quiet isolation. The townsfolk, though proud of their history and hospitable to strangers, looked upon the outside world with a kind of aristocratic haughtiness and no small degree of suspicion.

I remember the annual county fair at the edge of town, the watermelon feasts on Mr. Mumford's spacious lawn, the swimming at the Old Dam, cotillions in the Opera House in winter and dances in Arthur Fretageot's store in summer, and the rattle of Fount Hawkins's horse-drawn hack down Church Street, once a day, bringing a drummer or two to The Tavern from the spur-line railroad. But until the 1920's, New Harmony was content to live in proud memories of its past.

Then oil was discovered in the Wabash river bottoms.

Since that time, people in New Harmony have become rich who never dreamed of being rich, and others have taken a new lease on hope. Since that time, too, New Harmony has attempted to restore and preserve the relics of its past. The first of these attempts was by a state historical commission, which New Harmony soon discovered it did not cotton to. What the town likes much better are the individualistic projects of one of its native sons.

Indiana is always proud of its native sons, especially if they never forget, in their successes, to do right by their parents. Even the bandit Dillinger was forgiven a lot on the banks of the Wabash, because it was said that he was always kind to his folks.

Politics has always been in the Hoosier blood. There is a legend in the state that every baby born within its borders announces to the doctor with its first gasp of Indiana air: "While not seeking public office for myself, I will, if elected, serve my country and my party to the best of my ability." I have asked several Hoosier obstetricians if this is true, and I have never got a straight answer, perhaps because the obstetricians themselves had their eyes on public office.

Indiana claims two residents of the White House in the two Harrisons, although neither was a native of the state. And it has been called "the mother of Vice Presidents" because of the election of Schuyler Colfax, Thomas A. Hendricks, Charles W. Fairbanks and Thomas R. Marshall. In Eugene V. Debs of Terre Haute, it has produced one great political visionary and rebel; in Daniel Voorhees of the same city and Albert J. Beveridge of Indianapolis, two great orators; in Thomas Taggart of French Lick, a master of political organization and backstage planning. More recently, the name of Wendell L. Willkie has honored the scroll of Hoosier men in public life.

In the 1920's, Indiana forgot for a while Abe Martin's observation that "actions speak louder'n lodge jewelry" and, under the guise of "100 per cent Americanism" resuscitated the Ku Klux Klan. The Klan flourished cancerously in the state as it did nowhere else, but eventually the Klan was defeated and disgraced in the public eye.

Besides politicking, Hoosiers have two other traditions that distinguish them—providing their children with good educations and writing books. The one, I think, is responsible for the other.

No graduate of an accredited high school in Indiana today is more than twenty-five miles from an institution of higher learning. And it might be added that a very large proportion of Indiana's high-school graduates attend advanced classes of one sort or another after graduation. Besides Indiana University and Purdue, there are, scattered all over the state, many other colleges, large and small. At South Bend, there is the famous Roman Catholic institution of Notre Dame. At Greencastle, there is the Methodists' DePauw, and nearby, at Crawfordsville, is its ancient Presbyterian rival, Wabash. Franklin, founded by the Baptists, shares its name with the town near Indianapolis where it is situated. The Friends have Earlham at Richmond; the Lutherans, Valparaiso at Valparaiso and Concordia at

Fort Wayne. The Presbyterians have another school at Hanover, whose campus, on a high bluff above the Ohio River, is the most beautiful in the state.

Indiana's age of glory in writing came at the end of the nineteenth century and during the first decades of the twentieth. Those were the days of Lew Wallace, author of *Ben-Hur*, whose home in Crawfordsville is now a Hoosier literary shrine; of George Ade, Purdue's benefactor and one of its heroes; of Meredith Nicholson and Charles Major and Maurice Thompson; of Gene Stratton Porter, whose two homes in the "Limberlost" country have made rivals of the towns of Geneva and Rome City; of David Graham Phillips and finally—and most important in Hoosier minds—of Booth Tarkington and James Whitcomb Riley. During those prolific years, the writing fever was at such a height round Indianapolis that on one occasion a visiting lecturer from the East invited all the writers in his audience to join him on the platform, and the entire gathering swarmed up about him.

James Whitcomb Riley's name seems almost synonymous with the word Indiana. He wrote mainly in Hoosier dialect—and with such deceptive ease that thousands of Hoosiers have imitated him ever since. He wrote in the Hoosier tongue and about the Hoosier countryside in all its seasons, when there was "winter without and warmth within," as well as "wortermelon time" and that loveliest of all Indiana months, October, "when the frost is on the punkin and the fodder's in the shock."

But most important of all, Riley wrote about the pleasures of a Hoosier childhood, and that is what makes him The Hoosier Poet. For in Indiana, childhood is a long, long period of delight—a period so long, in fact, that most Hoosiers never completely outgrow it but retain throughout their lives something of its wide-eyed wonder and enjoyment.

Even Theodore Dreiser, in spite of his poverty on the banks of the Wabash and his later gloomy outlook upon life, had a happy Hoosier childhood. If you don't believe that, read his reminiscences in a rare book entitled *A Hoosier Holiday*. And Dreiser also helped his brother, Paul Dresser, compose the sentimental and nostalgic words of that famous Hoosier song, "On the Banks of the Wabash, Far Away."

Since Riley's time, there have been few Indiana writers whose works have been typically Hoosier, although there have continued to be plenty of Indiana writers. It seems hardly possible, for instance, that the sophisticated wit of George Jean Nathan is that of an Indiana man, yet it is. Lloyd Douglas demonstrates a certain preoccupation with the Golden Rule common among Hoosiers, but common also among Americans everywhere. Jessamyn West has artistically portrayed life among the Friends who inhabited the Whitewater Valley a generation ago, but Miss West left Indiana at the age of six, and lives now in California. The late Will Cuppy revealed his Hoosier background in his sense of humor, but it was not typically Hoosier like George Ade's or Kin Hubbard's. Jeanette Covert Nolan of Indianapolis is one of the very few Hoosiers I think of who have used Hoosier themes and at the same time remain in the state. The late Ernie Pyle, of course, was the only Hoosier writer of recent vintage who remained all Hoosier, wherever he went.

In other creative arts, Indiana has excelled chiefly in entertainment—on the radio and the stage and in the writing of popular music. It has produced three renowned composers in Paul Dresser, Cole Porter and Hoagy Carmichael; and in the theater it can boast of such stars as John Olson of Olson and Johnson, Joe Cook, Louise Dresser, Charles Butterworth and Red Skelton. To radio newsbroadcasting it has given several distinguished commentators—among them Elmer Davis, Edwin C. Hill and Claude Mahoney.

It is impossible to talk about Indiana without mentioning names. The state has probably produced more people who get into the news than any other region in the country. Indianans are more interested in people than in anything else. It is a part of their state pride.

Hoosier pride is a peculiar thing; it is not exclusively a pride in the size, the scenery, the antiquity or the climate of the state. It is more like the pride of a man in his home or the house he was born in. He is willing to admit that it may not be the best house in the block. He may even choose not to live in it any longer and he will grant that some members of his family have done wrong and deserve what they got. But he loves that house and that family, and the man who disparages them is in danger of losing his hide.

Indiana combines so many elements and traditions that it can appeal to the taste of Americans of all ages and backgrounds. It blends the Southerner's love of gracious living with the Yankee's industry and devotion to culture, and it assimilates foreign blood and foreign customs quickly, easily and hospitably.

As a result, Indiana strikes a homely American average in most aspects of life. The Lynds chose Muncie as the model for the famous *Middletown,* and even that other exhaustive study of human averages, the Kinsey Report, came out of Indiana. So comfortably American is this state that the most forgotten of all America's forgotten men was a Hoosier—Whistler's father.

Ohio

# by BENTZ PLAGEMANN

Ohio is the younger brother who stayed home. When the others had gone off, in search of adventure or fortune in the great world, Ohio is the brother who married the girl next door, raised a family, took care of the old folks, and inherited the family homestead when they died.

No one ever came to Ohio to look for gold. No one even came to Ohio to look for the legendary pot of gold at the end of the rainbow, or stayed there long if he carried the burden of great, impossible dreams. Ohio is the state of middle dreams, the state of normalcy, where it is always eight o'clock on Monday morning, and the factory whistle is blowing, and the school bell is ringing.

Ohio is neither East nor West nor South. It just sits where it is, and never shouts to make itself heard—it just speaks on in its calm, flat, unregional, unaccented, uninflected voice. But what Ohio says in that voice, and what it has said in the past, has affected you, for better or worse, and even whether you like it or not.

*Orville and Wilbur Wright built their first airplane, the one they flew at Kitty Hawk, in a bicycle shop in Dayton, Ohio. The Women's Christian Temperance Union began in Hillsboro, Ohio.*

Ohio was like that from the very beginning. An engineer and a minister helped organize the Ohio Company in 1786: Gen. Rufus

Putnam, and Dr. Manasseh Cutler. "No colony in America was settled under more favorable auspices," George Washington said gravely, when the sound, practical businessmen of the Ohio Company set out for the wilderness with their titles, deeds, and the patents signed by the Continental Congress. No claim jumping. No land grabbing. No hysteria. "I know many of the settlers personally," Washington added, "and there never were men better calculated to promote the welfare of a community." Welfare and community, strange words for frontier days. And then that word "promote." You hear those three words a lot in Ohio even today. And around Urbana, you can still find descendants of Richard Stanhope, the faithful Negro valet who was with Washington when he died, and who was given his freedom and four hundred acres in the new territory in return for his service.

*The first professional baseball team in the country was organized in Ohio. The Red Stockings. They still play. The Cincinnati Reds won every game that first season, 1869.*

You might almost say that Ohio wasn't settled; it was developed. It was never really what you might call pioneer country, and in answer to any protests I hasten to point out that the famous *Madonna of the Trail*, the statue of the pioneer woman put up by the Daughters of the American Revolution beside the old National Road near Springfield, Ohio, is walking west, and walking fast—*out* of Ohio. She was undoubtedly the wife of one of those restless, incautious men who weren't satisfied with a piece of land back East, or even out in Ohio. He wanted that pot of gold at the end of the rainbow. He was no Ohio man.

But go back a little way and you'll find the place where the Foos Tavern stood. Griffith Foos was a real Ohio man. He knew what he wanted.

Ohio was a business venture among many other things. It was that tavern, the Foos Tavern, on the old trail West at the end of the National Road; the Last Chance where you unhitched the horses, and the women and children got down from the Conestoga wagons. Ohio was the last warm meal, the last glass of ale at a bar, the last night's sleep in a bed. Ohio was the sensible, ruddy man behind the cash till in the tavern, and the mill where the flour was ground

for the bread, and the dry-goods store down the street, and the tin-
ner, and the wheelwright, and the grocery store.

*In Dayton, Ohio, James Ritty built his "Incorruptible Cashier," the
genesis of the National Cash Register Company. In a woodshed in
that same city, Charles Kettering put together his first self-starter,
possibly the most typical of all Ohio inventions. You don't have to
be told about Thomas Edison of Milan, Ohio, and the light that
didn't fail; or Charles Brush of Cleveland, who started the electrical
industry with his arc light; or Dietrich Gruen, tinkering with his
watches; and Rudolph Wurlitzer with his pianos and organs; and
William Proctor and James Gamble building the biggest soap factory in the world, in a state where cleanliness is still next to godliness.
Andrew Jergens made a pretty good thing out of his lotion, as Earl
Sloan of Zanesville did with his liniment.*

They taught me in school that Ohio is the mother of Presidents.
(In Virginia, I understand, they teach differently.) There were seven
of them. You remember what Grant looked like, but you might say
he was an exception. The others were Hayes and Garfield, the last
President to be born in a log cabin, and Harrison and McKinley and
Taft and Harding; four lawyers and a schoolteacher and a newspaper publisher. A faded memory of beards and business operations.
Our own Robert Taft was almost President. Toward the end they
called him Mr. Republican. They might well have called him Mr.
Ohio. He possessed to an almost classical degree the virtues prized
most highly in Ohio: to work hard and mind your own business,
never to abandon your convictions no matter who attacks you, or how
deluded they try to make you out to be, never to get excited. Robert
Taft couldn't understand why the people didn't want him to be President, but he died without making any fuss about it.

*William Holmes McGuffey wrote his famous Readers at Miami
University in Oxford, Ohio. What the McGuffey Readers taught is
still bred in Ohio bones: the virtue of hard work; the sure reward
of that virtue.*

The bounty of Lake Erie presses down on the top of Ohio, and the
state bends with its weight, and at the bottom the river flows, the
Beautiful Ohio, where the moonlight glows, where the barges float

**WASHINGTON, D.C.**  The stately Jefferson Memorial, framed by the Capitol's famed cherry trees.

**ILLINOIS**  (*center spread*) The colossus of Chicago—miracle of the midwest.

**VIRGINIA**  The Blue Ridge Hunt gathers in front of the stunning façade of Carter Hall, near Berryville.

by, carrying the hard-earned wealth down to the great Mississippi.
Ohio stands straight between its straight borders, plain and full of
common sense.

A lot of people came here and stayed awhile, or moved on, or were
taken in, but Ohio doesn't change. It's like the old homestead where
now the younger brother lives with his family. There isn't much style
about the old house—Ohio has always been a little suspicious of style
—but it's in excellent condition, and in the spring, when the rains
come, the lilac still blooms in the dooryard. Inside in the parlor where
the shades are drawn so the sunlight won't fade the Brussels carpet
you will find all of the old treasures and curiosities of the house. The
magnificent Greek Revival homes with their Adams doorways dream
on the commons of the New England villages of the Western Reserve. The Shaker chairs are there, and the old houses where the
slaves hid on their way to Canada and freedom in the dark night of
the Civil War. The Underground Railway, they called it. The Indian Mounds are there, and the monument to Perry at Put In Bay in
Lake Erie. "Don't Give Up the Ship," the banner said. The Mormon
Temple at Kirtland is there, the stucco of its surface struck into fire
by the setting sun, on the far hill where it stands. The women brought
their china and glass to be ground in with the sand and pebbles so
it would catch the sunlight.

Platt R. Spencer's tombstone is there, in Geneva, with his name
carved on it in the style of handwriting he developed and which
everyone in the country once had to learn. The Spencerian Hand:
"the tip of the little finger and the ball of the hand touching the surface of the desk as the loops are made." The monument to Betty
Zane is there, the girl who carried the gunpowder in her apron.

The curiosities and the treasures are there, but no one pays undue
attention to them. Very few people look to the past in Ohio. They'd
rather take you outside and show you the improvements, and you
will probably have to ride into town to see the post office and the
new junior high school and the latest factory.

*The Standard Oil Company was begun in Ohio. John D. Rockefeller
once gave me a bright new dime when we got off the streetcar together at the same stop on Euclid Avenue in Cleveland. I took it
home and put it in my bank. I was a very small boy, but I was an
Ohio boy. I hadn't wanted to take the dime, because I hadn't done
anything to earn it, but I supposed you had to humor people when*

*they got old and careless with their money. "Little boys are never*
*tired," my grandmother said to me one hot summer Ohio day, when*
*I came in from play and threw myself on the sofa in the back*
*parlor. I was up and out again, mowing the lawn, before I had time*
*to bounce. I got a much more respectable dime for that.*

You sleep well in Ohio, your brother's house. You know you are
safe there. Everything is under control. The foundation of the old
house is dry and sound, and the roof is good, and the flashing and
the drain spouts and the insulation are checked every year, and the
storm windows are up if it is winter, or the screens in summer, and
it is all so clean, in a favorite Ohio phrase, that you could eat off the
floor.

How proud they would be if they could see it now, the men who
made Ohio what it is! They knew what they wanted when they came
to Ohio, my great-grandfather, and the great-grandfathers of my
neighbors. You can come and look at it, but when you look at it you
must remember clearly that what you see is what they wanted for
their children.

The towns are all beginning to look very much alike now. There
is an airport on the outskirts, and near that there is a development
of new houses, all very much the same. The horizon is smoked with
the factory chimneys, and in town you will find that every Main
Street is the same. There is a J. C. Penney store, and a Woolworth's,
an A&P supermarket, a Sears and Roebuck order office, and a Sohio
station on the corner with its wide apron of cement washed down
and its pumps gleaming, and the young man who works there is leaning on the door of a convertible, talking to a pretty girl. There is a
Bell Telephone office, a Light and Power Company office, a Western
Union office, a Hook and Ladder Company, a Police Station, and a
YMCA with a sign out in front, in winter, telling you when the next
basketball game will be held. There is a movie theater, and if you
want to drive a short distance you can go to the next town, because
the same picture will be showing there.

And afterward, when the picture is finished, and the stores are
closed and their windows are darkened, the light will spill out from
the corner drugstore and you will hear the juke box playing in there,
and the laughter of young people, Ohio's children. They are loved
and cared for, Ohio's children.

*The 4-H Club Movement was begun in a basement room in the courthouse in Springfield, Ohio; and the Community Chest was a Cleveland idea. Every year the big thermometer stands on the corner of Ninth and Euclid in Cleveland, in front of the Cleveland Trust Bank, and it stands there like the conscience of its citizens until the red marker climbs to the level they have set for themselves for contributions.*

The men who came to Ohio were not the "Pike's Peak or Bust!" men, or the "California, Here I Come!" men. They were farmers and shopkeepers and shoemakers and tavernkeepers and tinkerers, and they didn't count on miracles; they asked only for the land's bounty and equal opportunity for all. They were sound men who respected themselves and who knew what they wanted for their children. Well, they got it. They succeeded. It's all here now. This is what Ohio is. And this is what you must keep in mind when you look at Ohio today.

Let us begin with the pretty girls of Ohio, with their thin, light skin; so fair, often, that the small veins show blue at the temples. (This is to be a very unconventional tour of Ohio, as you can see.) But you imagine, after a while, that you would know an Ohio girl anywhere, with her alternate directness of manner and her shyness —unrelated to coquetry—and the charm of her matter-of-fact way.

Ohio girls don't use the circumstance of their sex in the ordinary exchanges of living, and perhaps that is why they are direct one moment and shy the next, as if they recall unexpectedly now and then that they are women, too, as well as human beings. In Ohio, at a social evening, the men talk together and the women talk together, and if any sustained mixed conversation is required of them they seek each other out afterward with a kind of relief. You will think of that in towns like Youngstown, where the women hurry along the city streets, usually alone, carrying a package or a shopping bag, and probably a list in their pocket, half completed.

The young men of Youngstown, on the other hand (or for Youngstown read Warren, or Canton, or Akron, or Mansfield), the young men wear a very different air as they stroll the streets between shifts at the mill, or during the slack periods when they are laid off. They walk with the unconscious arrogance of admitted lords of the universe in twos or threes or fours, advancing abreast down the sidewalk, so that the hurrying women with the shopping bags must pass close to the shop windows where the mohair living-room sets, and the dinner china with garlands of flowers stamped on a cream-colored background are displayed under the neon signs. They seem unaware of each other, the men and the women, and the young men, walking, or stopping to talk in groups, are loud and uninhibited. But, oh, the sweet, shy, pretty girls, with the clear, white skin, and the fine, light hair. "My land!" you hear one say, as she runs into a friend on the street. "My land, what are you doing here?" And if you are Ohio born you feel a quickening of the blood at that old, familiar phrase. My land, where the men work hard at their jobs, and the women work hard at theirs, and where they meet, the men and the women, and where they are fulfilled, through their children.

Houses are women's things in Ohio, and everything in them is a woman's own, from the paper on the walls, and the furniture, and the rugs, and the pictures, down to the china spoonholder, shaped like a flower, on the stove, where you put the spoon down after you have stirred the broth. You can almost feel that nothing in the history of the world has ever been as clean as these Ohio houses, with their waxed floors, and vacuum-cleaned rugs, and the piece of paper placed on the linoleum inside the kitchen door, to catch any dirt that is on your shoes when you come in the back door; and everything in the whole house picked up and put away, with the newspapers tied in bundles for the Boy Scouts to collect, and the windows washed on the outside, and the curtains laundered and ironed and put back up the very same day.

*It is seven-thirty of an evening at the Inn in Oberlin. The members of the Chamber of Commerce, in meeting, have just finished their dinner: fruit cup, breaded veal cutlet, apple pie, and coffee, and now they have settled back for the speaker, after listening to The Barber Shop Quartette sing* Back Home in Indiana, *and* Lady of Spain. *The speaker of the evening is a Cleveland department store executive, a typical Ohio citizen, treasurer of his local March of Dimes. The title of his speech is "The Customer Is Always Right." The wife of the president of the Chamber of Commerce is distressed about the audience. "The wives were invited tonight," she explains, "but most of them were too exhausted by their spring housecleaning to come. Of course you couldn't hold your head up in this town if you didn't turn out your house in the spring."*

Oberlin is a college town. Oberlin College was one of the first colleges in America to accept Negro students, but in some ways it is even more significant that Oberlin was the first college in the world —repeat, first college in the world—to accept women students on an equal basis with men students.

Which leads us to the reflection that Columbus, Ohio, produced James Thurber, possibly as a demonstration of the impartiality and balance of nature. Mr. Thurber has devoted his years to curbing the excesses of college-educated women, much as, in nature, the hummingbird keeps us from being overwhelmed by gnats.

It was in Oberlin, too, that Mrs. William Stevenson, wife of the new college president, had to be gently and tactfully told after her arrival that it was considered rather pretentious to allow the maid to answer the telephone if it rang while she was at home herself. "Just let it ring until you get to it yourself," she was told.

The world of the men of Ohio is the world outside. You see them, on Saturdays or Sundays, or in the early evenings, the young husbands and family men, in their old faded Army or Navy clothes, endlessly occupied in all the yards of all the new houses. "They say you're lucky if you've got a good lawn by the time the house is paid for," says young Jim Freeman of Springfield, a Navy veteran, a fireman, working outside on his day off from the Engine House. "We've got good drainage here," he says. "No basement problem. And we changed the floor plans two feet out on the side to give Barbara more closet space," he adds, looking with pride at the garden patch ready for spading, now that spring is here, and at the clothesline poles he put up for Barbara, and at the stacked screens, ready to be put up now that the storm windows can come down.

If the lives of men and women together in Ohio seem sketched out in terms of black and white, without nuance, it is well to remind one's self that Ohio is an industrial state, and that there is always that whistle blowing at dawn. You imagine the young married women at their dressing tables at night, scarcely looking at themselves in the mirror as they take off the make-up, their husbands already in bed and the alarm clocks, set, beside them. Tomorrow night they may all go shopping at the new suburban shopping center, to buy food for the week, or spring clothes, or a new television chair; Jim and Barbara and Cindy and little Joey, happy people, having come to their own terms with life, the parents possessing, in exchange for their hopes and dreams and aspirations, what are surely the healthiest, and the best fed and dressed, and the most indulged children in the world.

But let us look at some of the towns and cities. Let us take as our point of departure Sandusky, that port west of Cleveland on Lake Erie, because it is pleasant there, and if you know New England it will seem familiar to you. The Marblehead Peninsula is rather like Cape Cod, and you cross to it over the water from Bay Bridge to Danbury. There are islands in the bay, and small boats dance on the clear blue waters in the spanking breeze, but in spite of the familiar names there is something alien to New England here, and suddenly you know what it is. This is fresh water, this vast inland sea stretching away to the horizon, and instead of the taste of salt in the air there is a clear, cool, woodland scent.

This is wine country too. In the commercial wine cellars of the city you can see casks which have been in use since the middle of the last century. Not all of the wine cellars are in the city. You can take a boat out to Kelleys Island, or Middle Bass (where the club-room of the winery is called "The Silenium"), and sit in cool, dark comfort and sample the local product.

Sandusky is a German city, with its brisk air and parks and churches in gray native stone, and the beer is excellent in the restaurants where the good lake fish is served, walleyed pike, and bass, and yellow perch, fresh from the water. The sweet dessert wines are good, the muscatel, and Tokay, and white port. If you want wine, incidentally, you go to the corner drugstore, where you will find the bottles displayed along with the tooth paste and the headache remedies. To buy hard liquor you go to a state store and fill out a form which even asks for your name and address.

East of Sandusky you skirt along the lake shore, seeing the white caps of the waves through the sand dunes and the groves of trees. You cross Old Woman Creek where the rare American lotus grows, its chinalike flower rising on a snaky stem some six or eight inches above the flat green leaves. You cross the Vermilion River, named for the color of the clay in its banks, where the Indians came to paint their faces for war. You are in the country of the Western Reserve now, east as far as the Pennsylvania line, and south to a line just below Akron. The Connecticut people came here, and many a hidden village on a back road, with its dark, blind, old Greek Revival houses facing on elm-shaded commons, is more Connecticut now than Connecticut itself.

The Western Reserve is the architect's and the amateur historian's paradise, a region of America waiting to be discovered by the traveler; where every village has its unrecorded history and its tales and legends passed down from memory to memory. Through towns bearing such names as Norwalk and North Fairfield and New London, you drive in the "Firelands," a tract of land set aside originally for the people of Connecticut whose homes were burned by the British during the Revolution. Good dairy land, where the Classical Revival farmhouses bear the signature of their architects in such unusual details as recessed second-story porches, and fretwork on porticos and pilasters; outlined at night against the setting sun on land flat as the Texas Panhandle, lonely and austere, waiting for a Marquand to record their almost forgotten tales.

The Firelands are only a part of the Western Reserve; all of Northern Ohio bears the stamp of New England, and if you go on, northeast, beyond Cleveland, to Painesville and Willoughby and Mentor, you will find examples of the work of the architect Jonathan Goldsmith, houses whose pillared façades might well serve as a backdrop for O'Neill's *Mourning Becomes Electra.* The blood runs thin in some of these towns, and there is ancestor worship here as pious as any in Massachusetts, where Archibald Willard's *The Spirit of '76* (said to be the most reproduced painting in America) hangs in Abbott Hall, Marblehead, although Mr. Willard himself lived and is buried in Wellington, Ohio, and painted his picture there, in the Western Reserve. (He began it as a cartoon, he said, to be called *Yankee Doodle,* but when he had posed his models an "inspired look" came over their faces, he reported, and he himself was inspired to a solemn and heroic approach.)

Fragments of old stories, and the testimony of lost causes and faded dreams tempt you to turn aside at every corner in the Western Reserve. John Brown's body lies amolderin' in the grave, but his soul goes marching on in Northern Ohio. They will point out the graves of his mother and father to you in Hudson, that jewel of a village in Summit County where the old Academy is, arrested in time, with great elm trees shading the fine old Federal and Greek Revival buildings of soft red brick. John Brown lived in Hudson for twenty-one years; and down in Oberlin they talk of him still, and of their own native son, the Negro killed at Harpers Ferry. Or, in search of stories and the echoes of lost passions, go to Tallmadge, near Akron, where the magnificent Congregational Church stands on the com-

mon. The church was built in 1825, but before the church was built,
Delia Bacon was born there, in 1811, that wonderful eccentric who
died mad after she had succeeded in setting the whole literary world
on its ear with her sudden conviction that William Shakespeare
hadn't written all those plays after all, but two or three other men,
including someone of her own name.

You have to go nearer to Cleveland to see the sustained vigor of
the old blood, where a combination of natural resources and water
transportation and Yankee enterprise built the fortunes and the
manor houses on the heights above the city, and east of that, in the
Chagrin River Valley, where blooded horses take the jumps in the
paddocks, and where the polo fields glow softly like old, rubbed
velvet.

*It is Thursday night of the Symphony Season in Cleveland. In the
quiet passages of the symphony the audience is so still in its uphol-
stered seats in the muted house that you imagine you can almost
hear the whistles of the freighters as the ore is brought into the
twisted Cuyahoga, or the creaking of the cranes over the coal barges
as the night sky is stained by a great sudden flare of light from the
mills. After the concert when the audience goes home, it is not to
the Goldsmith houses of their ancestors, but possibly to the Norman
or Tudor houses of Shaker Heights, with their leaded, mullioned
windows, and the half-timbering, and the windows opening out onto
gardens, and onto streets named Winchester, or Westchester, or
Eaton, or Mannering; or to a "Lane," or a "Place."*

The people of wealth, who form the society of Cleveland and the
Western Reserve, are a responsible group, bred in the tradition of
obligation. They do not wear hair shirts under their discreetly tailored clothes, it is true; they do themselves well, and possibly even
better than is apparent to the eye, since the key for people of wealth
almost everywhere in Ohio is understatement. Ostentation has always been regarded as vulgar. The Livingstons and Hannas, the
Eatons and Hoyts and Ingalls, the Wicks and the descendants of
Cotton Mather do not produce younger sons given to drinking champagne out of slippers, but over the years they have learned the
practice, in their own discreet way, of what Thorstein Veblen called
conspicuous consumption. The mansard-roofed Gothic houses of Millionaires Row on Euclid Avenue in Cleveland have long been aban-

doned for Shaker Heights, or for the comfortable life modeled on the life of the English country squire, in the rambling white frame houses with their barns and rolling meadows in the villages of Hunting Valley and Gates Mills along the Chagrin.

A young man of society may waste his substance in hunting and polo, or in the somber, elegant rooms of the soot-darkened Union Club in town, as long as he turns up on Monday morning, clear-eyed and shrewd, at his office in the Hanna Building, or the Union Commerce Building or the Terminal Tower; and as long as he takes his place, and works at it, on the boards of the social agencies and charities, or the civic improvement groups, or the school boards, or the Symphony Society, or the Art Museum.

Equal responsibility is demanded of the young society matron, who is trained from the very beginning to take her place in the activities of the Junior League in no superficial way. She is expected to work, on the hospital committees, or the nursing committees, or on whatever necessary project is at hand, before she can relax with tennis or golf or garden-club activities.

The character of Cleveland society is, in its way, the character of the people of the state. Many of the great fortunes were made by men of background, conditioned to the uses and abuses of money. They brought their ideals of behavior with them; they set the tone in their manner of living for the others who followed. They do not, even today, lust after false gods; they waste no time in idle envy or emulation of New York or café society. It is a relaxed society, and not a closed one. The mere making or possession of money is no entree, but neither are doors closed to newcomers if they learn to take their place gracefully in the accepted, conservative, responsible pattern.

The firmly established, largely early German society of Cincinnati has experienced fewer changes and less influx of outside influence over the years, and for this reason it may be less flexible than society elsewhere in Ohio, and possibly even more comfortable in its way, with its combination of German *Gemütlichkeit,* and Southern graciousness and warmth. Newcomers to the city used to have it explained to them that "the Vanderbilts and the Astors of Cincinnati are the Schmidlapps and the Hickenloopers." German names still figure largely in Cincinnati society, although the German families no longer live in their wonderful *"Sauerbraten* Byzantine" houses in town.

Wealthy Cincinnatians have moved out to Indian Hill, or to the beautiful prospect above Eden Park, although the social life still revolves around the old, sprawling Country Club, which now sits with its rolling greens almost in the center of town. Here, too, the emphasis for social acceptance is on community responsibility. The Taft family, among others, has set a worthy example for years, and the Family Service Society of Cincinnati recently celebrated seventy-five years of service.

To write of society in Ohio, with a capital S, is a doubtful and rather awkward undertaking. The word is seldom heard in Ohio. The boundaries and the standards of behavior and the code of ethics of Ohio society exist only by tacit agreement, and if it is examined too closely it is likely to vanish, up a dozen avenues of laughter and astonished denial. For responsible as it is, discreet as it is in its activities and its pattern, it risks, knowingly, the disapproval of the defiantly plain, no-nonsense citizens who make up the major part of the state, and who mistrust a broad "a" more than they might mistrust a possibly counterfeit bill. Cleveland is cosmopolitan, and Cincinnati is cosmopolitan, and society there pays a certain penalty for its effort to live in a more fashionable world, or even for the rewards of trying to live in a larger world.

"Sometimes Cleveland acts as if it doesn't belong to Ohio at all," they will tell you in Columbus, or points south of Cleveland. The sons and daughters of wealthy Cleveland families are often sent East to be educated in New England boarding schools, or Ivy League colleges, "but anyone who has gone to an Eastern boarding school, or has a degree from a big Eastern college," they will say, "has a distinct disadvantage here." Towns and cities like Springfield and Columbus and Middletown and Dayton sit stubborn and foursquare on their old foundations, each feeling itself to be unique and self-sufficient, suspicious of the wary visitor, ready with a convenient chip for the shoulder if necessary, every man a king.

There are sections of these cities, and of cities such as Mansfield and Chillicothe and Zanesville and Washington Court House, which have a certain chauvinistic, 19th Century character, with dark, old, eclectic buildings under crenelated false fronts, and with cast-iron pilasters and pediments, and a Gothic-Victorian flavor. Civil War monuments stand in squares, and there are cast-iron fountains in parks, and iron urns filled with geraniums, standing amid plantings of canna lilies or yucca.

Here and there is evidence of some knowledge of a larger world beyond, often brought home to Ohio by the boys who have gone out to war; although it is difficult to account for the occasional "Latin Lounges"—the bars, lighted softly at night, where the boys in the black suède shoes woo the pretty girls with the fair skin, generally in groups of four or six, so that the courtship can be carried on with the comfort and support of one's friends. But you can dine in "Streets of Paris" cafés; and in hotel rooms all over the state you will find framed water-color prints after Dufy, the bright vigor made quaint, with top-hatted gentlemen and women in hoop skirts on the Paris dream streets.

Ohio is not the Middle West, as some deluded Easterners persist in thinking, but it may be that the Middle West begins here. In many respects Ohio is still the Last Chance Town, the place where you are supposed to get down from the stage, and change from your fancy clothes, and begin to talk and act like a natural man. Charles Dickens noted this, in his ill-tempered travels of 1842. Stopping at Colt's Exchange Hotel in Sandusky (it still stands; it is just down the street from the Dorn Winery, facing the lake), he wrote in his journal that the proprietor of the hotel "constantly walked in and out of the room with his hat on . . . and lay down on our sofa, and pulled his newspaper out of his pocket; and read it at his ease; I merely mention these traits as characteristic of the country . . ." An entry which still has the power to amuse the people of Ohio, who thought that Mr. Dickens ought to have known when he was being deliberately baited.

The old republican principles are still deliberately and defiantly practiced in Ohio, and the visitor will regard them as acts of ignorance or boorishness at his own peril. In Chillicothe today, for example, when a man alone hails a taxicab, the driver will open the door to the front seat beside him as he pulls up to the curb. He is not a chauffeur; he is a man doing a job. And you'd better look at him, too, before you decide to tip him. He may not like it; just as any man in Ohio may not like it if you call him by his first name too quickly. It is well to remember here the 18th Century dignity of "Mister," that democratic title which removed the "Esq." from the address on letters, and brought every man up to the same level.

But speaking of democratic and republican virtues, the practice of politics is still highly respected in Ohio. In the fine old State House in Columbus, where the battle flags are furled, with their frayed edges protected by black netting as they stand in the lighted cases, and where a plaque in memory of Andrews' Raiders is fixed to one wall, and where the enormous painting by Powell of Perry's victory at Lake Erie, familiar to all school children, hangs over the east stairway, a kind of mystical quality can almost be felt in the corridors.

Ohio is conservative, conservative, conservative. Ohio is so conservative it sometimes hardly seems to be breathing. You look in vain through almost any Ohio paper for adequate coverage of national or world news. "But it isn't really indifference," perceptive Ohioans will tell you. "Since Robert Taft died," they say, their tone suddenly empty with that genuine sense of loss with which one might speak of a death in one's own family, "we are waiting. We are waiting for our leadership in national and world affairs."

*It is night in Columbus, the State Capital, and at the Gayety Burlesque, Miss "Tiny" Burns, "petite, saucy and lovable," the posters say, is doing her grinds and bumps. The dusty, faded old house is almost empty. About forty in the audience, young people, boys and girls together in a group out for a laugh, and a few old creeps. Over at the Deshler-Hilton Hotel a contingent of businessmen has just arrived on a late train for the beginning of a convention in the morning. They have all been given Mexican straw hats with untrimmed edges, and name plates to pin on their lapels. They stand by the elevators, waiting, serious and tired looking, holding the Mexican hats and the name plates absently. As the bellhop picks up the men's bags he looks at the luggage labels carefully and addresses each man by name.*

The Pickaway Plains lie south of Columbus, and if you cross them at dusk, where the Scioto flows between its willow-shaded, dreamlike banks, you can almost imagine what this wonderful farm country looked like in the old days when it glowed with the campfires of eight Shawnee villages. You want to forget now that this is bloody land, fought for tenaciously, and that the Logan elm still stands, under which that Mingo chief stood to deliver his famous lament. "Who is there to mourn for Logan?" he said, after his family had been killed by the whites. "Not one."

You cross the Pickaway Plains to get to Chillicothe from Columbus, but if you go to Chillicothe with the memory of its romantic past you are doomed to disappointment. Chillicothe was settled by

Virginia aristocrats, and before the 18th Century had ended there were bookshops in Chillicothe, with stock from London and the East, and there were carriages on the streets, and fine houses with windowpanes of glass brought over the mountains.

Some of the old houses still stand, in the city, and on the hills around, but there are different émigrés in the city now, men who have come from the South with their families to work on the new atomic plant going up down on the road to Portsmouth and the river; enterprising men in an enterprising community, who shame you for wanting the city to have preserved more of its outlived past. But you can go to "Adena," if you like, the country house designed by Latrobe, and completed for Thomas Worthington in 1807, on a hill northwest of the city. The Duke of Saxe-Weimar visited there, and the Henry Clays came every summer, and Chief Tecumseh dined in the State Dining Room, and from this house, the legend goes, after a night of conversation and cards, Worthington and his friends stepped out into the cool morning air to see the sun rise over Mount Logan, and took it at that moment to grace the Seal of the new state. A good story, but unfortunately the house wasn't finished then.

Now "Adena," like Williamsburg, has been restored within an inch of its life, to an arbitrary point which probably never existed in its history, but you leave it with a sense of loss, and go back down toward the city, as the sun strikes its blind, sterile windows. The city is dominated by the magnificent Court House, built of honey-colored freestone in 1855, a Greek Revival structure with a superb portico, and with Mayan touches in the decoration of the stone lintels over the doors, and other detail so incisive and exquisite that from a distance the whole effect is rather like that of intaglio carving in a gem. Giants walked this land once, you think; and where are they now, the men with the vision who made this land?

The director of the Ross County Historical Society gave me the answer to that. "The vision is still here," he said, and from another hill above the city he pointed out the Mead Paper Plant below, constructed over a prehistoric stream. "For the water they need in their production of paper they have tapped a river buried long ago under the glacial moraine," he says. "Ohio is like that, taking its strength from its buried past."

With these thoughts of the past which, in Ohio, always lead back to the present, you think of Youngstown again, that apotheosis of mill towns, a city where almost nothing is beautiful except those things built by men without any consideration of beauty. The steel mills spread through the valley of the Mahoning like a great shout of masculine defiance, looking, to the uninitiated, with their retorts and caldrons and condensers, like the dream of a mad scientist, and at night the sky of the city is bathed in a clear, cold, flickering light, intense but, at the center of the city, soundless, like a stage effect without thunder for the death of the gods. Even with the blind pulled, the hotel room is bathed in the thin, insistent light of the Bessemer converter, and if you look out you will see in this light torches of flame spurting into the sky, waste gases burning, and other waste gases ascending as smoke.

It is like a symbol of the melting pot itself, you think, and on the streets of the city the faces of the hurrying women and the confident men are new and raw and almost, it seems, without features; difficult to trace or place by racial background. Polish, Czech, Greek, Italian, Serb and Yankee; all are merging into a new visage, a face of light skin and clear flesh, with high color in the cheeks, but with the features still unformed, as if the stamp of the new race had not yet emerged from the soft, mixed clay.

The new race is largely a people without consciousness of background, or even of continuity in history, living on the buried past, living in the sound old house, but having, for the most part, cut themselves off from the abandoned patterns of their fathers. They face only to the future, and they must make up their new ways as they go along, but they possess for this a tremendous wealth of vitality as intense as the heat of the Bessemer converter in which the molten metal is cleansed. Everything they do is new, the clothes they wear, the way they hold their forks when they eat, even their speech, long lost from its Anglo-Saxon source. They do not know themselves yet, and they need isolation in which to develop, an isolation for which they are sometimes criticized. Other than that, in the stubborn old tradition of this Republic, they ask for nothing for themselves. The voice of Ohio is seldom raised outside of its own boundaries, and they are content to have it that way.

# PART IV *The Mid South*

# Washington, D.C.

## by ROGER ANGELL

One spring not too long ago, my wife and I made a trip south to inspect a piece of riverbank real estate of which we are part owners. Along with several hundred thousand of our fellow deed holders, we passed a pleasant April week inspecting our property—asking questions of our tenants and foremen, taking down familiar books from the library shelves, refreshing our memory of old monuments on the estate and admiring the new outbuildings, rereading cherished family letters, and even poking about in the attic. It turned out to be a good idea, this week of rediscovery. We came home in possession of many bright new scenes and rare faces, with the recollection of many moments of seriousness and some of unexpected hilarity, with the feeling that we had learned much about the past and perhaps a little about the present. Best of all, we returned with the happy feeling that our personal fortune was larger than we had known. I recommend the same tour of inspection to everyone who owns a similar share in the city of Washington, D.C.

For an American, Washington is the finest tourist city in the world. There are several reasons for this large claim, but one of the most valid is the fact that Washington is a hedgehog. The fox, you will remember, knows many things, but the hedgehog knows One Big Thing. Applying this old country adage to the realm of cities, one realizes that New York is our finest fox and Washington our one true hedgehog. The complicated, fascinating fox demands a lifetime to study, but if you have only a week or a weekend for your research, the stolid, one-track-mind hedgehog is for you. If you are a tourist, go to Washington.

For all its size, Washington has but a single purpose, a single business—government. It is an artificial creation—a company town, a housing project, a planned city—and for this reason the visitor can see it plain, with few of the confusions which assail him when he enters a city or a village which has grown up on its own and has taken its character from the thousand obscure pressures and subtle nudges of history. But if Washington has unity, it is still not simple; it is not a town to be cracked in an afternoon. It is the city of the One Big Idea.

As you first walk about Washington, you discover countless monuments to this idea, and the figures and words, carved in stone, of men who have believed in it. Seeing the monuments, which are mostly large and mostly marble, you are impressed and reassured by the durability and simplicity of the idea. But then, hours or days later, an important thing happens to you. Watching the capital going about its immense daily labors, watching it at work—in offices and committee rooms and great forums—you come to realize that the One Big Idea is not yet proved. You see that it is still a new concept and one that is besieged daily by countless pressures and problems and the need for difficult decisions. Here, for me, lies the excitement of Washington: in the constant testing of this Big Idea, in the trying out of this brash and dangerous notion that free men are wise enough to govern themselves.

We started with the monuments and the marble. Early on Easter Sunday morning, we taxied to the Washington Monument. It was a fine place to begin, at the exact center of Washington and springtime and tourism—except for one thing: we could not get in. There above us, the immense white paperweight leaned into the spring wind, all 555 feet 5⅛ inches of it, inviting us to elevation and observation, and here on the ground were at least 555 fellow Americans, all standing in a ragged queue that extended from the portal entirely around the foot of the Monument, and all obviously inviting us to get the hell to the end of the line and wait our turn for the elevators. For some reason, we were not annoyed. We abandoned our plans for the summit, and walked slowly around the little hilltop, cricking our necks as we peered upward, shading our eyes as we stared off east and west toward the Capitol and the Lincoln Memorial, both of them quivering slightly in the early morning sunlight, and both more lovely, for all their familiarity, than the heart had remembered. Here, enjoying this carefully contrived, classical and sentimental landscape, I realized (as I was to do again and again on succeeding days) how much of Washington is a cliché—and what a beautiful cliché it is, retaining always its capacity to stir you and to arouse the expected feelings of quiet pride and proprietary excitement. And I was even glad about the crowd of sight-seers, for I suddenly realized that I would be worried about a country whose citizens had become so sophisticated and so bored with the obvious and the patriotic that it could not muster a long line of tourists around the foot of a national shrine on a fine Easter Sunday morning.

We circled the Monument, studying the cars parked around it (bearing license plates from Tennessee and Texas and Montana and Missouri and Vermont and Virginia); admiring the Easter bonnets from Bangor and Boise, the Bon-Ton Shoppe and Saks Fifth Avenue; collecting bits of conversation and accents from East Boston, Puerto Rico and the Great Smokies (the woman who said "White Hoose," we decided, was probably from Virginia). When we walked down the hill to camera range and unshipped our cameras, we found a man beside us on the grass engaged in the same occupation. He was trying to arrange his wife and three restless children and the Monument into A Good Composition, and he was having his troubles. Finally the younger girl began to cry and the photographer lost his patience. "Dammit, Edna," he yelled to his wife, "tell her to shut up. This is for the album!"

But the holiday mood, bright and indestructible, persisted. Down at the Tidal Basin, a strong breeze whipped in off the Potomac, ruffling the waves, which were full of fallen cherry blossoms and, peculiarly, dead fish. A group of soldiers and their girls were stretched out on the grass, eating popsicles, and further on we came upon two Waves sitting under a cherry tree with their shoes off. The President, I had read, was attending divine services and planned a little golf later in the day, and here came another golfer—a secretary who passed us at a brisk pace, wearing tartan shorts and carrying her clubs on her back. Congress was in brief Easter recess and Congressmen were reported to have gone home to see their families and visit constituents, to roll Easter eggs instead of logs. It occurred to me that they might have done better to stay in Washington, for clearly, most of their constituents were here—walking around the Tidal Basin, photographing the cherry trees and the fishermen, lining up for rides on the swan boats, carrying souvenir booklets and hotel-room keys and post cards, and planning to call upon their Congressmen.

We found eleven buses drawn up in front of the Jefferson Memorial, one of them loading up with a troupe of small and cheerful Japanese, another debouching two dozen YMCA men from Mansfield, Ohio, all of whom were attired in Bermuda shorts and Argyle socks. Except for that scene, though, I found the Memorial, which I had never visited before, to be a disappointment. I liked the challenging, dangerous words on the walls (". . . laws and institutions must go hand in hand with the progress of the human mind. As that becomes more developed, more enlightened, as new discoveries are made, new truths discovered and manners and opinions changed, with the change of circumstances, institutions must advance also to keep pace with the times . . ."), and I liked the cool and constant breeze moving through the open colonnades. But I could not help thinking that Jefferson, the architect and patrician, the man of Monticello, would have preferred a statue six feet high instead of nineteen feet, and would have voted for his beloved Virginia brick instead of for glaring white marble.

The Lincoln Memorial was better. Here we found the crowds larger than ever—and somehow less noticeable and obtrusive. Beneath the slim pillars, beneath the soft light falling through the marble ceiling, and, most of all, beneath those great hands and tired, infinitely distant eyes, the hurrying, holidaying, chattering, picture-snapping swarms of our fellow visitors seemed tiny and inconsequential and perhaps only unintentionally boorish. And when at last we began to grow annoyed with the jostling and the heat in the temple, with the whining discussions about ice cream, and with the ugly position of reverence tourists assume when they bend over to focus their cameras, we walked out of the hall and around to the back of the building. Here we were suddenly and totally alone, in cool stone and among the lovely shadows made by fluted columns. We sat down on the new grass, beside rhododendron and pine, and lit cigarettes and wiggled our toes and watched an airplane climbing the bright April air above Arlington. And here, in a moment, I recovered my composure. I thought about Lincoln's face and the words of the Second Inaugural on the wall inside, and I found that I was glad to be a tourist in Washington in the spring.

Government is Washington's first business, its *raison d'être,* but it has a mighty sideline which is now enjoying a permanent and increasing boom—tourism. More than four and a half million tourists come to Washington during the year . . . a figure that has increased by a quarter of a million in the last three years. Over half a million high-school kids descend on the city like eager juncos every spring. Most of them are seniors, traveling in groups, who have raised the money for their expedition through food sales and variety shows back home, and who travel to the capital by bus from as far away as Maine and Oklahoma. With their water pistols, their brush-cuts and pony-tails, their bright sense of history (heightened by Miss Zinsser's course in American Government back home), and their incredible energy, they are Washington's most identifiable and indefatigable visitors.

Then there are conventioneers—members of some 330 conventions that assemble here annually, ranging from the Lions to the WCTU to the Daughters of the American Revolution. The DAR, I discovered, are known as poor tippers but hard workers. "Sometimes I think those old girls must rest up all year for their trip here," one cabdriver said to me. "Because they never get tired. They sure are *strong!*" He shook his head reminiscently. "Big, too," he added.

In spite of the fact that most of Washington's prime attractions are free (or cost a dime or a quarter at the most for admission), these various visitors combine to spend more than 250 million dollars a year in the city. If this figure seems too large to hold in your hand, ponder the following statistics, based on one sidelight of tourism: one photo-finishing agency in Washington processed *14 million* black-and-white snapshot prints one year, plus over 100,000 rolls of color film. *In a single day* one April, at the height of the spring invasion, the same agency processed 112,300 black-and-white prints. Add to this all the color film exposed, all the business done by the other photo agencies in Washington, and all the films that are taken back home to be developed, and you begin to have some idea of the size of Washington's profitable, camera-toting locust swarm.

The fact that so many of these tourists persist in visiting Washington in the spring (almost a million and a half of them in April and May alone) annoys the city's merchants and innkeepers, who would prefer a steadier, year-round business. But I think they are wrong. Washington is perhaps the most beautiful springtime city I have ever seen. It has space, it has air, it has light—a soft and extraordinary April glow that seems to hover just above your head as you stroll the side streets. The city appears to have more trees than Paris, and all the many dozens of parks and circles and squares and malls are alight with geraniums and azaleas, with plum and quince and crab-apple blossom. Coming out of your hotel in the early morning, you turn the corner onto one of the great avenues, and your heart is lifted by Washington's great white distances, by the subtlety and sweep of the genius of L'Enfant, the city's designer.

Forget the crowds and the Kodaks and the conventions; this is Washington's time of year. In the morning, the Government girls pack the long yellow and maroon buses inward bound from Rosslyn and Arlington, filling them with new white straw hats and the hope-ful scent of *Arpège*. In the evening, a visiting high-school senior from Waycross, Georgia, walks hand-in-hand with his steady under the heavy, dark trees on 16th Street, and you are charmed by their slow and graceful accents. In the afternoon, the girls from the Cathedral School turn out for softball practice near 34th Street, wearing bright yellow gym suits, and at the same moment a freshman Congressman from Indiana appears on the floor of the House sporting a new pair of perforated white shoes and carrying in his hand a speech in honor of his State Flower.

Every well-prepared visitor should bring more than his camera and traveler's checks with him to Washington. He should bring along a lively sense of the past. He can acquire this only by reading about the city before he comes here—in any one of a dozen or more books about Washington. His imagination thus prepared, he will be able to see more than simply what comes before his eyes. He cannot then commit the all too common and unfortunate error of believing that Washington's past is what he sees in its monuments—a past that is heroic, impersonal and without human error. I don't think it much matters what particular aspects of Washington's short, furious and often preposterous history he chooses to remember.

It is possible, for example, to look at the "Hobbyhorse" statue of Andrew Jackson in Lafayette Square with a certain lack of rever-ence if you remember that this statue always made Lincoln laugh out loud. . . . Or, walking this same sleepy square, you might choose to recall that this was where the flamboyant Representative Dan Sickles shot and killed his best friend, Philip Barton Key, the son of the author of *The Star-Spangled Banner,* in a fit of rage over Key's illicit relationship with Mrs. Sickles. Dan Sickles pleaded temporary insanity (the first defense of its kind in this country), was acquitted, and went on to become a remarkably second-rate Union general, and to lose a leg at Gettysburg. . . . If you admire the cold, clean beauty of the Washington Monument, then study the original plans for the edifice, which called for a Roman temple and a statue of George Washington riding in a chariot and wearing a toga. And then go on to read how the Know-Nothings managed to postpone the completion of the Monument for decades, because Pope Pius IX had sent a block of marble to be incorporated in the structure. And don't forget that the Monument killed one United States president—old Zachary Taylor. President Taylor attended Fourth of July ceremonies, in 1850, at the foot of the unfinished Monument, where he demolished a bag of cherries while sitting in the hot sun, and washed this down with a pitcher of cold milk. Not surprisingly he was dead within the week. . . . Perhaps you like to believe the unverified story that Andrew Jackson spoiled L'Enfant's magnificent Pennsylvania Avenue by his highhanded settling of the dispute as to where to put the Treasury Building. The legend says that he planted his cane in the middle of the avenue and proclaimed, "Put it here!" . . . But it *is* true that during a slavery debate in 1856 Senator Charles Sumner of Massachusetts was bodily attacked on the floor of the Senate by Representative Preston S. Brooks, who beat him unconscious with a cane and almost killed him.

And always, there are the more vivid pictures from the past, scenes of sadness and sleeplessness and mortal struggle. . . . Robert E. Lee praying all night in his bedroom in the Lee Mansion at Arlington, after he had been offered the field command of the Union Army at the beginning of the Civil War. . . . Julia Ward Howe getting up in the middle of the night in her bedroom in the old Willard Hotel to write *The Battle Hymn of the Republic,* just after visiting the Union encampments outside the same Lee Mansion in Arlington. . . . And Abraham Lincoln sitting up at night, too, to write a long letter urging courage and resolution upon one of his hopeless commanders of the Army of the Potomac—McClellan or Burnside or Hooker—and then tearing up the letter before morning. . . . Woodrow Wilson dying by inches in the White House as his dream died with him. . . . And the silent crowds standing outside the White House where Lincoln lay dead at the end of a great war; and the other, equally silent crowds outside the same house where Franklin Delano Roosevelt lay dead toward the end of another. . . .

Somebody once threw a cat off the top of the Washington Monument. It spun, volplaned, did several half gainers and tucks—and landed, uninjured, on all fours. Several years later, when the cat finally died (probably of boredom), somebody had it stuffed and sent it, of course, to the Smithsonian Institution. The Smithsonian, to the best of anyone's knowledge, has never thrown *anything* away, and for this reason it has been called the Nation's Attic—a description which cannot be improved upon. Like all attics, it is eminently worth a periodic visit. (But let it be clear here that the keeping of trivia and memorabilia is only part of the Smithsonian's job; it runs no less than four museums and art galleries, has a crackerjack department of ethnology, and operates the first-rate National Zoological Park.)

What I like best about the Smithsonian's Arts and Industries Building is its magnificent seediness, its incredible juxtapositions. If you want to see General Sherman's uniforms and Charles A. Lindbergh's *Spirit of St. Louis* at the very same instant, here they are, right next to each other. Here is a tremendous doll's house from 1914 next to Mamie Eisenhower's wedding dress. Here is an exhibit showing how artificial graphite is made, here is a working model of a 1928 Willys engine, and here (buzz!) are some live bees. Here, presumably for purposes of thoughtful comparison, is a Mexican oxcart spang next to the *John Bull* steam engine. Had enough? Or shall we go on and see the scale model of an asphalt-making machine and ponder the influence of the sewing machine upon history?

One good thing about the Smithsonian: you can quit wherever you please, for nobody has ever seen all of the Institution's thirty-million-odd keepsakes. My last and most cherished memory of the place was the sight of a young man and woman wearing identical black jodhpurs, black leather windbreakers and glass-studded kidney belts. They were incredulously examining a pre-1910 motorcycle, and were laughing fit to bust.

The only real way to see the Capitol building is to join one of the guided tours there. Any visitor who fails to do this will become instantly and hopelessly lost among the endless gilded corridors, the double staircases, Senators' barbershops, and the appalling statues of

Phil Kearny, Huey Long, Henry Clay, Elizabeth Cady Stanton and other assorted American deities. All day long in the Capitol, these squads of guided tourists pass each other in the halls—schools of mackerel behind their pilot fish, their eyes on the ceilings and their mouths slightly open.

I went to the Capitol prepared to think about politics and history, and found myself instead thinking about art. For the "official art" in the Capitol is absolutely overpowering, and most of it is overpoweringly bad. Not all of it; I admire the Senate Chamber and the old Supreme Court Chamber; and the President's Room, with its deep colors, its frescoes, its too-big chandelier, and its black leather chairs, is a florid, rococo delight. But the rest—the crawling Brumidi frescoes, the overblown pageants in oil, the Italianate corridors, the stone statesmen in double-breasted suits—must be seen to be disbelieved. Oddly enough, they did not upset me in the least. I had the same feeling about the building itself. The Capitol is all wrong: there are too many banks of stairs, too many wedding-cake tiers of columns; the dome is much too heavy, and the building's best profile, the East Front, faces in the wrong direction. But I could not, for all that, find the Capitol anything but beautiful. I was touched by the rather pathetic bravery of our Government in having set out so confidently to surround itself with nobility and Great Art, and impressed by the dimensions of its effort and the gallantry of its failure.

Later on, I mentioned this feeling of mine to a friend who is an old Washington hand. "I know what you mean," he said. "Come to think of it, I guess I love the Capitol too." And then he pondered for a moment. "I think the Capitol is like the face of somebody you have known and loved for a long time," he said at last. "You *know* that the face isn't beautiful, but you come to think of it as beautiful because of the admiration you feel for the person's fine qualities and for what he has done in his lifetime."

The place in which to recover from the gaucheries of the Smithsonian and the aspirings of Brumidi is the National Gallery of Art. Here is the quietest place in Washington, and one of the richest and most diverse collections of art in the world. Here you find the quality that is so rare in official Washington buildings—attractiveness. The pictures are beautifully hung and lighted, and you walk almost for miles through rich, cool glades of color, and linger gratefully in the galleries containing your favorite works and periods (for me, the Chester Dale Collection of 19th Century French painting). In the

National Gallery one finds oneself, as in so many other buildings in
Washington, reflecting upon the individuals behind the institution,
the human causes and caprices behind all that marble. The Gallery,
the gift of Andrew W. Mellon, is culture bought by capitalism. It is
the last, breath-taking (and perhaps atoning) gesture of an old-style
American millionaire. It is the American Success Story made respectable, graceful, gentle and possibly immortal. What could be
more amusing, more American, more National than this?

The splashiest show in Washington and the favorite with youngsters is the tour of the Federal Bureau of Investigation. I enjoyed it
—the death mask of John Dillinger (who was perhaps shot deader
than anyone in history), Ma Barker's last stand, the Nazi spies out-
witted, the queer money and bad checks traced to their source, and
all those busy, anonymous agents behind glass looking into micro-
scopes and examining what?—Human blood? Fingernail scrapings?
Prussic acid? Telephone slugs? It is a highly moral show: Crime
Never Pays, all the crooks are dead ducks or about to be, and you,
the law-abiding American citizen, are always on the winning side.
Every tour winds up in a Hollywood finish—with a satisfying burst
of Tommy-gun fire and the silhouette of the wrongdoer, at the other
end of the range, punctured like a commuter's ticket. For me, in fact,
the Warner Brothers overtones of the F.B.I. tour became so strong
that I expected at any moment to see Pat O'Brien and J. Edgar
Hoover hurry down the hall past us, with their snap-brim hats down
and their shoulder holsters bulging, and then to see them return, a
few minutes later, carrying the bullet-torn body of James Cagney
between them on a shutter.

"Washington is the greatest town for shop talk in the world," said
a Government executive to me at a cocktail party. "I know that shop
talk is an awful disease, but I think it's better than small talk any
day. You have to remember that all of us here, all the hundreds and
hundreds of thousands of us, are working in the most fascinating business in the world. And another thing: I think that people work
harder here—put in more hours of tough work—than in any other
town I've ever seen. That's why all the entertaining is at home, like
this. That's why all the parties break up at nine or ten in the evening.
That's why Washington has no real night life."

This enthusiasm, this intensity (with the grain of self-doubt), this
"awful disease" I encountered among everyone I met in Washington.

Plus the rumors. Washington, as I have said, is the biggest company town in the world, and at every Washington party or gathering I attended, the rumors, the inside dope, the anecdote about what the Senator said to the Admiral, flew about the room with the speed of light. And everybody, both the men and the women, was *doing something* and was identified by his job as much as by his name. ("She's Hell's Canyon," I was told upon being introduced to a pretty, redheaded lawyer.)

And yet for all their contagious and exciting excitement with government, for all their pleasure at being "in on" things and at attending upon and assisting in the making of great decisions, Washingtonians are quick to tell you that they live in what is, in many major respects, a small town. In the same week, three separate people—a Library of Congress curator, an investment banker who has lived in Washington all his life, and a man who had come to work for the Voice of America only two weeks before—all paid the identical tribute to their city: they praised its comfort, its relaxed day-to-day life, its stability, its love of families and gardens, its addiction to slow-going, good talk; all three used the adjective "Middle-Class." And a fourth person, the wife of the Voice of America man, said the same thing in a different way. "I hate it," she said. "It's exactly like Toledo, and I spent years and years of my life just trying to get away from Toledo."

Undoubtedly Washington is closer in many respects to Toledo and Grover's Corners and Main Street than it is to London and the Quai d'Orsay. One explanation for this is that a vast number of Washingtonians have come here from elsewhere and, while they work for the Government, remain no more than semipermanent visitors. There are fifty state societies in Washington, all of them active. For residents of what is today the number-one capital of the world, Washingtonians still show much of the exaggerated chauvinism and accompanying doubt that marks the small-towner. They will boast that the city now has seventeen radio stations and that culture is on the rise ("Have you visited our Contemporary Arts Institute?" . . . "You *must* go to the new Arena Theater!"), while at the same time deploring the lack of a truly great university in the city and squirming over Washington's insatiable fascination with high Society.

But I think many of the doubts are uncalled-for. No city can be really parochial when it has two newspapers of the caliber of the *Star* and the *Post and Times-Herald*. No town can be hick when it includes among its citizens the largest permanent assemblage of newsmen and reporters in the world. The same factors which make for impermanence and lack of continuity in Washington are also responsible, as one lawyer pointed out, for much of its strength. "There is no inherited position here," he said. "The competition and the demand for brains is greater today than ever before. Dilettantism is simply unknown now. A man can rise in the Government just as fast as his ambition and ability will take him. What we have here is an unstable society, under tremendous pressure, and that, to me, is a healthy society."

One thing is certain: nobody who has worked for the Government at a responsible level ever quite recovers from Washington. "They don't go back to Pocatello"—not really, not even after retirement, discouragement or political defeat. A friend of mine who used to work for the Department of Interior told me of once seeing an old, defeated, out of office, Middle Western senator who had returned to attend a committee hearing in Washington. The ex-senator came into the high-ceilinged committee room before the session, wandered vaguely about, and then pointed to the table at the end of the room. "That's where I used to sit," he said to nobody in particular. "That's where my name plate was." There were tears in his eyes. And then my friend, a former New Dealer who is also out of office and out of Washington, smiled and said: "I know how he felt. I feel about Washington these days the way Frenchmen felt about Paris when it was occupied by the Germans."

Settle back in your seat in the Senate Gallery, rest your chin in your hands (but don't lean on the railing—Against the Rules!), and watch your Government at work below. At work? If this is work, you decide at once, you'd like to be paid for the same easy duty. A dozen senators are scattered about the great room; two are standing to be recognized; someone is talking—presumably for pure pleasure, for no one seems to be listening. Two of the club members come in through the swinging doors, stare languidly around, and exchange a joke. A third strolls out, biting the tip off a fresh cigar as he leaves. The faces below leap up at you into recognition, out of newspaper photographs. ("There's the Veep!" . . . "Who's that in the Chair—?" . . . "There's our senator.") But what are they doing? Surely this is a joke—an expensive, bad joke.

But stick around; listen and learn. And remember that this is only the showcase of the system—the visible tip of the huge legislative ice-berg. And work *is* being done, you begin to realize, amid all the lan-guor, the politeness and the introduction into the Record of a tribute to a retiring judge in Oklahoma. After half an hour, you have heard remarks on a dozen totally diverse and often important subjects— the tax problems of aviators imprisoned in China, the number of life belts to be carried on river steamers, a major Postal Bill, the tension in the Formosa Straits, the possible effects of lingering radiation, a bill for the relief of John Otter, Indian. You find that you cannot keep your eyes off the Majority Leader, for he is on his feet every minute, hard at work, his hands on the controls. He confers at length with his opposite number; he walks back six rows and whispers with a colleague, who then hurries out; he summons a page and loads him down with papers; he nods to the chair; he signals for a roll call. You become aware of a subtle, efficient system of communications. A senator wanders in, seemingly without reason, and takes his seat. A moment later, another senator rises and asks a long and difficult question about a pending appropriations bill, and the man who just came in, a member of the committee that reported out the bill, rises and answers the question in detail. There are mutual thanks; the work goes on.

The Senate does its public work to accompaniment of politeness, protocol, long-windedness and a system of complex and cumbersome rules, but I think there is as much reason for pride as for annoyance in this apparent inefficiency. For democracy and free speech are rarely truly efficient. Quick enactment of legislation is railroading; it is dictatorial. Freedom must go slowly; it must take time for the expression of doubt, for disagreement, even for demagoguery. Pride comes from our realization that the system works nevertheless. The Big Idea is preserved by the rules, and its daily work gets done in the end, even though we are bored to death by its droning voice, its maddening slowness. And all that official politeness down there on the floor ("I yield to no one in my admiration and esteem for the distinguished senior senator from ——") is more than merely charm-ing and old-fashioned. It is a discipline, a highly necessary habit, that allows human and hard-working men to get their work done in a respectable manner, without the intrusion of violent personal and partisan feelings. It is the same rule of excessive politeness that keeps the overcrowded, too proximate Japanese from flying at each other's throats. Watch the Senate at work: it is humankind at work under rules and restraints; it is civilization.

To witness the real labors of Congress, to be instructed (and probably not entertained), one goes to a committee hearing. We went, on a rainy afternoon, to the Senate Committee on Government Operations. We sat beside two elderly ladies carrying reticules, two regulars who had been first in line outside the committee room and who took pages and pages of shorthand notes throughout the long afternoon—self-appointed secretaries keeping tabs on The System. There were no points of order, no disagreements, no drama. We listened to an engineer and heard terribly detailed testimony about the letting of Government contracts for the construction of grain elevators in Pakistan. Like the senators, I tried to pay attention and fought against sleep in the hot room, and then I wished, suddenly and sharply, that this hearing could be seen coast-to-coast, too, in every living room and tavern in the country. For this was the real thing —the painstaking, dreary and vital detail work of a Government whose responsibilities had suddenly spread to the other side of the world, into a corner of a country that most of us could not even place on a map.

There was nothing dreary about the Supreme Court. I was lucky to get in that day, and I shall remember my afternoon there as long as I remember anything about Washington. We stood in line, several hundred of us, to be admitted to the high chamber, for this was a big day—the first day of hearings on the methods whereby desegregation would be carried out in the nation's schools. There was something in the air that morning; you could almost taste it—the flavor of history, the smell of fresh earth as the past was turned under. Almost a year earlier, the Supreme Court had rendered its decision outlawing segregation. But it had posed some questions—How shall it be done? How fast and by whom?—and we were there to see these questions argued.

The doors opened at last and we filed in and sat in silence—lawyers and plaintiffs and attorneys general and citizens, the passionate and the expert and the merely curious—and stared ahead at the high bench and the four columns and the red curtain behind. The press was clustered, four deep and some even standing, along one wall, prepared to relay the tidings to Toledo and to Grover's Corners and to the south side of Chicago and the south side of Mississippi. We waited there upon the power of the law and upon the rights of a few young elementary-school scholars—*Oliver Brown and Twenty Others v. The School Board of Topeka, Kansas.*

Then there was a stir, the black-robed figures appeared, and we rose and heard the ancient, scalp-prickling words of the crier: "Oyez, Oyez, Oyez! . . ." and "God save the United States and this Honorable Court!"

The preliminaries over and the earlier decisions rendered, the attorney general of Kansas arose, and we were at once plunged into details—exactly how the school districts of Topeka had been altered in the last year. The personalities of the nine men facing me made themselves felt with extraordinary power: Warren, looking like a teacher, a polite schoolmaster who hoped there would be no error in recitation . . . Frankfurter, a sharp-eyed terrier, swiveling in his chair, pointing, interrupting, asking questions . . . Douglas, a scratcher and a fidgeter, his pale eyes wandering the room . . . the new boy Harlan, unnaturally quiet and watchful . . . the veteran Black, slumped low and looking pale and exhausted.

The lawyers rose and sat, the quietly phrased recommendations and counter-recommendations succeeded each other, the legalisms swirled about us, and the fervor and anger and hopes of the audience seemed to rise and fall in almost-visible waves.

But no one raised his voice, least of all the lawyers and justices, for no one, I suddenly realized, knew the answers. At that moment, the magnitude, the difficulty and the power of the Big Idea struck me almost like a blow. The personalities meant nothing; the decisions—which would affect the lives of millions of Americans—were yet to be made. Here was simply an assemblage of responsible men, all stricken with very evident self-doubt, all under immense pressure, all trying to bring the order of law to the barbarism of passions and prejudices, all searching for the hard answers to some terribly hard questions. This was the moment that brought Washington alive for me. It made me proud, and it scared me.

At the end of that day, our last day in Washington, my wife and I again went to the Washington Monument. It was windy and cool, and another rainstorm was making up over the river. We got at the end of the line, which was short now, and waited there, with dust and bits of old newspapers whirling about us and the sky getting darker by the minute. But we were still not to get in. The last elevator-load of sight-seers came down, and the guard closed the gate and came out and said, "Closing time, folks. You all come back in the morning."

We stayed on there for another minute, standing in that darkening and artificially dramatic moment before a storm, and watched the lights going on in the White House and in the great office buildings along Constitution Avenue and, away off, in the Capitol. We watched the big buses loading up and the homeward-bound, five-o'clock traffic piling up. But I found that for the first time in that April week, I wasn't thinking about Washington. I thought instead about the rest of the world and how it waited now, at every moment, upon this young and self-conscious and wonderful city. I thought of San Francisco and Moscow and Rome and Jakarta and Bogota and Brazzaville all listening on the other end of the wire, all waiting for the decisions that would have to be made here tonight and tomorrow and the next day. I had a notion that all of them, perhaps even Moscow, were hoping that they would be the right decisions; that someone would choose wisely again, and that the One Big Idea—the idea that men could rule themselves—was still in business.

# $\mathfrak{M}$aryland

## by JAMES WARNER BELLAH

I don't doubt for a moment that almost anyone can move to Baltimore, go into the insurance business, raise a family and lead a reasonably normal life, untroubled by the ghosts of gentlemen in white-sapphire stock buckles, with lace at their cuffs and scabbarded blades under the tails of their velvet coats. But it is far better to allow for their presence, for when the winter fog smokes in from the Chesapeake Bay they are quite likely to fall into step beside you, stand you a rum cobbler at thruppence a merry round, or deftly beguile your lady—if her smile invites. For you cannot hide Maryland under gasoline pumps and Coca-Cola signs—too much of its past is still present to be reckoned with.

Slice the geographer's scalpel across Maryland from southeast to northwest and you come up with a cross section of terrain that is more delightfully varied than in any other state of the Union. Two thirds of Maryland is tidewater. For thirty-two miles of Worcester County the open Atlantic pounds the outer Maryland shore. West from the ocean, the creek-laced Eastern Shore spreads its low and fertile acres to the Chesapeake Bay, a broad land-bound sea that divides the state in twain. West from the Chesapeake the land rises at once, breaks into intermediate rolling valleys and rises again toward the Appalachian Range, which spines the western reaches of Maryland. But before the Appalachians are reached one must traverse the great valley of Washington County. About thirty miles long and twenty wide, this valley is as magnificent in scenery as the storied Shenandoah and as productive as any soil in the world.

Caught as Maryland is between the Republican might of Pennsylvania, the coal baronies of West Virginia, the paternalistic Du Pontism of Delaware and the vast and ancient inertia of the Old Dominion, it is astonishing that her intrinsic character did not long since become hopelessly hybrid. Especially as she embraces, geographically speaking, the District of Columbia. But somehow Maryland has not lost her character. It is a part of her life today as it was her salvation in years gone—a hardy, forthright heritage of self-respecting, well-mannered individualism.

When one speaks of the character of a people, one speaks in intangible generalities that must be brought to earth. There were grand old men in Maryland in my youth. One comes to mind above all others as the epitome of the Maryland way of life: a man in his nineties, as slender and straight as when he surrendered his battery at Appomattox. For thirty years his wife had been bedridden with an arthritis that had stiffened her frame into almost complete immobility. One evening, returning home from the cheer of his club somewhat later than usual, he heard her call, "Is that you?" He stepped to her bedroom door in the dignity of older times, bowed gallantly and said, "And whom were you expecting, my dear?" The twinkle and the tenderness, the subtle compliment and the denial of pain in the memory of gayer years—either the nuance is there for you or it is not.

Charles I, whose towering contempt for the British Parliament eventually cost him his head, gave Maryland—lock, stock and barrel—to his friend George Calvert, first Lord Baltimore, with absolute proprietary powers in matters of government. A scant six years later, in 1638, the sturdy colonists of Maryland moved to take the reins of government in their own hands. They looked upon the right of self-government as so inalienable that, prior to the Declaration of Independence, they defended it vigorously against all comers—the proprietary Calverts, the Royal Governor, the British Parliament, the Crown and the Continental Congress as well. Playing no favorites.

George Calvert himself was a Roman Catholic, but religious tolerance was one of his ideals. The first Maryland law to further it was passed more than three centuries ago. Negroes were enfranchised in slave-owning Maryland sixty years before the Civil War. In 1810 all property qualifications for suffrage were abolished.

Now this is not put down as mere historical record, it is listed as clinical data on a people who progressed swiftly from absolutism to the democratic way of life long before the latter phrase was coined.

I think the reason for it is twofold. The early settlers were of British stock—yeomen sprinkled through with a generous helping of gentlemen. Each knowing the other's tricks and neither impelled too much by a desire to hang witches or to make proselytes. But far more important was this: Maryland is an extremely pleasant part of the world to live in. Marylanders enjoy it immensely and always have. The climate is temperate in the main, the terrain varied, the horses are fast and well blooded, the Chesapeake is a sailing man's paradise and the *spécialités* of food are of such gastronomic legend that to bring Duncan Hines into the discussion would be tantamount to the Gospels rewritten by H. L. Mencken. So with the bounties of God their heritage, Marylanders—from the beginning—lived and let live in self-respecting, well-mannered individualism. They still do.

The climate saves the state from the malarial apathy of the deep South. On an August day, Baltimore heat can addle one's pate beyond the capacity for much else than a frosted julep, but it seldom attains to the cloying steam-room humidity of swamp-built Washington. The vast broad stretch of the Chesapeake's upper reaches is a firming hand on temperature. Nor does a man often freeze to death in the Chesapeake duck blinds, for even late fall kisses Maryland with the courtesy due an old mistress. And winter, especially on the Eastern Shore, is seldom the season that locks Pennsylvania roads tight on occasion, or that drenches the deeper South in tepid rains until all joy leaves one's being. It is a winter of content.

Let us come into Maryland from the south, as General (then Colonel) Washington often did "for the horse races at Annapolis Towne"—where he lost his lace-ruffed shirt more often than he won. The Maryland Jockey Club—1743—the oldest racing organization on the continent and quite possibly the oldest sporting organization of any kind in the United States, held its original meetings in Annapolis, not moving to Pimlico until 1870.

The town of Annapolis today is one of the most amazing architectural olla-podridas in America. Almost literally between Nick the Greek's and a filling station one will come upon a fabulous example of southern Georgian—still shaded by its ancient elms and not infrequently still occupied by the family that built it seven or eight generations ago, when Annapolis enjoyed perhaps the most brilliant and cultivated society in the colonies—certainly one of the wealthiest, due to its sea-borne commerce, until Baltimore became a port of entry during the Revolution.

By no means has the city's vitality deteriorated with the years. It is a thriving place that has lived through history and with it, coming into these times as a prosperous modern town of small businesses, light manufacture and Bay fishing—with shiny middle-priced cars and well-dressed stenographers in its ancient narrow streets.

Again the anachronism, because those streets are still called Duke of Gloucester, Hanover and King George's, and from the thriving business district rise the spire of St. Anne's Protestant Episcopal Church—a state church in the time of the Royal Colony—and the white dome and pillared portico of the State House built four years before the Revolution and still the seat of government of the State of Maryland.

St. John's College—one of the nation's oldest educational institutions, occupies twenty-six acres in the heart of the older part of town. It began as King William's School, founded in 1696. McDowell Hall, its main building, was erected in the 18th Century as the residence of the royal governors and is still in use. St. John's College bears emphasis, for in an age of specialized education, it is devoted solely to the liberal arts, basing its instruction on the tutorial and seminar rather than the lecture system and endeavoring to educate broadly. Limited to three hundred undergraduates, it is coeducational and non-sectarian and was the first college in Colonial America to prohibit religious discrimination.

Of the United States Naval Academy on the Severn, little can be said that has not already been said. But for those who go down to the sea in ships, either in mind or in body, there is a must at the Academy—the museum of ship models. In days more ancient than our own the building of a ship began with the building of an exact model—the scale being usually standard at one quarter inch to one foot. The model was completed in minute detail to the last copper spike and the last small block of the running gear and was workable throughout. Portions of hull planking were left off for access to interior structure, and portions of decking were removable for the same reason. The model thus became a dynamic three-dimensional blue-print, and the yardmaster worked from it.

The collection of these admiralty models at the Naval Academy is probably the most representative in the world. Most of the little ships whose full-scale counterparts made empire—as well as the ships that challenged it and made the challenge stick—are there. His Majesty's Ship of the Line *Britannia*, 100 guns, and the *U.S.S. Constitution*, *H.M.S. St. George*, 96 guns, and the *Half Moon* and the New Bedford whaler *Niger*, the *U.S.S. Maine*—a whole miniature history of the sea in precise detail.

The worth of the collection in dollars is impossible to estimate. It can be pointed out that such and such fifty-four-inch model would bring $70,000 in the right collector's market, and that $1,000,000 might cover the entire collection. But this is not actually so. So few men are left who can build such ships and time is so short for them.

Leave your car and walk through the Academy grounds to the Museum. Stop at the monuments and read the inscriptions to the men who rose to manhood in the years of other crises, and you will come away more confident of the future, a little lighter of step, a trifle higher of chin. The youthful apprentices you pass will be on the bridges and in the conning towers and cockpits in the years to come, nor will they give up one ringbolt of the ship, either, in their good time.

I never come into Baltimore but once again the fundamental Maryland character comes to mind—self-respecting, well-mannered individualism. Edward Bouchet owned one of the first automobiles in town—a turn-of-the-century Panhard with an open basketwork tonneau and a folding rear step. A thunderous machine of many intrinsic hazards in a day of rutted dirt roads and wooden-planked bridges. Edward and my father and uncle once started for Annapolis in the juggernaut, but a few rollicking miles on the way, my uncle, who had been in the tonneau, turned out to be with them no longer. They retraced their route several miles and found him waiting where a particularly vicious bump had catapulted him. With commendable tribal loyalty to his younger brother, my father suggested to Edward that thereafter he drive more carefully. "Come, come," Edward said. "The car is insured. Everyone who gets into it is insured. Anything or anyone we hit is insured. Why spoil the sport?" Self-respecting, well-mannered individualism.

Baltimore in its older parts is an ugly town unless you love it. If you love it, its personality shines through the scabrous overlay of modern trade and even that attains to beauty by association. Again, even in the old town there are still vignettes of what the city was in the heyday of the Baltimore clipper. Mount Vernon Place still retains a touch of older dignity that would be hard to trump in any other city of the world. So does Washington Place.

There were two Baltimores prior to 1729 but neither one of them took. The exact site of the first is still subject to archaeological debate, and of the second only scant ruins remain. The third and present began life on the north shore of the head of tidewater on the Patapsco River at the point where Jones Falls empties into it and at a time in history when the tobacco and grain planters of the upper Chesapeake country needed a sea terminal nearer than Annapolis. The city grew up around this port function, which still is its modern blood of life. The Patapsco is a deepwater estuary that branches into four arms within the city and offers better than a hundred miles of water front for shipping facilities.

As there were three cities, so there have been three distinct periods in Baltimore history, each leaving its indelible mark upon the modern metropolis. The first was the clipper-ship era, which it knew alike with Boston, New Bedford and Falmouth—when the shipmaster was king of Charles Street, strolling it with a carven gold knob to his ebony stick and a fine powdered wig to his gnarled and weather-beaten head. The fortunes of many old Baltimore families were founded in that period. Boys went aboard Baltimore clippers through the hawsepipe and fought the hard fight aft to the quarterdeck. Shares of cargoes, shares of ships, ships themselves and then whole lines—with the golden profit piling high in vaults blazoned with the old house flags, and no faint shadow of the income tax to lay bony finger upon it.

The second period is stark. The political sentiment of Baltimore was Southern in 1861. Occupied almost from the start by Union troops, the city was harshly disciplined for its political convictions. Its lush trade was disrupted and dissipated by the Union war effort. Private fortunes were broken and pride humbled. Unlike Richmond and Atlanta, Baltimore never had its gallant moment of lost glory. It never took the field for its honor, but lay rather in chains throughout the conflict. The city never fully recovered until after the great fire of 1904.

The final period is today's—Bethlehem Steel's, Alcoa's, United States Industrial Alcohol's and Glenn L. Martin Aircraft's—a teeming metropolis whose telephone book lists branch offices of almost every important industrial operation in the country. It is a prosperous city and a pleasant one. A hard-working city and a playful city. It is a city that graces the fine romantic pen of Van Wyck Mason and the dour vitriol of H. L. Mencken. While the fumes of commerce lace the Bay fog of autumn and tarnish the moon, some of the older men still fence, engaging the sons and grandsons of men they started crossing blades with years ago in the *salles d'armes* of the city. For it is a fencing town still, and beyond New York, Los Angeles, New Orleans, Philadelphia and Chicago, fencing towns are hard to come by, for the sport has no gate to support it, only die-hard devotees, it being an axiom that one must be an accomplished fencer to enjoy watching.

Not so with horses, and Baltimore is a horse town too—with Pimlico the shrine, almost in the heart of the city. The Maryland Jockey Club moved its meetings from Annapolis to Pimlico in 1870, and since then the track has echoed to the hoofbeats of the finest horses of our times—Man o' War, Equipoise, Challedon, Gallant Fox, Citation, Tom Fool, Whirlaway, Count Fleet and Native Dancer. The Preakness gives precedence only to the Kentucky Derby. In fact Man o' War declined the issue in the Derby to wait for the Preakness. And it was at Pimlico that the famous meeting between Seabiscuit and War Admiral took place. "If it's Seabiscuit, take his bit and bridle, Mowbray—and ask him what he'll have."

Laurel has a comfortable sound. Havre de Grace used to tinkle gaily but Pimlico has a joyous whipcrack authenticity—a staccato of turf tradition that has clung to it through the long years and still does. The Futurity, the Pimlico Special, the Dixie, the Baltimore Spring Handicap, the Preakness, the Black-Eyed Susan. *Pimlico.*

In 1650, one Robert Brooke arrived in the Colony from England. He traveled well. With him, in additon to his household and servants, he brought the leading blood of his stable and the cream of his pack. So fox hunting was first introduced to the North American Continent —and the blood of that now-ghostly pack has remained with the Brooke family for three centuries. I would say also that their grand manner of travel had remained unchanged as well, for in an 8000-ton freighter out of Londonderry for Baltimore the winter of 1929, I occupied the next stateroom to a sixteen-hand Irish hunter consigned to one of the distaff descendants of the Brookes in the Green Spring Valley. I wish no misconception made of my use of the word stateroom. There were eight staterooms off the boat deck. Six were occupied by ship's officers. I had the seventh. The hunter had the eighth.

Steeplechasing dates in America from June 7, 1865, at Paterson, New Jersey; but organized hunt racing in the United States today is the history of the Maryland Hunt Cup, the most widely known of the amateur meetings. Long before that unknown Englishman shouted, "Let's race to yon steeple," meaning in a straight line regardless of intervening obstacles, some mad Irishman had invented the Wild Goose Chase, which one supposes called for racing cross-country under the line of flight of an actual wild goose. One likes to believe so anyway, for there is a demented Irish grandeur to the concept. Whatever—the steeplechase in Maryland bears closer affinity to the Irish version than to the English. Some fifty years ago, members of Green Spring Valley Hounds invented a "pounding race" which was a game of mounted follow-the-leader. By competition, casualties and cussedness, they eventually developed a club champion and having done so, looked to greener fields. In 1915 the meeting began to take place annually near Glyndon, on the Worthington Valley estate of J. W. Y. Martin, Esq. From those days to the present, the Maryland Hunt Cup holds almost the same interest nationally, in the field of amateur racing between flags, as the Kentucky Derby and Maryland's own Preakness on the flat. Although the date varies each year, devotees hold standing reservations at the Belvedere Hotel for the Hunt Cup weekends, whenever they fall.

Baltimore is the sacrosanct portals of the Maryland Club at the corner of Charles and Eager streets, where the cooling Tom Collins at one time held military rank. A small one being a Lieutenant Collins, the others progressing in glass size to general-officer rank—and retirement. It is the Bachelors Cotillon, which ranks with the St. Cecilia, and horse-drawn vegetable wagons, hawking still, of a Saturday morning. It is the old Shot Tower in the heart of town and the Baltimore Orioles in the hearts of their fans, and it is the modern Negro housing projects of the city's slum-clearance program.

Baltimore is also Johns Hopkins University. Although the school is known the world over for its primacy in medicine, this fame somewhat shadows Hopkins' other departments. In the College, the basic policy is strong emphasis not on required courses, but on the unity of knowledge, and on the integration of fields of man's activity with other related fields, so that the undergraduate's horizon of understanding widens steadily as he progresses toward his ultimate specialization. The college itself is in Homewood—a beautiful suburb of the city—and has been planned so well in land purchases and bequests that its quiet academic atmosphere will be preserved for years to come.

Baltimore is also the Dandy Fifth Regiment, now Federally designated the 175th Infantry of the 29th Infantry Division. Its Armory is well worth a long hour, for the regimental history in trophies, battle honors and relics is the history of the United States.

Like New York's Seventh, the First City Troop of Philadelphia, and the Richmond Blues, Baltimore's Fifth is a tradition in the land. A military unit with a record of combat second to none. In some respects a hereditary family responsibility and in others a gentlemen's club. Its military history is unbroken since 1774. With the Blue Hen's Chickens of Delaware it took the brunt of Washington's rear-guard action at Long Island. In 1814 it successfully defended Baltimore against the same British force that burned Washington. Baltimore was *not* burned, and the next day one Francis Scott Key observed that the national colors on the Fort McHenry ramparts were still at full staff. (If "the rockets' red glare" ever confused you, they were Congreve rockets, which were the forerunner of the bazooka and used tactically in much the same way.) In the First World War, the Dandy Fifth fought through the miserable and mist-skeined Argonne, and in World War II it hit the Normandy beaches and continued across Europe to make junction on the Elbe River with the Sixth Cavalry Division of the U.S.S.R.

What are such things as battle honors? An empty parade of past glories? I think not. Rather they are a spiritual bank account passed on from grandsire to sire and son against a time of further threat—which is to say today, in this land of the free and home of the brave.

The University of Maryland sprawls ruggedly in white concrete and red brick across College Park, south of Baltimore on U. S. 1. It is a living, personal monument to almost fifty years of effort on the part of Harry Clifton ("Curly") Byrd, the University's president from 1936 to 1954, when he resigned to enter the Democratic lists for governor. A state university in the broadest sense, Maryland serves well the basic and varied educational needs of the state.

North of Baltimore on U. S. 40, in the northeast corner of the state, lie Havre de Grace and Elkton. Of Havre de Grace one need say nothing to those for whom the sound of it sparks the eye of memory. Of Elkton, a thriving commercial town of late years, one need only say that state law has dimmed its Gretna Green reputation. Time was when every road to Elkton bore signs offering to facilitate marriage, each sign promising to cut more of the necessary time and tape than the preceding sign. Package deals of clerk, minister, witnesses, and flowers were offered on a price-war basis. But times have changed. One can still be married in Elkton, but it is no longer the haven for hasty or exhilarated nuptial decision.

To the west of Baltimore, in fact from well within the city limits, the land begins to rise abruptly into the Piedmont, or the eastern slopes of the Appalachian range. This is the threshold of the old agricultural upland of the state, still rich in grains and dairy products, apples, forests, tobacco and fine cattle. Many of the old upland towns still stand with their main-street façades much the same as they were in the days when the brick was handmade to build them: Taneytown, Thurmont, Hagerstown, Cumberland and Frederick of the Barbara Fritchie interpolation, where the immortality of the old girl is secure today in the sales of Barbara Fritchie candy (story free).

This Western Maryland country, rising as it does into the Allegheny Mountains, offers as magnificent a spread of natural beauty as any other terrain in the East. Adequately road-netted throughout, the western counties still offer a certain primeval majesty to the tourist and a paradise to sportsmen. The farms are prosperous small farms in the main, with the little towns comfortable in the present and breathing still a faint buckskin odor of the past: Indian Springs, Accident, Mount Savage, Funkstown.

There is breathlessness to Western Maryland after one crosses the Appalachian Trailway—a sense of quiet expectance in this meeting of past and present. Skirting the winding road ahead is a young man in a brown coat and the scarlet cap of a hunter, his rifle shouldered for safety over the fences. But it needs only the memory of yesterday to change the scarlet to coonskin and the .30–.06 to a Lefever long rifle for the fact to come alive again that he is following Indian spoor, not the track of white-tailed deer.

There are twenty-three counties in Maryland—plus Baltimore, which is not part of a county—and with no exception each one offers some private monument of the days of the Cavalier colony—a great house, perhaps, such as Carrollton or Wye or at least a manor house where someone seated his family in days gone, when land was the essence of wealth and servants were to be had by indenture or purchase in any quantity necessary to comfort.

Carrollton, which originally embraced 17,000 acres of extremely choice and varied lands, was the seat of Maryland's senior Catholic layman in his time, Charles Carroll the Signer. On these lands, at Tuscarora, stands the Old Carroll Mansion which, being built of native limestone, is extremely well preserved. The Darnall House is the oldest seat in good condition still standing on the manor. It is at Rocky Fountain and is one of the ancient landmarks. St. Joseph's Church, also on the manor, is well worth a visit and a prayer and a coin dropped in the alms box. The original seat of the Carrolls was, however, in Howard County at Doughoregan Manor, a magnificent two-story great house over 300 feet long from wing to wing. It is there that the original Charles Carroll is buried, in the family chapel.

This is in no sense a guidebook to these old homes, for dozens of such works are readily available, but one or two others should be mentioned in passing, as particularly outstanding monuments of a past way of life, just as legitimate in its time as the subdivision and the FHA loan of today. For prospect, perhaps no house excels Tulip Hall. It commands West River, looking across a broad stretch of Chesapeake Bay to Kent Island and a long run of the distant haze which is the Eastern Shore. Sotterley, in St. Marys County on the Patuxent, is built in the floor-plan shape of the letter z, a design unique in the state. And finally, for present purposes, Homewood in Baltimore—the house Charles Carroll, of Carrollton, built for his son Charles. This house strikes the architectural keynote to the modern Johns Hopkins University which has developed around it. It is distinctly Jeffersonian in concept and is one of the finest houses to be found anywhere in the world.

From the earliest days of the colony there was a necessary geographical separation of the Western Shore and the Eastern Shore of Maryland by virtue of the broad reaches of Chesapeake Bay. The years crystallized this into cultural and economic differences until today there is strong political schism. You are an Eastern Shoreman first and a Marylander second, and if you are a Western Shoreman first and a Marylander second, you probably follow the Mencken doctrine that all Eastern Shoremen are stubborn and slightly, shall one say, reactionary?

Until very recent years, the flat red soil and sandspit of the Eastern Shore was a fishing and agricultural community throughout its width and length, if one excepts the sea-food canneries and the fruit-preserving enterprises that came into being shortly after the turn of the century. The Pennsylvania Railroad has for years operated a main line down the center of the peninsula from Wilmington to Cape Charles in Virginia, but branch lines to the smaller towns were sketchy, hectic and far between. They operated with charming informality. If a farmer's barn was on fire, the train to Oxford has been known, as late as the early 'thirties, to stop while the engineer organized his passengers into a bucket brigade to put the fire out. His reasoning was fundamental. The immediate fact was the fire. There would be no train behind him until the next day and it made no difference when he arrived in Easton or Oxford because none of his passengers were expected until the train got in.

Informality has been characteristic of the Eastern Shore since the earliest days. It is not necessarily laziness or sloth, nor is it for studied effect. Only an Eastern Shoreman fully understands another and beyond that he has small concern for the outside world, although he nods to it in native courtesy as it passes by. His land is good land for small farming, the mourning dove flies in season, as does the duck. He tongs his oysters when the urge is on him, the crab comes up his creek to grow a new shell and the terrapin grows in his own or a neighbor's sequestered bed. His name is Goldsborough or Tilghman or Lloyd somewhere in his ancestry, and that gives him his land by inheritance for over three centuries. Therefore he feels he has the right to live upon it as he sees fit and to raise his glass in the gallant toast—"Here's to Eastern Shoremen, where'er they may be dispersed."

But of recent years his ancient bailiwick has been invaded. When the Chesapeake Bay Bridge was opened, the Eastern Shore became part of the rest of Maryland almost overnight. When the ubiquitous Du Pont interests put in a nylon plant at Seaford, Delaware, the handwriting was firm upon the wall; the economy of all Caroline County, Maryland, was converted literally overnight from agriculture to manufacturing.

It is inevitable that under the lash of commercial necessity much

of the ancient charm of the Eastern Shore before long will belong
to the memories of very old men—and to history.

How many miles of tidewater wash the Eastern Shore has never
been accurately determined, for each one of its rivers is Bay-
drowned by the tide, as are their hundreds of branching creeks. Talbot County alone enjoys over 900 miles of tidewater lands. In Talbot
three miles by road would at one time bring me from my house to
my neighbor's, whereas the same journey was ninety-four miles by
boat.

This is why Maryland's oldest yacht club—the Chesapeake Bay
Yacht Club—has its clubhouse two miles from the nearest water and
has never had a water station. The members kept their boats at their
own anchorages, and established their clubhouse at the most central
meeting point—Easton, the county seat.

The Miles River Yacht Club is possibly the more active organization at present. Its clubhouse and water station are on the lower
Miles, at St. Michaels, which is an ancient town, almost completely
of the past. From here one can chug up half a dozen creeks by small
boat and see the land still as it was in the days of the Calverts, the
rough-cut creek banks broadening to wheat and cattle acres, with
an ancient manor house still standing—sometimes in sad disrepair,
more often modernized and lived in by more recent owners who
carry on a replica of the pleasant living that the original owners
knew.

The premier manor house of the Eastern Shore is Wye House in
Talbot County. It is not a particularly beautiful structure, but it is
imposing. Wye is a "five-part" house of wood, which is to say it has
a central block and a corridor leading off from each side to an end
wing. In Joan Lloyd's day its interior was much as it had been left
by the Lloyds when year-round residence was discontinued. In the
office to the right of the main entrance there were cabinet drawers
sheafed thick with ancient parchment plantation transactions from
days long before the Revolution. Used only as a summer home, Wye
was nevertheless alive with living. The priceless knife boxes still
stood on the buffet and the portraits of long-dead Lloyds looked
down through a faint gray veil of mildew, due to a lack of winter
heating.

The house looks across the old bowling green to the brick and
lofty arched window bank of the orangery, which is perhaps as fine

a piece of architecture as you will find in all America. There are almost three miles of box hedge in the garden, and eight generations of Lloyds lie in the family cemetery.

The Chesapeake retriever is a Shore dog. In point of legend he is probably the first American dog ever bred, for it is generally conceded that he sprang from a *mésalliance* between a Newfoundland bitch who leaped from the rail of an early Colonial ship and swam ashore and a dog from an Indian encampment, breed unknown, who met destiny with her.

If the bar sinister is part of the retriever's heritage, so, too, is heart. He is a lion in his own country. As the pups of Highland sheep dogs start for the Grampian flocks at six weeks, the Chesapeake pup starts for salt water. He is the complete amphibian. He will submerge his head entirely for his first solid food and has been known in maturity to dive to six or eight feet. He sights his game rather than smells it, because water kills scent. His thick, tight-gnarled coat, with self-generated lanolin, keeps him from waterlogging. He can swim for miles in icy waters and would retrieve a DC-6 if it would float behind him. When there is no shooting, he goes for busmen's holidays and you may meet him swimming miles offshore, and there will be mild reproof in his gentle golden eyes if you take him aboard.

He is a gentleman who will lie by your fire and dream with you without talk. He will guard your children when they toddle near the water—less in fear that they cannot swim than in concern that they may drown before they can hold a gun and fulfill their destiny—and his.

The Chesapeake log canoe, the skipjack, the ram and the bugeye are indigenous to the Bay country and you will still see the bugeye on occasion. Her masts rake aft decisively, which is her distant identification. She is extensively broad-beamed to allow for her shallow draft, which was necessary so that she might push well up into shallow creeks to load agricultural freight in the old days of sail. The broad beam kept her seaworthy for outer Bay navigation, for the Bay, like the Great Lakes, is restless water and its sudden squalls and heavy seaways must be met with respect and consummate seamanship. The Bay has myriad minor victories on its long record of ships one will pass no longer.

For a century past, the entire lower peninsula has lived on borrowed time in the march of commercial development. This was a delightful interlude, for it left the Eastern Shore of Maryland as a living museum of what life had once been in these United States. There are a few horses and rigs on the roads, a hazard to the automobile, right up to today. Customs and manners and habits remained much the same as they had been throughout the 19th Century. There was a legitimate landed gentry and a solid, self-respecting yeomanry, and life just was and it was nice to live it—and it was only seven hours by car from New York.

Half a century ago New Yorkers began to discover it. Mr. Sheiffelin Schuyler purchased Bruff's Island in Talbot County and made a delightful home of it, taking the county to his heart and becoming more a part of it than he was of Schuyler, Chadwick and Burnham in later years. Others followed him, finding in the Shore a place of casual delight and a gentle backwater in which to relax. Pittsburgh and Philadelphia families came down and purchased old manor houses, first to summer in, but more often than not, for permanent homes. The Chryslers and the Raskobs came, and in recent years retired regular officers have found it a pleasant place in which to dream of battles they will never fight again.

It is of the very nature of Maryland and of the Shore that there was no rabid attempt to exploit the influx. Land prices rose with the arrival of money, but not outrageously. There was no boom. One could be taken if one were careless—but not too badly. One's manners and address were the passport and if one seemed a good sort, one was taken to the bosom of the Shore.

The Eastern Shore as it was, and as it still is to an extent, was a charming accident of history. It was Pleasant Valley with the marks of horse's hoofs on the grand staircase because one of the last owners was so attached to his hunter that he was known, on occasion, to ride upstairs to bed on him. It was turkey shoots in the fall and fox hunts *to clean out foxes*—with the hunt on foot, on bicycles, in Model T's and on mules, with the only fillip to decorum being one or two red (not faintly pink) sweaters for warmth. It was the Washington Hotel in Princess Anne ("Built 1744, in the Reign of King George II"), with account books running back to the days of £/s/d, and a double staircase to accommodate ladies in hoopskirts. It was old Col. Oswald Tilghman saying, "I have every expectancy of going to Heaven when I die, for I have never cheated at cards, never killed a man who didn't have an even chance of killing me, and never told a lie in my life—except, of course, to a woman." It was sleepy courthouses

and World War I names on the American Legion honor roll that were
identical with those on the Confederate memorial next to it. It was
Cadet Robert E. Lee's initials scratched on a window pane at Wye
House with the diamond of betrothal of a girl who did not marry
him.

So if it is high time that the oil refineries move in, then they must.
And if the fishing grounds must be churned sterile by the screws of
tugs and liners, and broad meadows be scored by the steel rails of
marshaling yards, and if the manor houses must make way for low-
cost real-estate developments, there is still a moment left to raise
the glass once more and raise it high *"to all Eastern Shoremen, no
matter where dispersed"*—and snap the stem.

Come back with me now across the whole state and pin me down,
if you can, to that which I have assiduously avoided except in titil-
lation—food. The ruffed grouse still runs in Garrett County, with the
wild turkey and the white-tailed deer in Allegany. There are terrapin beds along the Miles and the Choptank—where the legal size
is secondary to the succulence to be enjoyed for a slight infringement
of the law, and the soft-shelled crab comes to Hunting Creek like
the willing bride in youth. The Bay oyster is still the most delectable
this side of anywhere, and a dozen fresh in a pint of pale is still the
finest breakfast in the land when the vapors of a rugged night cling
to the soul.

I will mention no "best" restaurant; some are better, but those
worse cease to exist forthwith. Food anywhere is always what the
eater demands, and Maryland food is so dear to the Maryland palate
that criteria of quality are pre-established. The crab, the oyster, Bay
and offshore fish are a gourmet's delight in almost any hole-in-the-
wall in Maryland's Bay towns. For terrapin one had probably better
wait to reach Baltimore—and I am fully aware that I take my life
in my hands when I say that.

The original and fabulous recipes of Maryland were, in the beginning, the recipes of its homes, kept from generation to generation
in the old kitchen books. More often they were never written down,
for literacy was not a primary virtue of cooks. They were house
dishes. Duck is seldom served in braces, but in dozens rather. Oysters
come by the barrel—or the more delicate bushel. Soft-shelled crabs
in heaps, and if a dish is to be run down for future duplication, its
original source material will probably read "add to taste" or "don't

leave in the oven too long." There is esoteric pride in Maryland cooking and justly, because Maryland hospitality, of which Maryland food is a basic ingredient, has almost completely done away with extreme old age as a cause of death.

But then again, in Maryland, extreme old age has its own definition. I call to mind another grand old Marylander who was wont to start his day with a prebreakfast noggin while he shaved himself with straight edge. Then his doctor told him to have done with the breakfast tot, and word of it reached his boy Sam. There was no drink the next morrow. The old man bellowed down the service stairs in no uncertain terms: "I've been having that whisky peg every morning for sixty years and I've lived to be eighty!" And Sam, quaking even in the whites of his eyes, "I know, suh—but doctah say ef you hadn't, you'd be almost ninety now!"

Of oyster races we must have a word, for it is one of the few events I have ever excelled in. The Chincoteagues would come up the Shore by the barrel, consigned to two eaters, in the heyday of the sport. He who consumed the lesser number raw, paid for the whole. I had done moderately well in the preliminaries—well enough to take on the champion. In pregame quarterbacking I made inquiries and got the supreme accolade—"Mistuh Van is an oyster-eatin' man, but yo're the oysterish."

But it is of terrapin that I wish to speak particularly. You may have it in season almost anywhere in Tidewater Maryland and it will be excellently prepared if you choose the most reputable places in the same careful manner you would choose a lady to wife. But few have had it at its supreme best, as I did when the late Murray Lloyd Gainsborough prepared it for me in Candlewood silver, working by spirit lamp under a portrait of his gray-kepied grandfather and using eighty-year-old amontillado. The equation is mathematical. *Terrapin Maryland is as the youth of the terrapin is to the age of the sherry.*

But then again, I don't doubt for a moment that almost anyone can move to Maryland, go into the insurance business, raise a family and lead a reasonably normal life.

#  Virginia

## by CLIFFORD DOWDEY

One afternoon, some years ago, I was slumped on a New York terrace, feeling poorly, trying to soak up some of the thin warmth. It was spring by the calendar, but there was no fragrance in the air, no lilt, and I mentioned to a friend who had stopped by to see me that I felt nostalgic for the sweet, mellow warmth of the Virginia spring.

What was it about Virginia that exerted such a pull on its sons, my friend asked, and I began to explain it.

Three hours later, he said, "It's five o'clock. Let's go have cocktails."

"You forget I'm sick," I protested.

"You forgot it," he said, "when you started to talk about Virginia."

Love of their land is native to all Virginians, whether they live in the flat, river-drained Tidewater of the East, the richest and most populous and oldest part of the state—where the whole country (America as well as Virginia) began—or in the green, rolling middle country of the Piedmont, the "horse country" that's become a sort of Left Bank for equine-minded millionaires; or in the mountain country of the west, the loveliest part of the state, which includes the magnificent and fabled Shenandoah Valley, the Blue Ridge Mountains, the more rugged valley of the southwest, and the Alleghenies climbing into West Virginia and forming a border with the state which broke off from the Old Dominion.

Even to the most urban Virginian, his state is the land. For its first two and a half centuries Virginia was primarily agricultural, and into my time, I knew no one who did not have kinspeople on farms. We visited them in the summer, driving from some small, wooden depot in a surrey, long after cars were commonplace. On the hot, fragrant land, with its strange murmurous sounds, we were laughed at for jumping at the sight of a harmless black snake and forced by pride into unequal tests of strength. Yet when our country cousins visited us in the city they were welcomed with no spirit of vengeance. Even as children we sensed that they represented the enduring nature of our country—Virginia.

Virginians have an almost universal habit of defending anything about their state with: "Why, it's always been that way." Yet, however bitterly it may be lamented in Virginia, the Old Dominion does change, though changes have to be measured by the ages rather than the years. The main point, of course, is that the character of the state does not change, has never changed, and the people resist any change which might affect that character.

The regional culture of Tidewater, the Piedmont and the mountain country varies widely, even to accents; and interests of the three sections not infrequently clash head on. But, though regional natives may regard one another with polite wariness, or even veiled disapproval, the variety of the regions forms for the Virginian a physical self-sufficiency within his own borders which goes a long way toward explaining his character.

It is not that the state boasts of any single physical glory which some other state doesn't have more of or better; it is simply that to the Virginian everything is here. He has the sea and the mountains, the rolling countryside and the flat, relatively plain stretches of Tidewater. Indeed, the native's attachment to his land is not always because it is beautiful, but because of its association; it was settled by people of his blood, and their blood is in the soil.

In my own Tidewater, the beauty is largely in the eye of the beholder. When a family, like my own, has lived almost 350 years in an area covered by four counties, some magic of association accrues to the land. Yet, many people without personal associations also respond to the magic in the hot, miasmic countryside, as if they too can sense the ghosts in the heavily scented mists.

There is almost a lushness in the wildly growing honeysuckle and creeper, in the ivy on red-brick walls, the pink and white dogwood, the redbud, the splashes of azalea, the slumbrous crape myrtle, the roses, and the fragile lavender of wisteria against iron-grill balconies. Some of the world's finest gardens, now in their third century, grow in Tidewater. Spring comes early, in a sudden flowering, and the summers are long, too long, ordeals of damp, steamy heat.

The dampness comes from the water that drains the low-lying land. In the early days of the planters, water was everything, since it carried their tobacco. And water was everywhere, all flowing toward the Atlantic: brooks into streams, creeks into little rivers, and big rivers into the Chesapeake Bay. The big rivers begin with the Potomac, which forms our northern border with Unionist Maryland (except for the two counties on the Eastern Shore of the Bay; and very vain they are of their separateness). The pleasant Rappahannock, across which Washington threw the silver dollar, flows through the middle of the state. Next come the York and the James, and between them lies the Virginia Peninsula, running 100 miles from Richmond to the Bay.

Though the Peninsula was first known nationally in the Civil War, when McClellan tried to take Richmond from there, the narrow, once-fertile strip was the beginning of our country—and I mean both my native state and the whole nation. There on the swampy, malarial island of Jamestown was born the Virginia idea, for Virginia is both a place and an attitude.

The Virginia idea, it must be clearly understood, was not what is today called the American Dream. The Virginian did not dream of a democracy, with its literal meaning of the rule of the people. His dream was to found an aristocratic republic, in which superior individuals would emerge to rule the many.

While his concept of a social order was the first in America, it influenced only Southern states, to which Virginians migrated in frontier days. The rest of America adopted the New England order so completely that it even swallowed the Puritan myth of founding the country at Plymouth Rock in 1620, thirteen years after its actual founding at Jamestown. One of the reasons for the Virginian's indifference to this historical distortion is some doubt in his mind that he wants the United States attributed to him. Having no more promotional zeal than a desiccated member of some old-guard club, the Virginian even permits his children to celebrate Thanksgiving in the style of the Pilgrims, though he knows that the first Thanksgiving in America was celebrated at Berkeley Plantation, up the James River from Jamestown, in 1619—well before the Puritans had even sailed for Virginia and been blown off their course.

To begin at the beginning, the first Britishers to establish a permanent colony of English-speaking people on this continent arrived in Virginia in 1607 in three small ships of twenty, forty, and one hundred tons. Unlike the *Mayflower* descendants, Virginians do not agree even on the names of the ships. One was definitely *Discovery,* the second either *Goodspeed* or *Godspeed,* and the third either *Susan* or *Sarah Constant.* This uncertainty exists because the Virginian, for all the jibes at his "looking backward," has a casual acceptance of his past. To him the past is a continuous stream that flows into and interweaves with the present. Because the same people have been in the same place for three and a half centuries, he can be forgiven if he takes legends about his past for granted rather than trying to prove them. But, as a result, he lives under some awesome misconceptions—though even the misconceptions form part of the attitude.

For instance, the Virginian accepts as dogma that the first settlers to arrive in the naked wilderness were all younger sons of great British families. By record, few great British houses sent sons to Virginia in 1607, and none left any descendants in America. Indeed, not one of Virginia's distinguished families can trace its ancestry to *any* of the 104 tough-bitten adventurers who arrived on those first three ships. A kinsman of my ancestors, Humphrey Blount, came in the first waves, but he was killed by an Indian arrow in 1613. Others died of starvation or malaria, and still others went back to England.

Despite the high mortality of America's first pioneers, others kept coming. More Blounts came, in 1619, and founded one of the half-dozen families who derive from what is called "the early adventurers"—those who came before 1622. These early adventurers were a curious cross section of British life. They were artisans and cutthroats, farmer sons of the minor country gentry, an assortment of minor rogues, London clerks and adventurers such as Captain John Smith, that great swaggerer and agile penman whose life was saved by Pocahontas, and a collection of the useless who could write "Gent." after their names as a symbol that they were above gainful employment. All came as the Forty-Niners went to California two and a half centuries later—to get rich. But they differed from all other American pioneers (except those of South Carolina). They came with the aristocratic dream. As early as 1648, a newly success-ful adventurer was commended because "he lives bravely, keeps a good house, and is a true lover of Virginia." That "true lover" was the ultimate test. It meant identification with the land and accept-ance of the responsibility for the social order.

Even while these "early adventurers" were fighting Indians, starva-tion and malaria, with the dying outnumbering the survivors ten to one, they peered over their crude palisades and dreamed of the grandeur of plantations to be wrought from the rich land. While their London backers were abandoning hope of the Colony's survival, men were staking out plantations in this Indian-infested wilderness, and laying the foundation for an aristocratic society.

The might of their dream is attested by the enduring nature of the society they erected, complete with its myths and legends and dogmas. Nor was the superior individual they expected that society to produce an idle fancy: in its full flowering, the Virginia Dynasty produced more great men in a comparative time and place than ever before or since on this continent. Men who would have been giants in another time and place were overshadowed by such contempo-raries as Jefferson, Washington, Patrick Henry, George Mason, John Marshall, Madison, Monroe and the Lees.

They risked their lives in a Revolution, yet their dream never changed: they wanted freedom from a British king, personal liberty, but no change in their order. Jefferson, because of his grotesquely misinterpreted democratic ideals, was regarded as a dangerous rene-gade by his own family. His cousin, the brilliant eccentric, John Ran-dolph of Roanoke, spoke more typically when he said, "I am an aristocrat; I love liberty; I hate equality."

By 1775, the Colony had spread far beyond the fortified little set-tlement on Jamestown Island, and the capital had shifted to Wil-liamsburg, midway between Jamestown on one river and Yorktown on the other. During the Revolution the capital moved to Richmond, then a trading post at the head of tidewater on the James River, and the splendor of plantation life on the Peninsula began to decline. The rule of the planter class, which instead of giving leadership had clung to its privileges in personal uses of power, was ended, along with so much else, by the Civil War.

"The war," as Virginians still refer to it, was not a matter of two armies fighting to a decision. For an entire decade the state was fought over, lived off, and ruled by occupation forces. Its civilization was destroyed more totally than that of any avowed enemy of the United States.

The planter class, for all its power, had been unable to swing Virginia into the secession column—until Lincoln called on Virginia for troops to invade her sister states. Then, with the soil they loved threatened by invasion, the people themselves rose against the Yankees. In an unsurpassed rush of volunteering, they formed the nucleus of the greatest army man for man in the Western world—Lee's legendary "Army of Northern Virginia." Robert E. Lee, a disbeliever in slavery and a nonsecessionist, became a god of the South not only because he fought off six Union armies and their generals (including Grant), but because he personified the patriarchal leader of the legendary aristocratic society. From that Virginia society came other members of the planter class, like Jeb Stuart and A. P. Hill and the great fox hunter, Turner Ashby; there came members of the then unprivileged class, like Stonewall Jackson and Dick Ewell (a schoolteacher's son whose grandfather had been an intimate of George Washington); there came professional soldiers like Joe Johnston and "Prince John" Magruder and George Pickett.

Virginia lost its ruling class (the good with the evil), its manpower, its wealth, its place in the sun. It did not lose its glory, for the Army of Northern Virginia had no habit of defeat. The state's educated class and its virile young were sacrificed in a cause that was lost, but the only state marker of defeat you'll find in Virginia is on the last retreat that ended at Appomattox Court House.

In coming back from the total wreckage, with cities and even college buildings burned, Virginia started with nothing. Freed Negroes and dispossessed planters followed lean mules on adjoining fields under the merciless sun. Or they trekked in carts and on foot in a melancholy stream into the rebuilding cities, seeking any kind of work.

When my grandfather first came to Richmond, he had only the clothes he had worn at Appomattox. As buttons bearing Confederate insignia were forbidden, and he was too poor to buy buttons or pins, his patched gray jacket was held together by thorns. The Confederate buttons (which I still have) were kept as a secret badge of honor.

Instead of the conquest changing the Virginian, it clarified and accentuated all that he already was. He brought to the city his courtesy, which deepened in this time of trouble; he brought his manners, which grew softer in his gentleness to his fellows; he brought his proudest inner possession, a sense of honor.

There were some with the greed to take advantage of the distress of their countrymen. Even during the brief lifetime of the Confederacy, some cold-headed operators suspected the Rebels' future and hoarded their gold. They broke the creed; they were not true lovers of Virginia. The true lover went down the financial drain and, like virtue, this has its own reward to his descendants.

During the physical and financial rebuilding of Virginia, new powers emerged and took up where the lordly planters left off. Their rise was in the Virginia tradition of the rule of the many by the superior few, for they were superior in about all that counted in those desperate days—money.

It was not until a half century later, in the Great Depression, that the arrogant grip of these neo-Bourbons was cracked by young ambitious Virginians with their way to make and nowhere else to go; yet with all their energy and determination, they could not have done it without help from the North. Under the enchantment of the Virginia way of life, Northerners began buying up old places so that they could live as the planters had. They have come in such numbers that we called the movement "the second invasion." Incredible as it seems to those of us who went North, they come to Virginia for opportunity! They are ambitious for a place for their families rather than for personal fortune.

The center of Virginia's parochial society has always been the family—indeed, the state is something of a family. The basis of this is not, as is commonly thought, "ancestor worship," though certainly there are awesome bores on the subject who reverently muse over familiar genealogical charts in some personal telling of their beads. The family is simply the thing of value, as is wealth (or conspicuous consumption) in a money society. And those qualities regarded most highly by a Virginia family, in addition to honor and gentle manners, are lack of suspiciousness and of pushiness.

It is these standards, as clearly understood and as unarticulated as an unwritten code, that have attracted the new Northerners. In Tidewater, we have been particularly fortunate in those from the North who have bought the great river plantations which grew from the Jamestown dream. By restoring these places to their ancient splendor, they are making the Virginia peninsula even more appealing to visitors.

This narrow strip of land, between the James and the York rivers, contains Jamestown, the first settlement, of which little more than the ruins of the church remain. Across the peninsula, at Yorktown, are the breastworks where George Washington won our independence. And between the two, Mr. Rockefeller's $61,500,000 dream shows Williamsburg as it was in Colonial days when it was capital of Virginia.

In conducting informal tours for friends from the North, I have found that nothing so stirs the visitor, so evokes the past, as the river plantations, those individual principalities which formed the dynastic society of Virginia. Today, these show places—Westover, Brandon, Berkeley, Shirley and many others—are open to the public during Garden Week, April 21–28, and the grounds may be seen the year around.

Probably the purest evocation is captured at Westover, where the house of most classic beauty in Colonial America was designed by that learned dandy, William Byrd II. He collected the largest library in the Colonies, was a good writer himself, and his love of elegance was matched by an infallible taste.

The neighboring Berkeley Plantation is open the year around to visitors, and was originally the home of the Harrisons, one of whom was a signer of the Declaration and another was a President and the grandfather of a President. The lawn is so vast that McClellan's army of more than 100,000 camped between the house and the river, on the retreat from Richmond. Under the influence of its repose, a Union general and his bugler experimented with a new "Lights Out" bugle call which, sweeping through the Union army, was adopted as "Taps."

Taps had long since blown for the grandeur that was Berkeley when the present owner's father bought it as a summer place around the turn of the century, and started his son on the career of returning a plantation to its former glory.

Similar houses are owned by similar converts all over the state, though some remain in the possession of the original families. Descendants of the famous "King" Carter still live at Sabine Hall, built in 1730, which continues as a working plantation; and their neighbors the Tayloes still occupy the charming Mount Airy. Both of these show places are in what Virginians call the Northern Neck, where

George Washington was born at Wakefield and Robert E. Lee grew up in the now state-owned Stratford Hall.

The Neck is bounded on three sides by water—on the east by Chesapeake Bay, on the south by the Rappahannock, on the north by the Potomac—and until bridges and highways were built in recent years it remained, quite deliberately, inaccessible. Perhaps the least known region outside the state, it has the steadiest influx of Northerners who come to settle with neither horses nor old houses on their minds. They are substantial people and they blend without a rift into an order that has never been disturbed even by a railroad.

Though no state of its size includes larger areas of water, and no state was more influenced in its development by the use of waterways, Virginians as a whole were not a seafaring or water-minded people. Of course, fishing, for food and sport, has been a part of Virginia life since Jamestown, and boating has long been a pleasure to many, but it is distinctly within my memory that yacht clubs became fashionable along the countless waters that flow into the Bay.

The slow turn to water sports has a counterpart in Virginia's failure to see the full possibilities of its magnificent Hampton Roads. This immense harbor, with its fifty miles of shoreline, serves Norfolk and Portsmouth on the south bank of the James and Newport News on the north shore. But the shipyards and navy yards have drawn thousands of that "restless proletariat" which the planters feared from the beginning, and which the gentry still fear. As a result there is a stalemate between those who want to change nothing and those who want to change the existing order. And the Hampton Roads area—with nearly one fifth of the state's population and more than one fifth of its purchasing power—has been grievously neglected.

While the Northern Neck is similar to the Peninsula, physically and culturally, both being parts of Tidewater, a marked change comes in the Piedmont, now called "the horse country." The land of the Piedmont is open and rolling, with limestone deposits essential for good grass and for building strong bones. But actually the whole state is horse country. The first Thoroughbred to be imported to America for breeding (Bulle Rock, in 1730) stood near Richmond, and the two greatest Virginia money winners were bred in the Shenandoah Valley and in Hanover County, the land of Patrick Henry.

Racehorses for the commercial tracks, however, are not the abiding interest of Virginians. In typical anachronism, horse to them means "hunter"—a Thoroughbred trained to hunt, to be shown as a hunter, and to race in steeplechases where the prizes are cups and the glory local. As deep in my memory as the legends of the Confederacy are pictures of red-faced women, in severely tailored black hunting clothes, jumping sidesaddle at local horse shows, and of the beauty and excitement of colored silks fluttering in the autumn wind as gentleman riders maneuvered their horses for the start of a race over timber.

In steeplechases, *aficionados* stand beside a jump, and I remember my father holding me up and I wildly shaking as he forgot me to yell to a friend who had fallen right before our eyes: "Go on, Ira, you're still good for second money!"

We rode in childhood, and those who didn't ride knew about horses, as kids today know about automobiles. And, as with kids today, some of us never loved anything else so much. Those who earn their living in other ways make horses (hunters) an avocation. And natives of the so-called "horse country" (more properly hunt country) can support themselves by serving as trainers and riders of hunters for the equine-minded millionaires from the North.

The Piedmont has the best hunter show in America at Warrenton, one of the oldest and probably the best breeding show at Upperville, and long-established horse shows and racing around Leesburg, Middleburg, Culpeper and Berryville. And in those areas are the breeding farms of Mrs. Dodge Sloan, Mike Phipps, Paul Mellon and—at Montpelier, the former home of President Madison, near Orange—of Mrs. Marion du Pont Scott, one of our greatest converts.

The social *éclat* of the horse probably extends from its association with the plantation culture. Since all things in Virginia change by the ages, the native is just facing the fact that horses might, after all, be an anachronism.

From George Washington to Harry Byrd, Defenders of the Faith have been essentially defenders of the status quo. Yet George Washington led a revolution for which he would have been hanged had it failed and Harry Byrd introduced a minor social revolution when he induced industries to come to Virginia. Resistance continues, however, to large-scale industrialization which would change the social structure. "It's better to have more, scattered small industries," Senator Byrd once said. "They are the backbone."

The sharp cleavage between entrenched wealth and the rest of the population does not exist in a state where the drayman (as an actual example) might be the cousin of a former President—and not boast about it either. Families long distinguished produce clerks who prefer scholarship, or hunting, or the bottle to a more solid success. At the Richmond German, a dance assembly at which young ladies are presented to society, the clerk will appear in seedy evening clothes where the tycoon in finest raiment may not enter.

Because of the prevalence of this gentry, there is a body of voters who would so bitterly resent being referred to as "the people" that no demagogue has held power in the history of the state.

The setting of the University of Virginia is in that blandly enchanting countryside of Albemarle County, in the Blue Ridge foothills, where the spirit of the Sage of Monticello mingles with the aura of horse-shows and fox-hunts, old houses and new fashion. The old part of the university—the center unit of Jefferson's design—is probably unequaled by any other American college for its original and classic beauty. There are many colleges in the state—William and Mary, second oldest in the country; Washington and Lee; V.M.I., the only college in the country to possess a battle flag, won at New Market in the Civil War; Hollins and Randolph-Macon, Westhampton and Mary Washington, and the rare loveliness of Sweet Briar. But the university, on its evocative grounds at Charlottesville, exemplifies an undercover struggle between entrenched privilege and the vitality of a people.

This endless struggle is as old as the Old Dominion, though you will never hear a Virginian refer to it on the outside. They all join the myth which goes, "befoh de wah we had plenty of slaves." In the same way the Confederate Army had, as far as I know from listening to stories about my friends' ancestors, only two privates—Margaret Mitchell's grandfather and my own. We had a club called "Sons and Daughters of Men in the Ranks," but we had to take in Yankees to swell the membership.

Once I tried to disentangle history from the legend, in a lecture I gave to a woman's club in Richmond. I praised the courage and the hardihood of our pioneer ancestors who made reality out of a dream. I was nearly run out of town. They were no more eager to be reminded of their rough beginnings than is the lady who has recently escaped from the other side of the tracks.

So provincial-minded is the Virginian that once when I referred to "the Valley," I was astonished at a Mid Westerner who asked, "What Valley?" To the Virginian, there is only one—the Shenandoah. It was the first Great Valley of this country, through which the later-day (18th Century) pioneers passed to the then distant west of Kentucky, and where a unique culture developed among the fugitives from the plantation class in Tidewater and the migrant Dutch, Mennonites and Quakers from Pennsylvania.

The hardy Pennsylvania Dutch placed their impress on the Valley with their self-sufficient farms and self-reliant frontier democracy, but they, too, were swayed by the Jamestown dream. Though it was not plantation country (with slave labor and money crops), the fertile limestone soil yielded a fat competence which gave to the Valley people a continuity of sturdy individualism with manners indistinguishable from those of lordly Tidewater. Like the rest of the state, they have a great love of their region, but unlike most of the state, they live in an area of physical beauty by any standards. Lying between the Blue Ridge and the Alleghenies, it is a magnificently contoured country where, in the 100-odd miles from Winchester to Lexington, tourists enter pre-Revolutionary towns with time-mellowed red brick houses built flush on the street.

During the Civil War the Valley suffered a devastation so complete that the executioner, a coarse little man named Sheridan, reported that "if a crow flies over the Valley, he'll have to carry his own knapsack." The Valley people had survived Indians before Yankees, and they took in stride the burning of their barns and houses, the running off of their stock—even the loss of their men, who were the nucleus of Stonewall Jackson's army.

If I were going to visit the Valley for the first time I would start on the Skyline Drive, running along the crest of the Blue Ridge, from which you can see the whole incredible panorama. In the Blue Ridge are the only people who speak Elizabethan English in America. Their ancestors were fugitives from the planter control of Tidewater, and they built a rude, aristocratic republic in the hills. They created mountaineer baronies, in a wild version of the James River plantations—for they, too, held the attitude, in their way. They made love and moonshine, played old ballads on the zither, and, illiterate and unknowledgeable of the world, survived with pride and good manners.

These hill clans also held their rude domains southward in the misty Blue Ridge, where Virginia borders Tennessee. This is the land

of John Fox's *Trail of the Lonesome Pine,* of the laurel and rhododendron, galax and hemlock and dogwood, of fine beef cattle, of
deer and bear, wild boar and wild turkey, quail and possum and
rabbit. This handsome country could well become a new garden spot.
The rolling green hills offer the coolest area in those truly epic summers which may be one explanation for the lack of dynamism in the
Old Dominion.

French aristocrats found a haven here from the Revolution, building the lost town of New Paris; Sherwood Anderson found a sanctuary here; and here Bob Porterfield found a unique success. Bob
had gone to New York to take a fling at the theater. When the depression struck, he returned home with a troupe of hungry actors,
and an idea. Abingdon offered him the use of the opera house in the
century-old town hall, with the jail underneath the stage, and the
Barter Theater was born. Nobody made any money that first summer
but they all ate high on the hog. When one of the patrons brought a
young pig, Bob Porterfield raised it and from successive litters produced hams, with which he pays royalties to such playwrights as
Noel Coward and Robert Sherwood. Only G. B. Shaw returned the
ham with the querulous protest, "Don't you know I'm a vegetarian?"
It became the first state-sponsored theater in the country, and one of
its functions today is to take "live theater" to people all over the
state.

Virginia also takes art masterpieces to the people in the nation's
first Artmobile—an air-conditioned trailer provided by that institu-
tional department store, Richmond's Miller & Rhoads, with paintings
belonging to Walter Chrysler, Jr., and operated by the Virginia
Museum of Fine Arts, one of America's finest small museums.

To the West are the Alleghenies, and to the northwest the counties
which seceded from the mother state during the Civil War and
formed West Virginia. When the dividing line was drawn down the
Alleghenies, the story goes, Unionists gave the surveyors such lavish
hospitality that they drew what amounted to a drunken line, veer-
ing east whenever they came to a particularly desirable spot, such as
White Sulphur Springs with its Greenbrier.

The Virginia part of the mountains is the nearest thing, after the
Shenandoah Valley, to the truly spectacular in the state. Certainly
the valley running from Warm Springs to Monterey is one of the
loveliest in our land. This whole section is filled with springs, though
most of the spas, which go back to post-Revolutionary days, today
are ghost towns. You can visit perhaps a dozen abandoned spas

where the grandees and their ladies once waltzed to Strauss after taking the sulphur baths; I never look at these places of vanished grandeur, like Old Sweet and Sweet Chalybeate (Cal-lib-e-at), without a yearning that they might be resurrected. But then there would be neons and gambling-hells, and the ghosts would slink away.

Today there is a new fashion in these hills—fugitives from the cities walk the quiet streams, fishing and lolling, and hoping that no one discovers their favorite spots. There are long-discovered places here, too, that are never out of fashion, like the Homestead at Hot Springs. In these resorts, as in the whole state, there is nothing of what is called "night life," and the Virginian who has tasted the entertainment of New York may groan despairingly at the lack.

In the state that invented the lavish table, where into my grandparents' day dinner lasted from 2:30 to 5:00, its capital was designed for gracious living. Built on a succession of hills rising above the James River and dominated by the white-pillared capitol planned by Jefferson when he was governor, Richmond with its "city villas" (as Dickens called them), was, in the words of a foreign visitor, "a charming, small world capital." Most of the villas are gone now, victims of "progress," and a tourist needs a guide to find the survivors which still evoke the vanished era. With them went the bars, and the hotel restaurants, which survived five Union armies—but not a Methodist bishop named Cannon who brought prohibition to Virginia, and, under stress of World War I, to the United States. Today, even in Virginia's citadel, good food can be found only in homes—and then without taint of French sauces.

Virginia food is both indigenous and a result of the war. In their desperate poverty, the three things they had were corn, hogs and greens. From these came the batterbread, the pork and sausage, and the turnip greens cooked in hog fat. To these were added that curious squash called simlin, a combination of black-eyed peas and stewed tomatoes, fresh- and salt-water fish (with roe herring as a breakfast dish and shad roe as a delicacy), game and fowl, "local beef" and "local liver," fruit and melons, crabs and clams and all varieties of oysters, of which the best are baked with ham, and ham itself—which is a separate subject. The pale meat sold as "Virginia Ham" is a Northern product. The true Virginia ham comes from peanut-fed hogs, and the meat is dark, very strong, and most Virginians can afford it only at Christmas. With a small hot biscuit, it is the favorite of all cocktail hors d'oeuvres.

The thin, crisp biscuit, and all hot bread, takes the place in the

Virginian's diet that sauces occupy in that of the European-minded
gourmet. No Virginian, no matter where he lives, ever forgets the
hot rolls on his mother's table.

In this, as in all things, the Virginian remains uninfluenced by
what other people do or like. In drinks, his bourbon comes from
native corn, and if you offer a simple Virginian Scotch, he'll say, "No,
I prefer whisky." For my own martinis, I can rarely find a customer
(unless a Northern visitor) and this includes the after-church hour of
a very light drink. I refer here to the Episcopal Church. The after-
church drinking hour of its communicants goes back at least to the
early 18th Century when William Byrd at Westover became so overwhelmed with Sunday guests, some of whom stayed on for the following Sunday, that he caused the church to be moved. You can still
see it, small and simple and wholly charming, and wonder how so
few communicants could have caused one host so much trouble.

The ruralites who voted prohibition to Virginia are no longer in
numerical predominance, but they are so solid, so impassioned, and
so traditional, that no bloc is strong enough to defy them. They are
supported by the bootleggers who flourish in a state where alcohol
may not be served in a public place—but only bought by the bottle
in a state store. The poor people say: "You can't buy a drink in Virginia: you have to buy a drunk." The rich belong to clubs in which
bartenders serve them as long as the members keep bottles in their
lockers.

This blight of the rural rule on night life does not apply to the
cities' Negro population. Since the Negroes have no intention of
abiding by a law they regard as manifestly absurd, the police are
said to permit orderly, established fleshpots to remain open. To walk
down famed and wide-open Second Street in Richmond after midnight (when the rest of the city is as silent as a graveyard) is to
discover one of the complexities of "segregation" in a traditional society composed of two thirds white and one third Negro.

Between the educated, privileged Negro and the ignorant there
is a chasm deeper and wider than anything in white society. As everything in Virginia extends from the past, this is an extension of the
historic cleavage between the house people and the field hands. But
the drivers of Cadillacs are sometimes black people of field-hand
heritage who toot imperiously at Negroes of obviously gentle background.

The Negroes have made an art of manners. Except for some of the

hostile young and those who stand stiffly on the dignity of new privilege, they equal the whites in courtesy and friendliness, and between
the two races there exists a casual intimacy outsiders find difficult
to believe. My nurse Edmonia, who had been my father's nurse, had
before that been my grandmother's companion, and the two girls had
come to Richmond together after the Civil War at the age of sixteen.
As Edmonia and my grandmother grew old together, a silent rivalry
developed between the old ladies. They occupied adjoining rooms
and they vied with each other for the most presents—handkerchiefs,
petticoats, stockings, even the bright patches which went into the
quilts they made. When they died, the drawers of their bureaus were
crowded with objects they had never worn and which seemed to
settle the rivalry at a draw. I remember them with enduring love, as
my daughters will remember Lucille, their younger version of Edmonia. This is not offered as any pious benediction on "the race
problem," but only as a statement of things as they exist in a world
changing too fast.

This, then, is the culture which has endured without essential
change for nearly three and a half centuries, and which, in the words
of Senator Byrd, expects to continue a long time yet. It gave America
its greatest revolutionary leaders, it produced more presidents than
any other state, it gave to the Confederacy Robert E. Lee, the
nation's supreme military leader—yet it makes no great American
claims. It is Virginia.

The people of no other state are more passionately identified with
their own land place. When traveling abroad and asked their nationality, they will invariably reply, "I am a Virginian." In fact, I
know of one internationally famous gentleman who carried this to its
ultimate parochialism. When he was presented to the Court and the
King asked where he was from, he replied, "Fauquier County, sir—
the upper end."

In *The History and Present State of Virginia*, written in 1705, an
observer said, "Here is the most Good-nature, and Hospitality prac-
tis'd in the World, both towards Friends and Strangers. . . . If there
happen to be a Churl, that either out of Covetousness, or Ill-nature,
won't comply with this generous Custom, he has a mark of Infamy
set upon him. . . ." To our strength and weakness, this could be
written today. For even in changing by the ages, Virginia does not
change in the attitude.

# West Virginia

## by JOHN KNOWLES

Many people who have not visited a state think of it as a particular color; for me Florida is bright yellow, Louisiana russet, Alabama clay red. I believe that many who have not seen my home state, West Virginia, think of it as gray. But in fact it is the greenest of states—mountains like tight green clouds, valleys of every shade of green with rivers of plated green moving through them. Lining the banks of the Kanawha River, which flows across the southern part of the state, are gray coal mines and chemical plants in gray towns; but everywhere the natural green encroaches against them, as though to squeeze out the thin line of industry separating the green of the mountains from the green of the river. And right now, in the fall, vivid colors are breaking out from the greenness to bring the whole state alive. Day by day these big hills are brightening, the hues increasing in intensity until you can almost hear the clashing brightnesses—trees of burning scarlet and gentle yellow vying on the hillsides among the rocks and evergreens.

West Virginia is a lovely state to look at and an odd one to think about. Many Americans seem not to be really sure it exists. "West Virginia?" new acquaintances exclaim hazily when I tell them where I'm from. "How far do you live from Richmond?"

This is a very tactless question, and I reply distantly that I have no idea how far I live from Richmond, but that I live seventy-five miles south of Wheeling, and two hundred miles north of Charleston (West Virginia). This rarely helps them to place me geographically, but it clears the air of that specter which haunts the state, the memory of that outraged, abandoned mother, Virginia.

We West Virginians are very tired of being considered inhabitants of just a dominion of the Old Dominion; we would like to make it clear that our state has been independent for ninety years. Some residents take a very strong line about this and always refer to it in conversation as *"West—By God—Virginia!"* We know it is the state people forget when trying to memorize the fifty, that it's the state they aren't sure whether they've driven through or not, that it's one of the hillbilly states. Nevertheless, West Virginia stands right in the middle of American history and development, and has caught and held a great deal of both within its impossibly irregular borders.

The result is a stew, a conglomeration of old-new, radical-conservative, Southern-Northern, rich-poor, ridiculous-dignified American characteristics. That is why West Virginia is "pivotal" politically and gets so much attention during Presidential campaigns. No one can call the turn here; like a completely open-minded man, the state has made a habit of accepting both sides of our national arguments, indiscriminately including Yankees and Rebels, Bourbons and labor agitators, old-stock mountaineers and Sicilian coal miners, beauty and unsightliness. You think you have it when you see the steel mills, the coal mines, the great chemical plants; you think again when you hear the Southern accents, feel the relaxed pace of life, the lazy laissez-faire sociability. Then you see a log-cabin mountain family and you don't know what to think. What you may finally conclude is that this ignored little state somehow incorporates the major elements of life throughout the nation.

On the map my state is probably the funniest-looking state in the Union; it resembles a pork chop with the narrow end splayed. The square southwestern corner of Pennsylvania divides northern West Virginia into two panhandles, one dwindling up between Pennsylvania and Ohio and the other extending eastward like a limp arm between Maryland and Virginia. The northern panhandle, which contains Wheeling with its heavy steel production, points a symbolic finger at the industrial northeast. The quietly rural eastern panhandle curves back toward the Old South. And this is the dual role of the state, bustlingly industrial yet lackadaisically Southern.

But both panhandles spring from the hillbilly heart of the state, the steep little Allegheny Mountains to which old farms and forests cling, and through which dirt roads connect such unassertive villages as Romance and Kentuck, and Losie and Chloe. The names of these quiescent mountain settlements tell something of the state: Alice, Burnt House, Thursday, Shock, Lost Creek (pronounced "crick"), Cucumber, Cyclone, Hurricane, Gip, Heaters, Hominy Falls, Coco, Quick, Lone Cedar. West Virginians are a literal-minded breed, and if Gip seems to be the most appropriate name for their town, that's what they call it, without apology.

I have always wanted to humor those people who insist on finding Li'l Abner in every farm youth, whose ears ring with imagined buckshot on every country road. I've always wanted to bring one of them into my state over a back road with the properly grimy name of Blacksville Road. You approach the Mason-Dixon line from Pittsburgh over a fine Pennsylvania highway, a smooth, wide strip of cement gliding gracefully through pleasant farmland. Suddenly this show-off road ends. There is a kind of dropping sensation; the car springs, which have been relaxing, are thrown into violent action. There is a sharp left turn, a sharper right turn, a stop sign. You are in Blacksville, West Virginia.

Beyond the stop sign you encounter your first real West Virginia turn, a tight hairpin curve starting up the side of a mountain. Reaching the top you plummet straight down into a narrow valley. Now you are really in the hills of West Virginia and the scenery is chaotic. There are few orderly perspectives in this state; the great geological upheavals which buried vast fortunes in minerals underground threw up hills, ridges and mountains every which way on the surface. Valleys start east, turn north, end going west. Hills rise in steep juxtaposition, forested so thickly that it seems you could walk on the treetops. Wide meadows tilt at improbable angles with haystacks perched on them like rakish hats, fences running busily down, around and over, trying to organize the disorder.

As you follow the wanderings of the Blacksville Road, narrowed by now to the interesting West Virginia width of one-and-a-half cars, cows appear grazing almost directly above, while on the other side you look down the chimney of a farmhouse. Surely West Virginia has the only cornfield which is entered by stepladder, the only mule which must be hoisted by block and tackle to the fields. The famous story of the city motorist in the hill-farming country has at least poetic truth. He is driving along the bottom of a steep-walled valley when there is a sudden flurry of dust ahead. He pulls up, and as the cloud settles he sees a rather battered farmer stamping his foot in anger. "What in the world happened?" asks the motorist.

"That's the third time," replies the farmer disgustedly, "I've fell outen that cornfield this mornin'."

The Blacksville Road is stereotyped West Virginia. But presently you wind along a little stream, a "run" as it is called here, pass through a 100-year-old covered bridge, and enter Fairmont, my home town. Here the myth of West Virginia the mountain wilderness must die.

Fairmont is the seventh largest city in the state. The houses are wired for electricity. The streets are paved. This is an important center in the richest bituminous-coal seam in the world, but there are no mines to be seen, they are all in the outlying districts. John L. Lewis commands allegiance underground, and a publication called the *Southern Social Register* attempts to hold sway above. On Saturday nights, good old mountain music twangs out from local hot spots, while in the high-school auditorium the Fairmont Symphony Orchestra plays Mozart. The town has drawn inhabitants from everywhere, Alabama drawls mingling easily with the heightened diction of Massachusetts. Italians, Russians and Poles were brought in to work the mines early in this century, and now their children and grandchildren are being assimilated into Fairmont.

I suppose all these influences make Fairmont a confusing place culturally, but it has a special, typically West Virginia atmosphere which blends them all comfortably. The best term I can think of to describe it is laissez-faire, which would be translated there as "let it be." I saw it most clearly in action one day when I was sixteen. At the time I was taking out a girl who was very attractive but not very mechanically minded, and one afternoon she inadvertently drove her family's new sedan into a grocery store.

"That's terrible," said her mother when she heard of it. "And you children wanted to use the car tonight, didn't you?"

We admitted as much, rather hopelessly now, in view of the accordion folds in the car's front end.

Her father, less easily discouraged, drove the car around the block. "It won't turn left," he reported, "but it turns right well enough."

"That's wonderful," said her mother. She handed me the keys. "*You* do the driving," she said, "and don't try to turn left."

We spent a fine evening going from place to place in large right-hand circles. No one worried about the cost of the repairs. The car would get repaired eventually. And it did.

This balanced ease is one characteristic of West Virginia; another is the ghosts. In Fairmont we consort with the shades of vanished wealth. We grew up with their haunts around us: an empty mansion, modeled after Inverness Castle in Scotland, with crenelated towers and a swimming pool in the basement; pillared homesteads turned into dancing schools; gracious family residences become Red Cross headquarters, or the meeting rooms of the Women's Club, or torn down to make way for gasoline stations. The time was the end of the '30's, and these were the homes built, and during the depression abandoned, by the coal "barons" of Fairmont.

The two most elaborate were within a couple of blocks of our home. Higate, which has become a rest home for nuns, was a majestic place behind its ornate black iron fence, with gravel drives curving through immaculate lawns, its boxwood hedges, tennis court, and the formal vistas of its landscaping. Coal was king in 1910 when J. E. Watson built it, and it was a kingly domicile, a half-timbered Elizabethan country manor house set down in the coal fields.

Next to it is Watson Farms, the original family place. The twenty-room main house ignores its setting just as blandly as the other great Fairmont houses do—it is Spanish Mission design. So are its gatehouse and the carriage house and the other outbuildings. But the grounds, rolling land thick with rhododendron and evergreens, used to be pure West Virginia, and it must have been a fine home at its height, just before the first World War. Clarence Watson was in the Senate then, and William Jennings Bryan came to visit him there.

Today the main house, the carriage house and barn have been broken up into apartments. New ranch-style houses have sprung up like toadstools on the grounds, and the original old log-cabin Watson home, freshly painted, is now a nice suburban residence.

It's all there on Watson Farms—the simple pioneer days, the lush impermanent boom, economic collapse, and then recovery to the pleasant broadened level of middle-class living in the 1950's. It's the social history of Northern West Virginia, and it suggests the social evolution of the United States.

The age of flight presents a real challenge in West Virginia, where nothing is flat except the river surfaces, and not always those. Charleston, the capital, has solved the problem by blasting the tops off three mountains, moving 9,000,000 cubic yards of earth, and setting down on the resultant plateau an $8,500,000 airport. This is Kanawha Airport, the city's current pride. It is served by four air lines and offers what is probably the most comfortable entrance to the state.

With a population of about 90,000 and over 200,000 in the surrounding metropolitan area, Charleston is the center of the state's most thickly settled area. It has more physical dignity than any other West Virginia city, not having been dropped in a hollow or perched on a mountainside. It extends back in an orderly manner from the north bank of the majestic Great Kanawha River, with a splendid, Chicagoesque shore front and a wide boulevard paralleling the river the whole length of the city.

Charleston has a cultural life in keeping with its urbane appearance; a symphony orchestra and even a chamber-music group are maintained, a little theater flourishes, public forums are held, touring Broadway plays come and are welcomed.

The Kanawha Boulevard leads on to the downtown center of Charleston, with the South Hills, a handsome residential district, overlooking it from the opposite bank. Motoring along this drive you pass a symmetrical red-brick house, Georgian colonial in design, graceful and refined in aspect—the governor's residence. And next to it, thoroughly overshadowing it, rises the large, impressive, extensive, ornate, three-winged, U-shaped, Corinthian-pillared, gold-domed, 300-foot-high, $10,000,000 State Capitol.

There are at least two reasons why a small state such as West Virginia should have so elaborate a capitol. One is that, until it was erected in 1932, the official headquarters of the state shuttled four times between Wheeling and Charleston, and the present edifice settles by its sheer size and immovability where the state government will sit for a long time to come. It is also the solidest and weightiest proof that the state is 100 per cent independent of Mother Virginia, a fact which we West Virginians hope to see gain general recognition.

You can also fly into Wheeling, up in the northern panhandle, your plane nosing down on the mountain-surrounded airport like a stalling dive bomber. This is West Virginia's third largest and perhaps best-known city, thanks to its pun-evoking name. (Sample gag: America's most difficult national project is Wheeling West Virginia.) But with its Northern orientation, this original capital of the state doesn't worry over the jokes and wheezes.

Wheeling Downs, the city's race track on an island in the Ohio River, is a beautiful sports center, with its bright grandstand and clubhouse, its landscaped grounds, its shining Thoroughbreds. During the fifty-five days of racing there, which end about October first, the city takes on a dashing air, slightly lawless and western, very big-time for West Virginia.

On the outskirts of town unrolls 808-acre Oglebay Park, a gracious old plantation turned into a municipal playground. For a city of Wheeling's modest size, Oglebay Park is a major accomplishment in recreational diversity. Outdoor operas, folk dancing, flower shows, turkey shoots, swimming carnivals, horse shows, carillon concerts, golf, tennis, riding, hiking and many other sports, symphony programs—it's a very diverse list.

Wheeling has too much to offer to mind being laughed at, and more than enough industries, 400 of them, manufacturing everything from stogies to steel, to be able to afford a few jokes at its expense.

You can come by train from Washington to Grafton, the noted northern West Virginia rail hub, but I cannot recommend this route. The trip could be spectacularly scenic, the train climbing up and plunging down the Alleghenies, curving around horseshoe bends like a dog chasing its own tail. But whenever the scenery has really caught your attention the train is sure to dive into some tunnel, and all becomes gray and black. I think it was Irvin S. Cobb who described this route as the longest tunnel in the world, interrupted by occasional air vents.

Arriving at Grafton will confirm all your worst fears about West Virginia. Here the first battle of the Civil War was fought, or rather not fought: the Confederates evacuated the town before advancing Union troops without firing a shot, pausing only long enough to burn bridges and mess up the town generally. Grafton has been disordered ever since, a gray, sagging place, its narrow streets crawling miserably up a steep hillside. Whatever isn't gray is black, and while it is a busy rail center, it has looked abandoned as long as I can remember.

Grafton is what some outlanders expect of West Virginia, and once they have seen it, especially if it is their first impression of the state, they often develop an irritating habit of gauging everything else by it. "Yes, this is nice," they'll admit when shown one of the state's numberless scenic beauties, "but of course I knew *everything* couldn't be like Grafton." For them, everything really is; West Virginia remains gray in their imaginations.

But I still haven't pointed out the real way to come to West Virginia. Coming by train to Grafton is not recommended, and the Blacksville Road should be attempted only by the most expert drivers. Come instead to Harpers Ferry, at the easternmost tip of the state, fifty-five miles west of Washington, D.C. Thomas Jefferson said the view here, where the Shenandoah River flows into the Potomac through a gap in the Blue Ridge Mountains, was worth a trip across the Atlantic. The main highway by-passes the Ferry now and you may miss the turn-off, but don't let that worry you for the moment. A few miles farther on is Charles Town and old West Virginia, the farthest outpost of the mint-julep country, the northern end of that gracious arc of pillars and soft accents and fine horses, the center of which is somewhere near Atlanta. In its most Rebel moods this area, the extreme eastern panhandle of the state, considers the West Virginians beyond the mountains a band of shirt-sleeved Yankee boors and still comes to a boil over the outrage of 1863.

In that pivotal year in our history, just ten days before the Battle of Gettysburg, West Virginia joined the divided Union. The eastern panhandle, overwhelmingly sympathetic to the South, had no wish to be in this oddity of a state, this secession from the Secession. But they were given no real choice. The Baltimore and Ohio Railroad passed through these counties, and the Government in Washington, busily carving West Virginia out of Confederate Virginia, tacked the eastern panhandle onto the new state so that the B & O would be officially in northern territory. Charles Town has never forgotten that it was railroaded into West Virginia.

In West Virginia the conflict was a civil war in the bitterest sense, a war within a state, with the battles lines of allegiance running down the center of main streets, through back yards and barnyards, and cutting cruelly through the middle of family homes. The eastern panhandle, politically in the North, its loyalties and men with the South, suffered most. Harpers Ferry was battered by successive captures and recaptures, Romney changed hands fifty-six times, Charles Town was ruined.

The old wrongs, the dead conflicts, have slowly taken the life from Harpers Ferry. The state recently bought more than 400 acres in and around the town and donated them to the country for preservation as a national monument. Harpers Ferry clusters around the base and climbs up the sides of a steep hump of land between the Shenandoah and Potomac Rivers; the rivers join just beyond the town, Maryland and Virginia are represented across the water by impressive cliffs, and the spirit of John Brown marches on here as nowhere else.

At a time when advocating the abolition of slavery was a most inflammatory attitude, Brown was the most militant of abolitionists. Fresh from the warfare in Kansas over slavery, he attacked Harpers Ferry in 1859 to free the slaves in that area. He also thought he might start a government of his own there, hustling Negroes by this route from Southern slavery to Northern freedom.

John Brown's raid, together with the war it forecast, arrested the development of the town. Harpers Ferry is motionless today; only about 800 inhabitants remain—there is no industry, no business section, no real vitality. Relics of the past are scattered carelessly through it, and nature has moved to take possession again. The handsome early 19th Century houses near the center of town are collapsing, undercut by floods, war and poverty. Old ladies slip along the silent streets, old men hole up with stray dogs in historic, decadent mansions.

Unless the visitor knows something about the raid and about the Civil War in this area, he will find Harpers Ferry only an uninteresting shell. On the bottom land between the town and the river junction, outlined in white flagstones on a sunken lawn, is the site of the Armory which was seized by Brown and his band of twenty-two men, and where they were besieged by United States troops under Brevet Colonel Robert E. Lee. Near the Armory site a small white monument has been erected in memory of John Brown, the great abolitionist and hero of the North. But you can't get away unchallenged with *that* kind of thing in ambiguous West Virginia, so close by it the United Daughters of the Confederacy have placed a boulder to Heywood Shepherd, loyal servant of the South. A Negro, Shepherd was stationmaster at Harpers Ferry, and failed to stop quickly enough when Brown's men cried halt. They shot him. "He exemplifies the character and faithfulness of thousands of Negroes," wrote the United Daughters in their inscription.

A little distance up the street, hewn out of native rock, are the steep natural stone steps which ran with gore during the Civil War. At the top of them is the sagging mansion of the founder of the town, Robert Harper, and beyond it, up a little trail, is the ruin of

St. John's Episcopal Church, which was used as a hospital during the war. The Gothic walls and empty windows remain, the roof is gone, four trees grow up through the nave and vines cling everywhere. Farther along the trail a great rock threatens at any moment to plunge down a cliffside into the Shenandoah River; Jefferson stood on it to make his remark about the view, which is a little obstructed now by the wild fingers of television aerials. It's a fine view, but mortifying as it is to contradict Jefferson, I don't think it was ever worth a trip across the Atlantic.

At the top of the path, on the grounds of Storer College, is John Brown's Fort. Actually a fire-engine house, the fort was down by the river when Brown was besieged and captured in it. After the raid it became famous, and was shipped to the Chicago Exposition of 1893 and moved here and there before winding up on its present site. It's a righteous little structure, one and a half stories high, with arched windows and topped by a cupola. It is a museum today, and also a kind of shrine to the man who achieved such an odd immortality there.

It's interesting that he chose this spot as the place where he could stand to move the whole nation. The raid was a typically West Virginia adventure, very small and irregular, presumptuous, almost silly; yet reverberating outward in all directions, forecasting the future, crystallizing a national dilemma.

John Brown in legend and Tidewater elegance in life dominate this northeastern tip of West Virginia. You will find the Old South in Charles Town today, patched up physically and emotionally, slaveless but still served by Negroes, horsy as ever. The magnificent manor homes built by George Washington's relatives around Charles Town are occupied once more; Claymont Court, erected by his grandnephew Bushrod, has been restored, and a swimming pool and one or two other modern touches added. But it remains antebellum, a spacious yellow-brick mansion with slave quarters attached to the main house by walled courtyards, and a wide veranda, which all plantation homes must have, overlooking a sloping terrace. "Visitors Welcome" reads a sign at the main gate, just as it should at a Southern home.

Apple growing and cattle have restored the prosperity of Charles Town, scenery has drawn the tourists, and horse racing is the main diversion. None of the national front-page horses appear; huge purses are not won. I don't believe the Duke and Duchess of Windsor have ever attended, but people from the panhandle, people from Virginia and Maryland and the District of Columbia enjoy it very much. My sister and a couple of her sheltered friends used to go alone to the races when they were fourteen and no one ever feared for their morals.

Ed Blake, editor of a local newspaper, has a reason for the courtly atmosphere of life around Charles Town. "Good soil," he said recently, "it always draws good people. This is the best farming land in the state, along with the Greenbrier Valley in the south end. They breed wonderful cattle there. Why, down in the Greenbrier Valley there's more bluegrass than in the whole state of Kentucky—and you can quote me on that." I do so with pleasure, and I believe it.

The Greenbrier Valley is another fragment of the Old South in West Virginia, and it has that vivid greenness which bluegrass produces. As in the eastern panhandle, there are the white wooden fences here, but they bring a serene simplicity to this landscape, they seem to be holding it together. It is completely unlike the pitching hills and distracted fences of northern West Virginia; here the hills are in order and at rest, the fences bright and changeless. And here, whitest of all, is the Greenbrier Hotel at White Sulphur Springs, where everything to be painted is painted white, leaving the lawns and shrubbery, the trees and surrounding hills in deep green. It is the vacation pride of West Virginia, and while it has always wished it were a Virginia resort again, as it was before the Civil War, we are glad to have it in our state.

Directly across the state, in the southwestern corner next to Kentucky, life is as different as can be found. Rustic living and revival religion set the tone, people are just folks, and horses are not for racing or riding, they're for work.

Logan, West Virginia, the center of this rugged country, has its own legendary figure—that scourge of the mountains, Devil Anse Hatfield. Captain Anderson Hatfield, as he is referred to on his tombstone, was almost John Brown's equal in righteousness and easily his equal in lawlessness. Both men conceived of themselves as bigger than life, both led bands of killers for reasons their instincts told them were good, and society brought them both to account—well, almost; Brown, who was of course the greater figure and ever uncompromising, was executed. Devil Anse kind of played along with society and died quietly in bed, at the age of eighty-two, from pneumonia. But long before that, he had been stripped of his power as chieftain of the Hatfield clan, the hated McCoys of Kentucky could walk with comparative safety along the streets of Logan, and society had restricted him, like a lesser Napoleon, to a patch of mountains around his home. He used to come into Logan on Saturdays from his farm, his beard spreading down to his chest, "a nice, quiet fellow," one of the elders of Logan told me.

I was glad to hear this because I was just a shade uneasy in Logan. People in Fairmont had filled my ears with warnings. "You'd better carry a gun when you go to Logan," they said. "Don't get drunk on moonshine, don't act like a revenuer, and don't talk Yankee." When I arrived in the narrow, jammed streets of Logan, with mountain bluffs surrounding the town like fortifications, I had a sudden uneasy feeling, as I got out of the car, that I might be lined up in someone's gun sights.

The old-timer briskly dismissed Logan's feuding reputation. Like everyone in that country today, he is anxious to forget the primitive past. Log cabins, he points out, have almost disappeared. The roads have improved to the point where horses are no longer needed to haul cars up the mountains during wet weather. Electricity is everywhere. The children go to school, and the men seldom carry guns.

"My father came here in '71," he said, "and it was quiet, peaceable, neighborly. There were a few fights, what I mean a man might get killed, just like anywhere. But nothing serious."

He spoke in the warm, expressive way of West Virginians, using a wide range of tone, slurring over a few words to descend emphatically on the important one.

"Devil Anse used to call on our family every couple of weeks," he went on, "and I was up to his house once, with my daddy. Very nice old man, Devil Anse was."

He told me that the Hatfield Cemetery, with a monument to Anse, was at Omar, a few miles away. I asked him to describe the monument but he said it was "just another stone to me, I didn't pay it much mind." So I went to see for myself.

On the road I had to stop at an intersection and a tall boy of about thirteen, with red-brown hair and the calm, fine-boned highland face came to the window of the car. "Goin' to Omar?" he asked.

I said I was, and without another word he got in. I asked whether he could show me where the Hatfield Cemetery was, and he said he could. We drove along in silence for a while, and then he said, "Pull in here."

I stopped, and the boy got out and pointed up a steep hillside. "The cemetery's up thar," he said.

I started up the rocky path and the boy followed. "Are you coming along?"

"Yup," he said. We climbed in silence, and at the top of the path saw a No Trespassing sign over the name J. D. Hatfield. Almost secure in the old fellow's peaceful picture of the hills, I went by it with only a momentary jouncing on the nerves, to look at the graves, perhaps thirty of them, ascending the cleared slope. Devil Anse, in white Italian marble, looms over the burial ground. He stands erect, in frock coat and leggings, gazing paternally across the hills. A lone fir tree stands beside him and two of his sons, killed on the same day, are buried at his feet.

"My aunt lies up thar," said the boy suddenly, pointing farther up the hill. I looked at her grave and the others, with withered wreaths on their markers, forgotten bouquets here and there, the grass overgrown all around.

This was the ending then of the bitter vendetta. On Devil Anse's monument his children are listed, among them Jonse, who started it all in 1882 by running off with Rosanna McCoy. Of course fighting had broken out before that between the McCoys on the Kentucky side of the Tug River and the Hatfields on the West Virginia side, but Jonse and Rosanna really ignited it. Then followed the ambushings, the kidnappings and slaughterings, the pitched battles, the burning of the McCoy leader's cabin, the ineffectual indictments (both families controlled law enforcement in their respective counties). Above the din of border warfare the governors of Kentucky and West Virginia argued furiously about who had invaded whose state, and who should surrender which feudist to whom.

The feud simmered down during the '90's, and the coming of the railroad to Logan in 1904 extinguished it. There was too much valuable coal up those narrow hollows to have them a battleground, too much good timber stood on the mountains to leave them forever a no-man's-land. Money dragged law and order willy-nilly into Logan County, and the day came when the Hatfields began laying to rest in their cemetery relatives who had died from natural causes.

The boy and I returned to the car and drove back down the road.

"Bob Hatfield's store," he said, pointing to a little homely country store at the side of the road. We stopped there and met Bob, a jolly fat man in rimless glasses wearing a shirt gaudy as a beach umbrella. He was filling a little girl's order and teasing her affectionately. "Sassiest customer I ever did see," he exclaimed about her to the world in general. I noticed the latest in chlorophylled, ammoniated tooth pastes on his shelves, and thought how far we were from Devil Anse. Then I heard a very un-West Virginia voice coming from the back room, and looking in, saw a television screen occupied by Bishop Fulton J. Sheen, lecturing on Freud.

Right then I abandoned the idea of finding any real mountaineers.

Driving away, I mentioned to the boy that, judging from laughing Bob Hatfield, the days of violence were over.

"Yeah, he's always jokin'," agreed the boy. But he added, "One time we's fishing on his land, and he took after us with a shotgun."

That night I drove away from Logan feeling that certainly it was peaceful and all the hillbilly clichés were wrong, but that like a quiet fire far down in a mine, a trace of lonely clannish implacability remained.

So it is in West Virginia—a chopped up, heterogeneous area where each part has only a limited understanding and not much admiration for the other parts. Considering its surface ruggedness, it is something of a tribute to western man that two million people settled there at all.

The Indians didn't try. They reserved it for animals, and judging from the game still there, it must have been a very happy hunting ground. Today armies of deer roam among the mountains and can be seen bounding across busy highways. Grouse, wild turkey, raccoon, black bear and other game fill the state with sport. On autumn days, with the mountainsides celebrating by lighting up the trees, and the lifting wind carrying animal scents and spinning leaves and the blurred crack of shotguns—on such days the notion of West Virginia as a gray industrial hole vanishes.

A state as historically, geographically and culturally ambiguous as West Virginia has a hard time taking a stand on most of our national issues. For example, West Virginia is unshakably on the fence with regard to Negroes. They vote, and they ride where they wish in buses. But they sit in the balconies of theaters, and accept other less obtrusive segregation. They are not second-class citizens and they are not first-class citizens.

The state straddles liquor with equally determined irresoluteness. West Virginia is dry, with liquor legally sold only in state-operated stores. But numberless "clubs" with a couple of dollars membership fee have sprung up where bars operate more or less openly. And then there are just plain bars, without any pretense at being clubs, doing good business. Gambling, rackets, political graft, all have their place in the West Virginia as in the national picture. Being such a compromise of a state, West Virginia is strategically placed to hold a mirror up to our national manners—the gyrations around the green tables of Nevada, the political scandals of New York, the racial inequalities of Mississippi, all are reflected there. Unselective like a mirror, West Virginia catches these images as well as the better ones.

Perhaps then if we could find the typical West Virginian we would have the typical American—what a boon he would be to all the poll takers and opinion samplers and everyone with something to sell. But I cannot find such an essence; it isn't John W. Davis of Clarksburg, who ran for President in 1924; or Louis Johnson of Clarksburg, who was Secretary of Defense for a while; or Jack Dempsey, who loosened up his championship muscles in the Logan coal mines; or Wheeling's gift to the Metropolitan Opera, Eleanor Steber. It's not Ed Blake or Bob Hatfield, or Wib Whited or anyone I know, and it undoubtedly isn't me.

There was a roving pioneer named Adam O'Brien who lived in West Virginia after the Revolution. I don't think he's this archetype, either, but there is something in his last sorrowful judgment of this region which carries across a century and a half. "Those varmints, the sheriffs and constables, are worse than the Indians," he exclaimed, "because you can kill Indians and you dare not kill sheriffs." Times have changed considerably since then—the Indians are gone, for one thing—but this still sounds very much like the natural, not too law-abiding, slightly irreverent voice of West Virginia.

# Kentucky

## by A. B. GUTHRIE, JR.

The typical Kentuckian is a goateed colonel with a thirst.

He is a barefoot mountain boy with an itchy finger on a flintlock.

He's the owner of a mortgaged plantation and a Thoroughbred foal with the look of eagles in its eyes.

He's a backwoods demagogue who can't spell demagogue.

He's a Southern gentleman.

He's a private enterpriser, a dealer in corn squeezin's, and no revenooer better show his nose.

He's Li'l Abner, Devil Anse Hatfield, the Little Shepherd of Kingdom Come, Private Tussie, Happy Chandler, and Gracious Living by Ancestry out of Bluegrass by Ol' Virginny.

He is all these things, and so, of course, he's none of them.

Kentucky?

It's a heaven of a place (or, to give proper order to an old comparison, heaven is a Kaintuck of a place).

It's a brier patch.

It's Dark and Bloody Ground.

It's bluegrass and juleps and women fair beyond the fortune of any other realm, not excepting the Egyptian.

It is eroded and sequestered hillsides; it is coal mines in the mountains; it is race tracks in the great meadow.

It's all these and none of them, typically, either.

If you must catalogue Kentuckians, go to the writings of the Rev. Mr. Timothy Flint, a New Englander whose summing up defies improvement after more than one hundred and twenty-five years. "The people of this state have a character as strongly marked by nationality as those of any state in the union," he wrote. After respectful passes at their origins, high spirits, courage and tendency to extremes he went on, "When a Kentuckian presents himself in another state, as a candidate for an office, in competition with a candidate from another state, other circumstances being equal, the Kentuckian carries it. Wherever the Kentuckian travels, he earnestly and affectionately remembers his native hills and plains. . . . No country will bear a comparison with his country; no people with his people. The English are said to go into battle with a song about roast beef in their mouths. When the Kentuckian encounters the dangers of battle, or any kind, when he is even on board a foundering ship, his last exclamation is, 'Hurrah for old Kentucky.'"

The resident is likely to divide Kentucky into three regions—Western, Bluegrass, and Eastern. The historian says there are seven natural geographical divisions—the Bluegrass, the Knobs, the Kentucky Mountains, the Pennyroyal, the Western Coal Field, the Jackson Purchase, and the Ohio River Flood Plain. The geologist argues for eight, and, by a stricter re-division, comes out with a total of thirteen.

Either of the two professional lists shows the geographical variety of the state and helps to explain the variety of humanity. The economist could follow with data underscoring the immense differences in per-capita income and natural wealth. The Bluegrass has been called the garden spot of the world. Burley tobacco, the farmer's big cash crop, thrives there as perhaps nowhere else. Beef and lamb grow prime. The Thoroughbred horse develops a stamina unequaled —from the intake of limestone from limestone waters, Bluegrass boosters will tell you. Lexington prospers uncommonly, largely from agriculture. Louisville and Jefferson County are in the big money. They produce or process paint, metals, cigarettes, whisky, beer, machinery, rubber, printing, meat, and chemicals. Paducah, Ashland, and Covington, like smaller towns along the Ohio where industry has tended to concentrate, can boast of factories and payrolls.

When the mines are operating, the coal towns in the eastern and western fields have money, if not always beauty; for coal is Kentucky's biggest export—the biggest, that is, if you exclude the brains the state ships out. Kentucky stands third among the states in coal production, surpassed only by Pennsylvania and West Virginia.

To the list of "have" communities must be added the cities, towns, and counties supported by Kentucky's multi-million-dollar tobacco crop, by the distillation of whisky, by the production of cattle and sheep and hogs, of small grains and corn, by the sale of clay and fluorspar and timber, by the presence of a chance factory or an oil field.

By contrast there are counties desperately poor, so poor that their often dense population can be accounted for only by the absence of known opportunity elsewhere and the countryman's unease outside his old surroundings. There are counties that can't raise enough tax money to operate properly the bare agencies of government. There are towns that can't afford to build sewage systems or to purify water contaminated by people farther up the creek who can't afford sewerage either. There are counties without a bank. There are patches of tobacco and corn on eroding hillsides so steep as to give pause to a goat. There are towns and counties without anything like adequate medical service. There are others without any dentists at all.

A Kentucky newspaperman despondently told me one day that he doubted that Kentucky should have been made a state. It was too various. Bounded for more than half its coast by the crazy meanderings of the Ohio River, it had no unity except touchy loyalty. More than that, its attraction in the west was to St. Louis, in the south to Memphis, Nashville, Knoxville and Chattanooga, in the north to Cincinnati. That last attachment, incidentally, gives to Covington a unique distinction. It's the largest city in the United States without a hotel more ambitious than a rooming house; Cincinnati, just across the river, exerts a corner on the trade. The newsman concluded that only Louisville, pulling on southern Indiana towns, and northern Kentucky, through the tolerated gambling joints that fleece the Ohio lambs, tended to reverse the outbound stream.

He was a little too optimistic. At least four of the clubs in Newport and Covington, including the lush spots, are owned all or in part by a Cleveland syndicate. Thus the stakes lost in Kentucky by Ohioans go back to Ohio along with the losses of Kentuckians.

Beverly Hills, built on a hillside a mile south of Newport, provides investment opportunities in the most elegant of surroundings. It is thickly carpeted. Its long, delicately illuminated oval bar glows with polished glass. Its dining room will seat eight hundred people. Its ceilings are artistically contoured. It puts on a floor show.

Upstairs is the business. Waiting for the man with the dice to roll an eight the hard way, I counted one chuck-a-luck game, two black-jack games, two roulette wheels, and four crap tables. The man sevened. "New shooter," the stick man crooned. "Get your bets down. New shooter coming out." Two dealers sold chips, paid them out and pulled them in. On a raised platform a spotter watched the turn of the dice. Chips sold from a dollar up.

Beverly Hills is just one of perhaps a dozen well-known gambling places and one of scores of spots, ranging down to what are called "Bust-out joints," where a man may risk a buck on a race or a roll of the dice.

Ten days after my researches the games closed down, victims of a combination of politics and righteous wrath. I have spoken of them in the present tense, however, thinking it risky to lay away patients with such demonstrated recuperative powers.

For a variety of good reasons northern Kentucky doesn't give to the state the popular characterization that, say, Butte gives to Montana or Reno to Nevada. One reason is the older and profounder conception of Kentucky as the arch border state, the hapless but difficult neutral of the Civil War, so riven internally that brother fought brother and father fought son, offended, violated, levied on by North and South alike. It was a state without a nation, a tieless territory of ferment, antagonisms, shifting indignations. If the Rebels made Federals of some Rebels, the Federals made Rebels of more Federals. Right after the war northern papers were calling Kentucky the most disloyal state of all. That charge may be argued, but not the statement that Kentuckians nevertheless were a sturdy and independent lot. And not the fact that nowhere was the internal conflict sorer.

Those experiences lie deep, if often unrecognized, in the make-up of Kentucky. The outward signs of the old schism are evident today. Eastern Kentucky, a community of small freeholders without slaves, sided with the Union; today, by and large, it votes Republican. Central and Western Kentucky, with their slave-worked plantations, were sympathetic to the South. Their present political preferences reflect the fact.

The United Daughters of the Confederacy object to "Civil War." They say "War Between the States," thus re-emphasizing the South's answer to a question grown moot. They don't like the Federal Government any too well, either. Lexington members were disturbed just a little while back by the indifferent care given the Confederate plot in the Lexington cemetery. The superintendent advised them that the Government would assume the upkeep if the Daughters would deed the plot to it. Already the Federal burial ground was under such an arrangement.

What! asked the ladies. Give anything to the Union! Never! They didn't either.

Such manifestations, though, are vestigial. Kentucky bears the scars of the 1860's, in places to be suggested later, but they don't hurt much anymore. No longer, except by courtesy to history, is this the arch border state. The rebel yell died with old Colonel Dick Redd, who used to sound off in his cracked voice as he rode his chestnut charger up and down the streets of a Lexington that already in the 1920's regarded him as a curiosity. The term, Yankee, rooted loosely in the old struggle has been extended to designate any rude outlander from beyond the Ohio River, and is employed by Democrat and Republican alike. The descendants of Union men suffer the praises of Stonewall Jackson and Robert E. Lee. I know Democrats who yield to none in their admiration of Lincoln. Negroes vote. They have ever since the War Between the States.

One afternoon I asked a half-dozen all-wool-and-a-yard-wide Kentuckians where I'd find a hotbed of the Confederacy. One said well, maybe Hopkinsville. One guessed, maybe, Danville. One said western Kentucky had a parcel of Rebels—he wouldn't know which town, though. One said he reckoned Lexington had about as much of the old spirit as any place. They agreed that feelings weren't what they used to be; too many things had come between.

The conflict today perhaps can be described best as one of traditionalism versus change. Even the tardiness with which the old political cleavage is yielding to the realities of economics reflects habit more than conviction. It is fashion, not passion. It illustrates not the border quality of Kentucky but the reluctance to change with the changing times.

Examples, big and small, evidence the sentiment that what was good enough for grandpa is good enough for me. Until quite recently Kentuckians built houses like those already built, shying away from experimental and functional architecture, from picture-window modernism. In about 1940, when Dr. Frank L. McVey, then president of the University of Kentucky, put up a flat-topped, functional home, the curious jammed traffic by his door. Business houses were slow to install air conditioning; you almost would have thought they figured to sweat this fancy out. New-fangled apparatus, the gadgets and gimcracks of industry, come late to the state. The citizenry insists on keeping a constitution adopted in 1891. One of its provisions, of course now inoperative under national law, denies suffrage and office to women. Another puts in the oath of office for officials and attorneys a solemn declaration that the oath-taker never has engaged in a duel either as principal or second.

Until the election of 1949 all public officers except the governor were held to a maximum salary of $5000 annually. Variously and reversely construed by the Court of Appeals, this constitutional provision raised hob. The trained men whom the state needed couldn't be suckered into services that paid so little. Public health, road construction, park development, education—nearly every service of state, indeed, was crippled by the limitation. Yet an amendment to liberalize it carried by less than 20,000, despite the efforts of both parties and the vigorous backing of the state administration. Even so, its passage was a great victory. Previous campaigns all had failed. So had a campaign for a constitutional convention. What if the constitution was old? one opponent asked; so were the Ten Commandments.

It is easy but not quite accurate to imagine the citizenry rigidly divided into sides, the traditionalists here, the progressives there, like teams in a tug of war. The split tends to run deeper, into the personality of the individual, who finds himself torn between old loyalties and new attractions and needs. On no issue is the line-up entirely ready-made.

Neither, by any means, are differences in attitudes altogether geographical, though one part of Kentucky is likely to regard another with suspicion, condescension, or even disdain. Tradition has its ancient lovers in industrialized Louisville and the manored Bluegrass as well as in the hinterlands to east and west. The cries for change rise from mountain and municipality.

Into the contest and its recurring results, however, enters the disparity of financial circumstance. By contrast with industrialists, Bluegrass planters, coal-mine operators and professional men in fat surroundings, there are thousands of men scratching for life on leached slopes and worn swales.

Five thousand dollars a year for politicians and professors! That's a fortune! The plight of these people creates a general insufficiency, despite the state's spotted riches.

East and south of the Bluegrass you come quickly to some of the less-favored land. If your route and time are right, you see occasional scrawny livestock, forlorn hillside corn, cabins weathering to pieces in ravines, women, maybe barefoot, in sacklike dresses. And children, of course. Children always. These sights aren't invariable but they're far from rare. Then, if you follow the road I took recently, you come to the coalfields and to Harlan.

Two young miners—Warren Till and Harold Coldiron—were waiting for me there. They were sharp and personable boys, so sharp and personable that it seemed a pity they should have entered an uncertain and static employment from which, the saying is, a man never escapes. They didn't feel that way, though, not altogether. Harlan was home. Other jobs were scarce and, by contrast, dinky. Fourteen seventy-five a day was good money, even if it didn't average out to a great deal, what with strikes and limited work weeks and all. More —and this was my inference—a man who didn't work in the mines might be suspected of cowardice.

Harlan is a small and busy town situated in the valley of the upper Cumberland. Out from it are clusters of uniform frame houses, mostly perched on stilts. These belong to the operators, or sometimes to private investors, and are rented by miners, few of whom own their own homes. Eastward along through the neighboring settlement of Evarts you catch glimpses of mine openings, rubbles of slate, and conveyers angled white on the hillsides. In the summer the valley is green and lovely despite these scars. In the winter, with the flanking mountains whiskered by leafless trees, it is pretty drear.

Here on a May day in 1931 was fought the "Battle of Evarts," a battle which touched off a decade of violence, bloodshed and terrorism. A group of mine guards led by a deputy sheriff encountered a crew of union pickets at an Evarts mine. Someone started shooting. Three mine guards and one miner lay dead when the party was over.

Before comparative peace came to Harlan more men died, the National Guard marched in again and again, the La Follette Civil Liberties Committee held hearings that astonished the nation, Governor Happy Chandler tangled with John L. Lewis, and representatives of the newly formed civil-liberties unit of the Department of Justice appeared on the scene. Meantime, there were wholesale indictments, trials, charges, reports. A state commission said after study, "It is almost unbelievable that anywhere in a free and democratic nation such as ours, conditions can be found as bad as they are in Harlan County."

We drove from downtown Harlan and followed a street like a neglected alley and came to a huddle of dwellings and a front porch where half a dozen Negroes had gathered to pass the Sunday morning. We got out and squatted on the ground and fell into conversation. Most of the Negroes were transplanted Alabamans, and most of them were mine-car loaders and got paid on a tonnage basis. Sometimes they earned more, sometimes less, than shift men.

"This man wants to know about coal mining," Warren said.

A small Negro with a cinnamon skin and yellow eyes and a face without illusion looked me up and down. "It's rough."

"What did you do while the strike was on?" I asked. The strike had ended a few days before.

"Several rabbits in these hills," he said.

The other boys nodded, grinning.

"And some fish in the river. We made out."

"Don' forgit miners' strawberries," someone prompted him.

"What are they?"

"Pinto beans. They go a long way."

I asked about working conditions.

"Ain't nothin' like it used to be," the small man said. "It's safe by what it was. Course, man was killed the day we opened up."

"You ever been trapped in a mine?"

He shook his head. "Got my eye knocked out, though, an' lost fifty-three days."

"How?"

"Slate fell on me. Knocked my eye clean out, but you wouldn't know it now. An' I had to wait while they took the coal out. Coal comes first. There I was, with my eye restin' on my bosom. By and by they come and got me." Unexpectedly he grinned, finding some kind of humor in the case.

"How do you load a car," I asked, "with a shovel or what?"

"Hands, shovel, crowbar, pick, anything." He stepped to the side of the house and picked up a scoop and came back and said, "Me,

I'm a small man. Ceilin' maybe ain't but so high." He held his hand a little above his waist. "Look, I can spraddle my legs out and shovel standin' up."

"What about the others?"

"I'll show you about us," a much bigger man said. He pulled up the leg of his Sunday pants. On his knee was a pad of callus like a pancake.

We had a look at a mine afterwards. It was almost head high at the opening, but quickly pinched down. We stopped before we had gone very far and looked, hunched over, into the tunnel dwindling ahead. There were occasional batteries of dim lights there and, unseen in the darkness, the belch of water. Outside, sawed and split to about fireplace size, were timbers to be used to keep roof and floor apart. Outside, too, was a string of mine cars, squat, wide jobs that looked like little scows.

The outlander is likely to think of the miner as a surly and difficult fellow. Not so. He may believe, and does, that sooner or later his number will come up, but he doesn't live in gloom. Like any fatalist, he lives day by day, enjoying himself while he can.

"A miner spends money when he's got it," Warren told me. "These house-to-house salesmen, they make a killing. A miner'll buy any kind of a gadget."

Out of their border-state experience, perhaps, Kentuckians impose a handicap on the co-operation that their problems demand—they're suspicious of the human animal, including one another. You have only to consult their law books to confirm this point. Neither the governor nor any minor officer of state may succeed himself. Neither may mayors of first- and second-class cities. The constitution lists twenty-eight special prohibitions and, for safety's sake, one catch-all restriction on the powers of the legislature. When, in 1947, a campaign for a constitutional convention was being waged, the antis contended that the state lacked men of sufficient caliber to draft a satisfactory instrument. That was a slander that should have made the pros victorious, but didn't.

The fact is that Kentuckians love politics but have little faith in its principals or performances, including the judicial; as a result, a kind of basic anarchy, the violence of individuality, persists, particularly, one concludes, in the hills and hollows to the east. The conclusion is supportable but still uneasy: in the race for national homicidal honors Kentucky cities outside the mountains have done pretty well through the years. An astonishing number of people carry pistols or blades, just in case. In old families with long years of education and social grace a dark strain of violence occasionally breaks out.

The lawmakers and the courts are duly indulgent. Under the law, crimes of violence are mitigated by the element of "sudden heat and passion." They are in other states, too, but there the offender has to prove provocation. In Kentucky he just has to show that all of a sudden he got mad.

Juries are equally considerate. Comparatively few homicides result in death penalties. At most the defendant is likely to be given a life sentence, which means he can be free in eight years if he's a good boy.

A great deal has been written and said about the mountaineer with his touchy pride and his readiness to act on his own. Outsiders sometimes talk as if every resident would shoot at the drop of a persimmon. Writers, with exceptions, go to extremes. They exaggerate the dark unpredictability of the mountaineer or they make him just too quaint for words, perhaps in the certainty that eastern editors will fall for either version. In neither case do they treat him as a human being, shaped by forces outside his command.

Beneath his usual reserve the mountain man is friendly and obliging. He is hospitable almost to the point of embarrassment to strangers. He has a mind, if an untutored one. In his hills he is frontier America; often he comes out to give leadership to community and state. The risk that a decently disposed and mannerly stranger runs in Kentucky Appalachia is too slight for consideration. It is with himself that the mountaineer has trouble.

He does have it there. No virtues explain it away. It exists—product of ignorance, isolation, poverty, background, social compulsion. Most of all, perhaps, social compulsion, which itself reflects background. At least one historian has ventured the belief that feuds trace directly to the indiscriminate guerrillaism developed by the Civil War. You don't hear of feuds any more, though the clan spirit survives, an injury to a man being considered a personal grievance by kinsmen down to in-laws and second cousins, but associated habits persist. There remain the unruly impulse, the recourse to gun or knife, the carrying of weapons. Warren Till told me—and maybe he was just having fun with a greenhorn—that as a high-school senior he, like his mates, carried a revolver to class.

A Lexington newspaperman and novelist who came out of the fastnesses of Clay County believes the compulsion on the mountain man is the fear of loss of face, the fear of being thought afraid. Scared, he has to prove he isn't. He's not by nature more violent than his outside brothers; he just answers to a different standard. We get back here to Warren Till and Harold Coldiron. They told me that rather than to have anyone think they were afraid to enter a mine they would go in even if they knew beforehand they would never come out.

The Kentuckian's love of politics and such by-products as courthouses and courtrooms and legislation appears to contradict the impulse to anarchy, but it is nonetheless real. No year goes by without an election—school, municipal, county, state, Federal—and nearly every one full-dress. The state abounds in buttonholers, some ambitious for office, some only fascinated. Courthouses ring with promises and denunications. Newspapers tear into the fray. Radios squawk.

It is fitting here to lament the good old days when the late Edwin P. Morrow and Augustus Owsley Stanley were having-at each other. Now there was politics, and there was oratory, and there was fun for everybody, including the antagonists, who got together before and after their debates, it was rumored, for a friendly cup. They were keen and witty adversaries who entered politics joyfully.

Over a Coke or around a fire, older observers of the political scene like to quote a crack of Stanley's. He had beaten Morrow by a nose in the 1915 race for governor. Four years later Morrow again was the Republican nominee. One of his targets was a textbook adopted under the administration of his friend, who could not succeed himself but of course was compelled to defend his record. Morrow said the book contained errors of grammar, which it did. He said the Democrats could not escape responsibility for putting a linguistic monstrosity in the hands of the innocent school children of Kentucky. Stanley, who was more scholarly than Morrow, had his answer. In swelling rhythms he described Morrow's own rhetoric: "Unrelated nouns in open concubinage are crowded into the same sentences, and poor bastard pronouns wander aimlessly through a wilderness of words, vainly seeking their lost antecedents, whom they resemble in neither gender, number nor person."

Morrow was elected, presumably not to Stanley's entire dissatisfaction. Stanley remembers that they "fought mightily" but "ate and drank like friends."

In Kentucky we have no men like them today. They were the last of the old-fashioned orators, the last, that is, who brought good nature and wit and skill to heightened language.

Kentucky normally is Democratic, but not so Democratic as never to leave the fold. Union organization, notably that of the Mine Workers, has increased the Democratic strength in recent years, though from any gain must be subtracted conservative defections from the New Deal and Fair Deal. One of these renegades, a prosperous landowner who liked to flash the highly perforated checks the Government sent him for fencing or conserving or growing or not growing or whatever, said he glued the checks together one time and put them through his player piano, and damn if they didn't come out, *Happy Days Are Here Again.*

What do you do in a state of such extremes? You do the best you can, or you live in part by myth. In any case, you enjoy yourself.

Satisfaction isn't necessarily bushels to the acre or gain on the hoof or production on the line. It can be laurel on a mountainside, the white shower of serviceberry, the wind ripple of bluegrass, the palisades of the Kentucky, the spring festival of redbud and dogwood, the long haze of autumn, the columned front of old Morrison Chapel in Lexington. It can be a friend and a julep and a mare in a pasture. It can be the blaze of old cherry, fashioned after Hepplewhite. It can be a place where walk the ghosts of better men and worse. It can be a stage in the great American journey, east to west, where Dan'l Boone and George Rogers Clark and frontiersmen and soldiers and seekers tramped history on the land. It can be a day at the Lexington Trots, at Keeneland, at Churchill Downs, at Dade Park. It can be old ham and beaten biscuits and fried chicken and corn pudding.

These things the Kentuckian knows how to appreciate. Problems exist, troubles arise, but these endure.

The Kentuckian walks down the street of his town and meets friends along the way, and they stop, wanting to know how things are, how's the family, why'n't you come and see us, who you pickin' in the Derby, let's have a cup of coffee.

Or he and his wife call on their neighbors at night and, leaving, hear the words, "Glad you came. You all hurry back." Answering, they say, "You all come and see us now. Hear?" The partings are standard, but the sentiment is honest.

An interest in people, dead and quick, tends to make conversation personal. Small talk, if you insist on that term, occupies dinner table, fireplace and corner-drugstore gatherings, if not to the entire exclusion of broader discussion. The tendency perhaps constitutes escapism; in any case it reflects a real curiosity about the individual, a real relish for human vagary. Local historians are as thick as chiggers. But they talk more about personalities than about events and their causes and consequences. And they may turn from the long hunters or Abe Lincoln or Jeff Davis or John G. Carlisle to the more recent and humbler "characters" that Kentucky somehow produces in abundance.

They may tell the story, perhaps apocryphal, of the late Dudley B. Veal, long-time Lexington city detective and later jailer of Fayette County, whose lack of formal education was balanced by imagination and vehemence. Out of his long experience Mr. Veal said he knew the world was round because every damn no-good that ever left Lexington always came back. Or they may trade information about a Louisville *Courier-Journal* reporter who wondered how it was that a black cow can eat green grass and give white milk that churns into yellow butter. For the benefit of his followers—apple-knockers and ridge-runners, he called them, including himself in the classifications —he'd tell whether a hen lays an egg because she wants to or because she has to, or explain why a hound trots with his hind legs out of line. With historians and nonhistorians alike the individual comes before the event. I've never heard one of them contend in defense that the proper study of mankind is man, but the principle seems to have some limited application here.

Man in the form of the local product gives to conversation and culture a provincialism that finds a prior and greater impulse in the feeling of Kentuckians for Kentucky. Any man who had a choice would be a fool to live in any other state. Even heaven can be no more than a Kentucky of a place. By contrast with the facts the Texan's loyalty to Texas becomes a benighted and amusing attachment, to be tolerated on the ground of ignorance. You got to excuse people who haven't had a chance to get around.

This contentment with place to the prejudice of problem, this satisfaction in an imagined isolation from the underprivileged, can be annoying. It's hard, though, to keep a broad social consciousness alive and prickly when candlelight lies soft on old silver, and aged wood whispers under the feeling finger, and women and men honor the ways of ladies and gentlemen and, over coffee or bourbon, the rich, warm anecdotes spill out. Gracious living? It is a name, but more than a name. It is relaxation, ease, escape. At its best it is manners without rigidity. It is hospitality without calculation. If part of it is worshipful of ancestors and the great, gone days, part of it is immediate and fresh, and all of it is beguiling. The jet missile, the hydrogen bomb, the cold war, these join the distant shadows when your host in Louisville or Lexington or Paducah or Ashland or wherever has a mind and the means to entertain traditionally.

There are exceptions to a rule which, though common, isn't general enough to be called a rule anyhow. Obviously not everybody breaks out the rare distillations or gives with the country ham or opens the door on ancestral Chippendale at the honk of a visiting horn. And not all of them by a long shot shy away from the state's debits in enjoyment of its assets. There's Harry W. Schacter, of Louisville, for instance.

Schacter, president of the second-largest department store in the state, thought public knowledge of problems plus democratic co-operation could rescue the commonwealth from half a century of decline. Around him gathered other people, few at first, who thought information more important than the reputation that the patriots would protect. They were professors from the University of Kentucky, farm leaders, newspapermen, representatives of civic, professional and labor groups. They called themselves the Committee for Kentucky. Their aim was to create "a moral climate in which things could happen."

In twelve widely circulated reports they washed the dirty linen. They told the sorry stories of education, agriculture, public health, welfare, housing, legislation, taxation. They discussed the constitution, manufacturing, natural resources. They said: Here's the situation; what do we do about it?

Protests resulted of course. Many citizens were indignant, not so much at the conditions as at the exposure of them. Chambers of commerce growled at the unfavorable publicity. Women's clubs were openly critical.

That response was to be expected. What was astonishing was the strength of the counter-answer. Moved by the reports, people began to concern themselves with the long-neglected troubles of village, city, county and state. Communities began to plan and to act. Officials of state began to give ear, the policies of state to reflect the growing concern. Items of improvement have been substantial if not revolutionary, but more substantial still is the growth in public attitude away from reaction and ostrichism and apathy toward recognition and adjustment.

The myths in which Kentuckians find comfort are the myths of fast horses, good whisky, juleps, old retainers, leisurely graces beneath ancestral porticos. Unlike most myths these have so much basis in fact that a quick condition must be set: These are myths only as the facts are extended and exaggerated.

Not every Kentuckian trots to the race track, his money pulsing in his pocket. Fewer still like a horse because it's a horse rather than a hot thing. Riding isn't a particularly popular pastime. Lexington, "heart of the Bluegrass," never has kept a commercial riding stable in business. It has no public bridle paths. Neither is the citizenry universally attached to the stirrup cup, the evening toddy and the short snort. Ninety of Kentucky's 120 counties legally are dry. More give indications of becoming so. The liberal connotation of horses, whisky and women runs up against the fact of morals-in-action. That is a thing that needs constantly to be remembered—the strength in the state of a Protestant fundamentalism that equates highballs and horse races with sin. Kentucky is the home of good whisky and fast horses, but much of Kentucky is not at home with it and them. Such is the human wish for distinction, though, that even the antis sometimes appear to find pleasure in the reputation the state enjoys among outlanders.

One substantial fact, as distinct from myth, is that Kentucky stands first as a breeder of the Thoroughbred or running horse. And not by accident. Some quality in soil or water must give to horses an extra speed and stamina.

The running horse and to a small extent the harness horse and saddle horse are important to the economy of the Lexington region and not unimportant to that of areas near Louisville, Covington and Hopkinsville. Horses and horse farms probably rank as the No. 1 tourist attraction. Man o' War, in his years at stud outside Lexington, drew more visitors than the tomb of Henry Clay, the first college west of the Alleghenies, the home of John Hunt Morgan, the residence of Mrs. Abraham Lincoln and the college quarters of Jefferson Davis. It used to be said that 50,000 people came to see him yearly. Tourists go now to see the heroic bronze over his grave. They ride to Calumet Farm, home of Whirlaway and Citation, and to Coldstream Stud, and to Mereworth, Elmendorf, Almahurst, Beaumont and Walnut Hall farms, and others that ring Lexington. A tour of them is rewarding in the visual dividend of rich fields, groves and paneled pastures with their mares and foals. And the sight of costly, manicured barns may impress you with man's humanity to beast.

Because Lexington is known as the center of Thoroughbred breeding, many of the uninitiated think the Kentucky Derby is run there. It isn't. It's run at Louisville's Churchill Downs.

Louisville is Kentucky's biggest city and, businesswise at least, its most important. Its residents estimate a metropolitan district that counts more than half a million. It lies on a low plain where the Ohio River broke over falls as lucrative to earlyday pilots, porters and towline hands as they were vexing to vessels and crews. The falls aren't impressive any more. The Government system of locks and dams has reduced them substantially.

Until about 1870 the city's prosperity rose and fell with river traffic, in which the steamboat made its first entrance in 1811. A good many northerners terminated their river journeys at Louisville—which accounts for the fact that the town still casts a lusty if not majority Republican vote.

"Louisville," says the Kentucky WPA guidebook of 1939, "is a border metropolis that blends the commerce and industry of a Northern city with the Southern city's enjoyment of living." It might have said that Louisville is a big, friendly, country town, notable by outward reputation as the home of the *Courier-Journal*, the Louisville Slugger and the Derby.

Even to the man without interest in the turf the Derby is worth seeing at least once, though massed humanity may keep him from catching more than a glimpse of the race. It is horse race, fashion show, spring festival, mob. Notables and nobodies mingle, touts and tycoons, owners and swipes, all beating inwardly to an excitement that old Colonel Matt Winn sedulously cultivated during a long lifetime. A kind of craziness afflicts people, so that even the Kentucky absentee is likely to stay close to his TV or radio until it's over. The crowd is so thick that women caught in its close squirmings lose hats and gain hysterics. More even than it is a horse race, the Derby is a spectacle, a human spectacle the like of which it would be difficult to duplicate.

A second substantial fact, again as distinct from myth, is that Kentucky does make a great deal of whisky, Kentucky in this case being a dozen producing counties among the one hundred and twenty. At times the state manufactured nearly half the whisky distilled in the United States. More, the stereotype of the Kentucky colonel with a cigar in one hand and a glass in the other finds some enforcement in fact. If it's inaccurate to say that Kentuckians are good judges of whisky, it's true that many of them are. Two colonels got to arguing one day about the taste of their drinks. One of them said the whisky had a metallic flavor. The other said no, it smacked of leather. To settle the dispute they drained the barrel, to find at the bottom a leather-washered tack. (The story would have more authority if Cervantes hadn't told it three hundred and fifty years ago.)

It is said of the fractious Thoroughbred that a touch of his blood betters any breed. By something of the same reasoning a similar virtue could be asserted for Kentucky. Through claim of birth or residence the state can boast a list of distinguished men, historical and contemporary, out of all proportion even to its present population of about three million. From this troubled, rich-poor, literate-illiterate, rewarding-distressing, politics-ridden commonwealth have come and still come notables in jurisprudence, national administration, military affairs, science, journalism, literature, education and the arts.

A few years ago three Kentuckians were justices of the United States Supreme Court, a representation that possibly no other state ever could claim. In all, Kentucky has sent nine men to the highest court.

There's no need or room here to call the roll of history. The list of military personages alone would run to dozens. And, anyhow, the distinction doesn't rest exclusively on ancient honors.

This story of the state has run a cycle. We are back to old Brother Timothy Flint, who cited the political squabbling, the clanships, the frequent recourse to violence 130 years ago. But he noted, too, the presence and continuing production of talent and leadership. In words dated only by style, in words that express a hope still current, he said of Kentucky:

"It can not but eventually feel the obligations imposed upon it, to manifest its possession of such men and such talents, by desisting from the petty struggles and broils of party and faction, and acting with a moderation, calmness, and dignity befitting its character."

# PART V *The South*

# ℑennessee

## by HODDING CARTER

One summer, a few years ago, an unhappy young Tennessee wife wrote a letter to Mrs. Jean Bruce, the advice-giving columnist of the Nashville *Tennessean*. Her father, complained the young woman, drank heavily—a gallon and a half each week end—constantly abused her mother and had so misbehaved one night that her husband had been compelled to slap him.

"That's a lot of whisky," replied Mrs. Bruce. "Maybe one day he will get too much. Until then you cannot do a thing if your mother does not want to help. . . . I hope your husband hit him hard. It's a pity that someone does not beat him up plenty."

Tennesseans can understand such advice, for theirs has been a tradition of robust living and forceful action throughout a long, honorable and combative history. It is more important to understand this tradition than to memorize statistics, if you want to know the people who came to Tennessee, the country they found and what they have done to it and it to them.

You profit little from learning that Tennessee's population is some 3,500,000, for example, unless you are also aware that fewer than 14,000 Tennesseans are foreign-born and that only a small per cent of the 3,500,000 were born outside of the state; that a majority of its people are the lineal and spiritual descendants of the land-hungry and prideful Scots-Irish and the yeoman English, implacable Presbyterians, Wesleyans and Baptists for the most part, who brought across the contested mountains the demijohn and the fiddle along with the Bible and the rifle, and who shared a bitter mistrust for the King, the Tory, the papist and the dissimilar in blood and tongue.

But the Tennessean's pugnacity is not unrelieved. Hillman, riverman, dirt farmer, he preserves a folkway of courtesy to the stranger.

Once, while lost on a hiking trip one chilly afternoon in the mountains near Sewanee, I came across a mountain home, a split-log, dogtrot house with a rock-and-clay chimney and a long, slanting gallery on which a middle-aged man was playing with a dog. I asked him for directions. He gave them explicitly, his narrow, chiseled face studying my own, and then, probably noting that I was cold, he asked me to have a cup of coffee. I sat on the porch with him, talking about the weather and the autumn hunting, until his sweet-faced wife brought us black coffee in large white mugs. On the wooden tray with the coffee were two pewter receptacles.

"Long sweetenin' or short sweetenin'?" he asked.

"Long sweetening," I replied. A relieved look came into his blue eyes. He handed me one of the two pewter containers. It was filled to the brim with sorghum molasses. "We like it thataway too," he said. I caught a glimpse of the short sweetening in the other container. It was white sugar, and the bowl was all but empty. But there was enough for a guest.

He was a mountain man. There are other Tennesseans. You will not be much the wiser for knowing that the length of Tennessee is a long 430 miles and its breadth about 120, unless you discover that in the rough parallelogram thus formed there is not one Tennessee but three: the East Tennessee of the mountain men, the Middle Tennessee of bluegrass and tobacco and livestock, and the West Tennessee that ends among the cotton plantations and diversified farms along the Mississippi, newer than the others and once shackled to a ruinous one-crop economy.

You need not think of Tennessee's total area of some 42,000 square miles as imposing, for thirty-three states are larger. But in few other places has American soil been so bitterly contested, so darkened by the lifeblood of defenders and conquerors, so vital to the extension and the preservation of a new, continent-spanning nation.

The American Revolution's success in the South was assured at King's Mountain, in South Carolina. John Sevier and his Tennessee

Long Rifles won that battle. The same Long Rifles broke the resistance and the hearts of the courageous Cherokee; Andrew Jackson's
Tennesseans destroyed the British at New Orleans in 1815, ending
the last European encroachment upon the continental United States;
wrested, with some illegality, Spain's Florida from the Dons, destroyed the Seminoles, and assumed a large measure of frontier security from the south Atlantic coast to the Mississippi.

In the Civil War, few states suffered as did Tennessee. Her divided people knew the ultimate horror of civil strife that pitted the
slavery-hating Republicans of the East Tennessee highlands against
their seceding brothers to the west. Historians agree today that it was
at Shiloh—a long, bloody year before Gettysburg and Vicksburg—that
the Confederacy was doomed. Tennessee gave the nation its first
postwar President, Andrew Johnson, a man whose conciliative spirit
was overwhelmed by the vengeful radicals.

In World War I, there was a mountaineer named Alvin York.
Though a conscientious objector, he became the nation's best-known
hero. In World War II, there rose on Tennessee soil a city named
Oak Ridge, a city of mystery whose ultimate contribution to human
destiny no man can predict. And it is only 180 years from the Long
Rifles to Oak Ridge's Museum of Atomic Energy.

In these and other directions, statistics by themselves grow mean-
ingless. Note that in the Great Smokies there are sixteen peaks of
more than 6000 feet. Does such information capture the intransigent
beauty of the rhododendron, high in the misty blueness, or the kin-
dred independence of the mountain folk? List the agricultural and
industrial products of a state that still relies principally upon the soil.
Can this recount the lately joined struggle against ignorant destruction of the land, or the zealous quest for industrial balance? Tennessee had, less than two decades ago, a per capita income that was
among the lowest in the nation. But no longer; the figure has
quadrupled. Can this reflect the miracle wrought by the Tennessee
Valley Authority, the miracle of water working for man in the creation of hydroelectric power for over one million consumers and for
nuclear fission, the miracle of flood control and assured water transportation, and land reclaimed and directed to forgotten usefulness?

Here, from just beyond the Appalachians to the Mississippi, was
the beckoning pioneer land, the free land of young America. Here,
in 1796, was created the sixteenth state; and long before the Decla-

ration of Independence at Philadelphia, angry Tennesseans proclaimed at Watauga an association of free men. Here, Daniel Boone broke through the Cumberland Gap, the long rifle cradled in his arm, seeking bear meat and deer and beaver skins and fertile valleys for those who followed. Here feudal, devout men built the split-log church and gave brave classical names to their first, one-room academies, and quarreled in the crude courthouses from which strode an Andrew Jackson, duelist, horse racer, warrior and despotic democrat. Here roamed forest clearers, Indian scalpers, corn-whisky drinkers and ballad singers.

Soft people died early on the frontier, their blood wet on the puncheon floor, the mother grotesquely inert beside the spinning jenny, the child forever asleep upon the corn-shuck pallet. Only the hard and the resolute survived. And so the Tennessee frontier marked its sons with resolution, frequently harsh and unyielding, for generation after generation. There is a likeness among them all: Tom Spencer, the seven-foot Long Hunter, and Cordell Hull, the log-rafter from the Cumberlands; Andy Jackson, the fire-eater, and Andrew Johnson, the Union Democrat; James K. Polk, the second of Tennessee's presidential triumvirate, who added mightily, through war and diplomacy, to America's domain, and Sam Houston who guided an empire of his own; Davy Crockett, the hunter and politician who died at the Alamo, and David Glasgow Farragut, the first full admiral in the American navy, who damned the torpedoes at Mobile Bay.

One of Tennessee's best storytelling governors, Bob Taylor, who knew the toughness of his people and the virtues they most admired, had a favorite story that had to do with a Tennessee archetype, Brother Billy Patterson, a new preacher, and Bert Lynch, the bully of the mountains, who picked fights with all comers.

"In his first sermon in Bert's neck of the woods," Governor Taylor would recall, "Brother Billy Patterson hurled his anathemas against Satan and sin and every kind of wickedness. He denounced whisky; he branded the bully as a brute and a moral coward, and personated Bert. This was too much for the champion. He resolved to thrash Brother Patterson, and in a few days they met. Bert squared himself and said:

"'Parson, you had your turn last Sunday; it's mine today. Pull off

that broadcloth an' take your medicine! I'm agwine to suck the mar-
row out'n them old bones o' yourn.'

"The pious preacher pleaded for peace, but without avail. At last
he said: 'Then if nothing but a fight will satisfy you, will you allow
me to kneel down and say my prayer before we fight?'

"'All right, parson,' said Bert. 'But cut yer prayer short.'

"The preacher knelt and thus began to pray:

"'O Lord, Thou knowest that when I killed Bill Cummings and
John Brown and Jerry Smith and Levi Bottles that I did it in self-
defense. Thou knowest, O Lord, that when I cut the heart out of
young Slinger and strewed the ground with the brains of Paddy
Miles, that it was forced upon me and that I did it in great agony of
soul. And now, O Lord, I am about to be forced to put in his coffin
this poor, miserable wretch, who has attacked me here today. O
Lord, have mercy upon his soul and take care of his helpless widow
and orphans when he is gone.'

"And he arose, whetting his knife on his shoe sole, singing:

> "'Hark! from the tombs a doleful sound;
> Mine ears attend the cry.'

"But when he looked around, Bert was gone. There was nothing
in sight but a little cloud of dust far up the road, following in the
wake of the vanishing champion."

Upon them all, the stamp of the frontier, the outdoor stamp. Tennessee is the land of the hunters of the coon and the possum and the
fox. It is a land where a mountain man may compete in a turkey
shoot today with a rifle fashioned by John Bull of Bull's Gap some
135 years ago; where the West Tennessee tenant may grabble naked
in a slough for a mess of fish and where the vacationing fisherman
and huntsman swap lies at Reelfoot Lake over a bottle of Jack
Daniel's whisky, that potent sour-mash distillation whose long-ago
creator remains a patron saint. And in the Cumberland Mountains,
the revenuers again stalk the resurgent whisky makers, who reason
that when the tax on corn liquor gets so high, it's time again for a
man to make and drink and sell his own.

There are other less innocent manifestations of the frontier's
stamp: The shameful, though limited, outrages of the Klan; the
sound and fury of Tennessee's politics, where factionalism and personal venom and the lethargy of the nonvoting majority are more

apparent than are issues; racial conflict in Columbia; the GIs' armed uprising in Athens; the long-ago evolution-law trial at Dayton. Distant people envision the mountaineer caricature and do not see the rising cities, the hopeful towns, the sure forging ahead.

In perspective, even the aberrations can be understood. Go back a short time, as time is reckoned in the history books and the recollections of men. Remember again the frontier, and remember also that this frontier was bloody and raw and that it began to recede only about 135 years ago. On this frontier, vices and virtues were alike primitive. Leadership, political or military, was violent, personal and immediate, and there was scant time for meditation upon good and bad. Culture, in its softer definitions, was a thing that came later. But not before the frontier had marked her sons.

What the Long Hunters saw first of Tennessee were the mountains, shrouded in blue haze, guarding the eastward approaches, north and south.

Some of the hunters surrendered to the beauty or the primal independence of the mountains, and settled among the giant tulip poplars and beside the cold, quick streams of the Great Smokies and the Cumberlands. Their more restless fellows roamed the Land of Peaceful Hunting, slaying the bear and deer and bison, or possessing and clearing the fertile valleys and plateaus and lowlands beyond the eastern peaks. But all who came by way of the eastern passes remembered the mountains: remembered the flame azalea, the purple rhododendron and the dark leaves of the laurel that grew along their slopes. Here was East Tennessee, a land of great heights and twisting, narrow valleys and solitude.

The settlers and travelers and adventurers who came northward along the Natchez Trace to Middle Tennessee remembered best the rich plateaus and rolling bluegrass country, lying between the eastern and western loops of the Tennessee River; a gentler, more fertile land than the mountain valleys, a land where a man might prosper and build a great house among the oaks and the cedars, with the iris and yellow jasmine and honeysuckle thick in the woods that border meadow and field. Here was the pulsing heart of a state.

Once during the war I swapped some homesick bragging overseas with a young Tennessean, a fighter pilot in the Ninth Air Force.

"There's only one place worth living in, and that's Middle Tennessee," he said. "When I get out I'm going back there. I'm going to marry a Nashville gal. I'm going to buy some Middle Tennessee land and raise Tennessee Walking Horses and Tennessee babies. I'm going to cure Tennessee hams with Tennessee hickory, and I'm not going to drink anything but old Jack Daniel sour-mash Tennessee whisky. And if my wife ever talks about leaving Middle Tennessee, I'll drag her clean over to the Tennessee River and drown her. Hell, I'm so homesick I could root for the University and I'm a Vanderbilt man."

The later settlers found a third Tennessee; a country to be reached either by long, overland journey, or roundabout by water or land or both. Here was West Tennessee, a land of black bottom lands and river swamps and long, undulant valleys between unimposing hills. Here was a lusher, wilder growth; lilies and Indian rye, orchids and wild rice and cypress. Here was proper earth for cotton's planting, a land to which the slave could be brought, where the river outranked the overland road or the mountain pass, and the price of cotton determined the price of man.

Give me the rivers, says the West Tennessean, the borderline Cumberland, the Tennessee, and the yellow Mississippi, the lush bottom lands and the wonder of Reelfoot Lake. In the narrow, eighteen-mile-long lake live the alligator gar, the huge spoonbill catfish, the savage water moccasin, the terrapin and a profusion of game fish. To dark Reelfoot wing the mallard and teal and the Canadian goose, the bittern, the rail and the purple gallinule. Here soar the bald eagle, the blue heron and the fish hawk; and in the forest tangle the coon and opossum hide from man. Reelfoot is a sportsman's heaven today.

Middle Tennessee is more tranquil than its rivals; it is a land where man's own mark seems permanent and nature more normally lavish. But on the eastern borders of this more placid countryside rise mountains, too, the rugged, outer plateau of the Cumberlands, and there is no softness to beauty here. This middle land is girt by the Tennessee River, tamed now and reshaped and bent to man's full use; but the river once spelled travail and blood. And here men seem to remember the past most lovingly, though they are not bemused by it; and it comes to life readily, in a score of towns, a hundred landmarks, a thousand folk tales remembered.

Here, in Middle Tennessee, a man can speak unashamedly of culture. To the colleges and universities of Nashville come annually about 9600 nonresident students, white and Negro. In Nashville, a symphony orchestra flourishes, and a children's museum, one of the most beguiling in the country. Middle Tennessee is the cosmopolitan region of the state. It seems also to rest upon the firmest foundations. The Middle Tennessee farmhouse is solider and more extensive than its counterparts to the east and the west. Its landowners appear to be more secure, its folkways and even its sports more deeply rooted.

East Tennessee, Middle Tennessee, West Tennessee. So much in each of which a man might boast. The refashioned river itself; Fall Creek Falls, with a water drop of 256 feet, the highest east of the Rockies. And Lookout Mountain dominating Chattanooga and Moccasin Bend, a lofty rock-faced promontory carved through thousands of years by the downrushing Tennessee. From Lookout Mountain, a man can see seven states on a clear day. If he is a good Tennessean, he will prefer the nearest.

And within the state, he will prefer his section and the city which dominates it. Time was when the four principal cities of Tennessee could be defined by characteristics as well as by location. This is less true now, for a common industrialization tends to level their differences. They share a determination to grow, to industrialize.

Nevertheless, certain differences persist. Nashville, the second largest city and capital of the state and of Middle Tennessee, has a serene, Athenian quality, as if it were more attuned to its eight universities and colleges than to its industrial plants. A Nashvillian speaks more readily of his city's book houses and writers, its symphony and its statelier past, than of its more material promise. Memphis lacks this quiet assurance, for it grew from a brawling boom town on the river to the state's largest city so hurriedly that it has hardly had time to assess itself. Energetic, clean and preoccupied with its almost incredible industrial expansion, Memphis seems—despite its Beale Street, its heavy Negro population, its Cotton Carnival and a commanding position as the deep South's cotton-trade center—more like a bustling Midwestern city than the mecca of Mississippi planters.

Chattanooga and Knoxville have more in common than do the others. They are only 100 miles apart, the one lying on the border of Middle and East Tennessee and the other in the shadow of the Great Smoky Mountains. Chattanooga derives spiritually and economically from both sections; it profited after the Civil War because perceptive Northerners, sensing the industrial advantages of her location, joined hands in a real reconstruction, so that cosmopolitan

Chattanooga became one of the first of the South's industrial cities. Today it shares with diversified Knoxville the benefits of being in the heart of the TVA country; both prosper in no small part because of TVA's reclamation and recreational enterprises.

Gentleness and compassion were not among the virtues of the early Tennesseans. Courage and hardihood were. And the tough breed which survived produced a hero's roll: Nolichucky Jack Sevier, who was the first governor of the unique, independent state of Franklin and six times governor of Tennessee; Evans and Isaac Shelby, scourges of the Southern Tories; James Robertson, revered even in his lifetime as the father of Tennessee; Colonel John Donelson and the surviving companions of the unbelievable winter voyage by flatboat and pirogue down the Tennessee to the Ohio and up the Cumberland to the site of Nashville; Daniel Boone, blazing the Wilderness Road; Davy Crockett, roaring, fighting drunk on the Memphis bluffs.

But none of them left such a mark as did a spare Carolinian, a redheaded lawyer who came riding into Tennessee near the end of the century. In Andy Jackson were reflected all the vices and virtues of the Tennessee frontier. He dominated his adopted state for thirty years, and all the United States for half as long. Duelist Andy Jackson, who feuded with Calhoun, and dipped unwholesomely in land speculation with his friend John Overton, encouraged the rape of the Cherokees, and bossed Tennessee's politics down to county and town, and spoke for the common man; childless, pain-wracked Andy Jackson, playing the flute in The Hermitage at Nashville, for his neighbor's children to dance by, and dreaming of his dead love.

It is not implausible to conjecture that had Jackson been in power a generation later he might have avoided the Civil War; for he had a spirit that could cow the South Carolina cockerels and the venomous abolitionists of New England alike. But he was dead in 1861, and across his state raged the desperate fury of civil strife.

Most of Tennessee had been lukewarm to secession. Its mountain Republicans had actively opposed withdrawal from the Union. And Tennessee had been the last state to secede.

But this sane reluctance did not spare it from some of the most terrible destruction of the war. From the capture of Fort Donelson in February, 1862, to the battle for Nashville in December, 1864,

Tennessee was a battleground. Bloody, decisive Shiloh . . . Murfreesboro, Chattanooga, Lookout Mountain and Missionary Ridge . . . Chickamauga . . . and Franklin.

In Tennessee, Grant experimented in the strategy of the bludgeon, and Sherman condoned sack and pillage. And Nathan Bedford Forrest, slave dealer and cavalryman, with his "critter company" baffled and enraged the overwhelming forces of conquest and occupation.

"Two hundred recruits wanted," Forrest advertised in the Memphis *Appeal* soon after disastrous Shiloh. "I will receive 200 able-bodied men if they will present themselves at my headquarters by the first of June with good horse and gun. . . . Come on, boys, if you want a heap of fun and kill some Yankees. (signed) N. B. Forrest, colonel commanding Forrest's regiment."

Tennessee, the last state to leave the Union, one of the longest occupied and worst ravaged, became the first to re-enter. Her debasement under the Reconstruction governor, Parson Brownlow, a fanatical loyalist, was not so long-lasting as was that of many of her sister states; but it was complete for its duration. And out of the humiliation and desperation of the disenfranchised white, rose the ghostly Ku Klux Klan, born as a prankish fellowship of young Confederate veterans, and expanded and diverted to an awesome, extralegal striking force against misled Negro and predatory carpetbagger and scalawag.

The story of Tennessee has another chapter. The Bible rested also on the log mantel beside the powder horn, and when the town sites were cleared, the preacher-teacher came to instruct in reading and writing and figuring and piety. The frontiersman hungered for more than land. He coveted for his sons what he had lacked on the seaboard and beyond the ocean.

The culture of Tennessee is oriented in part toward the wilderness past, in part toward what the wilderness denied. Its folklore relates to storied fighters and hunters, patriots and orators; though the mountaineer's individuality is being lost as the highway and the radio, the craft shop and the newspapers intrude, the Tennessean takes pride in the olden virtues of the mountain people, in the ballad preserved and the riflemen's turkey shoot and the fiddler calling the reel. In these and less subtle ways is evidenced the frontier temper, the agricultural base, the rural savor of the state's lifeway.

In a state that was once prostrate and has been long exploited there are now forty-nine institutions of higher learning. Twenty-eight of them are colleges and universities, seven are professional schools, five are teachers' colleges and nine, junior colleges. Eight are for Negroes and these include the noted Fisk University, Meharry Medical School and Tennessee Agricultural and Mechanical College, one of the largest Negro institutions in the world. All three are in Nashville.

The record of educational expansion is impressive, and all the more because of the small and harassed beginnings. The first regular school west of the Alleghenies was not opened until 1780, when a fighting preacher named Samuel Doak began conducting graded classes at his farm near Jonesboro. It was not until Reconstruction that a public-school system began to compete with the little academies, in great part sectarian, that for almost a hundred years afforded the young Tennesseans their only schooling. The public-school system is weak still, for almost everywhere there are too few schools and too great a difference between the best and the worst. But that, too, is changing.

The origins of some of the institutions of note are of more than passing interest. The splendid University of Tennessee began as Blount College in 1794, one of the earliest nonsectarian and co-educational schools in the United States. Vanderbilt University, founded as a Methodist Episcopal church school, was later endowed by old Cornelius Vanderbilt, renamed in his honor and made nonsectarian. The proud little University of the South at Sewanee in the Cumberlands, was founded by the Protestant Episcopal Church just before the Civil War. Bishop Leonidas Polk, one of its founders, went to the war as a general, and Union troops burned the new college down to its cornerstone. It was rebuilt principally with British contributions. At Bell Buckle is Webb School, unique among Southern preparatory schools, whose classical-minded founder, "Sawney" Webb, was the father of preparatory-school education in the South. Near Monteagle in the Cumberlands is the Highlander Folk School, a training school for industrial leaders, founded by Myles Horton, which works closely with the mountain people in preserving the old crafts. At Nashville is the principal teaching-training school in the South, George Peabody College for Teachers, which, as the University of Nashville, received a large bequest from the estate of George Peabody of Massachusetts, and like Vanderbilt, took the name of its benefactor. And at Nashville also is Fisk University for Negroes, which was founded after the Civil War by the American Missionary Association, and has prospered from its own indomitable purpose and a lasting

good will. There is a happy symbolism in the announcement that
Fisk, whose first students were former slaves who studied the sim-
plest of curriculums, has recently received one of the best modern-
art collections in the United States, including works of Picasso, Rivera,
Cézanne and Georgia O'Keeffe. It is a long way from *Swing Low,
Sweet Chariot* to the Fisk art gallery.

A cosmopolitan diversity reflects the origins and objectives of these
Tennessee institutions. Contrarily, the creative spirit in the state has
been largely regional in outlook. Writing fares best among the arts.
Out of Tennessee in the recent past have come T. S. Stribling, the
hill realist, Harry Harrison Kroll, John Porter Fort, Leland Crabb
and Jennings Perry; and from West Tennessee, Roark Bradford, and
sensitive Anne Goodwin Winslow, of Raleigh. It was from West
Tennessee that Joseph Wood Krutch went to New York. And young
Peter Taylor is a Tennessean.

Of all these Tennessee contributors to the arts and letters, I would
single out the late Roark Bradford, the gentle, honest interpreter of
the Negroes of the lower Mississippi Valley. The ignorant intelligent-
sia suspected him on the grounds that he mocked the Negro. The
evaluation was shallow and unjust. He never caricatured or ridi-
culed the primitive, amiable folk whom he knew so well. He laughed
with them and not at them, and the laughter which he set down was
as real as the Mississippi.

I suppose that I am prejudiced, because he was my good friend,
and because he gave me some newspaper advice long ago which
I have tried to follow.

"Don't go after the ordinary folks," he said. "Most people get hurt
often enough without having writers go out of their way to hurt
them. Go after the people who do the hurting."

In a nation so extensive as ours, the American of one region often
finds it difficult to understand the people of another. What little he
thinks he knows is frequently true only in part or is a cruel caricature.
So with the notion of Tennessee as a tragicomical area populated
by shaggy-eared mountaineers, book-burning fundamentalists and
political monstrosities, a backward land of social absurdities and racial discrimination, where the Klansman, the political boss, the landowner and the fundamentalist conspire against economic and moral
evolution.

Begin with the position of the Negro in Tennessee. Among the
Southern states Tennessee is unusual in that its Negro population

does not constitute an omnipresent problem, nor do its politicians emphasize the racial issue to any appreciable extent.

A clue to this relative tranquillity lies in the composition of early Tennessee agriculture and the accompanying role of the Negro slave. A majority of Tennessee's farms—and even its western plantations—have always been relatively small. The farmer and planter owned but few slaves, and were in direct contact with them; and this closer, individual association had a humanizing effect upon master and slave alike, so that compassion was developed in the one and a more diverse capability in the other.

An obvious result of the small-farm composition of Tennessee was a lower ratio of Negro to white than elsewhere in the cotton South. The Negro was never in a majority in Tennessee, and today the state's 550,000 Negroes are only one sixth of its population, the lowest proportion in the Deep South. The social taboos are rigidly observed, but, particularly in Middle Tennessee, the Negro enjoys a happier status as landowner, voter and independent citizen than do his brothers in most of the rest of the South. More hopefully significant than anything else, perhaps, is the number and the quality of Tennessee's educational institutions for Negroes and the general acceptance of Negro suffrage.

But statistics on educational development cannot indicate the personal, human element of white-Negro relationships in Tennessee—nor the friendship and respect that are accorded the outstanding Negro. It is unlikely that any Tennessee citizen is more esteemed than Dr. Charles S. Johnson, the president of Fisk University, a patient, scholarly scientist and educator whose faculty is bi-racial and whose school is the meeting ground for a yearly interracial conference of men of good will and hopeful purpose. I doubt that any Tennessean is more liked by his patrons than is aged Aaron Taylor, custodian of the state law library, the only Negro in the United States to hold such a post.

Nor was any musician, in or out of Tennessee, more loved than the late William C. Handy, the timeless genius of the mournful blues—young Bill Handy, Alabama-born, who refused to follow the steps of his minister father and grandfather, preferring the "sinful music" of the rivermen and the improvisations of his first battered cornet; gaunt Bill Handy, hungry roustabout and day laborer, heading north on a freight train at twenty-one with the blues moaning in his head, to sing and play for dimes in saloons of Chicago.

As for the ballot, Tennessee has offered less resistance to the Negro

vote than has any other Southern state with the possible exception of
Virginia.

The rioting in Columbia in 1946 is still an open wound. In the back
country, hoodlums in masks and sheets prowl on occasion again,
and men dare to boast that they are Klansmen. But their numbers
are few and their vicious beatings and intimidation have claimed as
many white as Negro victims.

Such matters make headlines. Others do not. In Nashville I talked
with a young Fisk student, a war veteran who planned to be a
teacher. We discussed a city election in which he had voted. He
waved his hand expressively at the campus.

"That's all we're asking," he said. "A decent, equal education, and
the ballot. We can win everything we deserve to win with schools
and the vote. And we won't scare anybody when we do it."

The headline curse extends to Tennessee's politics. To the casual,
distant critic, Tennessee politics means the shrewd, vitriolic Edward
H. Crump of Memphis who rode herd over his city for forty years
and for fifteen years bossed his state. It means eastern Tennessee's
election-day gunfights, and the pitched battle in Athens between
young veterans and the thugs of the county machine which sought
to steal the election. It means the poll tax, and the oldest unamended
constitution in the United States—not a comma changed since 1870
—a hopelessly outdated document which denies duelists the right to
hold office, forbids the election of a minister to the legislature and
relieves the citizen of the duty to bear arms "provided he will pay
an equivalent to be determined by law."

Certainly self-government in Tennessee suffers greatly from indifference, petty venality, and factionalism. More than one governor,
senator and congressman have been the creatures of the autocratic
Red Snapper of Memphis. How strong has been his hold, up to the
recent past, is humorously illustrated by the story of a gubernatorial
candidate who had expected Ed Crump's backing and after happily
announcing his candidacy, learned that the Memphis machine would
support his opponent. "Man," commiserated a friend, "that sure puts
you out on a limb."

"Limb, hell," observed the wretched candidate. "I'm out on a twig."

But it is also fair to point out that Mister Crump's town is not boss-
ridden in the corrupt sense that characterized Hague's Jersey City

and the Kansas City of Pendergast. Memphis is a well-run, orderly, and relatively uncorrupt city—though that itself is dangerous, since it made Mr. Crump's totalitarian regime so attractive. And the boss man got his comeuppance some years ago in 1948, when the progressive Estes Kefauver won the United States senatorship, and Gordon Browning, once a Crump-backed governor, whom Crump hated most of all, became governor again.

The angry campaign was vividly Tennessean. Crump compared Browning to Judas Iscariot and called Kefauver the darling of the communists. But when the smoke cleared away, Kefauver and Browning were elected.

Most Tennesseans resemble their fellow mortals elsewhere in effecting a workable compromise between religion and human frailty. This adjustment with reality is in the heroic tradition. A group of Memphis ladies of more than a century ago whose little Presbyterian church was heavily in debt decided to organize themselves into a sewing society and hold a fair at which their handiwork would be sold. Near the church was a saloon owned by a generous citizen named Hart. The saloon was better equipped for holding a fair than was the church. So the ladies went to Mr. Hart, who readily consented to let them use the saloon. While the devil looked the other way, the Presbyterian ladies sold $700 worth of their work; and it may be hoped that the gentlemen of the church thenceforth gave Mr. Hart their patronage.

Even the most unearthly character in Tennessee folklore made much the same kind of compromise. She was the Bell Witch, the spirit of old Kate Batts who after her death harried John Bell, his family and even his good friend Andy Jackson because she fancied that she had been cheated in a land deal. The Bell Witch didn't restrict herself to hounding them alone, but spent her spare time attending every revival in Robertson County, moaning and shouting with the best; and raiding the county stills and getting unbelievably drunk. Since there were about as many stills as there were revivals, she must have been the busiest spirit in occult history.

The Bell Witch's divided devotion to the spiritual and the spirituous was not without more earthy emulation. The religious fervor, particularly of rural Tennesseans, is nevertheless real, and the majority of churchgoers worship simply and unaffectedly. Yet some do not. Tennessee has no monopoly on the masochists whose interpretation of Biblical passages leads them to extraordinary and sometimes fatal lengths; but these extremists do seem to thrive mightily in the Tennessee back country, and their performances are enough to chill the believer and the skeptic alike.

Once I witnessed a Holy Roller revival held in a field at nighttime, and the preachers and performing laymen—eight or ten of them—stood behind a long table on a crude, roofless platform. On the table burned yellowly a half-dozen kerosene lamps, the only illumination except for the stars. The five hundred or so worshipers and curious spectators sat on soap boxes, logs and the ground itself. It didn't take the preachers long to work themselves and many of their audience into a gibbering frenzy. Leaders and participants alike broke into the weird unintelligible supplication that they call speaking in the Unknown Tongue; and as the frenzy increased, men and women began grunting and moaning and laughing insanely. Here and there transfigured believers jerked uncontrollably, a chant of "Oh, sweet Jesus, sweet Jesus" keeping time with the gyrations. The lamps were white hot. At the climax, the preachers lifted the searing lamp globes from their bases and fondled them with their bare hands.

It is difficult sometimes to laugh without also marveling. And sometimes one wonders at the laughter. A quarter of a century has passed since the trial of young John T. Scopes in Dayton, a pleasant, hill-girdled little Tennessee city, tree-lined, thriving, remote from the outside world. No other event in Tennessee's history brought it so much notoriety.

Among the citizens of Dayton was George Rappleyea, a distinguished engineer, who in the spring of 1925 found himself vexed by a new state law which forbade the teaching of any theory of man's beginnings that ran counter to the Biblical story of creation. It occurred to Mr. Rappleyea that it would be good publicity for Dayton if a test case were to be made there. In a Dayton drugstore, he suggested to young John Scopes, a Northerner and biology teacher in the high school, that he put his head on the chopping block. Rappleyea would bring charges against Scopes. Scopes agreed.

Dayton got all the publicity that the little group had bargained for, and more. Overnight, John Scopes became a martyred hero to the Eastern press, and Tennessee a target for derisive onslaught. The American Civil Liberties Union rushed to Scopes' aid; Arthur Garfield Hays and Dudley Field Malone joined the defense forces. They

were to be overshadowed by Clarence Darrow, who had also immediately volunteered his services. The state prosecutors found a no
less notable ally in William Jennings Bryan, who in his later years
had increasingly concerned himself with the defense of fundamentalist beliefs.

With the trial, Dayton became a carnival town and a crank's
paradise as fundamentalism mobilized against the invaders, twice
damned as atheists and Yankees. Across the main street hung a banner: "The Sweetheart Love of Jesus Christ and Paradise Street is At
Hand. Do You Want to be a Sweet Angel? Itemize Your Sins and
Iniquities for Eternal Life. If You Come Clean God Will Talk Back
to You in Voice." The little city's pretty streets were lined with
peanut, hot-dog and lemonade stands. Quasi-religious barkers peddled pamphlets bearing such provocative titles as "Hell and the High
Schools," and "God or Gorilla?" In the hot July night, revivalists
shouted from beneath swinging lanterns, and white and Negro minstrels sang the praises of the Lord.

Darrow and Bryan, once political allies and friends, shouted their
contempt for each other in the sweltering courtroom and on the lawn
to which court was moved. "Bigots and ignoramuses," cried Darrow.
"The only purpose Mr. Darrow has," spoke the tormented Bryan,
"is to slur at the Bible." Once they came near exchanging blows.

The audience movingly and unexpectedly gave Dudley Field Malone the greatest ovation of the trial when he pleaded for the
defense:

"There is never a duel with truth. The truth always wins and we
are not afraid of it; the truth is no coward. The truth does not need
the law. The truth does not need the forces of government. The
truth does not need Mr. Bryan. The truth is imperishable, eternal
and immortal, and needs no human agency to support it. . . ."

The jury found John Scopes guilty, as he and his associates expected. He was fined $100. Five days later William Jennings Bryan
died in his sleep on a Sunday afternoon, exhausted in mind and body
and shocked to the breaking point by the savage disbelief of his
adversary.

The case was appealed to the State Supreme Court which up-
held the constitutionality of the statute. But the court made further
appeal impossible. It found that the trial judge had erred in assess-
ing the $100 fine, as that should have been the jury's prerogative, and
recommended a nollepros to the Attorney General.

"The Court is informed," the Chief Justice said, "that the plaintiff in error is no longer in the service of the state. We see nothing to be gained by prolonging the life of this bizarre case."

The Attorney General accepted the recommendation, precluding appeal to the United States Supreme Court. And the law remains on the books.

The ballad's tune is Old English, but the words are as new as a miracle that came into being only twenty-seven years ago; and above them throbs another and wordless song, the ballad of water at work for man. Here is man's ballad, as genuine as any that was handed down from mountain father to remembering son:

> *My name is William Edwards.*
> *I live down Cove Creek way,*
> *I'm working on a project*
> *They call the TVA.*
>
> *The government begun it*
> *When I was just a child,*
> *But now they are in earnest*
> *And Tennessee's gone wild.*
>
> *Oh, see them boys a-comin'*
> *Their government they trust.*
> *Just hear their hammers ringing,*
> *They'll build that dam or bust.*

The clean, purposeful dams tower high in the land of a continuing miracle, the land of the Tennessee Valley Authority. "You can't tear those dams down," said Wendell Willkie, who tried, as president of Commonwealth and Southern, to keep them from rising; tried understandably and with conviction, in a gigantic battle of economic concepts and of survival. He lost his fight, but not his stature. Tennessee won the fight and gained also in stature; and in the long run no American has been in reality a loser.

Consider first the valley of the Tennessee. Its area is four fifths as large as all England. Upon the mountains which shadow the sources of the Tennessee there fall annually 6000 tons of water to the acre. From the mountains, the water seeks its own level, rushing down the green slopes in a thousand creeks, into a host of small rivers, and thence into the Tennessee. In the wake of the eroding water, two and a half million acres have been lost. Another four and a half million have been reduced to submarginal usefulness. The Tennessee, roaring downhill—it descends nearly 600 feet from Knoxville to Paducah—was no friend to the harassed valley.

For almost a hundred years the shoal-infested river into which the mountain rainfall emptied has fascinated and challenged the engineer, the dreamer and the land planner with its potential power, its defiance of the navigator, its unpredictable rampages. No agency, public or private, seemingly possessed the resources, the vision and the capability to conquer the perverse, unorthodox river.

And then, early in his first term, President Roosevelt asked for the creation of a Tennessee Valley Authority. The long fight of Sen. George Norris of Nebraska neared an end. The TVA's objectives were to be "maximum flood control, maximum development of the river for navigation, maximum generation of electric power consistent with flood control and navigation, proper use of marginal lands, proper methods of reforestation of all lands in the drainage basin suitable for reforestation, and the economic and social well-being of the people living in the basin."

Before the end of 1949 TVA had its millionth consumer. Not customer, but consumer, for TVA sells only to municipalities and cooperatives and these sell to the million customers.

"Maximum generation of electric power. . . ."

This is what the President of the United States said on August 6, 1945: "It is an atomic bomb. It is a harnessing of the basic power of the universe. The force from which the sun draws its powers has been loosed against those who brought war to the Far East."

Two days later, Colonel K. D. Nichols, district engineer at a place of which most Americans had never heard—a place in Tennessee named Oak Ridge—added a little more to the awesome story that the world was piecing together.

"The nearby sources of electricity in large amounts from the TVA has been the chief factor in locating the plant at Oak Ridge," he said.

A model for military brevity. Behind it lay the saga of new, urgent dams, completed far ahead of schedule out of men's sweat and guts and lives—massive Fontana and Kentucky and Douglas and Cherokee—so that more power might be generated in the Tennessee Valley. Behind it the unwritten history of a secret city that sprang up in a place called Happy Valley, a remote, unsettled and peaceful region eighteen miles from Knoxville. Behind it, the key to victory in an awesome race among nations. At the peak of what was known as the Manhattan Project, 75,000 people lived in the guarded, austere settlement, themselves ignorant of the task at which they labored and conscious only that its purpose was dreadful, vital, linked to the winning of a war that seemed so far away.

Oak Ridge is, in great part, still a place of mystery, but it is now an open city too. Its population, shrunk to a stable core has begun an orderly growth. Permanent homes and business buildings rise; it has its own newspaper; and almost in the shadow of the guarded plants women work their rose gardens, and men sit in their shirt sleeves on cool porches.

And there is one especial place in Oak Ridge where the visitor can say, "This is understandable, this is American, this is part of my past, part of my children's future—I pray." Surprisingly, it is the Museum of Atomic Energy, the first permanent center devoted to telling only the story of the atom.

I do not say there is reassurance in the scale models, the maps and the diagrams which depict and superficially explain the plants in which U-235 is separated, the uranium chain-reacting pile, the preparation of radioisotopes and the creation of power from nuclear energy. But there are two moments in the museum which all can understand. The first comes when a guide asks the visitor for a dime. The dime is made radioactive before the donor's eyes and returned to him in a souvenir mounting. The second comes in the exhibit for the youngsters. There the atom-splitting process is explained in cartoons and dialogue by Dagwood and other beloved cartoon-strip characters.

*Step right up, folks, see the atom demonstration, only twenty-five cents for adults, five cents for children—and dear God, let it go on like this. . . .*

Visionary Senator Norris could not have foreseen the outcome of his struggle "waged on behalf of the common people against the combined forces of monopoly and human greed." The distant enemy which TVA helped destroy had carried monopoly and greed to a far ghastlier extreme than the Nebraskan who loved humanity could have even imagined. Nor could he have envisioned or understood more hopeful ends, the promise of the radioactive isotopes from the laboratories of Oak Ridge, for the healing of man and the enrichment of society.

Maximum generation of electric power. . . . A great cloud over Hiroshima, a secret weapon that is secret no longer, a crossroads that branches from Happy Valley in Tennessee to the outer reaches of the earth.

Surely David Lilienthal was thinking of such matters long ago, in his first speech on the social implications of TVA.

"Those who believe that things as they are cannot be improved will wonder why we are concerned with a better planning of economic and social life," he mused. "But those with a sense of humanity, who see all about them want in the midst of plenty—factories idle while men need the products which manufacturers want to produce, millions of farmers desperate because they have produced too much while other millions of men go hungry for lack of these very crops— those who see these distressing facts and are perplexed and troubled by them will join in any intelligent effort to bring a bit more order into a world which so desperately cries for it."

A bit more order. Fields rustling with green, thick pastures where once the red gullies tore away earth's life. . . . White-faced Herefords and heavy-uddered Jerseys where a cotton farmer once told the tax collector to take the land and be damned. . . . The sheen of a fat bass in the sunlight on Norris Lake. . . . The tinted-glass windows of small factories, and large, in a valley that once begged for industry at any cost . . . the yellow glow of electric lights, high on a mountainside at night, the hum of the washing machine and the refrigerator in a tenant's cabin, the swelling deposits, the proud towns . . . the stately parade of the steel transmission towers of TVA . . . the red and yellow and green lights on the switchboard of the control room at Chickamauga. . . .

"We wanted those dams to have the honest beauty of a fine tool, for TVA was a tool to do a job for men in a democracy," said David Lilienthal.

People have to play even while they work out their destiny—and that means, among other things, that you don't need to approve TVA in whole or in part to enjoy it. Ask anyone who has gone on the annual TV-Ho! cruise upriver from Paducah to Knoxville, 630 miles of fun and adventure and surprise.

*On the waterfront of river-wise Paducah, a Negro baptism ceremony among the willows; beyond the shrieking penitents, the oil barges, the present that is background for the past. . . . Lake Ken-*

*tucky, a long, blue 184 miles from Kentucky Dam to Pickwick; and
on it a trim small ketch, heeling to a sudden squall, its sails rare yet
on the transformed river. . . . Storm-whipped whitecaps scudding
across Lake Pickwick, toward the overtaken foothills, while the
smaller craft, shepherded by the TVA and Coast Guard patrol boats,
make for the snug, well-marked safety harbors. . . .*

We came ashore the first night, in a warm, drenching rain, at Johnsonville. The rain couldn't halt the first of the catfish and hushpuppy
receptions for the most pampered voyagers in the history of navigation. The rain just made the fish and the barbecue, the crisp hot
cornmeal slabs and coffee taste better.

*Always in Tennessee the past intruding upon the present.*

*On this site, General Forrest and his cavalry ambushed a Federal
flotilla, sinking some gunboats and supply boats and capturing others.
The sunken craft lie deep now beneath the higher waters of the lake,
and far from the newer shoreline, too deep for boys to dive, as they
once did, for mementos of the dead; and on the shore here will rise
a generative force a thousand thousand times as powerful as ever
were the broken boats that strew the river bottom.*

The first night, Johnsonville. The second, Pickwick Landing, where
the dead fish bobbed crazily as we rose in the swirling waters of the
lock; where in the sheltered cove, the voyagers sang and fished and
swam in the dying rain; where only a few miles from Shiloh battlefield—so green and tended now above its buried thousands—a mammoth automobile carrier churned upstream with its glistening load.

And then the thriving little cities of Alabama, where the river
curves southward, loops eastward and rises again toward Tennessee.
Chickamauga Dam at Chattanooga, in the shadow of Lookout Mountain after the mountain-girt passage that they rightly call the Grand
Canyon of the Tennessee. Watts Bar. And great Norris Dam.

*Everywhere the pride and the confidence, the friendly hosts talk-
ing of plants and pay rolls and a burgeoning agriculture. Everywhere
the fish fries, the barbecues, the whole-souled entertainment of
friendly people who want you to know how far they've come and
how much further they intend to go. And everywhere the pleasant
shock of contrast. Boys swim yet in the subdued waters, bobbing distantly in the waves of the Diesel-powered tows. Men in skiffs fish
within earshot of the droning turbines at Wilson Dam, the nucleus*

*of the noble dream; the hillman's cabin looks down upon the nitrate plant; the workmen on the new country club can see below them the long-ragged farm that now responds to guidance, and Knoxville, journey's end.*

# North Carolina

## by OVID WILLIAMS PIERCE

North Carolina begins with the brightness of sea sands and ends with the loneliness of the Smokies reaching in chill and cloud to the sky. It stretches from the break of the Atlantic to the still of mountain coves, from sunlit capes to shadowed valleys five hundred miles away—from the low river-fed acres of the Coastal Plain to the rocky Piedmont and on to the hanging slopes of the Blue Ridge.

The state's outer banks are long golden strips of sand pointing into the Atlantic to form treacherous capes—Hatteras, Lookout and Fear. Nothing can dramatize their remoteness from the rest of the world so much as storm. This was true especially at Nags Head in the days before bridges and highways, when the sense of isolation there was almost complete. But the Coast Guardsmen gave you ample warning: in hoods and raincoats they rode the beaches on horseback, stopping at the old cottages (then there were long stretches of sand and sea oats in between) and telling the silent little groups on the porches the news that had just come in.

For two days the beach had been deserted, even in front of the old Arlington Hotel. People gathered on the porches and wore sweaters and jackets against the dampness and chill. Wind-whipped waves filled the air with spray. And there, just a little way over the sand, was the dark, tortured, twisting sea.

The terror of this day was the height the water reached. If you stood midway between house and beach, you had to look up at the waves. They rose unbelievably above you, held their towering height for a second, then in crash and thunder and torrents of spray rolled higher and higher over the beach. And all the while you knew the real winds were still at sea, that during the night they would lash across the sands, already a diminishing strip beneath you, and carry the Atlantic over into Albemarle Sound.

So, during the long night you watch through the blackness. Kerosene lamps in the windows, hardly more than match flames, intermittently identify the cottages which lonely watchers have not yet abandoned to night and wind. The circle of yellow light within the thin walls of your cottage is like an island now riding in blackness, spray and roar. Once or twice you look out at the black, beaten shapes of the houses near you and can only wonder what the storm has done.

But first light brings calm and view of another world. Waters of the Albemarle and Atlantic have met. To the east, out to sea, to the west, across the Sound, the surface of the water is unbroken, a great glittering mirror now to hold the sky. The long stretch of sand which bore a strip of road, a path to the outside world, has been washed from the earth. Hotels, cottages, garages, chicken coops, which rose out of the sand on stilts, are now sliced from the bottom, low and flat. Even the great dune along the highway, Jockey's Ridge, a little mountain of sand, is an island with the water lapping round it, diminishing its command of the earth.

You know that in a short time people will begin to appear on this unpeopled scene, to break into the unworldly emptiness with tentative exploratory surveys, two or three in a boat, to assess what the night has done. Just for a moment longer will this silence hold. Already there in the distance is a boat. Two men are rowing, one is standing, pointing across the mirror of water that stretches as far as he can see.

You are a visitor. As you look out over the little hills of sand spotting the horizon, it comes to you again with a shock of surprise that this rib of the continent, reaching down from Nags Head, past Oregon Inlet, down and down to Hatteras, Lookout and Cape Fear, has been closed to the world for almost two hundred years.

On the stretch from Whalebone Junction to Hatteras there are seven tiny villages like beads on a string, hardly more than clusters of houses around a store or two. They've had no governments, no taxes, no jails. A hard-surfaced road has recently made them accessible. But earlier the only chance of approaching them through the sand was to follow the daily mail truck, with its tires nearly flat, and not allow it to get too far ahead. With it out of sight, you were faced with a bewildering maze of disappearing tracks across a desert of sand. Far in the distance, the village itself was hardly more than a mirage, simmering in glare and heat.

Inhabitants of this region still speak with a Devon accent, a full-vowel dialect to carry against wind and "toide." Their songs, for the outsider, need almost as much translation as Chaucer:

> The noight was doark and hoizy,
> When the Pickodully Doizy
> Went daown with the cap-tun and the cre-uw.
> Oi'm sure the water drow-uned 'em
> For we never, never found 'em,
> And Oi know they didn't come ashore with Oi.

Folk tales in the region are endless. In the stories the old pirates, Stede Bonnet and Blackbeard, who would frequently retreat through the inlets to safe waters, live again. So, too, are the land pirates remembered: those who hung the lantern on the old nag's neck and made her walk the beaches at night, hoping that her light would be mistaken for a beacon which would lure lonely ships upon the sands. A headless horseman gallops the dunes. Virginia Dare, the first child of white parents on this continent, appears at midnight reincarnated as a white doe, for those who know where to look. Offshore, there is a phantom ship, a modern Flying Dutchman that has never been named. In the little village of Rodanthe, Christmas even now is celebrated on Twelfth Night.

An old man, ninety-one, ninety-five, he couldn't remember—nobody left to tell him—was sitting in a cottage on the mainland. Far out across the Sound lay the little spot of sand which had for eighty years been his home. Yes, grandchildren made him come to the mainland. Lost his wife seven years ago. Now he was just waiting, just looking out over the water, as though the place where he'd done all his living had been swallowed up in the earth. Falling mustaches framed his chin; his eyes blinked.

You call it a ghost town—Portsmouth? Hunh, once it was all the world. His father? He shook his head. Had tried to find out too late where he came from. Trouble was, hadn't nothing been written on paper. Memory was all.

Sure, out there, every man had to do everything. Hunt, fish, carpenter, plant, save lives at sea in storm. Doctor, preach and bury. Found three dead men in my time, one of them caught in a net. Just like they come from another world, so far as anybody could say. No questions asked. No law to ask it, not in them days.

Ghosts? Didn't believe in 'em himself. Plenty did. Couldn't tell another man what was or wasn't, not on the outer banks. Every man made his own world. Bring a man dying in a sailboat across the water at midnight, wind and no stars, is ghost enough.

Did he ever expect to cross the Sound again to see what was left? The old man blinked again, a little confused by the question. Go back? He shook his head slowly.

But now North Carolina has embraced its ragged fringes. Long bridges reach across the glare of the Sounds, ferries ride the choppy inlets; and hard-surfaced roads, like spines down wind-blown strands, bear the traffic of the world outside into this lost corner of earth. Kitty Hawk, Nags Head, Hatteras, Ocracoke Island, have all become a summer world of beaches, of swimming and fishing. In the last few years the stretches of summer cottages, filling stations, motor courts, cafés, hotels with concrete aprons for parking, dance halls opening to the sea, have reached deeper and deeper into the old desolation of sand.

At night during the summer months on Roanoke Island (reached now by bridge from Nags Head to the east), hundreds of people assemble at the Waterside Theater for a performance of *The Lost Colony*, a pageant by Paul Green, which celebrates with dignity and insight North Carolina's first story, the story of the 117 men and women who settled the "Citie of Ralegh" on this spot in 1587, only to vanish without a trace, leaving nothing but the cryptic word CROATOAN carved on a tree, not as a key nor as a guide but as a token, perhaps, that the dark soil of American forests had already received English blood.

For this last scene the forlorn little group of colonists assembles mid-stage. They shoulder their bundles and packs. Already the site which they have cleared—this "Citie of Ralegh"—looks abandoned, its fires cold. One by one, they turn away. But, suddenly, with the banners of England flying, their voices raised to God—"We walk this way of death alone"—they march into the forest, which is waiting to receive them, to hide them forever from later years.

Now the stage is darkened, and the audience feels the silence reclaiming the land.

Then, as if by a miracle of timing, over the Sound, far down the beach, lights from a great granite shaft play across the sky. It is the Wright Brothers National Memorial Monument rising from Kill Devil Hill, marking the site of the dunes from which Orville and Wilbur Wright sent man's first power-driven plane into the air. On December 17, 1903, their fragile machine flew for twelve seconds, one hundred and twenty feet. On a fourth try, it flew eight hundred and fifty-two feet into windy space.

The audience still sitting in the darkness of Elizabeth's century looks for a brief moment with fresh wonder upon its own.

The Coastal Plain of North Carolina lies between the Sounds and the fall line, a distance of a hundred and fifty miles inland up the broad muddy rivers. This area of lowland, crossed by the Chowan, the Roanoke, the Tar, the Neuse, the Cape Fear, like so many highways to the sea, is the Old South of North Carolina, the agricultural South of river plantations, of small towns, of counties predominantly Negro, of long stretches of nothing but swamp, heat and pine.

The Great Dismal Swamp, lying at the upper edge of the Coastal Plain (and across the Virginia line), is thirty miles long and averages ten miles in width—a quagmire, a vast spongy surface that is neither water nor land. For two hundred years lumber companies have tried to subdue it but the swamp remains as inaccessible, at its secret heart, as it ever was. Sunlight can barely filter through the density of its inner growth: cypress, black gum and juniper. Stained for centuries by the leachings of trees, the water has become a deep wine. The region is in fact an unearthly darkness lying across sunlit land.

Perhaps this secret swamp is a symbol in an area where the past still presides visibly upon the landscape, where the past still looks out from abandoned oak groves, from the skeletons of old resort hotels, from chimneys rising starkly in the middle of plowed fields.

Perhaps this untracked path across the east is a symbol, too, of the Negro world, which for so long has coexisted with that of the white but which has remained forever closed, a river, its banks ever widening, mysterious, uncharted, across the Southern states.

Just off the highway near Halifax, an old Negro was sitting under a shed in his back yard. He was weaving a cane bottom on a kitchen chair. Obviously this was something he could do now without having to move around. He had all his paraphernalia conveniently within reach. Even his chair had been placed to miss the sun, which lay neatly at his feet.

"Uncle Jim."

His hand jerked, but his face showed no surprise. Many stood here to watch, many from the passing world.

"You don't know me?"

"Naw-suh." He was intent again on his chair. "Sit down. Company welcome here. Folks stops all time. From way off. Can't remember countries. Kentucky and Baltimore. Which country you?"

When I told him, knowing that it was the place of his birth, he took both hands from his work, holding the palms out toward me, as though to reject what he'd heard. "Hish yo' mouth. Sweet Jesus, I know." Then he looked at me hard, finally nodding. "To be sure, to be sure."

And, so, we were a part of that most lasting fraternity, sons of a remembered place and time. Recent faces, recent years had hardly the substance of reality for him. These days now were merely the shells of empty moments around a remembered living core—a core made of people larger than life.

"That was Miss Julia said that. Miss Julia, to be sure. Her pa was the one married the second time. Yas-suh. Married him a rich lady from way off. Kin see 'em right now in that surrey, coming into town. Folks didn't think he done right, marrying so soon. Wouldn't even pay no calls out there. Just like they'd be turning against Miss Cora, lying in her grave under the cedar tree for not more'n a year, Miss Cora that had been the prettiest lady of anybody's remembering around here. Couldn't understand how come he done it, was what it was. Lawd! Lawd!"

Finally he looked up, shook his head sadly. "Don't nobody know what we talking 'bout."

Was it only the magic of remembering which made the lives of people of this post-Civil War generation seem more dramatic, their manners more distinctive, that made them "characters" capable of dominating a place and time?

In any case, people in eastern Carolina have lived under long shadows of old figures, belonging now to time and myth.

The surest sign of the past in the eastern counties is an oak grove, an old company of trees, rising like a great tent swollen with wind. Mounds of brick and clay show where chimneys stood. But nobody will be there to give the grove a name.

Yet in the heart of the back country, completely hidden from view, at the end of a strangled road, stands the shell of a once great house—windowless, porchless, long since gray and warped, open to wind and rain—but containing still (if it has not been sacked) rare pine flooring, fine cornices, medallions clinging to water-soaked walls.

You will be surprised, as you stand there on this spot from which life so long ago fled, when a little Negro boy pulling a sardine can at the end of a string appears from behind the house. He is as startled as you. For a second he is incapable of retreat. Then he is gone, his boat of a sardine can abandoned.

In a moment the others come, no nearer than they must, just out from the corner. They make a little group, as though they moved as a body around this silent place. The mother is surrounded by a half dozen children holding to her skirt and to one another. She is neither young nor old. She will speak your language, but she knows another of her own. She is out of time, belonging neither to the crumble of the world in which she survives nor to that which your presence has brought to this isolated place.

A little off to the side, beyond the limits of the yard, three or four dark cedars are drawn together in a group, as if forever bound in retreat. A tangle of vine has almost completely claimed them. Underneath that choking green the graves lie—nameless even to them who watch the hanging cemetery gate.

"Lady ain't gonna sell this place. Ain't never gonna sell. Gonna stay here until lady dies. Ma say her pa 'longed to lady's pa. Us gonna stay here until lady dies." The Negro woman speaks with a deadened monotony, delivering a part rehearsed, revealing in her words the seekers who had stopped here before.

As though disbelief on your part provoked her, she adds, "Ma tell you. She tell how come can't nobody buy."

She turns then, indicating for you to follow.

Three or four rooms, opening upon a porch which makes an L at the back, have been kept nearly habitable by makeshifts of patchings: tin in lightless windows, loose planking for walkways across gaps in the flooring, a discarded automobile seat for a porch chair.

Here, enthroned, sits Ma. Even the approach to her is somehow deferential. "Ma, here man. Tells him lady ain't gonna sell."

She begins shaking her head. "Won't 'low no selling, lady don't. Says old Jane die here. Says keep dis place for old Jane. Bring lady, too, some day, that graveyard. Then time for old Jane to go. Old Jane sets here watch. Waiting for lady to come back home. Den old Jane go too. Don't live after lady. Dey sell. Sons, daughters. Watches now, waiting for time. Keep ghost off nighttime. Puts knife graveyard gate."

Old Jane sits presiding over a little realm as dark as time. It is hard for you to believe that not too far away runs a great highway bearing the traffic of the world.

Of course, Old Jane's diminished kingdom of lady and spirits is an exception. But it is true that, since the War Between the States, the second and third generations of owners have moved to town. Many old sites have been cut into small farms. In Halifax, Northampton, Warren and Bertie fine old houses have been dismantled and shipped north. In some cases Northern money has come in and saved old houses for the South. Many a mansion would be lost except in fiction but for outside help.

So, if this part of North Carolina is no longer a land of country sites, it has become a land of little towns. Some are raw and ugly under the Southern sun. But there are, too, the old towns: the county seats of softness and charm, of wide shaded streets, empty in the noonday sun except for some old Negro passing by, of pleasant white houses with green blinds drawn, of old heavy trees without motion in August heat, of Confederate monuments on lonely watch now in un-used parks, and of molding yellow courthouses with square clock towers and cupolas enveloped in the fluttering shadows of pigeons and sparrows.

But the most striking feature of the little eastern town—something common to them all—is the straggling fringe of houses known as "colored section," spilling over into a ravine or clustering around a dead-end road, each bearing a name: Scott's Bottom, Harper's Field, Smith's Stretch.

In winter these sections look cold and deserted. All doors on the sagging porches are shut. A broken pane is stuffed with newspaper. Thin smoke rises from a chimney here and there to remind you that some of the older residents don't go out to work. But in spring when doors and windows are open, the road out front is everybody's yard. The air is alive with swinging clotheslines, colors flapping in the sun, the misty smoke of a pot boiling, thick smoke of trash fire, and white and pink of fruit trees flowering (all winter they've been no more than black wet sticks).

But the ragged edges of the towns are buttressed with new brick schoolhouses, shiny and sharp-angled and surrounded by gleaming yellow buses, too bright in the Southern sun, buses that started early in the morning to gather the little groups of Negro children waiting far out in the country at mailbox, crossroad and store.

It would be a mistake to assume that this eastern half of North Carolina has only the past to give the state, only the remnant of a plantation culture. This east has for long been growing and marketing one of the greatest shares of the world's tobacco, so here, too, is the area of the markets: Kinston and Greenville, Wilson, Henderson and Rocky Mount, and dozens of lesser size.

All have round their outer edges flat sprawling warehouses with acres of cement flooring and cavernous doors—doors to which in the fall the farmers will deliver load after load—wagons, trucks and trailers piled high—of "golden leaf"—the labor of months, actually, from the last of the winter to the fall of the year. No farming requires harder work, longer hours or greater skill.

A farmer who looked to be about sixty-five was standing in the doorway to one of the big tobacco warehouses in Rocky Mount on the day the market opened.

"Been coming all my life," he said to me. "Started coming in a wagon. Them days coming to tobacco market was a business and a holiday too.

"See that street here. Now ain't nothing but automobiles as far as you can see. Folks can get in 'em and go home or go to a café. Don't have to bother about nothing to eat. Used to be folks would bring something to eat to you. Sell it, I mean. Had stands all up and down this street. Great big tubs of barbecue, corn bread. Great big tubs of lemonade, hunks of ice floating around in it as big as your head. Sell you anything else too. They was folks that didn't do nothing but study ways to get your money. Money you done work the whole year for. Got it sometimes too. Would roll dice. Would even sell you oil land.

"Them days, got here, we had to stay a while. Us boys come sitting up on a top of a load of tobacco with the mules pulling us durn near all night long. Get here little 'fore sunrise, time to put tobacco on the floor. Warehouse had stables for the team. A little liquor passed around. See folks you hadn't seen in a year. Man, it was better'n August meeting any day.

"Now, got to wait till they tell you to come. What day. Just like you got a 'pointment with the doctor or something. Tell you when they got floor space for you. Man, I reckon it is better. I seen wagons lined up on this street here for a mile back—all waiting to get in and unload. But, seems like, waiting warn't so much of a burden them days as folks make out it is now."

Inside there was a sudden pulling of the crowd toward a corner of the warehouse. A group had formed at the head of the first row: the warehousemen, the auctioneer, the buyers. They were assembling as a machine now, every man having a part. Suddenly, as a group, impatience gripped them. "All right! Let's go! Let's go!" And the machinery was in motion, the chanting, sinuous rhythm of buying and selling had begun.

If this eastern half of North Carolina is self-contained, agricultural, and living within reach of its past, it is a proper complement to the Piedmont, a higher, rockier land, cut by sharper, swifter streams— the Yadkin, Saluda, Catawba and Broad. This is the region of cities, not farms; of factories and mills, of youth and growth, not of decaying houses standing miles and miles from any town. And all the roads lead here, to Raleigh and Durham, to Charlotte, Greensboro, Winston-Salem—and to Chapel Hill.

If North Carolina has a center, it is the town of Chapel Hill. But when the site for the university was selected in 1792, it was less of a center than a frontier. The rolling Piedmont and the unknown mountains rose to the west. The old towns of the east were behind it, lost in the distance and the green of the land.

What has Chapel Hill become in the South today?

My guide, a member of the faculty recently retired and a man whose affection for the university is balanced with understanding, sat across from me in a quiet pleasant corner of the Carolina Inn. Outside, Chapel Hill's great old trees properly shaded the veranda across the front, diminishing the urgency of the students' cars that filled the village streets.

Was there any other place which could claim Chapel Hill's title as "The Capital of the Southern Mind"?

"Suppose you name the place." And he pointed out the work that had been done by The Institute for Research in Social Science, under

the late Howard Odum. Nowhere had more searching studies been
made of Southern life; nowhere could a survey of a culture have
been made more objectively, especially of a region for so long mis-
represented and misunderstood.

How about the Carolina Playmakers?

Here was a subject close to his heart. Certainly. A significant part
of the intellectual ferment for which the university is known. Frederick Koch, it was, who began it. What he had to say was that a man
should write about himself. On this proposition the whole creative
movement started. The mountains of the west and the cotton and
tobacco farms of the east—areas which had rarely had any spokesmen
except in the rhetoric of their orators pursuing the ghosts of Northern
armies long after the Civil War, now had ably trained, devoted writers to interpret them realistically for the rest of the world. The Playmakers, reaching the farthest limits of the state, helped to make folk
drama a graceful, natural voice in everyday life.

Even a partial listing of Koch's students is impressive: Thomas
Wolfe, Jonathan Daniels, Frances Gray Patton, Bernice Kelly Harris.
Oh, yes, my informant went on, it was here that Wolfe wrote his
first play, *The Return of Buck Gavin*. Not a good play, but a start.
As a matter of fact, he was the only boy in Koch's first class. But
there was something about Tom Wolfe that should be corrected, a
false notion arising, perhaps, from the vast loneliness which so concerned him as a novelist. He was not a recluse. Not a tormented
spirit shunning others and in turn being shunned. Tom Wolfe, on the
contrary, was one of the most conspicuous men on the campus. He
acted in his own plays. He debated throughout his college years,
certainly without any show of shyness. He joined practically everything there was to join on the campus, social and honorary. And he
was with his other accomplishments something of a clown. It is safe
to say that none at the time could foresee that this lad, down from
the mountains, six-feet-three with boyish face, would later command
the angels of Milton to look homeward and melt with rue.

For over fifty years the university has held the intense affection of
its people, a fact suggesting that there no longer exists a single school
but, perhaps, the myth of many, made out of the needs and imag-
inings of different men. Old students not only want to return to
Chapel Hill to live but many of them do. Elderly couples, retired and
well to do, have found the village charm. Writers have made there a
considerable colony.

But the really important thing—the conversation continued—was that the university had survived as a great liberal institution, in an area where one wouldn't expect to find it. No one man could do it, could make a university. The university was the sum of all its people living in pursuit of ends unseen and knowing the purity of freedom of search.

Taking the winding road downward, away from the town, was like returning to an everyday world which had—quite surprisingly—known how to protect its citadel on the hill.

Barely twelve miles away another university lies hidden in the trees—Duke. Beginning at a circular drive, there is a long beautiful approach to the tower. The road rides high above the slopes and gardens below, which, in spring, drop down and down in terraces of color. The tower ahead reaches up, overlooks the forest around. Then, suddenly, to the right and left, the quadrangle, perhaps the largest university court in the world, has received you—a vast greensward enclosed by buildings of greenish-gray stone.

It is strange to pass a tobacco barn, a crossroads store, a little white church in a grove as fresh as a primer drawing, and to come suddenly to the center of this Gothic world. Here in the middle of the North Carolina woods is a re-creation of the Middle Ages, as complete as a town.

The story is that in 1925 James B. Duke looked over the forests around Durham and, coming upon this spot, exclaimed, "Here's where it ought to be." Here, accordingly, a complete university sprang from the woods.

The chapel tower reaches above the lesser towers. Arches and cloisters are worked into a unifying design. Flagstone walks cross the green. Chimneys and spires rising from the deep slope of moss-gray slate reach into the sky with the tops of the pines. And there inside the chapel are the bodies of the founders of the Duke dynasty, each marble sarcophagus as cold, as permanent as that of any European saint.

Comparison with the University of North Carolina is of course inevitable. By its very nearness to Chapel Hill, Duke has had a difficult role to play. To many, it has seemed to be a foreign thing on native soil. But Duke, too, is North Carolina—an old school, in fact, founded in 1838 as Union Institute, with a history of more than a hundred years of service to the South.

Now as you follow the serpentine road around the campus, you see the cars of all the states. Here is a school for the Eastern seaboard: New York, New Jersey, Pennsylvania, as well as the South. A little farther around the circle is the hospital area, one of the great medical centers of the South, a complete world within itself.

You can't help remembering again what a short time ago it was that Mr. Duke walked into this forest and said, "Here's where it ought to be." The making of a myth out of marble tombs inside the Duke Chapel seems not so strange as the story of this school translated from tobacco farms, from North Carolina land.

Quite abruptly, to the west, above this Piedmont plateau, above the mill towns, above the new highways endlessly bearing the traffic of a growing land, rises the ragged escarpment of the Blue Ridge. It rises suddenly. There it is before you, a great wall, the boundary of still another world: North Carolina's western fringe.

For a hundred years the isolation of this mountain region was as complete as that of the eastern sea-reaching strands. But now this heavily forested, cloud-wrapped land, too, has been embraced. The young have come out of the valleys to the mills and colleges of the Piedmont. Picture shows, beauty parlors, radios have reached to the farthest village to compromise old purities of manner and speech. And highways are bearing more and more of the world outside to regions which only a short time ago were known only in name.

One of the most beautiful drives in America is that along the Blue Ridge Parkway, coming out of Virginia, past Asheville to the Smokies below. Frequently high above clouds, the highway winds down and around the folds of the mountains, showing its own path far below, cuts gracefully through rock, and turns time and again above canyon and valley that unexpectedly open the world as far as you can see. The distance is a pale blue range above a range, hardly more than a deeper breath upon the sky.

Round the glittering lakes in sunlit valleys are dozens of summer camps bearing the names of Indians, mountains, waterfalls—names on swinging signs over rustic cedar gateways, on sweaters, on writing paper for weekly letters home. Little clusters of white shacks, tennis courts, bridle trails circle the shining lakes. The young are discovering themselves away from home, expanding with new-made friends as swimmers, riders, and sleepers under the night stars along old Indian trails.

Halfway up the mountains, on the verandas of the hotels, 19th Century white-frame buildings, all windows, row above row, rising out of rhododendron and laurel, the elderly are sitting in the circles of rockers—gray-haired ladies and a few gentlemen, wearing light coats against the chill. They have come up to spend the hot months, as they have been doing for years, to this same porch, wrapped in afternoon mist, to remember those once here, to whom the circle of chairs earlier belonged. Sisters and widows of the state's illustrious, theirs is a close-knit little clan, one of the last aristocracies to be found. Their tales, their recollections, reaching back and forth from plantation to town, touching here an old judge, there an old bishop, a governor or two, tell the story of a North Carolina that is just disappearing, that is, perhaps, nowhere more real than here.

A short turn off the Blue Ridge Parkway will bring you to such a retreat. The small hotel looks out through mist-hung trees across the valley to Linville. The clouds are not always beyond the reach of the trees, so the little terraced area of paths and mountain laurel is quite often shut off from the world, from the valley which lies just below, from the mountains rising beyond. The balsam and cedars are black with dripping chill.

But inside, in a great stone fireplace, a fire is burning. Two elderly ladies, removing their cloaks, are just returning to its warmth. Thickening mist has kept them from their walk. Beyond a point the path is completely lost as though it had disappeared into space.

For thirty years the older of the two ladies has been coming here, first as companion to an aging, distinguished husband, then with a companion of her own, a distant cousin. For years and years the hotel sheltered a closed society made up of those who remembered the lady's distinguished husband, and circled round her, perpetuating a former day. There was a time when all remembered him, when the lady received the deference of all. But with the years the circle diminished; and finally only the lady came, each year searching the new faces, but turning away always with increased bewilderment. How could such a time have passed so completely away, not even remembered today?

Below the hotel, on a hairpin turn down the mountain, in a little recess against the rock, there is a wayside stand. From overhead there is a fern-and-moss-lined trickle of water. Myrtle capping an overhang is dark and thick; it reaches up as far as you can see. The

mountaineer is sitting beside his display of wares, in this misty heart
of the mountains, already blue-shadowed in the afternoon. You wonder how he got there; there hasn't been a cabin for miles. Pottery
and baskets, cane-bottom chairs, blankets and rugs. The blankets and
rugs with bright flowery patterns are strung and waving as though
on a country clothesline.

These mountains have been called the greatest reservoir of folk
manufacturing in America. The long isolation of this region, inaccessible by water or roads, accounts for the fact that crafts have survived
here as in no other part of the land.

The same isolation also perpetuated Old English folk songs, kept
alive in memory here for over two hundred years, to be rediscovered
in our day by the outside world. Also, in some of these areas, off
from any beaten track, fragments of early English speech linger even
now: the pronoun *hit* is still extant; *Ey God,* from which "egad" presumably derives, is current; and so are *mazard,* meaning head; *poke,*
meaning bag; and *peart*—lively or well. Certainly these words are
disappearing. But it is interesting to note that the word "mazard,"
which appeared in the gravediggers' scene in *Hamlet,* should reappear in the mountains of North Carolina after three hundred years.

An estimate has been made that within one hundred miles of Asheville, the capital of these mountains, ten thousand highlanders are
making their living from pioneer handcrafts once pursued in isolation in places known only on maps. And crafts, it should be added,
practiced in need, to supply mountain cabins with what there were
no roads to bring. Hand loom and ax, needle and hoe, afforded a
self-sufficiency rarely more complete in this nation than in this mountain land.

Now summer visitors come from half the states, from the whole
Eastern seaboard, to well-organized handicraft schools, to study with
native craftsmen in metalwork, weaving, pottery, wood carving, mar-
quetry and dyeing, to learn from the natives the source of colors
from hulls, berries, sage and goldenrod.

"Oh, yes." An elderly man from Ohio was speaking. "I come every
year. See what I've learned at my age." He was weaving an intricate
pattern, one that required great patience and care. He looked up for
a moment, taking off his eye shade. "My wife and I started coming.
Better do this now than bother your children. Sleep up here? Never
slept better in all my life."

In Asheville, it isn't necessary any longer to search for the path of Thomas Wolfe. The same public libraries which wouldn't have *Look Homeward, Angel* upon their shelves now have his picture upon their walls. A historical marker rises near the busy traffic of Pack Square to point toward his old residence a block or two away. "Dixieland," once a boardinghouse run by his mother, is now a shrine.

For a group of visitors the author's surviving kin were standing on the steps of the house, answering questions, restating the story of the child and the youth. Inside, some of the little group which had come to pay its respects were looking at the bare, almost stark interior, at the plain, worn furniture. Glimpses of long-lost days were restored. Fragments of conversation were recorded. A schoolmate, a neighbor, a friend who received him when he returned—they all remembered. And you know you are present at the making of a legend, the legend of a poet who loved his mountain land.

On beyond, farther than Thomas Wolfe could see from the center of his town, rises the state's last wall—the Great Smokies, ancient, mysterious, forever remote, lying under purple haze. The Qualla Reservation, a tract of sixty-three thousand acres, lies in the heart of this forbidding land. This is the home of 3700 Cherokee Indians, the finally diminished corner of their earth. They are descended from rebellious Cherokees who refused to be uprooted by the white man and escaped from the bitter march to Oklahoma known as the "Trail of Tears."

Now the icy streams, the dark forests, the patches of corn are theirs. They are self-governing: a tribal council administers their affairs. But as you ride through the little town of Cherokee, on the reservation, it is a final humiliation that you see. All along the street, with beads and trinkets and drums and feathers, the Indians are waiting for tourists.

A mountain man was standing near me, seeing the moth-eaten finery of a Cherokee chieftain selling his baskets and pots—seeing him with the eyes of an outsider, as though for the first time.

"Played with him as a boy many a time." He nodded toward the now strange figure in the chieftain's role. "What made 'em different from us when we were kids? Nothing! Only him right there was the slickest trout fisherman you ever saw. *Walked* different from us, one thing—with toes pointing in a little. Go through the grass along them mountain streams, smoother'n a snake. Not make a sound. Could spot the trout he wanted, pick him out in clear water like looking through a glass bowl. Never showed himself against open sky. Always kept dark behind so the fish wouldn't see. What else was different? Nothing till he grew up and saw what he had to be."

And you know that these heirs of an old race, bedecked in gaudy headdress, with the dust and noise of the road enveloping them, are lost forever, belonging neither to the world of their forefathers nor to that of their neighbors outside.

Between these old mountains of the Cherokees and far Hatteras on the eastern shore, there lies a long stretch of land, three regions independent geographically which were for so long only in name a state. The Tidewater was closed to the Piedmont; the Piedmont to the Blue Ridge and Smokies beyond. Mountaineer, small farmer, planter; log cabin, growing town, river house; ax, mill, land. So the regions ran.

But these early diversities have in their longest reach helped to weld, to unite. North Carolina today has attained a degree of wholeness, a unity in its differences that is rare for any state. The past of the east is there to question the direction of the Piedmont, the Piedmont to define the withdrawing west. There is an aristocratic condescension of family toward a new aristocracy of wealth. In the colleges there is an enlightened intellectual liberalism pulling against an old conservatism of the Bible Belt. There is challenge of change against a counseling past.

In the village of Burnsville, high in the mountains, you find one of the earliest visions of a state that would someday be. In the middle of the town there is a pleasant little square. You approach the statue in its center, a little surprised to see that it is a naval figure. For the sands of Hatteras lie far away.

But there before you stands a forgotten hero of 1812—Otway Burns, captain of a privateer, a man of the coast surrounded now with hills.

The inscription reads: "He guarded well our seas. Let our mountains honor him."

# South Carolina

## by WILLIAM FRANCIS GUESS

Years ago, when school let out in June and at Christmas, my brother and I traveled from a cotton-mill town in Piedmont, South Carolina, to a cotton plantation in the coastal pinelands, from the red Catawba River in the north to the black Edisto in the south. It was a fine and fearful journey: we braved two clangorous trains and taxied alone through Columbia, our state capital, a city risen, we knew even then, from the ashes of Sherman's march northward from Georgia.

But it was a symbolic journey, too, as I think we also knew. It took us, at Columbia, over the "fall line," a visible drop in the land across our triangular state, dividing the stern Presbyteric upcountry from the easygoing Cavalier coast. It took us from the stoic presence of one grandmother, whose affection did not save us from labors with the compost heap, to the capacious lap of another, who sent Negroes with waffles and milk to sustain us while we watched the cotton gin.

Blood and affection, however, reconciled the differences for us. And training. We were taught to be South Carolinians, Ca-ro-li-ni-ans, mind you, and not, please God, the Tarheel slur, Calinians. (An impious people who even boiled their rice to a glutinous soup.)

An old Charlestonian may think of his city first and last, his heart bound to the palm-lined Battery, where echoes linger from the blasts

of the guns his forebears trained on two meddling foreign powers—
Great Britain and the United States. (The half-foreign power of
South Carolina seldom meddles.) But by and large the people of
this state are tribal in their loyalties, whether their ancestors shucked
corn in Pickens County or ruled slaves along the Waccamaw. There
are, to be sure, tribes within tribes, and Negroes might disclaim with
some justice any membership at all. Though once at a New England
school a young Harlem Negro remarked, "You know us two"—meaning himself and me—"will get along fine. We both come from good
South Carolina families." A romanticism, perhaps, but not a fiction,
and we did get along. Admittedly, however, we would not have
shared quarters in South Carolina, and in most encounters here he
would have done the getting along.

South Carolinians don't speak of themselves as a tribe, but their
sense of identity and kinship, their contented possession of a fair and
historic land, distinguishes their character as a people. To judge them
content with themselves, however, is not to challenge their fame
as a fighting race, mythically descended from General Sumter, the
Gamecock of the Revolution. Only an angry people, after all, could
claim such a record. They fired the first—if not the last—shot of the
Civil War, they died on the dueling field till 1880; and in wrath at
the Democrats in 1948 they helped dig a third-party grave for their
Governor Strom Thurmond, only to resurrect him in 1954 for the
U. S. Senate in a protest write-in jubilee remarkable in American
elections.

The people of this state are still strongly homogeneous, Protestant
and Anglo-Saxon, though the terms are obviously more cultural than
racial. Most have similar origins and traditions, and most are caught
up happily in vast intertwining kinships.

An alien soon trips on the tribal lines. Replying with accustomed
brevity "Ohio" to the ladylike inquiry of his hostess, "And where do
you come from, sir?" a visiting gentleman from the Western Reserve
got in return a blank "Ohio, uh-hunh," along with a Lord-help-me
rolling of the eyes. He said he felt like a casteless Hindu.

But that was surely not her intention. As a lady, she wished him
to feel at home, but people you know just don't come from Ohio,
and South Carolina conversations begin and end with the people you
know. If only he could have said Georgetown or Chester or Florence:
what sweet extended vistas then of piazza talk. Her sister Blanche
and his Aunt Cecile might have slid down the spiral fire escapes together at Winthrop College, gripping their skirts to thwart the male

dean below. Their Kingstree cousins might have summered with Mrs. McGregor at Pawleys Island. True South Carolinians, in other words, can talk endlessly about themselves and their state.

They cherish the theory of social cleavage, but in practice they mix a great deal, because they've all been poor together, at least since the Civil—or rather, the War Between the States. Most have hop-scotched together in the public schools, and most collegians have shared rooms in state institutions: the University, Clemson, Winthrop or the Citadel. They don't even begrudge the claims of lineage, even though a family tree may prove nothing beyond the indisputable fact of generation. "Nice" South Carolinians would rather die than admit belonging to the middle class. They're aristocrats or nothing, and many of them feel about outsiders the way Stark Young's planter (in *So Red the Rose*) felt about his Yankee visitors: "It's not so much that these people are not wellborn, they don't want to be wellborn."

But South Carolinians aren't stuffy about it. In fact, they can make fun of themselves, their shibboleths and proprieties in an often racy and perceptive talk. South Carolina talk can be admittedly special. If you never sat at a country table around hog-killing time, you won't admire, I suppose, a great lady talker's sketch of a county bachelor: "Look at old Archie, poor old thing—looks like a hemstitched chitlin."

Her kind is special, of course, even in South Carolina. I've sat entranced for whole August afternoons while she aired off the gnats with a palm-leaf fan and entertained a stream of callers. She and her husband kept open house, in the face even of calamity. Returning home one summer noon with the mail, he said, "Honey, guess who's coming." "I don't have to guess," she said, "I can tell by the look on your face it's Cassie." (Cassie was a pious female of the blood.) "Well," he said, "if you'll sit up and talk to her all day, I'll sit up and talk to her all night. But I can't talk to her day and night."

I've thought their sort was dying out, but just the other day a young woman said to me of a tiresomely stylish and talkative old lady, "Child, I ran into her last week on the street wearing one of those low-cut dresses that showed the little blue veins in her bosom. She gabbled at me so I couldn't stick in so much as a whistle, and I thought to myself, 'My Lord, she's gotten so old and shriveled there's nothing left but tongue, eyes and tongue.'"

In addition to genealogy, South Carolinians are addicted to romance, in politics as well as in love and religion. And the object and source of much of their romancing is the low country. Vestiges remain

here of the great indigo, rice and cotton plantations of Colonial and
ante-bellum days, and also the legend of a culture inspired by the
Fundamental Constitution of 1669, in which English planners for
Carolina ordained an elaborate aristocracy "that we may avoid erect-
ing a numerous democracy."

If you enter South Carolina from the north by the coastal route,
the former King's Highway, you will begin to feel the low-country
atmosphere not far below Myrtle Beach, perhaps when you see two
live oaks mingling their branches high over the road and trailing
Spanish moss like veils of mourning.

More than any other feature, perhaps, they enchant, though it
sticks in the craw of a local lady that a visitor from Altoona, Pa.,
inquired of those incomparable oaks at Brookgreen Gardens, "Why
don't they clean that stuff out of the trees?" For those who live there
the danger has been that the veils and soft airs from the sea cast too
opiate a spell: one might recline like a lotus-eater while the Doric
columns behind rotted away.

And some did after the spoilage of the Civil War, at least till Yankee wealth came seeking quail and ostentatious quiet; an invasion,
incidentally, that prompted a new criterion of caste: Yankee plantation owners could not be gentlemen because "gentlemen sell plantations, they don't buy them." And when an upcountry South
Carolinian, occupying a plantation in the early '30's, reached for his
checkbook to pay his food bill, the country storekeeper said, "Mister,
when you first come down here, we thought you was a rich Yankee.
But now we know you're just as po' as the rest of us. The check you
gave me last month bounced."

To many South Carolinians, however, plantation country is merely
beach country. Summer colonies dot the entire coast, and many of
the larger ones display increasingly swank establishments. (Many
white South Carolinians share the hedonism that was ascribed by a
Negro philosopher to his own race, "You white folks buy what you
need, but we colored people buy what we want and beg the rest.")

Myrtle Beach, the largest of these resorts, now offers such entice-
ments as a motel trying to look like the Governor's Palace at Williamsburg and a restaurant using the effete come-on "No fried foods
ever." So Myrtle Beach obviously gets a sizable out-of-state trade.
I can't imagine South Carolinians upholding a prissy aversion to fried
oysters and shrimp and red-horse bread (known as hush-puppies elsewhere) or, for that matter, fried chicken.

As a South Carolinian traveling the King's Highway I would have to stop off at Murrells Inlet, a curving resort shore on which a single line of cottages spreads in a quiet grove of oaks and longleaf pines. There's not a joint on the shoreline—no jukeboxes tear up the night. (Dancing collegians ride down the highway, take off their shoes and join in the barefoot frenzies at the Pawleys Island pavilion.) Nothing stirs after dark, in fact, but the occasional boat of a fisherman gigging for flounder by flashlight.

Most who frequent the Inlet own their cottages and go year after year to fish, to eat their daily catch of crab and shrimp and to sit on their screened porches and talk to the neighbors. The crab are especially plentiful, and you can laze in a boat and bring them up on a drop line or rake them out of the "pluff" mud in the marshes at low tide, a sport for the doe-footed, since a pause to puff on your cigarette can sink you in slime at least as deep as the grave.

At the Inlet I like to visit with "Miss Julia" Peterkin (Mrs. William Peterkin, but the polite usage is "Miss" for older ladies, married or single), the Pulitzer-prize author of *Scarlet Sister Mary,* who has moved down every summer from Lang Syne plantation at Fort Motte for half a century: I'm a little grieved now to find her in a louvered-glass breezeway: she looked more natural rocking on the porch of the old faded red house, with its wooden shutters and weathered roof sloping down like the brim of her wide straw hat. She regrets the change, too, I think, but as she said it would not have been proper to let a visitor cave in with the rotting floor. In other words Miss Julia is a South Carolina lady, in spite of her novelistic career and the excursions she used to make North into the ulcerated circles of the literati, but she's not a rose without thorns. Her wit pricks at fakery and sham, though she always remains within the limits of the aristocractic code she espouses.

And that code, with its "realistic" stratifications, may induce its own unreality. Thus, her novels of Negro life, for all the realism for which they were acclaimed in the '20's, were written out of sympathetic condescension, presenting the Negro as a human being, but leaving out the all-obtrusive background of white society.

But her stories are beguiling and poignant. Better in the telling, perhaps, than in the writing, for her voice is sweet and low, and her blue eyes are magnetic.

One she tells concerns a plantation laborer, a magnificent black figure who lost his legs to gangrene and afterward pined away in idleness, having to bear the pain of his wife's lovemaking to another man in the next room. And finally, sinking toward death, he said to Miss Julia on one of her visits to his sickroom, "Missy, please, please bury me in a man-size casket. You know I was six foot tall."

And there's the story of her Inlet cook, Wallace, an ageless little Gullah, who succumbed during the last war to the sumptuous wages at the Myrtle Beach airfield. Every weekend, though, he brought his pay home to Miss Julia to keep for him. Accepting the envelope one Saturday, she said, "Wallace, how do you know I'm not going to spend this money?" And Wallace replied, "Miss Julia, any little thing you want you jes' buy it for yo'self. You'se the only mamma I'se got."

From the Inlet on down the coast it's old-plantation country, a thirty-mile strip including the barrier Sea Islands and centering on Charleston. It is also a Yankee domain, a sort of vast private hunting preserve. Bernard Baruch, for instance—actually he's South Carolina born—bought up all but three of the plantations carved out of Hobcaw Barony, one of the feudal domains apportioned to the Lords Proprietors. Though Lord Carteret never occupied his Carolina lands, Mr. Baruch does from time to time; and his daughter, Miss Belle, occupies her private seat, Bellefield, in a state of seclusion which she guards with her commission as reportedly the only woman constable in the state; in fact, not too long ago she arrested a Georgetown citizen who tied up at her boat landing.

But I don't mean to paint her as an ogress. She probably takes at face value the classic American right to be left alone. And if she totes a pistol, she's in the vein of plantation women of older days—like my grandmother, who kept a loaded six-shooter by her bedside till the day she died at the age of eighty-one.

And this may be a good place to remark on the nature of plantation life, which I knew in a fairly modest form.

In the first place the plantation was big, by general American, if not by Texan, standards—500 up to 5000 acres. Its crops, mainly cotton, were grown by Negro tenants, forty acres to the family, living in weathered shanties. People I knew and liked and who I thought liked me went in and out of those shanties: the waddling cook, for instance, whose "toting" pan yielded up every afternoon a succulent slab of cornbread and who sometimes indulged my forbidden heart's desire to bang at the little pump organ in her front room, gorgeously papered with magazine pictures.

At the center of plantation life stood the "big house," sometimes manorial, comely in proportion and richly appointed but more often just big and comfortable, if drafty in the winter. But there were fireplaces in all the rooms and Negro boys to haul in "light'ud knots" and hickory logs. Plantation life was opulent and cultivated—at certain times and in certain places. There were hunt balls and races and libraries and trips to Paris, but these graces were fewer and less continuous than legend would have it. Both planters and their wives had to labor, in the first place, to make a wasteful system pay, since neither slaves nor share-cropping tenants toiled with philanthropic zeal. As an ante-bellum hostess remarked to a British visitor, "When people talk of my having so many slaves, I always tell them it is the slaves who own me . . . I'm obliged to look after them, to doctor them, to attend them in every way."

But if plantation life as most knew it wasn't so grand, it was rich and pleasant. At Christmas the family gathered, twenty-five or thirty strong, for a week, and ate and talked and laughed and shot fireworks and hunted partridges. We drank persimmon beer and ate ginger-flavored sausage and fresh squab and tipsy squire and all the cakes that are too much trouble to make any more: Lane and Lady Baltimore and Japanese fruitcake. On summer nights we ate, among other delectables, boiled pinders, green peanuts boiled for hours in salty water.

But plantation hospitality has declined with the flight of Negro hands, and you aren't likely to find twenty-five at Sunday dinner around the most baronial of boards. In fact, you probably won't be asked to dinner.

Old-plantation country is still quiet and thickly wooded, opening up best to the mannerly explorer. Some of the homes are on spring-tour display and some that aren't yield through the good offices of somebody who knows somebody. One plantation which welcomes the traveler is Mepkin, the old Henry Laurens (Revolutionary statesman) place near Moncks Corner, now a Trappist monastery. (To replace the vanished house Mr. and Mrs. Henry Luce, Mepkin's former owners, built a flat picture-windowed lodge which makes an arresting sight in the context of towering moss-hung oaks.)

Many planters formed summer colonies in the scattered islands of pineland in the low country. These were the nuclei of such atmospheric towns as Summerville and Pinopolis. Pinopolis seems quaintly retired from the world, its cottages turning their whitewashed shoulders to a single road meandering through a continuous grove of pines. A favorite local event the past few years has been a tilting tournament presented by the Pinopolis Lancing Association on the splendidly capacious lawn of the Doric-columned Gippy plantation house. These tourneys had been a fairly common low-country sport—with crownings of the queen of love and beauty, and bootleg corn flowing from the hip—but the Pinopolis affairs are conscious salutes to the past, making much of colonial finery and genealogical luster: blooded horsemen tilt at the rings in knee breeches and Cavalier hats.

A few miles from Gippy stands Mulberry Castle, the only "mansion" surviving of those built with the first crop of low-country fortunes in the early 18th Century, and, with its pseudomedieval towers, a fine example of Jacobean baroque architecture. And the road past Mulberry Castle plantation leads, as do all low-country roads, to Charleston, the region's Holy City, South Carolina's first capital and always in the minds of its own a kind of Greek city-state.

So much has been written of Charleston, and Charlestonians are so touchy, that you sometimes wonder what to say. Still, there is one very evident thing about Charleston: it is the most glamorous city in America, a city with an antique grace so discreetly guarded it makes one think of heirlooms in daily use, a city that has blessedly escaped both the bulldozers and the ministrations of antiquarian wealth.

Its colonial aspect seems less glamorous, however, than its fame for Castilian pride of birth. Old Charlestonians are admittedly complacent, but less remote often than the families of softdrink barons with villas at Myrtle Beach. Content with their own company, they can and do receive cordially; and sometimes they even mix their blue blood in marriage with outlander red. But the myth seduces. Most Americans are homesick for lords and ladies; they like to think that somewhere lofty beings fit their ideal of nobility. So what is Charleston more famous for than the St. Cecilia Society, the ball-giving social fortress which legend erects to Trojan heights of impregnability?

The myth is implicit in these doggerel lines:

> *In Boston the Lodges speak to the Cabots*
> *And the Cabots speak only to God;*
> *In Charleston the Pinckneys speak to the Rhetts*
> *And the Rhetts don't bother about God.*

When the fury of the 1938 tornado damaged the roof of a tony
Episcopal church, a wit explained: "God has been trying to get in for
200 years, and he finally had to come in through the roof." But to
counter the notion that it's all myth, take the notation that one of the
Middletons who was president of the College of Charleston made
in his diary nearly a hundred years ago: "When Edward, Prince of
Wales, visited in New York, he had the honor of dancing with my
cousin Hattie Aspinwall."

Old Charleston retains the aspect of an 18th Century town, the
area between Broad Street and the Battery has as many fine buildings
of the period as any similar plot of ground in America. Georgian
porticoes open from the street onto columned piazzas repeated for
one or two stories above, facing south to catch the breeze and overlooking walled gardens. Gardens where azalea hues are not nearly
so prized as the fragrances of tea olive and banana shrub or the
ambrosial bounty of a Turkey fig.

To offer a dissenting word on Charleston's culture is to risk turning
up the dampers of hell, but the truth is that neither in the past nor
in modern times has Charleston, or the state of South Carolina for
that matter, produced a major American novelist or poet or musician
or painter. And it is picayune to mourn the failure or to blow up the
minor literary figures into major ones. Because Charleston is a part
of the South and the United States, and her great novelist might well
be not William Gilmore Simms, good as he was for his time, but
William Faulkner or even Herman Melville.

I will try to atone by remarking that only Charleston, of all the
towns in the state, violates the restrictive liquor laws to offer the
visitor a civilized drink over the bar; and by quoting the late Ludwig
Lewisohn: "A race lived here that loved dignity without ostentation,
books and wine and human distinction. Its sins, which were many,
fade into the past. They were always less vulgar and ugly than the
sins of those who have come after."

Less than fifty miles below Charleston—longer if you drive by the
famous Magnolia and Middleton Place gardens—the town of Beaufort (pronounced Bewfort) clings to another curving bay with something of Charleston's grace. Many of its houses have an architectural
kinship, though their tiered piazzas generally face the street.

Most of them were built by planters to escape their often isolated
and dull establishments on the Sea Islands. They were saved from
General Sherman by their usefulness as quarters for Union forces

which occupied the town throughout the Civil War. Their owners scattered, and their descendants might still claim Beaufort to be an occupied town, since few of the planters had the cash left to redeem their homes from the vindictive Federal taxes.

But few clouds linger from the storm: the chief relics of the past in Beaufort are the piazzas looking out across the bay and the live oaks and such serenely neutral monuments as St. Helena's Episcopal Church (founded 1712), which lifts its Yankee-donated spire over dead Confederate soldiers. Men and women of three centuries lie there, but one thinks first of the soldiers; here, for example, is an inscription which almost unbearably epitomizes the old regime, its virtues, its graces, and its limitations:

CAPT. PAUL HAMILTON—20 years
(30 battles)

*Special Order*

On his last battlefield, he displayed as he has done on every occasion every quality which adorns the perfect soldier. In his death our cause has lost an ardent defender, his state a devoted son, and this brigade is called to mourn the untimely fall of a brave, a loved and honored comrade.

By order Wade Hampton
Brig. Gen. Commdg.

From Beaufort to Columbia you follow a route which many plantation refugees took in 1861 and units of Sherman's Army traveled in 1865. But Columbia these days dwells little on the past; it's too busy trying to merit its status as the largest city in the state. It sports not one but two "skyscraper" apartment houses and a real, live supper club with talent imported weekly from up North (no drinks sold by the house—you tote your own bottle).

A visitor in the previous decade called Columbia the "city of philosophy and flowers," a description still pleasing to old Columbians, who look upon their city as a sociable grove of academe, boasting such urbane institutions as the Kosmos Club, whose town-and-gown membership meets twice a month for dinner and a scholarly paper; and cultural attractions as a growing museum of art and a Town Theater that since 1918 has boldly mixed a little Ibsen with the usual Broadway froth.

These graces, though scarcely Athenian, are all connected in one way or another with the presence in Columbia of the University of South Carolina, now showing signs of ancestral vigor. As South Carolina College it had a first-rate reputation for liberal learning until the Civil War, when carpetbag rule and subsequent attacks on its aristocratic leanings pushed it toward futility. Today it is encouraging the growth of graduate departments, and it was one of the first state schools in the Southeast bold enough to give entrance examinations. The University's alumni, however, are more devoted to the facts of football and are generally satisfied if their team can beat Clemson on the State Fair's Big Thursday.

The intense rivalries of that match are sometimes reflected in legislative voting, especially in the wrangling over college appropriations. But wrangling is a prime note in all South Carolina politics, a note intensified by the county-to-county canvass, a Democratic-party requirement for joint debates since 1890. The canvass was conceived by Governor Pitchfork Ben Tillman partially as an honest move to inform the politically ignorant masses, but it quickly degenerated into a kind of medicine show with overtones of a gospel-camp meeting. Crowds would gather for all-day rhetoric, and when the steam was up, the wool-hat boys would urge on the favorites—"Go to it, boy! Burn 'im up!"—while their wives fanned the flies off the waiting fried chicken and jelly cake.

I knew the canvass in its already declining days, the '30's, but it still offered at least one of the old warhorses, Ellison D. (Cotton Ed) Smith, who rode to the U. S. Senate for more than thirty years on a wagonload of cotton, brandishing the buggy whip of White Supremacy. When he parted his lips and bellowed those long rhythmic periods of hypnotic sound and fury, "I—am—an—un—reconstructed Southerner—from the top of my head—to the heels of my shoes," his opponents might as well have climbed down from the stump.

Many of the intracounty canvasses had the obscene flavor of a two-bit carnival. The biggest clowns got the vote. I remember one who shouted in a humble precinct, "I'm one of you boys and you know it. I was born down here and raised down here and you know it. And, by God, I'm still one of you boys, even though I *have* moved up with a better class of people." It was so good they voted for him to the man.

But I don't intend to malign all South Carolina politicians. Many are able, educated men, and those who got by on clowning alone are surrendering to the competition of television.

Modern South Carolina politics may have given the state Pitchfork Ben Tillman and his successors, but the people of the Pee Dee section, several eastern counties lying along the Pee Dee River, gave the state David R. Coker, who in turn gave the world the "priceless boon of pedigreed seed." In his efforts to improve strains of cotton and tobacco and in his support of manufacturing interests, Mr. Coker (1870–1938) carried on in the tradition of Governor David R. Williams, the scientific farmer said to have introduced the mule to the South in the early 19th Century, and of his father, Major James Lide Coker, experimental planter whose benefactions made possible, among other things, the founding of Coker College for Women at Hartsville.

The upcountry proper spreads out northwest from the Pee Dee. Traveling from Columbia, you recognize it as you strike the long green hills of Fairfield County. Though the character of upcountry life still betrays a more rigorous and a plainer heritage, scattered towns and houses show traces of low-country ease; Camden, for instance, thinks of itself as a piny refuge of Charleston manners. The town's present distinction lies in its grove-shaded ante-bellum houses, and in at least one public building, the gracefully plain Presbyterian Church designed by South Carolina's only architect of genius, Robert Mills. Many of the country's fine race horses are trained in Camden, and fashionable South Carolina turns the spring Carolina Cup running into a "twenty-five-acre cocktail party."

But in Camden I always get an upcountry chip on my shoulder. I'm done with white columns and trailing moss and homesick for red waters and rain-gray houses and hickory-nut trees. I suffer the dual loyalties that author John Rice said moved his father, who would remark after some social humiliation, "I have often wished I had been a gentleman," but who when telling a favorite story of Tillman's jibe at a lordly opponent would become the proud, poor boy of his origins.

When I say rain-gray houses, I'm aware that most of the houses in the upcountry are painted. What I mean to imply is that the upcountry heritage returns to plain houses, plain living and a plain religion, much as the silver-service set of Rock Hill or Spartanburg or Greenville might wish to deny it. And I do mean plain, not debased and surely not humble, though pretension can't tell the difference. A Georgia lady, joined up with a preposterous band of bluebloods tracing their lines to the Magna Carta, visibly shrank when I told her the church of her ancestor was a plain, unpainted affair, suitable to a God-fearing people. I suspect she promptly dropped him and took up an ancestor of more acceptable denomination.

Cotton grows on upcountry hills as well as in the lowlands, though decreasingly now since competition from the deeper South has drained the profit away. The farms have always been small, generally under 300 acres, and worked not only by Negro field hands but by the owners themselves. But when the upcountry farmer as I used to know him came in from the fields at night he washed himself and sat down to a polite and plenteous supper, laid out, probably, on a walnut drop-leaf table handed down from his great-grandfather. His wife might have toiled as hard as he, but over a wood stove in the kitchen, not at his side in the fields. For she was a South Carolina lady, and ladies don't chop weeds in the cotton patch.

Those two went to church every Sunday, the Presbyterian or the Baptist, and sent their sons and daughters to college if they could squeeze enough money from the cotton. They believed in education but preferred the utilitarian variety. (Their folks had always been too righteous and poor to care much for the classical South Carolina College at Columbia, and Pitchfork Ben Tillman built Clemson and Winthrop to suit their needs.)

As a child I often visited such people; I recall especially one couple. Their home was a spacious cottage built about 1825, with dormers in the roof, a long front piazza and interior paneling of mellowed pine. They lived a simpler life than I knew in the low country, they had harder soil to dig their living from and less time and substance for pleasure; but they loved their lands, they enjoyed their neighbors and they ate well. They talked out of long, humorous and affectionate memories; and they ate hominy and fried smoked ham and corn bread and turnip greens and an ambrosial pie they made up for hot summer Sundays, preserved damsons or scuppernong peels and whipped cream on squares of cold piecrust. They admired plain speech and honest intentions and hated sham. But it was a peril to mistake them for humble people. Their ancestors had fought for their country and held it: they were as proud in their way as were the coastal gentry.

And they had their caste distinctions even as Charleston. My grandfather, for instance, loved to quote an old upcountry farmer's slyly discriminating record of his children's marriages. "My son Alex," he would say, "married Louisa Bolton, sister of Thad and Thomas Bolton —mighty fine men they are—and they live up thar. Now my daughter Lavinia, she married Evans Curtis—good man to make a crop, he is—and they live over thar. But my son Hap, by the Lord God Almighty, married Sadie Suggs, old Coot Suggs' daughter, and they live down thar."

Many of these upcountry people were Dissenters of such dissidence that they backed into whatever causes they joined. During the Revolution they could scarcely decide which tyranny they hated most, that of George III or of their highhanded brothers in Charleston. (At least George, they often thought, was farther removed.) And during the Secession period some wavered between the evils of greedy industrialism and the myth of injured chivalry, fighting ultimately in a cause they never made. My mother has a stack of old Aunt Hannah Wylie's letters which belabor the secession movement and often in language surprisingly Anglo-Saxon for a lady. She reports attending a secession debate that was "more like a cornhusking than anything I can compare it to" and ridicules the argument of Barnwell Rhett (South Carolina Senator, often called the "father of secession") that departure from the Union would make them rich. He was cheered, she says, for "every puke anecdote he told." She was a typical upcountry Scotch-Irish Presbyterian Dissenter.

But today the cotton-mill towns—Spartanburg, Greenville, Anderson, Rock Hill and Lancaster—characterize the upcountry perhaps even more than the small farms of Scotch-Irish Dissenters. Mills thrived on the hill country's two principal resources—water power, and poor whites in flight from their grudging corn patches to the northwest. They rattled down on their mountain wagons, the purest Anglo-Saxon stock in the world, in a pioneering migration from the servitude of poverty to the servitude of the looms. There were quarters for the family in villages around the factory and jobs for all, too, for children of eight and ten and pregnant wives and the lean, overalled men with ancestral blue eyes and the grave mouths of defeated pride.

These millworkers gave South Carolina its first proletarian element, that is a distinct and almost alien body within the body politic. And they became a proletarian political force as Negroes never could, if for no other reason than that they had the vote and Negroes didn't.

But, of course, for the more potent reason that they were free men reduced to a kind of slavery and knew it.

One of their bosses, the late Colonel Elliott White Springs, described their heroic record in his miscellany *Clothes Make the Man:* "They fought with Braddock on the Monongahela; they killed Ferguson at Kings Mountain; they went with their Cousin Andrew Jackson to New Orleans; they went to Mexico for Cousin James K. Polk; they flung the gauntlet at Cousin Abe Lincoln, and they refused to be reconstructed by Cousin Andrew Johnson; they joined their North Carolina and Tennessee cousins in the Thirtieth Division to break the Hindenburg Line; they saddled Halsey's white horse at Tokyo; and they are ready to take on Joe Stalin or anyone else who attempts to exploit them. Every spinner could be a Colonial Dame, a D.A.R., or a U.D.C., if she wished."

The point is they could not take on the mill owners, who in the old days did exploit them. And through isolation in the company villages they were made a race of social pariahs. In my boyhood they were "lint-heads" and "mill-tacks," set off by the mountain twang of their speech, their faded ginghams and overalls and their snuff-dipping suspicion of the world in general. But as I found out when my mother taught some of their daddies and mammas and grandmas to read and write, they were often kind, loyal and quietly self-respecting. Their increasing assimilation is one of the most striking notes of change in upcountry towns. You can't tell them on the street now from anybody else.

They get good wages today, of course, from their remote corporation employers as they did from such intensely personal bosses as Colonel Springs, one of the last of the old race of cotton-mill kings, who ran his tri-county empire from Fort Mill in the eastern corner of Piedmont, South Carolina. With a great many millions to his name and absolute control of the business in his restless hands, the colonel could afford the tribal South Carolina right to tell any man to go to hell.

When the unions moved up their big guns, the Flying Ace of World War I is said to have warned the help that if they chose the enemy's ranks, they could eat the enemy's chow. And they stood fast. In return for their loyalty they get most of the benefits unions have won and some they haven't, such as the use of resort facilities at Myrtle Beach and college scholarships for their sons and daughters.

In addition they got what is rare for industrial workers these days, the sense of laboring for a man rather than a machine, a man many have known all their lives and one who called more than a few by name. And they got a lot of free entertainment. The colonel was at heart a Princeton Triangle man who grew up to be a *College Humor* man in an age that had lost its taste for John Held, Jr., and Clara Bow. He was also, probably, just a writer gone wrong; the only personal boast in his *Clothes Make the Man* is that he once earned the highest price ever paid for a short story up to that time, sixty-two hundred and fifty dollars. He was modest enough not to remind readers of the several films made from his stories, including one called *Body and Soul*. He did, however, offer gratis to office visitors copies of his *War Birds*.

The ads he composed for his bed sheets sometimes looked as though they had strayed from old-time *Ballyhoo*, but they had the virtue at least of spoofing the slick pieties of Madison Avenue and apparently they sold the goods. I daresay they also pleased the help, as did, no doubt, his legendary local stunts. When his daughter was married, for instance, he had her descend to the Fort Mill plant in her wedding regalia and parade among the looms.

About twenty-five miles from the colonel's desk lies the site of the important Revolutionary battle, Kings Mountain, in which some of his forebears undoubtedly fought, and I'm sure he would agree with other South Carolinians that the battle was the turning point of the Revolution.

From Kings Mountain southwest you follow a stretch of what Jonathan Daniels called the Gold Avenue, the South's rich industrial artery from Danville to Atlanta. Of the cities in this area the almost twin towns of Spartanburg and Greenville are the fourth and third largest in the state, but Greenville, with more than a 20,000 lead over her rival, is so busy that, to hear the natives talk, their only worry is where the next million dollars is coming from.

Almost every approach to Greenville displays the brand-new plants of brand-new enterprises. On one of these approaches you pass a sign not only of Greenville's prosperity but of a kind of luxury South Carolina has never before been able to afford: a 1000-acre tract on which is rising a $22,800,000 plant for Furman University. That South Carolina Baptists, who support Furman, are raising such a pile of money testifies to their strength in the state and symbolizes their strength in the Greenville section, often referred to as the Bible Belt of the Bible Belt. It's so Biblically inclined, a bookstore proprietor told me, that the only important theft she ever suffered was a seven-teen-dollar copy of the Good Book.

Twenty-five miles southwest of Greenville a comfortable inn, super-modern in aspect, stands unexpectedly on a steep rise of the Clemson College campus. Built and operated by the college, the Clemson House is only one sign of a general face-lifting of the agricultural and mechanical college which Tillman pressured into being. The college is located on the grounds of Fort Hill, the John C. Calhoun estate left to South Carolina by Thomas G. Clemson, the Philadelphia scientist who married Calhoun's daughter. Though the college has a huge new agricultural center, it is probably giving more attention these days to supplying engineers for the state's new industries. Some time ago, for instance, it completed a new center for training in ceramics. But the most impressive change is the replacement of the old barracks with a dormitory of a thousand rooms, resembling the Gropius-planned Graduate Center at Harvard.

In its role as the state's chief engineering college Clemson was shaped by upcountry industrial needs. But it has always drawn students from every section, as Tillman might have ranted, "between the palm-lined shores of Hilton Head and the rock-ribbed brow of Caesars Head." It has furthered, in other words, that reconciliation between upcountry and low which the college aimed at in its early days by drawing together sons of the Cavalier coast and sons of the Calvinist hills.

It is fitting, therefore, that two symbolic houses should stand on the Clemson campus: Fort Hill, the home of John C. Calhoun, first and last an upcountry Scotch-Irish Dissenter, though he came to address the nation as spokesman of the slave-rich coastal sires; and Hanover, the transplanted home of Paul de Julien, a low-country planter who pioneered in the early 1700's on lands now lying beneath the Santee-Cooper power development's Lake Moultrie. The Calhouns epitomized the stern Scotch-Irish breed which settled the backcountry Carolina; and the de Juliens epitomized one strain of the French-English breed which wrought *Peu à Peu* ("Little by Little," the words Paul de Julien inscribed on a Hanover chimney) a graceful culture in the low-country swamps. (It is fitting, too, that Calhoun's wife, a low-country aristocrat of Huguenot descent, should lie among the hills her husband plowed as a boy and that the fierce old statesman himself should rest in her home city, Charleston, which came to love him as well as any native son.)

But if their energies flowered in different patterns of life, the two breeds shared courage and the love of freedom. And however science may belittle the claims of blood, South Carolinians have bravely defended the worth of theirs. And they will keep on believing—I know as one of them—that to be a South Carolinian born and bred, with Cavalier and Huguenot and Scotch-Irish blood in one's veins, is to stand not appreciably lower than the angels in the Great Chain of Being.

# Georgia

## by CALDER WILLINGHAM

*"Aha," said Cousin Virginia. "Come all this way to write us up, h'm? What's it going to be—the truth, or are you going to struggle real hard to find something good to say about old Georgia?"*

*"Aw, naow, hon," said Cousin Gary, with a broad and beamy grin. "Ain't nothing bad could be said about old Georgia. What you mean, the truth?"*

*"I mean," said Cousin Virginia, "that it's hot, dull, hellish and horrible, and couldn't possibly interest anybody who isn't so unfortunate as to have to live here."*

*"Aw, shucks!" said Gary. "Go on, hon. Shucks!"*

The heat of Georgia's flatlands has given its mountains a special meaning to Georgians. There in those hills is a cool green paradise of forest, lake and hidden, cloud-hung cove; of air like champagne, of waterfalls and rhododendron, and fieldstone fireplaces with logs burning on a summer night. It is fitting that any tour of Georgia, any "march to the sea" by an ex-Southerner such as myself, should originate in the mountains. That's how Sherman did it, and while I have neither his motives nor his destructive powers, his path is still a good one to follow.

Georgia is physically the most complex Eastern state. It is the largest east of the Mississippi; the city of Rome, in its northwest corner, is almost midway between Miami and Chicago. Its surface is a long, wide table sloping gradually down from the mountains to the sea. Tilt the table erect, North above and South below. High to the left and right are heavily forested mountains, separated by a region of hills and valleys that blend into a wide, gently undulating band. The line of demarcation is clearly visible: above the band are hills and mountains; below it, is an almost perfectly level area reaching to the swamps of Florida and the coastal tidelands of the Atlantic.

The mountains, the hills and valleys, the Piedmont belt, the coastal plain, and the tidelands and sea isles—these are the five geographic divisions of Georgia. Each is an area unto itself. Enormous differences in physical appearance, climate, occupation and way of life distinguish them. Such distinctions indicate the inexactness of the term "Georgian," and atop these distinctions must be added the crucial though diminishing contrast between city and country. The surprising thing is that, vast and varied as Georgia is, its people have a continuous identity as Georgians.

Let us go on a fishing trip, a Georgia fishing trip, to Jack's River in the mountains. There is no better place to settle life's deepest problems, and simultaneously drink hearty and discuss the fair sex far from the delicate ears of Southern ladies. Here is as wild a spot as you will find anywhere in the East. We will go from the heart of the valley-and-hill region deep into the mountains, over good highways to black-tops, and from black-tops to a forest-ranger road, and on to a mere wagon-trail excuse for a road, on till Cousin Billy's new car trembles and heaves as we head upward to the smoky blue hills.

The hills and mountains of Georgia occupy roughly a tenth of its area—a considerable piece of real estate. And note that they are *not* the "foothills" of the Smokies; they are too high and wild for that. They are a continuation of the Appalachian chain.

Wildflowers of incredible variety thrive on their slopes, with almost tropical masses of rhododendron and other flowering shrubs. The original hardwood continental forest, untouched by the glaciers that scoured New England, still grows here, a forest that once may have been world-wide: close relatives of trees found here grow today in China. Humus accumulated through the ages, Southern sunshine, and the torrential rainfall that gave both the Blue Ridge and the nearby Smokies their names, have produced a forest here that is taller, larger and more lush than the northern hardwood forest of New England.

At dawn, we drive from the deserted, gray streets of Rome to Calhoun. On either side of the highway we see rich farmland, rolling
pastures dewy-silver in the dawn, and fat, high-bred dairy cattle.
The earth is a shocking Technicolor red—not shocking to me, because
I was brought up in this country and regard bright red as the natural
color of earth; but shocking to those who think the "red hills of
Georgia" are a fable. No fable. Red. Very red.

On we go, past the Indian ruins of the Cherokee capital, New
Echota, where a type of the Cherokee language has recently been
discovered—or so I was told at Cousin Virginia's party. We are still
in pine country, the yellow or loblolly or field pine is everywhere,
but we see enormous willow oaks along the streets of Dalton, the
"chenille-bedspread capital of the world." This is a nice place to stop
and get a bedspread with tufts forming a multicolored outline of a
peacock, in case you happen to want such a bedspread. Millions do.
But we continue north on a black-top, on through the bright-gold
early-morning sunshine. Since this is a fishing trip, lazy Southern pro-
fanity comes into play, emanating a secret, delicious hilarity.

The scene is changing, the valley has become narrower and we
see blue mountains in the distance. We by-pass Blue Ridge in mid-
morning as the fishing language becomes all the headier. There is a
certain pure art to this talk, at times a kind of poetry; it is not really
vulgar, though all of us would collapse with horror if some madness
should drive us to speak this way back home.

The valley narrows again as we turn upon a smaller hard-top. We
are out of red-clay country now; the earth is brown. The mountains
are much closer, the farms wilder. It is already cooler. Then the hard-
top vanishes and we are on a good dirt road. We turn again, now
upon a road maintained by the Forest Service; it is narrow but passable, and we are rising and winding through unbelievably dense
woods. Tulip trees a hundred and twenty feet tall rise like high thin
columns on every side, with hickories, oaks, ash, maples, ironwood—
it would be hard for the car to fall very far down the steep mountainside, and that is a reassuring thought since Cousin Billy, our driver,
has tossed caution to the winds and gotten fully into the fishing spirit.
Later he will jump into the campfire, but fortunately this reckless
gay mood has not seized him yet.

The Forest Service road comes to an abrupt ending. A wagon trail,
a bear path—no, an indistinct foot trail that a bear once passed over
—winds ahead, jagged with boulders and writhing crazily this way

and that, a dark tunnel through the trees. On we go, lurching and jouncing through country that looks undiscovered even by the Indians. A mile, two miles, a hairpin turn and another car; back up, stop; pistol practice, down the old hatch, pile in, boys; a dip, a turn, and finally and amazingly we are at the Jack's River camp: there is the musty-smelling old cabin with its rock fireplace, and the river itself in the glade below. A quarter of a mile away is George Schuler's farm, and that is all; mountains like smoky giants stand all around and loom overhead. Gone are telephones, electricity, television, movies. We are among the bear and the deer, the mountain laurel and dark hemlock groves.

The Jack's River is a typical stream of the Southern mountains, as George Schuler is a typical Southern mountain man. The Jack's is fast-flowing dark water, filled with boulders and stones polished smooth. Trout pools are not so deep that they cannot be walked for the mile or so of the river that is fished. In midsummer, one sleeps under blankets here.

A flash flood once swept down the Jack's, isolating George Schuler and a group of city fishermen. The party half forded and half swam the stream and got back to camp, all but George, a little bright-eyed man in his late sixties, who stayed and slept on the ground, rose in the morning with the birds and crossed the stream at its normal depth.

"I'm too old a man," said George, "to drown right yet."

Mountain men for the most part swim as well as old British tars; water is regarded as a dangerous element in contact with the skin. Spending the night on damp ground, however, soaked to the bones, is nothing to worry about—so long as you don't make the fatal error of changing later into dry clothes: that's asking for pneumonia. The thing to do is "let 'em dry on ye."

What George lives on is a mystery. Fish, game, a few vegetables from the small mountain-ringed farm. Of course, some people in George's position might stir a little "smoke" once in a while, but if George has ever done that sort of thing, he has turned his back on it today. Whisky, says George, leads to disputes between man and wife. "We don't drink it," he declares, "nor make it ary one." A small, soft-spoken man with a hand the size of a doll's, clad in antediluvian overalls, George peers like a wise old woods creature from below a "wool" hat, a faint smile on his face. Perhaps he is thinking that fishing expeditions are an amusing joke.

Rome, in north Georgia, is the capital of the valley-and-hill region, a town built among hills at the junction of the Oostanaula and Etowah rivers, which form the Coosa. The town is known, among other things, for the nearby Berry Schools and College, a fabulous educational empire created out of nothing, except an iron will and vision, by Miss Martha Berry. The students are chosen almost entirely from the rural South and do not pay to attend; but they all contribute by working (in the field of agriculture, mostly), and thus gain experience along with book learning—an educational system widely admired for many reasons. The campus of Berry Schools has been called, with justice, the most beautiful in America. It is certainly one of the largest. Miss Martha, by the time of her death, had accumulated more than thirty thousand acres for the "grounds" of her schools.

I was born in Atlanta but grew up in Rome from the age of three, all through the depression years. I remember the vacant stores on Broad Street, empty and dusty in the oppressive heat of summer. Model A's coughing up and down the street by the war monuments. Red-necked farmers in faded and patched overalls leaning against the red brick buildings on the Cotton Block, hopelessness in their eyes, tobacco juice dribbling down the stubble on their chins, the shade an angled dark line across their wool hats, as their wives, gaunt and pathetic with two or three or four dirty little tow-haired children, walk down the hot sidewalk to the ten-cent store for stick candy. They go past the old Rivoli Theater, whose patrons' summer-bare feet may or may not get bitten, as my own were, by gigantic rats the size of fox terriers. Cowboy pictures, with Buck Jones and Hoot Gibson, are showing, along with Boris Karloff as *The Mummy*.

Outside, the sun bakes down with blinding power, a power that would put half of New York City in the hospital. The ultraviolet whams down like a physical force, and atmospheric "lazy lulus" shimmer on the horizon. The blue asphalt on Broad Street softens, becomes mushy, and black bubbles rise in the tar patches. It won't rain, though the air is drenched with moisture, because "it's too *hot* to rain." Hot is the word: it's a hundred and five, a hundred and six, a hundred and seven in the shade, and who knows what in the sun. There is not a breath of air, not the hint of a breeze. The heavy moisture will drift on to become rain in the mountains, replaced by more moisture from the Gulf.

Life is at a standstill. The burning days and wet nights pass in a kind of delirium. Businessmen huddle in little clumps at the dining room of the Hotel General Forrest. Here and there are the Blue Eagle signs of the NRA. An occasional truck of CCC boys rides by. The sun bakes down and nothing happens. The stores stay empty and dusty, the Coosa Country Club limps along, as the grass burns brown and the members resign or fail to send in their dues. Old trees die in the heat, the corn in the red fields outside town is withered and yellow and runted two feet high, the cotton sickly, the peach orchards a dismal yellow-green . . . and dust rises in choking clouds from every country road around.

Dust is in the tall willow oaks and hackberries on Second, Third and Fourth avenues, and there is no money anywhere. Store clerks struggle against suicide if they're fired from an eight-dollar-a-week job, the Elks Club almost collapses, while nice ladies sip ice-cold Coca-Cola at bridge parties and deplore home relief, which after all is so spiritually demoralizing—a man can always find something to do if he has a little git-up, even if it's only cutting grass.

Call it an area of basic economic weakness hit doubly hard by a national calamity, but there stand those dusty, empty stores, the plate glass all dirty and dead flies on the display counters, their feet stuck up in the air. We have one, an empty one, and there is no one to rent it. But there was someone, finally: a traveling magician, for a week. He makes sparks come out of an apple in your hand; it's *electrical*, that's what it is.

"A million volts, little girl, are passing even now through your body cells and fluids. Do you feel them emerge through the fibers of your hand?"

"Eek!" said the little girl.

"Folks, that there electricity has just leapt out of that apple through this little girl's hand, right through space and you have seen it your own selves, or call me a liar and a tadpole!"

That summer never ended; it went on forever. But somehow fall was there, and the rain came, and flooded West Rome, and there were nine thousand tons of mud distributed evenly over Fourth Ward.

The Rome of the depression years is gone as though it never existed. Now the stores on Broad Street are not only rented but are remodeled with new plate glass, curved brick and stainless steel. The old Rivoli Theater has vanished. A trim new dress shop stands in its place. The businessmen don't huddle now, they get together and

**GEORGIA** The Old South lives on—here Mrs. Lester Hardwick graces a lovely tableau of trees and sward and stately mansion at dusk.

**FLORIDA** (*center spread*) Lunch and drinks beside the pool at La Coquille, in Palm Beach.

**MISSISSIPPI**  A crossroad store slumbers under the hot noonday sun near Bentonia.

smoke cigars and slam each other on the back, and smile faintly at the memory of the grim past. There are several new millionaires, and quite a few new multi-hundred-thousandaires, not all of them from "nice old families," but it doesn't seem to matter so much any more.

Everything is different. Cousin Donald's employees at Lindale make more Lady Pepperell sheets than ever before at salaries many times depression pay; the huge General Electric plant has arrived; and a kraft-paper mill. Subdivisions spread in all directions. The war monuments are gone off Broad Street: there are too many cars, and not old Model A's but shining chrome-covered new cars by the thousands. There is no mud in Fourth Ward any more, because a levee has tamed the Etowah, the Oostanaula and the Coosa. On those acres of dismal mud have been built a housing project, a new state hospital and an entire new business district. The deserted, run-down country club is a paradise of emerald green, flourishing with new members. The country roads around town have all been hard-topped and dust doesn't blow into the town any more—only it isn't a town now, but a booming bona fide city. What's more, it isn't *hot,* either —why, the climate is downright balmy and delightful. It was the depression that was hot. And besides, with so much air conditioning, who cares if it gets mildly and healthfully warm now and then?

The Georgia Piedmont, an undulating plain that stretches like a huge band across the center of the state, was not only the scene of *Gone With the Wind* and *Tobacco Road,* it is also the most vital area of Georgia in an economic way. With the exception of Savannah, the largest Georgia cities are located in the Piedmont: Atlanta, Augusta, Macon, Columbus, Athens, La Grange, Milledgeville.

As a child, I remember riding on dirt roads through the Piedmont, past old homes of the "Tara" type, as well as past dilapidated, awful, unpainted shacks of poor tenant farmers. This was before the days of good road maps. You had to ask constantly where you were, how to get to your destination, if the road was passable, and if the bridge ahead would hold a car. This meant stopping at a farm house, having a glass of buttermilk with the farmer, praising his coon dogs, commenting on the weather, telling an anecdote about Uncle So-and-So who used to live in this area—all of this in the deep shade of the front porch, as cicadas droned and sang and hummed in the Georgia summertime. Finally the farmer would give his "calc'lations" about how to "git thar," and then a prolonged good-by-that-sho-was-good-buttermilk, and back into the Model A, whereupon the coon dogs that were friendly on the porch would go mad with indignation and come racing, and follow along howling and barking and snapping at the tires for three or four hundred yards.

I also can recall visits to old mansions in the Piedmont countryside, old columned brick homes spared for one reason or another by Sherman. Many of these had fallen almost into ruins. But there they stood, magnificent gnarled oaks and hackberries around them, needing paint and with leaks in the roof, musty-smelling, stamped with poverty. Why, I wondered as a child, was it always considered such a treat to take visitors out and show them "the old slave quarters"? Invariably, these were in even worse disrepair than the main houses, with tattered tar-paper roofs, bare dirt floors, broken windows and doors of rough-cut pine hanging askew on crude hand-forged hinges long gone to rust. What was so fascinating, I wondered, about this? Why that glow of quiet pride? "Naow, suh, Ah will take you and yoah li'l boy out to see *the old slave quarters*." And the solemn procession, as if on the way to behold the Holy Grail, would begin. I can see now the expression on my father's face as he looked solemnly at *the old slave quarters*, nodded with a grave air, and said, "H'm-m-m-m-m-m." Very noncommittal, but this was always considered an adequate response; the host, usually some old gentleman with rheumy eyes and white hair and perhaps a little yellowish goatee, would inevitably give my father a grateful look, and back then we would go, mission accomplished.

Yankees and new-rich Southerners (and a few old-time "family type" Southerners) have taken over these old homes now. They are remodeled and furnished in the best of taste. It's big medicine socially, heap big strong medicine, to have one of these places, especially if it was "in the family." This claim is not too hard to make. Southerners in general and Georgians in particular can establish a blood relationship with nearly anyone: "The cousin of some distant great-great-aunt, I will have you know, brought up a whole crew of wild niggers from New Orleans, and built Red Roof Hall himself. It's been in the family for years. . . ."

The city of Atlanta is the capital of the Piedmont, and thus logically also the capital of Georgia. Atlanta is perhaps not quite, to the Southeast, what Boston is to New England, but it is not far from it. Along with New Orleans and Houston, it is one of the great cities in the South. Georgia Tech, Rich's department store, Emory University, Agnes Scott, many other schools and many good hospitals help make Atlanta today the hub of Georgia, financially and culturally. This was not always true. Just yesterday, Atlanta was an ugly railroad center. The growth of the city, along with the industrialization of the Piedmont since the end of the depression, is probably the most spectacular development in Georgia in recent years.

Ralph McGill, the celebrated editor of the Atlanta *Constitution*, takes an interest in many things, including Georgia novelists. He takes them to lunch at the Capital City Club, and usually gets them buzzed.

This of course puts them in a mood to love Georgia, and to love Atlanta and the Capital City Club, and the Bobby Jones Golf Course, and the South—above all else, the South!

"We understand the South," says McGill, "you and I. It isn't a backward, benighted hell hole, now is it? Problems? Sure, tragic problems, but don't tell me the South isn't changing and growing. What's more, my friend, where else in this country are you going to find people who are kinder, more honest or more human than the people of this damned and condemned and glamorized and glorified state? Is it true, or not? Do we understand the South, and Georgia, or don't we? Be frank with me. Do we or don't we?"

"Ralph, we understand Georgia. I might not know much in this world, Ralph, but I know one thing. When it comes to understanding Georgia, Ralph, we are in there."

The brilliant comprehension of Georgia that Ralph McGill inspired at the Capital City Club is a bit dimmed now. Too bad. But I think, in all seriousness, that if other sections of the country listened more to Ralph McGill and others like him, many misconceptions about Georgia would vanish, or at least a more balanced picture of the state would prevail.

In any event, there is no doubt today that the buttermilk-on-the-porch Piedmont has disappeared. Today's sophisticated farm dogs wouldn't dream of barking at the cars that zoom down the new highways, and perhaps even the old slave quarters have collapsed into dust.

Savannah is one of the most attractive cities in the South for a number of reasons, one being the large number of separate, small parks scattered through the downtown area. Besides, one of the greatest trees in America grows well there, and Savannah has taken inspired advantage of it: *Quercus virginiana,* the great live oak. The city is graced with several major park boulevards of four lanes separated by double rows of spreading oaks. The majesty and charm and beauty of these trees defies description. They make Savannah one of the most pleasant places to live in the entire United States.

The city is "picturesque," too, and like other seacoast cities, has almost an Old World atmosphere. Much that can be said about New Orleans or Charleston can also be said about Savannah: quiet, "gracious" living, a highly refined society of old families, excellent restaurants, a dash of night life. Today, however, Savannah is in commercial turmoil. An old friend, whose insurance offices are located in truly Old World surroundings, expressed the thought that perhaps he should modernize; and when a man of his traditionalism, talks of modernizing, Savannah *is* in turmoil.

There are two especially remarkable sights in or near Savannah. One is the Bonaventure Cemetery, which surely must be the most eerily beautiful cemetery in the world. Its enormous, gnarled live oaks, with their almost horizontal limbs hung and draped and shrouded in Spanish moss, form a landscape like a fantastic dream. Outside Savannah, at the Isle of Hope, lies another dream realm: Wormsloe Plantation, regarded by many as the most fabulous home in the South. Wormsloe is the sort of place that, if used as the background of a movie, would provoke the ironic comment: "Hollywood exaggerates so." It is hard to believe that such a place exists, even if you are actually there, enjoying a Scotch and soda with its owner and discussing (of all things) modern American writing.

The central residence is built on eight hundred acres adjacent to the Inland Waterway. The entrance to the grounds is approximately a mile from the house, which is reached by a drive lined with live oaks that create an effect of unbelievable grandeur and magnificence. And on the grounds immediately around the house are even larger live oaks—huge, spreading, gnarled, moss-draped giants that overshadow gardens of azalea and other flowering shrubs. The house itself has a raised front porch with tall white columns and curved steps on either side. Inside, the marble mantels, the furnishings and family portraits are ante-bellum.

The setting for all this is a twenty-acre park lovely with huge oaks, camellia-japonica trees, climbing purple wisteria and a dense carpet of Algerian ivy. The estate also has many acres of junglelike wild forestland—tropical bamboo growth among palms and oaks—as well as a private yacht basin on the Inland Waterway and the ruins of pre-Revolutionary Fort Wimberley. Wormsloe, incidentally, is one instance of an old Southern home owned by the same family that built it originally.

The sea isles of Georgia, the "Golden Isles," are one step from Savannah. Exactly what Sherman did to them I do not know. Perhaps he went over and had a swim and thought about the hell of war. In any case, the sea isles are there, and they are utterly different from northern Georgia. There is no denying their beauty or their tremendous assets as vacation areas, but Sea Island, the best-known of the Golden Isles, seems hardly Southern or Georgian in atmosphere, since most of its "cottage" owners come from such places as Philadelphia. (Eugene O'Neill's old "cottage" at Sea Island is indistinguishable from others built in the same period.) The place reminded me of Beverly Hills plus a beach. It is frankly at the service of the well-to-do—of "correct religious background," as one of its publicity officials told me. The famous hotel there, the Cloister, is a splendid establishment with luxurious grounds, a superb beach and swimming pool, and wonderful food. It also offers riding, tennis, a beautiful golf course, and in general much solid comfort to those who can get in.

I asked a woman at the Cloister for information about nearby Jekyll Island, the one-time haunt of millionaires that is now a Georgia state park.

"Jekyll Island," she replied, "is of no interest, and I would not go there, indeed not. I haven't been there myself since the days when Jekyll was Jekyll. It's not Jekyll any more. It's now going to be run over by hordes of Georgia crackers, and I assure you, sir, that nice Northern people, if they read your publication, couldn't have the least interest in it."

I went to Jekyll, the island paradise of the day of J. P. Morgan, Sr. The story is that J.P. and a few of his friends assembled a squad of doctors from Johns Hopkins and told them, "Find the healthiest and most beautiful spot on earth. We want to buy it."

The doctors looked long and far. They found one promising area somewhere in the South of France, but then discovered that it was not for sale. They found another in Egypt, but Egypt was too far away. Finally the doctors settled on Jekyll Island, off the south Georgia coast not far from Brunswick, and thus was born the most exclusive social nonesuch of modern times, the Jekyll Island Club.

Millions of dollars were spent there to build "cottages" and a big gingerbread clubhouse. No one except a select group of the incredibly rich was allowed to set a foot on the island. To be invited there in the old days was It. But new days came and wore away the substance of the Club. Perhaps, as Cleveland Amory has remarked, the Club was so exclusive it bored itself to death.

Now anyone can cross the new causeway to Jekyll and its huge old "cottages" from an era that has passed. Even the ghosts of the Morgans, Vanderbilts, Bakers, Hills, Pulitzers, McCormicks, Goulds and Goodyears seem to have fled this beautiful island and its once sacrosanct beaches, and all the visitor feels is that the luxury of yesteryear looks a little silly now. Georgia's crackers, however, should enjoy the island's eleven miles of spectacular beach, down which J. P. Morgan, Sr., used to putt-putt grandly on his little electric scooter bug, if they only keep an eye peeled for the descendants of the 300 wild boars sent to him by King Umberto of Italy.

Those born and bred on the south Georgia coastal plain (which Sherman had the good sense to avoid) are more likely to admire it than outsiders. The landscape, as any motorist driving through to Florida knows, is rather depressing. There seems to be nothing in it except millions and millions of slash pines, used in the production of turpentine, and the vast Okefenokee Swamp, used as the background for Hollywood movies.

There is more than that, however, to the region, and one place to see its true appeal is in the virgin pine stands of the great estates around Thomasville. Many Presidents have come to the area to hunt quail. Incomparably the most delicious of all game birds of the South, quail are hunted here on horseback through slash and longleaf pine, even by north Georgians who can afford to make the trip. In fact, it is a kind of index of your financial standing in north Georgia; if you are anybody at all, you pile your bird dogs in the back of the station wagon and head for these southern happy hunting grounds.

Also in south Georgia is one of the most interesting places I saw in the entire state—the private project for public happiness known as the Ida Cason Callaway Gardens. Located not far from Columbus and southwest of Atlanta, the Gardens are beyond all question the most remarkable thing of this kind in Georgia. One finds here thousands of acres of magnificent forestland, a five-mile drive of excellent paved road, and wildflower, holly, magnolia and azalea trails; also superb fishing, a beautiful golf course as good as any in the South, a large and attractive clubhouse with excellent food, boats to rent, a sight-seeing barge, a miniature train for children, a country store with country-cured hams and water-ground meal and delicacies from everywhere, and much, much more, including a snow-white man-made beach. And what price admits you to all of this? Fifty cents.

The puzzle, to me, was why Cason J. Callaway, an extremely able and successful businessman, spent five years and millions of dollars creating beauty in the wilderness. I talked for many hours with Mr. Callaway.

"We have set out here," he said gently, "to build the most beautiful gardens till Gabriel blows his horn." He took me all over the premises. And he told me why he had done it all.

First, the Gardens are a memorial to Mr. Callaway's mother. Second, Mr. Callaway feels, "If our children have something pretty to look at, if they have some inspiration when they're young, maybe they will see what life can be. Our country needs great men, and maybe a Ben Franklin will come as a child and play here."

Finally, however, I came upon the real reason, the real truth. We were walking on the huge beach, as Mr. Callaway told me how many train-loads of sand it took to make it. The Gardens were crowded that day, and many, many children were running and playing near the water. In the midst of our conversation, Mr. Callaway turned and looked at them in silence. I stood there with him, reflecting that many of these south Georgia boys and girls had probably never seen a lake before, or beautiful white sand, or so many slides and toys and miniature trains. They could not imagine the painstaking care, the hours and days and weeks of planning, the labor of love that went into building this natural wonderland, but they were having the very time of their lives.

And then Mr. Callaway's deepest motive came out. "It just gives me a thrill," he said, "to see these children having so much fun." That thrill was in his voice, and in his eyes.

*"Well!" said Cousin Virginia. "Talk! Say something! What did y'all see, runnin' all around Georgia?"*

*"Saw the bes' ole state in the Union!" grinned Cousin Gary. He leaned forward with a grave air, polite and Southern; grave, and very solemn and soft. "Take yo' glass?" he said. "And get you another?"*

# Florida

## by BUDD SCHULBERG

Did you know that the northernmost part of Florida is south of the southernmost part of California? I didn't know it myself until I drove from Jacksonville to Key West and back along the Tamiami Trail to St. Petersburg and on up the West Coast last winter. Then I heard it all the time and not from the Chamber of Commerce either. I heard it from gas-station attendants, from a waitress in Kissimmee, in Punta Gorda, and motel owners from Wisconsin or Ohio who were tourists themselves just a few years back. The Florida Chamber of Commerce is not known for modesty or lack of civic enthusiasm, but every town I stopped in had a flourishing chamber of unofficial hosts eager to sing the praises of their adopted state. Here and there, of course, one encounters a native Floridian—a cracker in the pine country rolling west of Tallahassee; a third-generation descendant of a founding family of Sarasota—but since the state population has trebled from a million and a half twenty-five years ago to about four and a half million today, and is growing at the rate of fourteen thousand new settlers each month, your Florida booster usually turns out to be a fellow who finally got tired of Great Lakes winters, or just moved his family down from the Bronx.

Florida has the oldest history and the newest population of any state in the Union. The Spanish conquistadors came here a full century before the English exiles found haven in Massachusetts. In the

1820's the energetic (and often ruthless) American frontiersmen displaced the demoralized Spanish. But the real colonization of Florida is a 20th Century phenomenon. There were only half a million people in Florida at the dawn of the century. Miami was a sleepy subtropical outpost on the banks of the Miami River flowing out of the unknown Everglades. Today Miami is America's fastest growing city, and Greater Miami now has a population greater than that of all of Florida in 1920, on the eve of the first boom.

*First* boom, we say, because almost unobtrusively a second has spread across Florida. You feel it on the Keys, where the little fishing village of Marathon seems to change its architectural face at least once a week. You feel it on the road north from Miami, where recently open country has been transformed into a connected series of modern-house, middle-class communities, all the way to Palm Beach; there are new motels and modest houses even in that aristocrat of winter resorts, and not far from superexclusive Hobe Sound there's a new low-cost housing development. The East Coast has long monopolized the tourists and the building programs, and the West Coast—Clearwater, St. Petersburg, Sarasota, Fort Myers, Naples—has prided itself on its quieter rhythm, its more conservative recreations. But the West Coast is no longer a chain of relaxed and complacent water-front towns staring drowsy-eyed into the Gulf. The spectacular fifteen-mile Sunshine Skyway out of St. Petersburg across Tampa Bay is a symbol of West Coast initiative. Now motorists, no longer bottlenecked in St. Petersburg and Pinellas Peninsula, can stream south into Bradenton and on down the easy-riding Tamiami Trail. Dozens of Gulf Coast towns that slept through the first boom are feeling the effects of the second.

In the Everglades country in February 1955 buildings lots between Sarasota and Ft. Myers were offered for $250. Three months later those bargains had been painted out. The choice, newly cleared palmetto waste extending from the highway to the Gulf was selling by the foot now, and the little towns were doubling, tripling and quadrupling their populations. "We don't call it a boom," said a lady real-estate operator (from Massachusetts). *Boom* is still a dirty word in Florida, and 1926 was a black year. "In the twenties people were buying and selling land they never even bothered to see. A lot might change hands ten times in a week. *You* remember. But here on the West Coast we have what you might call a solid boom. Nothing

frantic or hysterical. But more northern visitors come here every season, and tourists on this coast soon get the retirement bug and shop
for land. Or they sell their businesses up north and look around for
something to do down here. Anyway, we're growing so fast that some
of the old-timers are afraid we're going to end up as hectic and over-
developed as the East Coast."

The Florida growth is so spectacular (25 per cent population
jump in five years) and the tourist business is so well publicized
(more than eight million vacationists a year make Florida the world's
all-time pleasure dome) that many Northerners think of Florida as
an overballyhooed vacation resort with crowded beaches and the
sound of midnight trumpets blending with the race-track bugles. Actually the almost four and a half million permanent residents and
the eight-million-plus vacationists are pretty well scattered in a state
with 3750 miles of coast line, from the broad beaches of Fernandina,
just below the Georgia line, down the 400-mile peninsula and up
the Gulf side 600 miles to the rolling white sands of Pensacola, near
the Alabama line. Seen from the air, Florida looks like a long jagged
finger reaching into the tropics and the Caribbean. It fails by a few
miles and a couple of degrees to qualify as on-the-level tropical, but
Floridians import the tropics in the form of vivid flowers, lush fruit,
varieties of palms and even a siesta-fiesta culture that blends nicely
with Northern energy to form a new kind of American. He brings
with him his Middle Western production skills and his New England
education, and he puts them to work, but not at the frantic clip he
knew back home.

"I saw my partner hurry up and die," a fifty-year-old motel owner
told me outside Tampa. "Right then and there I decided to sell out
my plumbing-fixture business and move down here. We had been
coming to St. Petersburg for our winter vacations, so last winter we
just stayed. Wouldn't go back now for a million dollars. I bought
this place, but I got some new ideas for building a better one. Next
winter I'll sell out when the market is high and build me the snazzi-
est-looking motel on the Gulf."

There's a world of difference between the upper and lower East
Coasts, between the Gold Coast and what they are beginning to
call the *Platinum* Coast, between the citrus country and the Everglades, the big-city bustle of Jacksonville and the Old South mansion-
house mood of Tallahassee—but this Northern-flavor-with-a-South-
ern-accent mood was one I encountered from border to border. The

billion-dollar-a-year tourist trade, the fusion of the Old South and the restless North is rapidly producing a new kind of state which is neither Southern nor Northern, Middle Western nor Western, yet with discernible elements of all four. In fact, Florida is to the United States today what the United States was to Europe a hundred years ago—a melting pot, a frontier, a place to improve your health or your luck.

Florida is the world's greatest amusement park, of course, and a hundred pleasure-seeking images crowd around my head as I write —from the guests in the Fontainebleau's La Ronde Room enjoying high-class opera, to gut-bucket-strip tease, to thousands of local Negroes and Northern tourists spending only time to pull the shiny black bass out of the Tamiami Canal between Miami and Ft. Myers. But what impressed me most was the dreaming of big dreams. People may lie on the beach and bask and doze but they don't go to sleep in Florida. There's something un-Southern in the atmosphere that calls men to jump over the moon. King-size frustrations, or youthful dreams of glory, no matter how grandiose or touched with madness, have a way of taking root and enjoying fantastic growth in Florida. In fact, you might say Florida has been built by obsessive Northerners as balmy as the climate they came south to enjoy. Or to put it more kindly, people of rare daring have found in Florida a last frontier to challenge their will and resourcefulness.

Take Julia Tuttle who, as a wealthy young widow about seventy years ago, landed her family from a barge at Fort Dallas, a Seminole trading post on the wild shores of the Miami. To this post she brought all her worldly goods, her extensive library and art collection, her imported china, piano, housekeeper and two Jersey cows. Julia Tuttle cleared the jungle undergrowth, planted a lawn, and began dreaming one of those Brobdingnagian dreams that seem generic to this part of the country. She looked at her virgin beach and uninhibited tropical growth and wrote a Northern friend:

*It may seem strange to you but it is the dream of my life to see this wilderness turned into a prosperous country and where this tangled mass of vine, brush, trees and rocks now are to see homes with modern improvements surrounded by beautiful grassy lawns, flowers, shrubs and shade trees.*

Like the pioneers who were to follow, Julia plunged ahead. She went to work on Henry Flagler, the restless Standard Oil tycoon who had brought his railroad and the first of his great resort hotels to St. Augustine. Flagler had thought of St. Augustine as his American Riviera, until he pushed his railroad down the coast to Palm Beach. The irrepressible Julia had made up her mind that the railroad must reach her beloved Miami. Flagler held out until the famous frost of '95, when Julia sent sprigs of orange blossoms to prove that her home-site lay south of the frost line. Miami was a frontier village with a few sand trails and a shabby row of pine shacks and tents when Flagler's railroad arrived there sixty years ago. Overnight the town began to grow as Julia Tuttle envisioned it, and the handful of fron-tiersmen who had tapped their temples when "Jack-ass Julia" passed found themselves in on the ground floor of what was to become the vacation capital of the world in less than twenty-five years.

Julia Tuttle died in 1898; twenty years later Miami was a flourish-ing town of 29,000, and her dream of a garden metropolis on the banks of Biscayne Bay was realized, though not even her prophetic soul could have foreseen a day when four hundred of the most luxuri-ous hotels in the world would create a gleaming seven-mile sky line along Miami and Miami Beach. Built literally in Julia's back yard is a beanstalk city of pastel skyscrapers with a Greater Miami popu-lation of one million and four million transients flocking in each year.

Flagler went on to indulge an even more precarious dream, the extension of his railroad to Key West, a hundred and fifty miles to the south, across a limestone necklace of odd-shaped islands divided by deep-water channels, many of them a mile wide and one demanding a seven-mile span. This venture was rightfully called Flagler's Folly—there were mosquitoes and heat and tropical storms and seemingly impossible engineering obstacles—but Flagler pushed his 4000 men to do the job in seven years, and Key West, that fine old island city, was connected to the mainland for the first time in its picaresque history. More than 700 men were washed away by storms, and ships and precious materials were lost, but in 1912 the "eighth wonder of the world" was completed, and Flagler, a dying man of eighty-two, proudly rode into Key West on his single-track dream line, an enter-prise that was doomed to operate at a loss until it was swept away in the terrible hurricane of '35. But old Henry's single-track obsession had doomed Key West's splendid isolation. The Flagler roadbed was used for the extension of U.S. 1 across the subtropical keys, and today Flagler's dream is vibrantly alive as the Overseas Highway, a breath-takingly beautiful drive of 130 miles between the Atlantic and the

Bay of Florida, comes tantalizingly close to turning your motor car into a boat as the islands fall away behind and you are surrounded by the sparkling sea, dotted with mangrove islands to the horizon.

There is something about Florida's lush and fertile climate that grows limes as big as oranges, that magnifies the size of the flame-red flowers of the royal poinciana, that multiplies the variety of wild orchids and blows up to near-bursting the expansiveness of human dreams. People had laughed at Julia Tuttle and Henry Flagler, and they laughed at John Collins when he built his rattly wooden bridge between Miami and Miami Beach some forty years ago. The Beach was a forsaken swamp, a playground only for mosquitoes. Collins ran out of money, and another irrepressible Floridian (from Indian-apolis), Carl Fisher, bolstered his sagging dream. Fisher had been racing most of his life, on bicycles, motorcycles, automobiles, and making money (Prest-O-Lite, and the Indianapolis race track which he founded), and when he got to Florida at the age of forty, he was badly bitten by the Florida dream-bug. They laughed when Carl Fisher had the idea that the despised sand bar could be turned into the world's favorite vacationland. Bridges had to be built, marsh had to be filled, canals and islands had to be made, and doubters had to be convinced. There were people who said Carl Fisher was pour-ing $50,000 a day down a sinkhole. He offered a city block free to anyone who would build a first-class resort hotel. Today the land he was offering free—with no takers—is worth thousands of dollars a foot.

The Julia Tuttle to Flagler to Collins to Fisher parlay started paying off in the Steve Hannagan era when Miami Beach and the bathing beauty in the scandalous one-piece bathing suit became interrelated symbols of escape from winter temperatures and Northern pressures. Now this incredible island, which harbors one fourth of all the hotels in Florida, has settled down to a sane, durable and expanding econ-omy. There is a substantial middle class living in semiluxury on the man-made islands of Biscayne Bay, and insurance companies are moving their national headquarters into the area. "It's just as easy to handle the business by mail or phone in a modern sun-lit build-ing. In five years," I was told, "this will be the insurance capital of the world."

But the old-time tradition (the 1920's are medieval history to the hopped-up 60-year-old Miami) of hoopla press agentry has not

flagged. When Miami Beach celebrated its fortieth birthday by opening the fifteen-million-dollar, fourteen-floor, fabulous-is-putting-it-
mild Hotel Fontainebleau, Leo Morrison, vice-president in charge
of fanfare, flew a hundred New York notables down. This hardy
group of later-day pioneers, rendezvoused at "21" for lunch and
liquids, were catered to on the flight down by the "21" staff, were
welcomed at a cocktail party in the new hotel's Salle de Josephine,
enjoyed an informal dinner—if such a thing is possible—in the gran-
diloquent Fleur-de-Lis Room, went to sea next afternoon in "a fleet of
private yachts," watched from private boxes the Fontainebleau Race
at Tropical Park and staggered down that evening to the Grand Bal
de Fontainebleau. That's the way it went from Saturday to Monday.

The Fontainebleau, a daring, massive elliptical structure was designed by Morris Lapidus, a sober architectural experimenter who
confessed that the Fontainebleau was fun to build but he wasn't sure
he'd choose it for his own vacation. "Personally I like smaller places,"
he said. "And of course I realize it's a little overdone inside. But"—he
paused and smiled knowingly—"this seems to be what the people
want." Guess Mr. Lapidus is right. The Fontainebleau's plush-ultra
565 rooms have been filled since it opened. Of course there is an established system of hotel social climbing, which permits tourists less
flush to bed down on the west side of Collins Avenue (away from the
ocean) where rooms are $12 instead of $40 but spend their days
roaming the Fontainebleau lobby, using the stationery, ogling the
guests, dropping in at the Caribbean-type Boom-Boom Room or even
paying $3 to sit in the Fontainebleau sun by the Olympic-size pool.
"Why should I pay forty dollars just to sleep here? I pay twelve down
the street and get the benefit of all *this*," a rotund New Yorker told
me in the Fontainebleau gardens (modeled on the gardens of Fontainebleau, with tropical embellishments).

"That's my biggest headache, sight-seers," Morrison complained.
"We have to station bellboys just to keep people from coming in and
feeling the drapes." The lobby of the Fontainebleau must be seen to
be believed. It's French Empire, of course, with certain modern improvements that were not available to Louis XIV. The furniture is
elegant French period reproduction with a smattering of *moderne*,
and there are pillars that are Greek and pillars that are Romanesque,
and some square ones covered with crackled gold- and silver-leaf
paper that are pure Lapidus. There are stone statuettes of Grecian
ladies wearing a wisp more clothes than the girlies (that's what they

call them) on Dade Boulevard. There's an 18th Century music room, and in the Fleur-de-Lis dining room the décor, according to the menu, is "designed to capture the spirit of the court elegance of the time of Louis XIV." The Sun King is there along with "various ladies and courtiers, symbolizing Sea Power, Land Power, Music and Court Pomp."

Every year in Miami Beach there is a new hotel and a new hotel joke about "this year's hotel." When it was the Fontainebleau, the story was: "In the lobby of the Fontainebleau, if you drop a quarter, you have to give the bellboy a dollar to pick it up for you." Pretty true too. One bellboy, who may be buying into the place any day now, told me he wanted to be a writer and was saving $50 a week during the season so he could take a year off and write a novel. "And boy, could I write a novel about this place," he said menacingly. The Fontainebleau also boasts the most luxurious ice-cream parlor in the world, the Bon-Bon Room. It's all delicate roseate pink and white, and gives you some idea what it might be like to get inside of a strawberry-ice-cream soda served in a milk-white glass.

"On this room and three straight strawberry milkshakes you can get drunk," I heard a guest cry out from a nearby booth.

Personally, I preferred rum at the ocean-front bar. I was perched there one afternoon when a freak storm blew up out of an ominous yellow-gray sky. In a few minutes there was a sixty-mile wind blowing, and hail as large as golf balls. Charley the bartender went on mixing fancy drinks, using the outlandish hail in his cocktail shaker.

"This storm must be doing an awful lot of damage," said a young lady schoolteacher from Chicago, who had saved an entire year for these few days.

"It's only going on at the hotel," the bartender insisted. "There's nothing the Fontainebleau won't do to amuse its guests."

As we prepared to leave the Fontainebleau for Happy Jack's Cabins on the fringe of the Everglades, we identified our car as a convertible Cadillac. "Are you kiddin'?" said the indignant bellboy. "Whaddya think we got down there except convertible Cadillacs?"

Followers of the Beach's hotel rat-race tell you the third year is the test for every new hotel. "The first year everyone wants to get in the act. The second year the momentum carries you. By the third year there is usually a newer, bigger or flossier hotel and the race is on." Never in world history has there been a building program like the boom on the Beach. On the West Coast, where there is more stability, a hotel remains as it was built, and even in modern Florida's brief history begins to take on a look of age and solidity. The John Ringling Hotel in Sarasota, the Vinoy Park in St. Petersburg, or the San Carlos over in Pensacola are first-boom hotels which have come to look lived-in and respectable. But a Miami Beach hotel is outdated in six or seven years, and must be remodeled inside and out to keep up with the new-look neuroses of the Beach's restless tourists.

North Miami Beach, which is neither a beach nor north of Miami Beach, is another of the many dream towns from the first boom that only now are springing to life. Boca Raton, Hollywood-by-the-Sea, Coral Gables, were all laid out in a spurt of Roaring Twenties optimism, with broad avenues, elaborate parks and stucco-elegant towers and archways. The collapse of the boom left them as perhaps the most unusual ghost towns in the world. Hollywood, for instance, had the widest boulevard in the country, and almost no population. The manic history of Florida's last thirty-five years is reflected in this community's rise, fall and phoenixlike rebirth.

Joe Young, who planned a full-blown metropolis north of Miami, poured million after million into his dream. Before there were houses he brought a symphony orchestra to his circular park in the center of the city; prospective settlers were brought down by the busload and lived in tents while they picked out homesites. The hotel was palatial and the paved streets and the sidewalks were wide enough and numerous enough for a city of 60,000. Joe Young was going to have his own Miami, but not even a fortune of forty million could contain this Bunyanesque dream, and when the boom suddenly blew up, Joe Young couldn't pay his cement bills. His largest creditor, Samuel A. Horvitz, from Cleveland, found himself in the real-estate business, and to this day Horvitz's company—Hollywood, Inc.— dominates the town. Hollywood was condemned as an impractical dream three decades ago, but now there are lines of new cars and busy shops along business streets that were thought ridiculously wide during the late 20's.

Because palm trees and tropical flowers were planted during the boom, Hollywood doesn't have the bare, sprung-up-overnight look of so many of the new boom towns spreading north from Miami. Its fine six-mile beach and adjacent deep-water harbor of Port Everglades, its location on the edge of the Gulf Stream between Miami and Fort Lauderdale make it an ideal resort-retirement city. So many New York policemen and firemen have settled in Hollywood that the sound of a siren is said to stir eighty per cent of the population to grab their old uniforms.

In the last few years American know-how has revolutionized the life of Florida. Two innovations—air conditioning and frozen orange juice—have brought stability to a land that previously lived it up from Christmas until the end of March, and then marked time until the next influx of Northern sun worshipers. Air conditioning makes Florida bearable through the summer (which loyal, transplanted Floridians insist is no hotter than New York or Philadelphia), and retirement developments are mushrooming along both coasts as Northern pensioners discover they can live longer, more comfortably and certainly more cheaply by investing in one of the $7500 (or $6990) houses multiplying in identical rows from Hollywood to St. Petersburg.

But man is the most industrious of all mammals, and the dream of dozing his life away in the sun soon tires. "I came down to die. Now I'm back in the building business and making as much money as I ever made up North." I heard those words at least a dozen times while wandering from Jacksonville to Key West and up the Mangrove Coast through the prospering beach-water towns from Naples to Clearwater.

At the Earl Gresh Wood Parade and Museum, in St. Petersburg, a dignified elderly gentleman showed us the remarkable wood mosaics of Biblical scenes, all worked in natural-wood colors from shiny black ebony to delicately tinted rosewood. I asked our guide how he got into this work. "I came down seven years ago as a retired minister," he said, "and after a year or so I got a little fidgety to be useful again."

A Midwestern industrialist by the name of Curt Joa has instituted the *Curt Joa Plan,* by which retired mechanics who no longer can stand the grind of a full working day spend a few hours a day teaching their skills to apprentices. Now men of sixty-five who had felt banished from productive society work twenty hours a week, and supplement their retirement checks. "I enjoy Florida twice as much now that I don't feel I'm on the rubbish heap," a seventy-year-old machine-tool craftsman at Lakeland told me.

Between Miami and Homestead we encountered a retired businessman who did not mind being outside the pale of productive society. He was as lean and brown as the Seminoles who once traveled this edge of the Everglades. He was on foot, and he pulled a covered wagon about six feet long and four feet high, just big enough to sleep in. On its side was painted, "Dick Cook, the Walking Man." Cook had been a contractor in Michigan, where he had suffered a nervous breakdown after a construction bid turned out disastrously. That decided him to chuck the whole thing and just walk. This was his fourth year and he had done nearly 20,000 miles. This year he's walking up one side of the Mississippi Valley and down the other. I pulled the wagon a few feet to get the feel of it; it was heavy. The life he had staked out for himself sounded like an endless highway of drudgery, but Dick Cook seemed happier than some of the crowd we had fallen in with at the Fontainebleau.

"You can't really enjoy the scenery when you're in one of them things," Cook said, pointing contemptuously at our resplendent rented Cadillac. Was he ever going to settle down again? "Yes," said this peripatetic marvel, "one of these years I'm going to build me a little shack in Marathon down on Key Vaca."

The first time I saw Marathon, it was a crudely built fishing village of a few hundred people, with a motel for the deep-sea fishermen. Today it's a glamour-tag area, Marathon Shores, headed by Key Colony Beach, a whole community constructed "from the ocean's depth" by a Detroiter named Phil Sadowsky and his associates: fine hotels and motels, marinas, restaurants, charter fleets, and an 18-hole golf course.

Side roads still wind through the mangroves to isolated lagoons known only to herons and bonefish, and some of the Keys retain the tropical-island-away-from-it-all feeling that captured my imagination just after the last war when I drove down the lonely highway into the heart of the Keys. But today the Carl Fisher fever has seized the Keys. The wild cry of the gull and tern is drowned out by the roar of giant dredges coaxing the waters of the Gulf into man-made channels so that advertisements can offer "waterfront lots with your own boat dock." The Keys were a hideaway, getaway land before the new boom, and beach property was being sold for taxes. Now they have been discovered. The rich-rich come ashore from their sleek eighty-foot ocean-going yachts to window shop at Marathon. Islets lying off the Overseas Highway are now a string of tropical suburbs and a fisherman's paradise.

Lying west of the Keys, across the island-strewn Florida Bay, the glades rolling west of Homestead, the unofficial Everglades capital, are being cleared, drained and reclaimed into black muck-rich farming lands. And west of this new tomato and celery belt is a tropical wilderness that has fascinated me ever since I cruised around virgin Cape Sable and followed brackish Shark River into the heart of the Everglades, through the Seminole State Indian Reservation.

This is one of the most remote and primitive areas in the United States. Here the resourceful Seminoles finally found sanctuary in the trackless sawgrass prairies (which they aptly called "grass water") out of which rise fertile hammocks, or islands, heavily grown with royal palms, mahogany, tamarind, the red-barked gumbo-limbo, and the cruelly beautiful strangler fig. Here the Indians who refused the indignity of being removed en masse to Oklahoma built their villages and planted their squash and bananas, confident that this insidious marsh country of the redbug and the moccasin would be theirs by default because it was the one section of Florida the white man could not endure. The only other inhabitants of these impenetrable mangrove swamps were squatters, outcasts, moonshiners who lived in shacks raised on stilts over the shallow Florida Bay flats at a now vanished community well-named Snake Bite, or in lawless little bands on the islands of Whitewater Bay.

The Everglades squatter may represent one of the last Americans uncontaminated by modern civilization. One day on the Keys I met a West Coast fisherman who told me of a fishing village at the edge of the Big Cypress Swamp where criminals were welcomed and Federal men dared not enter. "We got our own ways and our own laws," he said. "If you want to go in there I'll write you out a passport." The broken coastline from Naples to Cape Sable is last-stand country for ragged individualists, where the roots of the mangrove trees look like a thousand gnarled fingers reaching into the dark still waters of the silent glade rivers.

To preserve this timeless stretch of grasslands, sloughs and tropical vegetation, where the rarest of the long-legged birds still breed and perch in the giant cypress, and wild orchids in hundreds of brilliant varieties burst from old stumps and tree hollows, is the dream of still another transplanted Northerner. Dan Beard, worthy descendant of the founder of the Boy Scouts, is a scholarly outdoorsman who first dreamed of an Everglades National Park when he was sent here on a survey twenty years ago. He was convinced that if this strange wonderland of the pink ibis and the snowy egret, of the sleepy 'gators and the vicious crocodiles, of the wildcat and the almost extinct

roseate spoonbill was not protected by Government purchase and
National Park Rangers, it would eventually become just another piece
of Florida real estate. "We got it just in time," Dan Beard told us
when we stopped by his office in Homestead. "We have acquired
over a million acres in the Everglades; we have the squatter problem
just about licked; we have new roads and our new National Park is in
business. We're working to make it the most interesting wildlife sanctuary in the country." In a single year half a million tourists, including
many attracted by the Audubon wildlife tours, have entered this
primeval world to fish for tarpon, study the tropical growth and bird-
watch the droll, impressive, stilt-legged wading birds found here in
greater numbers than any other place on the globe. As the Park extends its roads and services, the once-dreaded Everglades may draw
as many visitors as now flock to Cypress Gardens or Silver Springs.

Dan Beard, a naturalist with no thought of personal gain, may
seem a very different type from city planners like George Merrick of
Coral Gables and Joe Young of Hollywood, but when he talks of
Florida he has something in common with these other pioneers.
"You'll find all over the state," he says, "a creative spirit, a youthful
daring, a frontier enthusiasm for new ideas. The Everglades, of course,
are a real frontier, but the whole state is a frontier. The bulldozers are
pushing back the tropical forest, and people go plunging into
schemes that would scare them half to death back home.

"I'm from Flushing, New York, but this Everglades National Park
is my home now. We're working hard to make it the most interesting
wildlife sanctuary in America."

Yes, in Florida the imagination has a way of busting out all over,
in shapes and colors as strange and vigorous as the blossoms of the
Bird of Paradise and the passion flower.

Millions who come to Florida to find the sun and idle winter pleasures hardly have time to appreciate the drive and the vision that
lie behind some of the state's favorite attractions. Cypress Gardens,
for instance, is a miracle in what has come to be the Florida tradition. Thirty years ago Dick Pope was a real estate and advertising man who had gone bust after the blow of '28. To stimulate
interest in the Winter Haven section Pope got the idea of developing
the cypress swampland around Lake Eloise into an incomparable
tropical garden. There were folks in Winter Haven who laughed at
him as "The Swami of the Swamp." Today this "swamp" is Cypress

Gardens, one of the wonders of Florida, annually attracting more than a million visitors who come to watch the water-ski ballets, and the spectacular ski-jumping from the lakeside grandstand, and to enjoy the beauty of the ancient cypress trees rising out of the water, with their fantastically shaped "knees" spreading around them like a family of elves, and the winding paths and waterways bordered by rare and brilliantly colored plants gathered from all over the world.

Lake Eloise is one of a hundred lakes in a five-mile radius, and the city limits of Winter Haven embrace dozens of fresh-water lakes connected by channels that make possible an unusual water journey of seventy-five miles. The coastal beaches have become so famous that one has to sail, ski, swim and fish these inland waters to realize that Florida has three times as many lakes as Minnesota. From the Georgia line down the middle of the state to 700-square-mile Lake Okeechobee, there are 30,000 lakes and an entirely different tourist world from that of either coast.

To these lovely inland lakes come the quiet-type tourists who like small-boat fishing for large-mouthed bass. Here tourists are sedately called "winter visitors," and the residents are proud that their quiet towns are as different from the elegance of Palm Beach as they are from the carnival life of Miami Beach. "This is the real Florida," you will hear them say.

Mile on mile of orange trees perfume the air, and you aren't surprised to learn that one third of the world's orange crop comes out of Florida, and three out of every four oranges grown in the United States come from Florida's citrus belt. My old home state of California has almost been pushed off the citrus map by the dynamic growth of Florida's breakfast-fruit business. Along with eighty-nine million boxes of oranges, it contributes nine tenths of the grapefruit (forty-two million boxes), all the limes and tangerines. "All the fruit juice you can drink for ten cents" is still a come-on for motorists.

In Florida ultramodern architecture is taken for granted. Because South Florida, especially, is a 20th Century phenomenon, it's naturally receptive to the idea of drive-in banks, bird-cage houses and even open-air churches.

Some years ago the Florida Power and Light Company brought down a trainload of bankers from New York to observe the industrial possibilities of a state with hundreds of miles of wide-open spaces. The bankers boarded the train in style, complete with Homburgs. A Florida press agent, with an eye for direct action, went through the train flinging the stylish chapeaux out the windows to demonstrate that Florida is still a fishing-cap, open-shirt country, even for Wall Street bankers.

"There's something about the place that relaxes your prejudices and opens your mind," a public-relations man told me at their state convention at St. Petersburg Beach.

"The chairmen of the boards of northern insurance companies and banks come down here and insist on modern designs for buildings that they wouldn't be caught dead with in Chicago or Detroit. It's like a businessman putting on a Hawaiian sports shirt and yellow slacks. The modern architects are having a ball."

They're building modern on the West Coast, too, but like everything else on that gentler, less commercialized strand, the architecture is less radical, less flamboyant. There are people of great wealth along this coast, hidden away at St. Armand's Key off Sarasota, at Captiva Island and Naples, but you will not find the conscious style of Palm Beach, or the upper-middle snobbishness of Venetian Fort Lauderdale. Simplicity and informality are the keynotes of the West Coast. The motels make no attempt to ape the grandeur that is Miami Beach, and the winter guests on the beaches of Clearwater, St. Petersburg and Sarasota-by-the-Sea, paying less than their East Coast cousins, seem to enjoy the contemplative recreations—sun-bathing, shuffleboard, shell collecting, bridge fishing, and watching the sun take its evening plunge in the Gulf of Mexico, leaving behind it a trail of purple and rose and gold.

St. Petersburg is a growing city, and Sarasota, with a younger, more cosmopolitan population, with its writers, painters, little theater, and the spangled atmosphere of the Ringling Circus, is expanding at such a pace as to alarm the "old settlers," like MacKinlay Kantor, who came down to Siesta Key when it was a slumbering island in the 30's. Kantor, not a man to express his opinions *sotto voce*, is convinced that "progress" may yet destroy the original, Southern, unhurried atmosphere of Sarasota. Sarasota is growing rapidly but soundly. "We can't help growing," says a prominent Sarasotan. "With Sarasota's natural beauty, with the circus in our back yard, with a great variety of interesting people, and the easygoing tempo everybody feels as soon as he arrives, with wonderful beaches and good schools, we're much more than just a nice place to spend a few weeks in the winter. The West Coast is the future of Florida and Sarasota is the future of the West Coast."

It's tempting but perhaps misleading to generalize about this beguiling border of the Gulf. It's the avenue of royal palms through venerable Fort Myers on the banks of the broad Caloosahatchee. It's the new medical center at Sarasota. It's the thousands of old men and women drowsing and chatting on the green benches of St. Petersburg. It's the sprawling trailer camp of Bradenton, a caravan city with its dances, sports events and community sings. It's Steak Capuchina at Tampa's superb Spanish restaurant, Las Novedades. It's Webb City in St. Petersburg, a "drug-store" with a public-relations director, a radio director, fashion models, a roof-garden floor show, Arthur Murray instructors, a beauty parlor and barber shop, a bakery, ice-cream and coffee-roasting plants.

The West Coast is also unspoiled Mullet Key, off St. Petersburg, which has only one old-fashioned white-frame hotel for the few guests who want to enjoy isolated beaches, superb fishing and the absence of automobiles. It's a sign on a motel between Bradenton and Sarasota, "We're from Indiana and Illinois—where are you from?" It's tall Florida cowboys rounding up the humpbacked, exotic looking Brahman cattle around Punta Gorda. It's the St. Louis Cardinals and the New York Yankees battling for the spring-training championship of St. Petersburg. It's the snub-nosed, orange-painted Greek sponge boats putting to sea from their "little Greek" harbor at Tarpon Springs. It's 300 species of fish from combative but inedible tarpon to delicious pompano and bluefish.

The West Coast is also the fresh-water rivers that flow from subterranean caverns in a continuous outpouring of hundreds of millions of gallons a day. It is Homosassa Springs, nature's giant fish bowl, where you look through a glass wall into a fresh-water pool alive with what seems to be an infinity of fish, including salt-water varieties like snook and jacks and sea trout that mysteriously leave their native Gulf for this fresh-water basin. It's Weekiwachee, with its daily flow of 144 million gallons of fresh, crystal-clear water, where "mermaids" perform a remarkable underwater ballet, working from a novel underwater stage. The West Coast is the teeming harbor of Tampa; the sleepy fishing village of Cedar Keys; and the fisherman's dream, Crystal River, halfway between Weekiwachee and Cedar Keys, in lovely, unspoiled Gulf country where St. Petersburgers go for a weekend's fishing and camping when they want to take a vacation from the tourists.

Farther up the coast, and halfway between Tallahassee and Tampa, is the mouth of the Suwannee River, the lazy, lovely, picture-book river that Stephen Foster never saw, the river that weaves its languorous way from Georgia's dank Okefenokee Swamp through the Old Florida of White Springs, a quiet, 19th Century health resort, past Ellaville, a once-prosperous river town now slumbering on the banks of the widely sung but little-known river, and other century-old cracker towns that had their little booms in the 70's and 80's and are now curled up in sleep.

The hundred-odd miles on the East Coast from St. Augustine to Daytona are urbanized, commercialized and suburbanized. The West Coast is still adventure country. The East Coast has had its adventure and is settling down to its orderly, civic comforts.

The Northern stereotype of Florida too often fixes on Miami Beach or some other highly developed beach-colony life. Actually there are a thousand Floridas, and as one of the five million who take the state over in the winter and spring (and even in summer now that Northern piggybank vacationists and Southerners by the hundreds of thousands flock to the Gulf and Atlantic to escape the inland heat) you have a choice of crowded beaches and a full calendar of organized activities or the peace of a deserted stretch of sand where you can cast a line into the sea and reel in—maybe a bonefish or a pompano, maybe only an hour or two of contentment as you daydream by some of the world's most pure blue, pure green waters. Or you may find your Florida in the crystal-clear depths of Rainbow Springs, as you stare in wonder through the submarine porthole at the other-worldly underwater scenery, while a local Negro guide describes what you are seeing in language that strikes the ear as deliciously original native poetry.

Throwing bread into the water to attract the smaller fish, he says, "Now look at the little sunnies come up to eat the bread. Now look at the big-mouth bass comin' up behind to eat the sunnies. Now if we're lucky we'll see the giant leopard-gar comin' out to eat the big-mouth bass. On the Rainbow River we say only the man can catch the giant leopard-gar and only the Good Lord can catch the man."

If New England lives on its past and the West enjoys a vibrant present, Florida basks in its future. It is the only state which claims tourism as its major industry and sunshine as its principal commodity. It is a state with a sunny disposition; people are constantly telling you how much better they feel. The population of other states is made up of people who were born there. Florida is peopled mostly by those who pulled up roots and moved there.

Except in the hibernating communities in the northwest corner, optimism infuses the atmosphere. One night my wife and I were trying to reach Collier City, still a primitive fishing port on the lower West Coast. The dirt road grew bumpier, rockier and narrower and finally, along the water front, became impassable. A sign said "Road under construction" but the legend under it wasn't "Proceed at your own risk." Instead it was, "A sign of progress."

"That is what I love about Florida," said my wife, Vicki. " 'Travel at your own risk' always sounds so dismal. This road looks dismal but you have to admire their attitude."

In increasing numbers people who come to Florida to play are coming back to stay, including the Schulbergs, who had been wintering in Florida for years but finally took the plunge and moved to Sarasota.

# Alabama

## by CARL CARMER

I had not seen the red hills of northern Alabama for more than thirty years when I returned to them on a Sunday in early June. I drove in from Chattanooga and took the little ferry that lurches across the Tennessee River into Bridgeport, just south of the Alabama state line. The freshets of spring had not entirely subsided and the water was still picking up a pinkish brown from the clay banks. On the road down from Bridgeport to Scottsboro familiar signs advised travelers to drink Dr. Pepper when thirsty and use Clabber Girl baking powder when baking.

Northern Alabama when I first knew it was a mountain country with a river running through it. Hill cabins perched dangerously on steep acres high above the Tennessee ("Fire your shotgun up the chimley and your punkin crop'll drop into the fireplace"). It was a land of fiddlers' conventions and all-day sings and square dances and court weeks. Few Negroes lived here—their homes were in the Black Belt towns where their slave ancestors had worked for rich white folks. The mountain people plowed their acres six days a week and on the seventh attended little unpainted churches where the wrath of a jealous God was expounded with emphasis. Now this area, because of the damming of the Tennessee River, is a lake country. The rutted roads that once ran near the river are gone, and blacktops run smooth along the ridges from which motorists look down on families picnicking beside clear water.

Scottsboro is larger and obviously more prosperous than in 1931, when nine Negro boys from counties to the south were tried in the Scottsboro Courthouse and found guilty of rape. To the west, in a valley, lies Huntsville—a city of old, pillared mansions and new, clean business buildings, and the road to Decatur, farther on, offers long foothills and dramatic views of rippling surfaces over which small boats skitter and water skiers swing in long arcs. Blue lake, blue sky, red earth, white blossoms, green grass—make sunny days garish. Neat motels have sprung up along the way. Planes drone into a modern airport at Decatur. The towns in this area are crowded with new dwellings, small and grim, a picture window staring from each cottage forehead. There are fewer cabins on the slopes. Many of the hill people now live in "housing development" suburbs and listen to artificial folk music on the radio. Their aerials, lifted by tall rods above their roofs, twist and curve like nests of mountain snakes.

Industry has brought its not always welcome blessings to this hilly region. Teeming cities make its farms sure of markets for their produce. Corn whispers over wide acres that used to grow cotton. Cows graze where once were stump-dotted marshes. Businessmen who have made fortunes in the town factories grow Black Angus cattle in the meadows above their country homes, and sell the beef to expensive city restaurants. The shining silo towers of dairy farms hold feed for herds of Guernseys, and milk trucks roll silver-colored tubes of white cargo along the highways. Fertile pastures and new crops—corn, peanuts, beans—have emancipated the white serfs of the old Alabama economy. And the land has added its concealed treasures. Portland cement, coal, iron ore have pointed the way to wealth in Birmingham, the state's largest city.

Not as old as Mobile or Montgomery, Birmingham labors under a sense of inferiority which the two other cities delight in fostering. "We don't scrabble so hard for a dollar as Birmingham does," they say. "We have age and cultural background. Birmingham is *nouveau riche* and acts that way." As a consequence this "Pittsburgh of the South" self-consciously, but eagerly, goes about improving its cultural standing. Its riches help, and it has rolled colonies of expensive and often beautiful homes up and down the suburban ridges of Red Mountain and Shades Mountain, each of which, according to the city's detractors, bears an example of Birmingham's culture.

On Red Mountain stands an enormous statue of Vulcan—sixty tons of iron coated with eye-dazzling aluminum paint. Though it is called the "second largest statue in the world," it hardly improves the general opinion of the city's taste. The huge figure, an early work of the Italian sculptor Giuseppi Moretti ("He is bored with whirling in his grave," says a former disciple), was a marvel at the St. Louis World's Fair, in 1904, before it arrived eventually at its 120-foot-high platform on the summit of the mountain. To Birmingham it is a symbol of the bigness of its major industry.

Shades Mountain has another memorial of Roman classic culture—Vestavia, a replica of the pillared temple of Vesta beside the Tiber River. The structure lures visitors to see the sculptured figures of Roman gods and goddesses in its interior. Built by an eccentric citizen who chose to live among his togaed servants as a Roman prince, it remains one of the city's major curiosities.

A newer attraction on the same mountain is The Club, a glass-walled building of neo-Miami character. Here patrons may dine listening to the music of violins and a mother-of-pearl piano and looking down into the valley where the steel furnaces flare in the night ("You get the same thrill that Nero got—the fiddles play while the city burns").

The grime of a steel city persists in downtown Birmingham. Only here and there does it give promise of the city its riches will erect. A new art gallery, happily situated among the buildings of the city government, a Little Theater that has existed long enough to establish a tradition, a few clean-cut towers of business—these are the beginnings.

I had planned, when I set out for Alabama, to write a nostalgic, atmospheric, sentimental piece about it. It was in Birmingham, my first stop of considerable length, that I discovered this would be impossible. Almost no one would talk of the past, not even the past of a quarter century ago.

"There's a new spirit here," a Birmingham businessman told me. "The reason? Money for one thing. And in the wake of that—air conditioning. I know you used to think that heat gave Alabamians some of their characteristics—quick tempers but slow movements and slow minds. Well, now our offices, our stores, our homes, our automobiles are cooled through all the hot months. Nobody is exposed to the heat any longer than it takes to walk from an office building to his car. And in some companies the ten-thirty Coke break has become a coffee break—just like in New York City. An air conditioner costs no more than a television set. And I've seen one-room shacks that have both."

"Negro shacks?"

"I guess so—though Negroes can stand heat better than anybody else."

The approach to Montgomery from the west was a long "strip," sure omen of entrance to an American city—motels (TV in every room), drive-in movies, curb-service stands offering frozen custard, palm-reading "parlors"—forming a one-story jungle of soiled concrete and neon tubing.

Montgomery, however, I found much as I had left it. There are few apartment houses. Most families live in homes of their own, be they elegant or simple. The wooden awnings that sheltered shoppers for a century on the main business streets of the town have disappeared, but the tradition of providing shade continues; many of the new and modern shops use variegated awnings or jutting wooden shelving to fend off the sunlight.

On a Monday morning I visited the State Capitol and found that the old building, domed and white, had become the center of a wide circle of other Government houses, also white. No one was moving about (the state legislature was not in session) and no wind stirred the misty sunlight that struck between the tall white pillars. I was reminded of the Civil War and of my limping grandfather who had tried to destroy this temple and its creed of slavery; and I recalled a passage from a poem by Marianne Moore—"white is the colour of worship and of mourning." There was something, I thought, which had departed—and the empty shrine seemed to be waiting for it to return.

That night, at a dinner in a Montgomery country club, I told a new acquaintance of the impression the white buildings had made.

"You're right," he said, "and what the capitol is waiting for is the homecoming of distinction and dignity and honor. A hundred years ago the Deep South was governed by gentlemen of family and of classical education, champions of the humanities. Now we live, with accidental exceptions, under the tyranny of guitar twangers, gallus snappers, baby kissers and sockless barbecue orators. Beneath that Yankee mask of yours you know as well as I do that white knights should inhabit those white buildings. We've got them, but they haven't a chance against politicians who call them sissies, dudes and eggheads in order to get the gutless clowns elected."

"Isn't that kind of talk subversive?" I asked.

"It's the juleps talking," he said, "but *in juleps veritas.* Let's get down to what we've been avoiding—all we think or talk about—segregation. When the National Association for the Advancement of Colored People sent that girl to the University of Alabama in a limousine all dyked out in orchids they were stupid. But the thoughtful people of Alabama were stupider. On the night before the disorders on the campus I called on one of the grand old jurists of our state.

"'What's going to happen?' I said.

"'Violence,' he said. 'The roughnecks will try to stop her.'

"'You and I are good citizens,' I said. 'We detest illegal violence. So what are we doing here?'

"'Sitting home and hoping the roughnecks will win,' he said. 'Instead of listening to the opinions of our best minds—arguments that even the Supreme Court would respect—we're letting a mob take over.'"

My companion paused for a moment, then said pathetically, "What do we do now? What do all the intelligent earnest Alabamians do now?"

"Don't let this hotspur upset you," said a nearby friend. "He's one of our local radicals. I know where there's another drink and a pretty lady waiting."

The next morning I saw the gardens of the city. Montgomerians take gardening seriously and their rich soil rewards them mightily. No artist would dare to combine so many clashing hues—the red of japonicas, the pink of oleanders, the coral of Roses of Montanta, the purple and scarlet of begonias—yet somehow, relieved by the yellow of Cape jasmine, the blue of larkspur, the white of magnolias, sweet olives and Cherokee roses, and the garish alternating tones of the azalea, Montgomery gardens are choirs of singing color.

Later I stopped at a cemetery—a green carpet of grass, dotted with headstones, stretching toward the summit of a gentle hill. I asked to be brought here, to revisit the graves of seven Royal Air Force fliers who had come to Montgomery's Maxwell Field for training during World War II. A storm of wind and rain had brought darkness early on the afternoon of May 21, 1942, and the young men, lost in a trackless sky, had crashed to their deaths. Now I read on the simple gravestones the moving epitaphs their families had chosen—"For love of Freedom," "That is forever England," "He left the Vivid Air signed with his honor."

Beside these markers stands a tall and startling monument. Hank Williams is the name on the stone, and carved below are a guitar, a few notes of music, a ten-gallon hat. Hank was an idol of the millions of young Americans whose emotions are stirred by hillbilly music. The titles of his songs are worked into the stone here, too, among them *Luke the Drifter* (he used to call himself that), *Your Cheatin' Heart, Kaw Liga, I'll Never Get Out of This World Alive.*

"He had Montgomery's biggest funeral," said one of my guides. "No church was big enough—so it was held at Cramton Bowl, our stadium. Boys and girls from here and Georgia and Mississippi and Tennessee crowded it to the brim."

"He was a natural," said the other, "an untutored Mozart. But money gave him a way of life that killed him."

In the six years I had spent in Alabama during the Twenties, no one could buy a good dinner there. Southern hospitality was no myth and home cooking was superlative—but restaurant food was heavy, greasy, tasteless. There has been a considerable change, at least in Montgomery, where nowadays a traveler can find the exquisite food that the great cooks of Alabama (white and black) provide daily and as a matter of course in family homes. At Leila Dowe's Blue Moon Inn, for instance, an old-style residence on Goode Street, the gourmet (if he orders in advance) may feast on crabmeat soup, chicken Country Captain, asparagus ring with mushrooms, and other delicacies that convince him he has dined in the distinguished plantation-house tradition.

I took a wandering journey through many byways on my way to Mobile. I passed Snow Hill and Rose Bud, where the road offered grotesque vistas of landscapes shrouded by a broad-leaved vine called kudzu. Like flames of green fire, its swift tendrils had licked over stumps and dead trees, hooding them with green, blunting their pointed tops, creating ominous sculptural patterns. Near Uriah and Blacksher the muddy overflow of Little River lay in shallow pools defended by battalions of jacks-in-the-pulpit. At State Prison Farm, just outside Atmore, the corn stood high and the wide level fields looked neat and fertile. The tiny Styx River laves the town of Bay Minette and a few miles beyond it lie seemingly measureless stretches of tall yellow-green grasses. Ocean odors permeate the air above them. A few houses stand very much alone and the landscape looks as if it had been painted by an artist who meant to emphasize their aloneness. Even in sunlight the impression is ominous—a sense of moving through the setting of a bad dream.

Suddenly the traveler is in a long gleaming tunnel that dips under Mobile Bay and emerges into Government Street. He feels the miracle—in a few seconds he has left a nightmare of the present for Mobile's dream of the past. The long and gnarled limbs of the live oaks shade the street, admitting occasional spatters of sunshine. The mottled pavement leads through an aisle of public buildings and houses that display their gardens and wrought-iron galleries where they may be seen. Smaller and more intimate than New Orleans, Mobile holds the enchantment of its Latin past but has not yet felt the compulsion to exploit it. The old thoroughfare is longer than it used to be, but building in its northern stretches has been in keeping with the city's tradition.

Mobile Bay tells the story of the new Mobile. One morning I sought out my old friend Earl McGowin, the Commissioner of State Docks, and we set out, water-borne, on a tour of the port. As the fog burned off we made out nearly thirty vessels, among them the Dutch *Gran Río,* bound for Haiti with a cargo of bedsprings and aluminum sashes; the *Hadrian,* Norway's largest vessel, her vast tanks cleaned out to receive wheat, milo, corn and beans; the Japanese *Kyowei Maru* discharging a mixed cargo that included two exquisite Chinese junks; the American *Sue Lykes,* bearing British automobiles and Scotch whisky; the Costa Rican *Spidola,* exchanging Colombian mahogany for Alabama coal; the Liberian *Yucatán,* ready to transport milk bottles, cotton cloth and chicken feed to Cuba. These were only symbols of the port's swift growth. The hundreds of ships that crowd its wharves during the year carry natives of almost every country in the world. This bay, most remembered by Americans for a romantic barbershop ballad, *On Mobile Bay,* is now as exotic and cosmopolitan as Marseille or Port Saïd.

The seas have brought riches to Mobile, and business booms. Progress is a watchword, but it brings a danger with it. Near Earl McGowin's office, later that day, I heard a woman say to her male companion, "They're trying to save the oaks on Government Street. They ought to realize no trees can stand in the way of progress."

That night I boarded a larger and more elegant craft which went speeding on the glittering ripples among the dark hulks of the freighters into boundless moonlight. The dinner served on board was memorable. The Negro chef and his assistant prepared crab-meat with a chopped-vegetable sauce of puzzling flavor, and then broiled large snapper throats, which I had never before regarded as the astonishing fish-course delicacy they are.

After coffee I went on deck to chat with a fellow guest. Suddenly he asked me point-blank, "Are you a spy for a Yankee magazine?"

"No," I said.

"I need to tell you something," he said. "Stop trying to strangle us. All those men and women inside are against segregation—but not for the reasons the Northern press howls about. If our group could only win a primary we could put up an argument Yankees might consider. Our best candidate won't run because he'd be beaten. I think we ought to put him up anyway and go down fighting. Then some of you ruthless and irrational fanatics might know we tried. Let's join the ladies."

I spent the night in Earl McGowin's cottage at Point Clear, on the east side of the Bay. Next morning, not far away, I saw a huge star-shaped structure—the Grand Hotel.

"They kept the name out of sentiment," said Earl. "The old inn on the same site was rambling and Victorian. What do you think of this one?"

We went over for a closer look. The place seemed to belie its name. There is no grandeur about it—only a concealed elegance. The colors—rust for the roof and green-blue for the walls—are muted. Blue water bounds it on three sides. There is an outdoor auditorium far out on Julep Point, and the golf club (near the main building) is paneled in natural woods. The boat basin is roomy. Whoever planned the Grand Hotel evidently meant it to lure people of dignity and taste. I found it restful.

The home of the McGowin family is at Chapman, a tiny cross-roads community south of Montgomery about sixty miles.

They live in a tree-shaded park stretching back from a white fence bordering the highway. Here a big brick house with white pillars still shelters Miss Essie, widow of the Greeley McGowin who built a prosperous sawmill business at Chapman. Behind the main house, in a long arc on the shores of a little lake, are the comfortable homes of his sons and their families.

When the late Greeley McGowin set his saws to screaming through Alabama logs at Chapman, he had at least three definite purposes in mind. One was to make money in the lumber business. A second was to keep a steady and lasting supply of logs moving into his mill by replanting the areas he had cut. A third was to provide his four sons with education of a superior sort. He sent them all to the University of Alabama and thence overseas to Oxford.

Dusk was settling as Earl and I approached the door of Floyd McGowin, eldest of the brothers. Inside were all the McGowin clan, a welcoming swarm. The McGowin wives are not only pretty but well read, so the conversation was gay and intelligent. After dinner my host took me into his library and we talked books. His interests ranged from Chaucer to Joyce—and his collection alone of the works and critical appraisals of Joyce struck me as extensive and important.

Hours later I sat with Earl on the terrace of his home while fireflies doodled on the blackboard of the darkness.

"Despite all you Yankees hear about us," he said, "Alabama is a booming state. The towns you used to love for their sleepy charm are awake and thrashing about. We have water—not only on the coast but on inland lakes and rivers now made navigable. We have electric power, lumber, oil, chemical plants. Being an ardent states' rights man I sort of hate to admit that our Federal air centers—such as Brooks and Maxwell Fields—stimulate our economy with big payrolls. Yankees may disapprove of us—but there's a lot of Yankee money invested here. When you were teaching at the University our percentage of illiteracy was high. Now we have almost wiped it out. If it weren't for——"

"For what?" I said.

"What's your solution of this integration business?"

"I have none. To me it's insoluble."

"That's the word," he said. "Let's go to bed."

Chapman is not the only small community in Alabama where intellectual interests and industrial vigor reach a high level. As I was leaving I remembered the pronunciamento of the late "Uncle Louis" Davidson, world traveler, bon vivant, sage of the Black Belt counties: "There are only two towns in the world where a civilized man may live happily—Paris and Uniontown, Alabama." Alabamians of education take pride in the cultural tradition of the pre-Civil War South, though too many of them believe that they have inherited it and so do nothing about it. The new culture—represented by museums, the interest in contemporary arts, the appreciation of William Faulkner (twenty years ago his novels were generally denounced here)—has almost no relationship to the old-time planter's preoccupation with the Greek and Latin classics or Shakespeare.

Back through the gargoyles of kudzu I went, through Pine Apple and Snow Hill and the wide Main Street of Selma ("Never a homely girl from Selma"). Westward then—through Demopolis, whose past claims a romantic Vine and Olive Colony of aristocratic refugees from the French Revolution (they tried their unaccustomed hands at growing wine grapes and olives, with little success) and whose present boasts "the liveliest Junior Chamber of Commerce in the state," and thence northwest into the old Black Belt town of Livingston. There was the courthouse on the old square, the drugstore that has borne the same family name for many generations, the "bored well" ("Drink from it for what ails you")—and finally the home of Pratt and Ruby Tartt, with Miss Ruby standing in the doorway.

It was years since she and I had had a good long talk, but we took up almost where we had left off. Miss Ruby was in her eightieth year when I visited her but she had defied her aging. We sat under a tree in her garden while Lizzie, her Negro cook, turned the smell of frying chicken into a promise of joy. Had I heard about Jesse, a local boy who went into the Army and took to boasting that he was a leading citizen back home? When two of his buddies happened to pass through on the "doodle," the one train that stops at Livingston, they got off and asked at the depot about their pal. No one knew him, and this they reported back in camp.

"I didn't say I come from smack dab up to the courthouse," said Jesse.

As we sat down to eat, Miss Ruby said, "By the way, I don't know how our train got its name but everybody calls it the doodle. Our only other train doesn't stop here, so it's called the through-doodle. One day a boy stepped up to the station master and said: 'Do the doodle come before the through-doodle do or do the through-doodle come before the doodle do?' The whole county has been chanting that one ever since."

On the next morning Miss Ruby and I returned to our old routine of seeking folk materials. We visited Gainesville, once the prosperous center of a cotton empire, now almost a ghost town. In a general store there, while the odors of tobacco, coffee, candy, snuff enchanted us,

Miss Beth (Mrs. O. K. Murray) sang for us an ancient English ballad each stanza of which begins with a question from a wife and ends with an unmusical answer in monosyllables from her husband. The woman draws from him the information that he intends to go downtown to get drunk and that on his return he expects her to have cooked a bushel of peas for dinner. When she remonstrates they— the peas, that is—will kill him the husband replies, "Let them kill me," and when she asks where to bury him he replies, "Throw me away." This is the last stanza:

> *The buzzards will eat you, my kind old husband,*
> *The buzzards will eat you, she called him aloud.*
> *The buzzards will eat you, my kind old husband,*
> *The best old fellow in the land.*

It ends with the husband's shout: *"Let them eat me."*

In Gainesville, too, we pieced together the materials of an early melodramatic story—one of the dark, plantation-house tragedies that Alabama porch-sitters have always delighted in.

In the early spring of 1847 a plantation owner took the river steamer *Lamplighter* to Mobile, where business and politics would detain him for several months. His lovely but frail wife he left in the care of his best friend, a distinguished physician. The smoke of the side-wheeler's stacks had hardly blown from the sky before the two left behind were lovers. Though he was himself married, the physician wooed the lonely girl "in prose and verse," and soon the couple could not conceal their wild infatuation. All Gainesville was set gossiping when the doctor began wearing a ring marked with his sweetheart's initials, having had it enlarged to fit his finger.

By late May a friend of the betrayed husband arrived in Mobile. The next upstream packet, the *Ophelia*, bore an armed passenger. Striding up River Street from the Gainesville dock, the planter shot his rival dead, then ordered his wife out of his home. The Alabama courts exonerated him for the killing and soon thereafter granted him a divorce.

The story, like an ancient ballad, has had continuing life for more than a century. Most Black Belt Alabamians have forgotten about Dancing Rabbit Creek Treaty, by which the Choctaws gave Sumter County to the nation in 1831. Few could describe the surrender of General Nathan Bedford Forrest and his dashing command at Gainesville in 1865. But the tale of the planter, the doctor and the beautiful but faithless wife is a folk legend that will be told as long as people live in Alabama.

I saved my visit to Tuscaloosa, home of the University of Alabama, where for six years I had been a professor, for the last few days before I set out for home. Long-time friends awaited me there, and I knew it would be difficult to look upon the old town objectively. When a man comes back after years to a place he has loved, nostalgia compels mourning over things that are no longer the same.

I arrived on a gray hour when the pavements were still shining from a recent shower and the clouds were breaking to show patches of blue. Immediately I felt grieved because many of the oaks—the Druid Oaks, the town once called them—had disappeared. Now a tall hotel—promise of comfort and elegance—stood in a cement desert streaked by white parking lines.

My room was pleasant, my dinner good, and I set out as once I had in 1921 to see the town. Tuscaloosa has grown more at its center than on its edges. The lawns that once separated its big houses are now occupied by small houses that shoulder their way into the narrow "frontage." The magic atmosphere I had felt long ago was gone. I had to remind myself that time dispels enchantment.

The University, which had held two thousand students, each known by name to President George Denny, now boasts an enrollment of eight thousand. Its new president—handsome Frank A. Rose —came recommended to the board of trustees as a former football player and former minister ("They needed both," say Tuscaloosans).

Gradually I became reconciled to the changes that disturbed me. As I sat on the back gallery of the Moody House, first of the pillared homes I came to love, I was reminded by its owner that the president's home—most beautiful of all Alabama houses—and the Gorgas house with its graceful iron railings, enchanted more students than ever. The old Governor's Mansion, built in 1829, is now beautifully restored and has become the University Faculty Club. I lunched with friends there the next day, and afterward we stood for a while on the steps beneath the second-story iron balcony that is shaded by graceful pillars.

"Back when Tuscaloosa was the capital of Alabama," said one of our party, "the old capitol building used to stand at the other end of the street. Do you remember when it burned in 1923?"

"Yes," I said.

"We all gathered here to watch the fire and old white-haired Judge Foster stood in front of us. Tears were streaming down his cheeks."

"I remember," I said.

"We used to live in the glory of our past," said my friend. "Now we live on the promise of our future."

# Mississippi

## by WILLIAM FAULKNER

Mississippi begins in the lobby of a Memphis, Tennessee, hotel and extends south to the Gulf of Mexico. It is dotted with little towns concentric about the ghosts of the horses and mules once tethered to the hitch-rail enclosing the county courthouse and it might almost be said to have only two directions, north and south, since until a few years ago it was impossible to travel east or west in it unless you walked or rode one of the horses or mules. Even in the boy's early manhood, to reach by rail either of the adjacent county towns thirty miles away to the east or west, you had to travel ninety miles in three different directions on three different railroads.

In the beginning it was virgin—to the west, along the Big River, the alluvial swamps threaded by black, almost motionless bayous and impenetrable with cane and buckvine and cypress and ash and oak and gum; to the east, the hardwood ridges and the prairies where the Appalachian Mountains died and buffalo grazed; to the south, the pine barrens and the moss-hung live oaks and the greater swamps, less of earth than water and lurking with alligators and water moccasins, where Louisiana in its time would begin.

And where in the beginning the predecessors crept with their simple artifacts, and built the mounds and vanished, bequeathing only the mounds in which the succeeding recordable Muskhogean stock would leave the skulls of their warriors and chiefs and babies and slain bears, and the shards of pots, and hammer- and arrow-heads and now and then a heavy silver Spanish spur.

There were deer to drift in herds alarmless as smoke then, and bear and panther and wolves in the brakes and bottoms, and all the lesser beasts—coon and possum and beaver and mink and mushrat (not muskrat: mushrat); they were still there and some of the land was still virgin in the early nineteen hundreds when the boy himself began to hunt. But except for looking occasionally out from behind the face of a white man or a Negro, the Chickasaws and Choctaws and Natchez and Yazoos were as gone as the predecessors; and the people the boy crept with were the descendants of the Sartorises and de Spains and Compsons who had commanded the Manassas and Sharpsburg and Shiloh and Chickamauga regiments, and the Mc-Caslins and Ewells and Holstons and Hogganbecks whose fathers and grandfathers had manned them, and now and then a Snopes too because by the beginning of the twentieth century Snopeses were everywhere: not only behind the counters of grubby little side-street stores patronized mostly by Negroes, but behind the presidents' desks of banks and the directors' tables of wholesale grocery corporations and in the deaconries of Baptist churches, buying up the decayed Georgian houses and chopping them into apartments and on their deathbeds decreeing annexes and baptismal fonts to the churches as mementoes to themselves or maybe out of simple terror.

The Snopeses hunted too. They too were in the camps where the de Spains and Compsons and McCaslins and Ewells were masters in their hierarchal turn, shooting the does not only when law but the Master too said not, shooting them not even because the meat was needed but leaving the meat itself to be eaten by scavengers in the woods, shooting it simply because it was big and moving and alien, of an older time than the little grubby stores and the accumulating and compounding money; the boy a man now and in his hierarchal turn Master of the camp and coping, having to cope, not with the diminishing wilderness where there was less and less game, but with the Snopeses who were destroying that little which did remain.

These elected the Bilboes and voted indefatigably for the Vardamans, naming their sons after both. Their origin was in bitter hatred and fear and economic rivalry of the Negroes who farmed little farms no larger than and adjacent to their own, because the Negro, remembering when he had not been free at all, was therefore capable of valuing what he had of freedom enough to struggle to retain even that little and had taught himself how to do more with less: to raise more cotton with less money to spend and food to eat and fewer or inferior tools to work with; this, until he, the Snopes, could escape from the land into the little grubby side-street store where he could live not beside the Negro but on him by marking up on the inferior meat and meal and molasses the price which he, the Negro, could not even always read.

In the beginning, the obsolescent, dispossessed tomorrow by the already obsolete: the wild Muskhogean—Chickasaw and Choctaw and Natchez and Pascagoula—looked down from the tall Mississippi bluffs at a Chippeway canoe containing three Frenchmen—and had barely time to whirl and look behind him at a thousand Spaniards come overland from the Atlantic Ocean, and for a little while longer had the privilege of watching an ebb-flux-ebb-flux of alien nationalities as rapid as the magician's spill and evanishment of inconstant cards: the Frenchman for a second, then the Spaniard for perhaps two, then the Frenchman for another two and then the Spaniard again and then the Frenchman again for that last half-breath before the Anglo-Saxon, who would come to stay, to endure: the tall man roaring with Protestant Scripture and boiled whisky, Bible and jug in one hand and like as not an Indian tomahawk in the other, brawling, turbulent, uxorious and polygamous: a married invincible bachelor without destination but only motion, advancement, dragging his gravid wife and most of his mother-in-law's kin behind him into the trackless wilderness, to spawn that child behind a log-crotched rifle and then get her with another one before they moved again, and at the same time scattering his inexhaustible other seed in three hundred miles of dusky bellies: without avarice or compassion or forethought either: felling a tree which took two hundred years to grow, to extract from it a bear or a capful of wild honey.

He endured, even after he too was obsolete, the younger sons of Virginia and Carolina planters coming to replace him in wagons laden with slaves and indigo seedlings over the very roads he had hacked out with little else but the tomahawk. Then someone gave a Natchez doctor a Mexican cotton seed (maybe with the boll weevil already in it since, like the Snopeses, it too has taken over the Southern earth) and changed the whole face of Mississippi. Slaves were clearing rapidly now the virgin land, lurking still—in 1850—with the ghosts of Murrell and Mason and Hare and the two Harpes, into

plantation fields for profit where he, the displaced and obsolete, had
wanted only the bear and the deer and the sweetening for his tooth.
But he remained, hung on still; he is still there even in the boy's
middle-age, living in a log or plank or tin hut on the edge of what
remains of the fading wilderness, by and on the tolerance and sometimes even the bounty of the plantation owner to whom, in his in-
tractable way and even with a certain dignity and independence,
he is a sycophant, trapping coons and muskrats, now that the bear
and the panther are almost gone too, improvident still, felling still
the two-hundred-year-old tree even though it has only a coon or a
squirrel in it now.

Manning, when that time came, not the Manassas and Shiloh regiments but confederating into irregular bands and gangs owning not
much allegiance to anyone or anything, unified instead into the one
rite and aim of stealing horses from Federal picket lines; this in the
intervals of raiding (or trying to) the plantation house of the very
man to whom he had been the independent sycophant and intended
to be again, once the war was over and presuming that the man came
back from his Sharpsburg or Chickamauga majority or colonelcy or
whatever it had been. Trying to raid, that is, until the major's or
colonel's wife or aunt or mother-in-law, who had buried the silver
in the orchard and still held together a few of the older slaves,
fended him off and dispersed him, and when necessary even shot
him, with the absent husband's or nephew's or son-in-law's hunting
gun or dueling pistols. The women: the indomitable, the undefeated,
who never surrendered, refusing to allow the Yankee *minie* balls to
be dug out of portico column or mantelpiece or lintel, who seventy
years later would get up and walk out of *Gone With the Wind* as
soon as Sherman's name was mentioned; irreconcilable and enraged
and still talking about it long after the weary exhausted men who
had fought and lost it gave up trying to make them hush: even in
the boy's time the boy himself knowing about Vicksburg and Corinth
and exactly where his grandfather's regiment had been at First Manassas before he remembered hearing very much about Santa Claus.

In those days—1901 and '02 and '03 and '04—Santa Claus occurred
only at Christmas, not like now, and for the rest of the year children
played with what they could find or contrive or make, though just
as now, they still played, aped in miniature, what they had been
exposed to, heard or seen or been moved by most. Which was true
in the child's time and case too: the indomitable unsurrendered old

women holding together still, thirty-five and forty years later, a few of the old house slaves: women too who, like the white ones, refused to give up the old ways and forget the old anguishes. The child himself remembered one of them: Caroline: free these many years but who had declined to leave. Nor would she ever accept in full her weekly Saturday wages; the family never knew why unless the true reason was the one which appeared: for the simple pleasure of keeping the entire family reminded constantly that they were in arrears to her, compelling the boy's grandfather then his father and finally himself in his turn to be not only her banker but her bookkeeper too, having got the figure of eighty-nine dollars into her head somehow or for some reason, and though the sum itself altered, sometimes more and sometimes less, and sometimes it would be she herself who would be several weeks in arrears, it never changed: one of the children, white or Negro, liable to appear at any time, usually when most of the family would be gathered at a meal, with the message: "Mammy says to tell you not to forget you owe her eighty-nine dollars."

To the child, even at that time, she seemed already older than God, calling his grandsire "colonel" but never the child's father nor the father's brother and sister by anything but their Christian names even when they themselves had become grandparents: a matriarch with a score of descendants (and probably half that many more whom she had forgotten or outlived), one of them a boy too, whether a great grandson or merely a grandson even she did not remember, born in the same week with the white child and both bearing the same (the white child's grandsire's) name, suckled at the same black breast and sleeping and eating together and playing together the game which was the most important thing the white child knew at that time since at four and five and six his world was still a female world and he had heard nothing else that he could remember: with empty spools and chips and sticks and a scraped trench filled with well water for the River, playing over again in miniature the War, the old irremediable battles—Shiloh and Vicksburg, and Brice's Crossroads which was not far from where the child (both of them) had been born, the boy because he was white arrogating to himself the right to be the Confederate General—Pemberton or Johnston or Forrest—twice to the black child's once, else, lacking that once in three, the black one would not play at all.

Not the tall man, he was still the hunter, the man of the woods; and not the slave because he was free now; but that Mexican cotton seed which someone had given the Natchez doctor was clearing the land fast now, plowing under the buffalo grass of the eastern prairies and the brier and switch cane of the creek and river bottoms of the central hills and deswamping the whole vast flat alluvial delta-shaped sweep of land along the Big River, the Old Man: building the levees to hold him off the land long enough to plant and harvest the crop: he taking another foot of slope in his new dimension for every foot man constricted him in the old, so that the steamboats carrying the baled cotton to Memphis or New Orleans seemed to crawl along the sky itself.

And little steamboats on the smaller rivers, too, penetrating the Tallahatchie as far up as Wylie's Crossing above Jefferson. Though most of the cotton from that section—and on to the east to that point of no economic return where it was more expedient to continue on east to the Tombigbee and then south to Mobile—went the sixty miles overland to Memphis by mule and wagon; there was a settlement—a tavern of sorts and a smithy and a few gaunt cabins—on the bluff above Wylie's, at the exact distance where a wagon or a train of them loaded with cotton either starting or resuming the journey in the vicinity of Jefferson, would have to halt for the night. Or not even a settlement but rather a den, whose denizens lurked unseen by day in the brakes and thickets of the river bottom, appearing only at night and even then only long enough to enter the tavern kitchen where the driver of the day's cotton wagon sat unsuspecting before the fire, whereupon driver, wagon, mules and cotton and all would vanish: the body into the river probably and the wagon burned and the mules sold days or weeks later in a Memphis stockyard and the unidentifiable cotton already on its way to the Liverpool mill.

At the same time, sixteen miles away in Jefferson, there was a pre-Snopes, one of the tall men actually, a giant of a man in fact: a dedicated lay Baptist preacher but furious not with a furious unsleeping dream of paradise nor even for universal Order with an upper-case O, but for simple civic security. He was warned by everyone not to go in there because not only could he accomplish nothing, he would very likely lose his own life trying it. But he did go, alone, and talked not of gospel nor God nor even virtue, but simply selected the biggest and boldest and by appearance, anyway, the most villainous there and said to him: "I'll fight you. If you lick me, you take

what money I have. If I lick you, I baptize you into my church":
and battered and mauled and gouged that one into sanctity and
civic virtue then challenged the next biggest and most villainous and
then the next; and the following Sunday baptized the entire settlement in the river, the cotton wagons now crossing on Wylie's hand-
powered ferry and passing peacefully and unchallenged on to
Memphis until the railroad came and took the bales away from them.

That was in the seventies. The Negro was a free farmer and a
political entity now; one, he could not sign his name, was Federal
marshal at Jefferson. Afterward he became the town's official bootlegger (Mississippi was one of the first to essay the noble experiment,
along with Maine), resuming—he had never really quitted it—his old
allegiance to his old master and gaining his professional name, Mulberry, from the huge old tree behind Doctor Habersham's drugstore,
in the gallerylike tunnels among the roots of which he cached the
bottled units of his commerce.

Soon he (the Negro) would even forge ahead in that economic
rivalry with Snopes which was to send Snopes in droves into the
Ku Klux Klan—not the old original one of the war's chaotic and desperate end which, measured against the desperate times, was at least
honest and serious in its desperate aim, but into the later base one
of the twenties whose only kinship to the old one was the old name.
And a little money to build railroads was in the land now, brought
there by the man who in '66 had been a carpetbagger but who now
was a citizen; his children would speak the soft consonantless Negro
tongue as the children of parents who had lived below the Potomac
and Ohio Rivers since Captain John Smith, and their children would
boast of their Southern heritage.

In Jefferson his name was Redmond. He had found the money
with which Colonel Sartoris had opened the local cotton fields to
Europe by building his connecting line up to the main railroad from
Memphis to the Atlantic Ocean—narrow gauge, like a toy, with three
tiny locomotives like toys, too, named after Colonel Sartoris' three
daughters, each with its silver-plated oilcan engraved with the
daughter's Christian name: like toys, the standard-sized cars jacked
up at the junction, then lowered onto the narrow trucks, the tiny
locomotive now invisible ahead of its charges so that they appeared
in process of being snatched headlong among the fields they served
by an arrogant plume of smoke and the arrogant shrieking of a
whistle. It was Redmond who, after the inevitable quarrel, finally

shot Colonel Sartoris dead on a Jefferson street, driven, everyone believed, to the desperate act by the same arrogance and intolerance which had driven Colonel Sartoris' regiment to demote him from its colonelcy in the fall elections after Second Manassas and Sharpsburg.

So there were railroads in the land now; now couples who used to go overland by carriage to the River landings and the steamboats for the traditional New Orleans honeymoon could take the train from almost anywhere. And presently Pullmans, too, all the way from Chicago and the Northern cities where the cash, the money was, so that the rich Northerners could come down in comfort and open the land indeed: setting up with their Yankee dollars the vast lumbering plants and mills in the Southern-pine section, the little towns which had been hamlets without change or alteration for fifty years, booming and soaring into cities overnight above the stump-pocked barrens which would remain until in simple economic desperation people taught themselves to farm pine trees as in other sections they had already learned to farm corn and cotton.

And Northern lumber mills in the Delta too: the mid-twenties now and the Delta booming with cotton and timber both. But mostly booming with simple money: increment a troglodyte which had fathered twin troglodytes: solvency and bankruptcy, the three of them booming money into the land so fast that the problem was how to get rid of it before it whelmed you into suffocation. Until in something almost resembling self-defense, seven or eight of the bigger Delta towns formed a baseball league, presently raiding as far away—and successfully too—for pitchers and shortstops and slugging outfielders as the two major leagues; the boy, a young man now, making acquaintance with this league and one of the big Northern lumber companies not only coincidentally with one another but because of one another.

At this time the young man's attitude was that of most other young men who had been around twenty-one years of age in April, 1917, even though at times he did admit to himself that he was possibly using the fact that he had been nineteen on that day as an excuse to follow the avocation he was coming more and more to know would be forever his true one: to be a tramp, a harmless possessionless vagabond. In any case, he was quite ripe to make the acquaintance of the league; it began with that of the lumber company, which at the moment was taking a leisurely bankruptcy. A lawyer had been appointed referee in the bankruptcy: a friend of the young man's family and older than he, yet who had taken a liking to the young man and so invited him to come along for the ride too. His official capacity was that of interpreter, since he had a little French and the defuncting company had European connections. But no interpreting was ever done, since the entourage did not go to Europe but moved instead into a single floor of a Memphis hotel, where all—including the interpreter—had the privilege of signing chits for food and theater tickets and even the bootleg whisky (Tennessee was in its dry mutation then) which the bellboys would produce, though not of course at the discreet and innocent-looking places clustered a few miles away just below the Mississippi state line, where roulette and dice and blackjack were available.

Then suddenly Mr. Sells Wales was in it, too, bringing the baseball league with him. The young man never did know what connection (if any) Mr. Wales had with the bankruptcy, nor really bothered to wonder, let alone care and ask, not only because he had developed already that sense of *noblesse oblige* toward the avocation which he knew was his true one, which would have been reason enough, but because Mr. Wales himself was already a legend in the Delta. Owner of a plantation measured not in acres but in miles and reputedly sole owner of one of the league baseball teams or anyway most of its players, certainly of the catcher and the base-stealing shortstop and the .340-hitting outfielder ravished or pirated, it was said, from the Chicago Cubs, his ordinary costume seven days a week was a two or three days' beard and muddy high boots and a corduroy hunting coat, the tale, the legend telling of how he entered a swank St. Louis hotel in that costume late one night and demanded a room of a dinner-jacketed clerk, who looked once at the beard and the muddy boots but probably mostly at Mr. Wales' face and said they were filled up: whereupon Mr. Wales asked how much they wanted for the hotel and was told, superciliously, in tens of thousands, and—so told the legend—drew from his corduroy hip a wad of thousand-dollar bills sufficient to have bought the hotel half again at the price stated and told the clerk he wanted every room in the building vacated in ten minutes.

That one of course was apocryphal, but the young man himself saw this one: Mr. Wales and himself having a leisurely breakfast one noon in the Memphis hotel when Mr. Wales remembered suddenly that his private ball club was playing one of its most important games at a town about sixty miles away at three o'clock that afternoon and telephoned to the railroad station to have a special train ready for them in thirty minutes, which it was: an engine and a caboose: reaching Coahoma about three o'clock with a mile still to the ball park: a man (there were no taxis at the station at that hour and few in Mississippi anywhere at that time) sitting behind the wheel of a dingy though still sound Cadillac car, and Mr. Wales said:

"What do you want for it?"

"What?" the man in the car said.

"Your automobile," Mr. Wales said.

"Twelve fifty," the man said.

"All right," Mr. Wales said, opening the door.

"I mean twelve hundred and fifty dollars," the man said.

"All right," Mr. Wales said, then to the young man: "Jump in."

"Hold up here, mister," the man said.

"I've bought it," Mr. Wales said, getting in too. "The ball park," he said. "Hurry."

The young man never saw the Cadillac again, though he became quite familiar with the engine and caboose during the next succeeding weeks while the league pennant race waxed hotter and hotter, Mr. Wales keeping the special train on call in the Memphis yards as twenty-five years earlier a city-dwelling millionaire might have hacked a carriage and pair to his instant nod, so that it seemed to the young man that he would barely get back to Memphis to rest before they would be rushing once more down the Delta to another baseball game.

"I ought to be interpreting, sometime," he said once.

"Interpret, then," Mr. Wales said. "Interpret what this goddamn cotton market is going to do tomorrow, and we can both quit chasing this blank blank sand-lot ball team."

The cotton seed and the lumber mills were clearing the rest of the delta, too, pushing what remained of the wilderness farther and farther southward into the V of Big River and the hills. When the young man, a youth of sixteen and seventeen then, was first accepted into that hunting club of which he in his hierarchal time would be Master, the hunting grounds, haunt of deer and bear and wild turkey, could be reached in a single day or night in a mule-drawn wagon. Now they were using automobiles: a hundred miles then two hundred southward and still southward as the wilderness dwindled into the confluence of the Yazoo River and the big one, the Old Man.

The Old Man: all his little contributing streams levee'd too, along with him, and paying none of the dykes any heed at all when it suited his mood and fancy, gathering water all the way from Montana to Pennsylvania every generation or so and rolling it down the artificial gut of his victims' puny and baseless hoping, piling the water up, not fast, just inexorably, giving plenty of time to measure his crest and telegraph ahead, even warning of the exact day almost when he would enter the house and float the piano out of it and the pictures off the walls, and even remove the house itself if it were not securely fastened down.

Inexorable and unhurried, overpassing one by one his little confluent feeders and shoving the water into them until for days their current would flow backward, upstream: as far upstream as Wylie's Crossing above Jefferson. The little rivers were dyked, too, but back here was the land of individualists: remnants and descendants of the tall men now taken to farming, and of Snopeses who were more than individualists: they were Snopeses, so that where the owners of the thousand-acre plantations along the Big River confederated as one man with sandbags and machines and their Negro tenants and wage-hands to hold the sandboils and the cracks, back here the owner of the hundred- or two-hundred-acre farm patrolled his section of levee with a sandbag in one hand and his shotgun in the other, lest his upstream neighbor dynamite it to save his (the upstream neighbor's) own.

Piling up the water while white man and Negro worked side by side in shifts in the mud and the rain, with automobile headlights and gasoline flares and kegs of whisky and coffee boiling in fifty-gallon batches in scoured and scalded oil drums; lapping, tentative, almost innocently, merely inexorable (no hurry, his) among and beneath and between and finally over the frantic sandbags, as if his whole purpose had been merely to give man another chance to prove, not to him but to man, just how much the human body could bear, stand, endure; then, having let man prove it, doing what he could have done at any time these past weeks if so minded: removing with no haste, nor any particular malice or fury either, a mile or two miles of levee and coffee drums and whisky kegs and gas flares in one sloughing collapse, gleaming dully for a little while yet among the parallel cotton middles until the fields vanished along with the roads and lanes and at last the towns themselves.

Vanished, gone beneath one vast yellow motionless expanse, out

of which projected only the tops of trees and telephone poles and
the decapitations of human dwelling-places like enigmatic objects
placed by inscrutable and impenetrable design on a dirty mirror;
and the mounds of the predecessors on which, among a tangle of
moccasins, bear and horses and deer and mules and wild turkeys
and cows and domestic chickens waited patient in mutual armistice;
and the levees themselves, where among a jumble of uxorious flotsam the young continued to be born and the old to die, not from
exposure but from simple and normal time and decay, as if man
and his destiny were in the end stronger even than the river which
had dispossessed him, inviolable by and invincible to alteration.

Then, having proved that too, he—the Old Man—would withdraw,
not retreat: subside, back from the land slowly and inexorably too,
emptying the confluent rivers and bayous back into the old vain
hopeful gut, but so slowly and gradually that not the waters seemed
to fall but the flat earth itself to rise, creep in one plane back into
light and air again: one constant stain of yellow-brown at one constant altitude on telephone poles and the walls of gins and houses
and stores as though the line had been laid off with a transit and
painted in one gigantic unbroken brush stroke, the earth itself one
alluvial inch higher, the rich dirt one inch deeper, drying into long
cracks beneath the hot fierce glare of May: but not for long, because
almost at once came the plow, the plowing and planting already
two months late but that did not matter: the cotton man-tall once
more by August and whiter and denser still by picking time, as if
the Old Man said, "I do what I want to, when I want to. But I pay
my way."

And the boats, of course, they projected above that yellow and
liquid plane and even moved upon it: the skiffs and scows of fishermen and trappers, the launches of the United States Engineers who
operated the Levee Commission, and one small shallow-draught
steamboat steaming in paradox among and across the cotton fields
themselves, its pilot not a riverman but a farmer who knew where
the submerged fences were, its masthead lookout a mechanic with
a pair of pliers to cut the telephone wires to pass the smokestack
through: no paradox really, since on the River it had resembled a
house to begin with, so that here it looked no different from the
baseless houses it steamed among and on occasion even strained at
top boiler pressure to overtake, like a mallard drake after a fleeing
mallard hen.

But these boats were not enough, very quickly not near enough, the Old Man meant business indeed this time. So now there began to arrive from the Gulf ports the shrimp trawlers and pleasure cruisers and Coast Guard cutters whose bottoms had known only salt water and the mouths of tidal rivers, to be run still by their salt-water crews but conned by the men who knew where the submerged roads and fences were for the good reason that they had been running mule-plow furrows along them or up to them all their lives; sailing among the swollen carcasses of horses and mules and deer and cows and sheep to pluck the Old Man's patient flotsam, black and white, out of trees and the roofs of gins and cotton sheds and floating cabins and the second-story windows of houses and office buildings; then—the salt-water men, to whom land was either a featureless treeless salt marsh or a snake- and alligator-infested swamp impenetrable with trumpet vine and Spanish moss, some of whom had never even seen the earth into which were driven the spiles supporting the houses they lived in—staying on even after they were no longer needed, as though waiting to see emerge from the water what sort of country it was which bore the economy on which the people—men and women, black and white, more of black than white even, ten to one more—lived whom they had saved; seeing the land for that moment before mule and plow altered it right up to the water's receding edge, then back into the River again before the trawlers and cruisers and cutters became marooned into canted and useless rubble too along with the ruined hencoops and cowsheds and privies; back onto the Old Man, shrunken once more into his normal banks, drowsing and even innocent looking, as if it were something else besides him that had changed, for a little time anyway, the whole face of the adjacent earth.

They were homeward bound now, passing the river towns, some of which were respectable in age when South Mississippi was a Spanish wilderness: Greenville and Vicksburg, Natchez and Grand Gulf and Petit Gulf (vanished now and even the old site known by a different name) which had known Mason and one at least of the Harpes and from or on which Murrell had based his abortive slave insurrection intended to efface the white people from the land and leave him emperor of it—the land sinking away beyond the levee until presently you could no longer say where water began and earth stopped: only that these lush and verdant sunny savannas would no longer bear your weight. The rivers flowed no longer west, but south now, no longer yellow or brown, but black, threading the miles of yellow salt marsh from which, on an off-shore breeze, mosquitoes came in such clouds that in your itching and burning anguish it would seem that you could actually see them in faint adumbration crossing the earth; and met tide and then the uncorrupted salt: not the Gulf quite yet but at least the Sound behind the long barrier of the islands—Ship and Horn and Petit Bois, the trawler and cruiser bottoms home again now among the lighthouses and channel markers and shipyards and drying nets and processing plants for fish.

The man remembered that from his youth too: one summer spent being blown innocently over in catboats since, born and bred for generations in the north Mississippi hinterland, he did not recognize the edge of a squall until he already had one. The next summer he returned because he found that he liked that much water, this time as a hand in one of the trawlers; remembering: a four-gallon iron pot over a red bed of charcoal on the foredeck, in which decapitated shrimp boiled among handfuls of salt and black pepper, never emptied, never washed and constantly renewed, so that you ate them all day long in passing like peanuts; remembering: the predawn, to be broken presently by the violent near-subtropical yellow-and-crimson day almost like an audible explosion, but still dark for a little while yet, the dark ship creeping onto the shrimp grounds in a soundless sternward swirl of phosphorus like a drowning tumble of fireflies, the youth lying face down on the peak staring into the dark water watching the disturbed shrimp burst outward-shooting in fiery and fading fans like the trails of tiny rockets.

He learned the barrier islands too; one of a crew of five amateurs sailing a big sloop in offshore races, he learned not only how to keep a hull on its keel and moving but how to get it from one place to another and bring it back: so that, a professional now, living in New Orleans, he commanded for pay a power launch belonging to a bootlegger (this was the twenties), whose crew consisted of a Negro cook-deckhand-stevedore and the bootlegger's younger brother Pete: a slim twenty-one-or-two-year-old Italian with yellow eyes like a cat and a silk shirt bulged faintly by an armpit-holstered pistol too small in calibre to have done anything but got them all killed, even if the captain or the cook had dreamed of resisting or resenting trouble if and when it came; the captain or the cook would extract the pistol from the holster and hide it at the first opportunity (not concealed really: just dropped into the oily bilge under the engine, where, even

though Pete soon discovered where it would be, it was safe because
he refused to thrust his hand and arm into the oil-fouled water but
instead merely lay about the cockpit, sulking); taking the launch
across Pontchartrain and down the Rigolets cut to the Gulf, the
Sound, then lying-to with no lights showing until the Coast Guard
cutter (it ran almost on schedule; theirs was a job, too, even if it was,
comparatively speaking, a hopeless one) made its fast haughty eastward rush, going, they always liked to believe, to Mobile, to a dance;
then by compass on to the island (it was little more than a sandspit
bearing a line of ragged and shabby pines thrashing always in the
windy crash and roar of the true Gulf on the other side of it) where
the Caribbean schooner would bury the casks of green alcohol which
the bootlegger's mother back in New Orleans would convert and
bottle and label into Scotch or Bourbon or gin. There were a few
wild cattle on the island which they would have to watch for, the
Negro digging and Pete still sulking and refusing to help at all because of the pistol, and the captain watching for the charge (they
couldn't risk showing a light) which every three or four trips would
come—the gaunt wild half-seen shapes charging suddenly and with
no warning down at them as they turned and ran through the nightmare sand and hurled themselves into the dinghy, to pull along parallel to the shore, the animals following, until they had tolled them
far enough away for the Negro to go back ashore for the remaining
casks. Then they would heave-to again and lie until the cutter passed
back westward, the dance obviously over now, in the same haughty
and imperious rush.

That was Mississippi too, though a different one from where the
child had been bred; the people were Catholics, the Spanish and
French blood still showed in the names and faces. But it was not a
deep one, if you did not count the sea and the boats on it: a curve
of beach, a thin unbroken line of estates and apartment hotels owned
and inhabited by Chicago millionaires, standing back to back with
another thin line, this time of tenements inhabited by Negroes and
whites who ran the boats and worked in the fish-processing plants.

Then the Mississippi which the young man knew began: the fading purlieus inhabited by a people whom the young man recognized
because their like was in his country too: descendants, heirs at least
in spirit, of the tall men, who worked in no factories and farmed no
land nor even truck patches, living not out of the earth but on its

denizens: fishing guides and individual professional fishermen, trappers of muskrats and alligator hunters and poachers of deer, the land rising now, once more earth instead of half water, vista-ed and arras-ed with the long-leaf pines which Northern capital would convert into dollars in Ohio and Indiana and Illinois banks. Though not all of it. Some of it would alter hamlets and villages into cities and even build whole new ones almost overnight, cities with Mississippi names but patterned on Ohio and Indiana and Illinois because they were bigger than Mississippi towns, rising, standing today among the tall pines which created them, then tomorrow (that quick, that fast, that rapid) among the stumpy pock-age to which they were monuments. Because the land had made its one crop: the soil too fine and light to compete seriously in cotton: until people discovered that it would grow what other soils would not: the tomatoes and strawberries and the fine cane for sugar: not the sorghum of the northern and western counties which people of the true cane country called hog feed, but the true sweet cane which made the sugarhouse molasses.

Big towns, for Mississippi: cities, we called them: Hattiesburg, and Laurel, and Meridian, and Canton; and towns deriving by name from farther away than Ohio: Kosciusko named after a Polish general who thought that people should be free who wanted to be; and Egypt because there was corn there when it was nowhere else in the bad lean times of the old war which the old women had still never surrendered; and Philadelphia where the Neshoba Indians whose name the county bears still remain for the simple reason that they did not mind living in peace with other people, no matter what their color or politics. This was the hills now: Jones County which old Newt Knight, its principal proprietor and first citizen or denizen, whichever you liked, seceded from the Confederacy in 1862, establishing still a third republic within the boundaries of the United States until a Confederate military force subdued him in his embattled log-castle capital; and Sullivan's Hollow: a long narrow glen where a few clans or families with North Ireland and Highland names feuded and slew one another in the old pre-Culloden fashion, yet banding together immediately and always to resist any outsider in the pre-Culloden fashion too: *vide* the legend of the revenue officer hunting illicit whisky stills, captured and held prisoner in a stable and worked in traces as the mate to a plow mule. No Negro ever let darkness catch him in Sullivan's Hollow. In fact, there were

few Negroes in this country at all: a narrow strip of which extended
up into the young man's own section: a remote district there through
which Negroes passed infrequently and rapidly and only by day-
light.

It is not very wide, because almost at once there begins to the
east of it the prairie country which sheds its water into Alabama
and Mobile Bay, with its old tight intermarried towns and plantation houses columned and porticoed in the traditional Georgian manner of Virginia and Carolina in place of the Spanish and French
influence of Natchez. These towns are Columbus and Aberdeen and
West Point, and Shuqualak, where the good quail shooting is and the
good bird dogs are bred and trained—horses too: hunters; Dancing
Rabbit is here, too, where the treaty dispossessing them of Mississippi
was made between the Choctaws and the United States; and in one
of the towns lived a kinsman of the young man, dead now, rest him:
an invincible and incorrigible bachelor, a leader of cotillions and an
inveterate diner-out since any time an extra single man was needed,
any hostess thought of him first.

But he was a man's man, too, and even more: a young man's man,
who played poker and matched glasses with the town's young bachelors and the apostates still young enough in time to still resist the
wedlock; who walked not only in spats and a stick and yellow gloves
and a Homburg hat, but an air of sardonic and inviolable atheism,
too, until at last he was forced to the final desperate resort of prayer:
sitting after supper one night among the drummers in the row of
chairs on the sidewalk before the Gilmer Hotel, waiting to see what
(if anything) the evening would bring, when two of the young
bachelors passing in a Model T Ford stopped and invited him to
drive across the line into the Alabama hills for a gallon of moonshine
whisky. Which they did. But the still they sought was not in hills
because these were not hills: it was the dying tail of the Appalachian
mountain range. But since the Model T's engine had to be running
fast anyway for it to have any headlights, going up the mountain was
an actual improvement, especially after they had to drop to low gear.
And coming from the generation before the motor car, it never occurred to him that coming back down would be any different until
they got the gallon and had a drink from it and turned around and
started back down. Or maybe it was the whisky, he said, telling it:
the little car rushing faster and faster behind a thin wash of light
of about the same volume that two lightning bugs would have made,

around the plunging curves which, the faster the car ran, became only the more frequent and sharp and plunging, whipping around the nearly right-angle bends with a rock wall on one hand and several hundred feet of vertical and empty night on the other, until at last he prayed; he said: "Lord, You know I haven't worried You in over forty years, and if You'll just get me back to Columbus I promise never to bother You again."

And now the young man, middle-aged now or anyway middle-aging, is back home, too, where they who altered the swamps and forests of his youth have now altered the face of the earth itself; what he remembered as dense river-bottom jungle and rich farmland is now an artificial lake twenty-five miles long: a flood-control project for the cotton fields below the huge earth dam, with a few more outboard-powered fishing skiffs on it each year, and at last a sailboat. On his way in to town from his home the middle-aging man (now a professional fiction writer: who had wanted to remain the tramp and the possessionless vagabond of his young manhood but time and success and the hardening of his arteries had beaten him) would pass the back yard of a doctor friend whose son was an undergraduate at Harvard. One day the undergraduate stopped him and invited him in and showed him the unfinished hull of a twenty-foot sloop, saying, "When I get her finished, Mr. Bill, I want you to help me sail her." And each time he passed after that, the undergraduate would repeat: "Remember, Mr. Bill, I want you to help me sail her as soon as I get her in the water": to which the middle-aging would answer as always: "Fine, Arthur. Just let me know."

Then one day he came out of the post office: a voice called him from a taxicab, which in small Mississippi towns was any motor car owned by any foot-loose young man who liked to drive, who decreed himself a cabbie as Napoleon decreed himself emperor; in the car with the driver was the undergraduate and a young man whose father had vanished recently somewhere in the West out of the ruins of the bank of which he had been president, and a fourth young man whose type is universal: the town clown, comedian, whose humor is without viciousness and quite often witty and always funny. "She's in the water, Mr. Bill," the undergraduate said. "Are you ready to go now?" And he was, and the sloop was, too; the undergraduate had sewn his own sails on his mother's machine; they worked her out into the lake and got her on course all tight and drawing, when suddenly it seemed to the middle-aging that part of him was no longer in the sloop but about ten feet away, looking at what he saw: a Harvard undergraduate, a taxi driver, the son of an absconded banker and a village clown and a middle-aged novelist sailing a homemade boat on an artificial lake in the depths of the north Mississippi hills: and he thought that that was something which did not happen to you more than once in your life.

Home again, his native land; he was born of it and his bones will sleep in it; loving it even while hating some of it: the river jungle and the bordering hills where, still a child, he had ridden behind his father on the horse after the bobcat or fox or coon or whatever was ahead of the belling hounds, and where he had hunted alone when he got big enough to be trusted with a gun—all this now the bottom of a muddy lake being raised gradually and steadily every year by another layer of beer cans and bottle caps and lost bass plugs. And the wilderness, the two weeks in the woods, in camp, the rough food and the rough sleeping, the life of men and horses and hounds among men and horses and hounds, not to slay the game but to pursue it, touch and let go, never satiety—moved now even farther away than that down the flat Delta so that the mile-long freight trains, visible for miles across the fields where the cotton is mortgaged in February, planted in May, harvested in September and put into the Farm Loan in October in order to pay off February's mortgage in order to mortgage next year's crop, seem to be passing two or even three of the little Indian-named hamlets at once over the very ground where, a youth now capable of being trusted even with a rifle, he had shared in the yearly ritual of Old Ben: the big old bear with one trap-ruined foot who had earned for himself a name, a designation like a living man through the legend of the deadfalls and traps he had wrecked and the hounds he had slain and the shots he had survived, until Boon Hogganbeck, the youth's father's stable foreman, ran in and killed it with a hunting knife to save a hound which he, Boon Hogganbeck, loved.

But most of all he hated the intolerance and injustice: the lynching of Negroes not for the crimes they committed but because their skins were black (the lynchings were becoming fewer and fewer and soon there would be no more of them but the evil would have been done and irrevocable because there should never have been any); the inequality: the poor schools they had then when they had any, the hovels they had to live in unless they wanted to live outdoors: who could worship the white man's God but not in the white man's church; pay taxes in the white man's courthouse but couldn't vote in it or for it; working by the white man's clock but having to take his pay by the white man's counting (Captain Joe Thoms, a Delta planter though not one of the big ones, who after a bad crop year drew a thousand silver dollars from the bank and called his five tenants one by one into the dining room where two hundred of the dollars were spread carelessly out on the table beneath the lamp, saying: "Well, Jim, that's what we made this year." Then the Negro: "Gret God, Cap'n Joe, is all that mine?" And Captain Thoms: "No, no, just half of it is yours. The other half belongs to me, remember."); the bigotry which could send to Washington some of the Senators and Congressmen we sent there and which could erect in a town no bigger than Jefferson five separate denominations of churches but set aside not one square foot of ground where children could play and old people could sit and watch them.

But he loves it, it is his, remembering: the trying to, having to, stay in bed until the crack of dawn would bring Christmas; and of the other times almost as good as Christmas: of being waked at three o'clock to have breakfast by lamplight in order to drive by surrey into town and the depot to take the morning train for the three or four days in Memphis where he would see automobiles, and the day in 1910 when, twelve years old, he watched John Moissant land a bicycle-wheeled aileronless (you warped the whole wing tip to bank it or hold it level) Bleriot monoplane on the infield of the Memphis race track and knew forever after that someday he too would have to fly alone; remembering: his first sweetheart, aged eight, plump and honey-haired and demure and named Mary, the two of them sitting side by side on the kitchen steps eating ice cream; and another one, Minnie this time, granddaughter of the old hillman from whom, a man himself now, he bought moonshine whisky, come to town at seventeen to take a job behind the soda counter of the drugstore, watching her virginal and innocent and without self-consciousness pour Coca-Cola sirup into the lifted glass by hooking her thumb through the ring of the jug and swinging it back and up in one unbroken motion onto her horizontal upper arm exactly as he had seen her grandfather pour whisky from a jug a thousand times.

Even while hating it, because for every Joe Thoms with two hundred silver dollars and every Snopes in a hooded nightshirt, somewhere in Mississippi there was this too: remembering: Ned, born in a cabin in the back yard in 1865, in the time of the middle-aged's great-grandfather, and who had outlived three generations of them, who had not only walked and talked so constantly for so many years with the three generations that he walked and talked like them, he had two tremendous trunks filled with the clothes which they had worn—not only the blue brass-buttoned frock coat and the plug hat in which he had been the great-grandfather's and the grandfather's coachman, but the broadcloth frock coats which the great-grandfather himself had worn, and the pigeon-tailed ones of the grandfather's time and the short coat of his father's which the middle-aged could remember on the backs for which they had been tailored, along with the hats in their eighty years of mutation too: so that, glancing idly up and out the library window, the middle-aged would see that back, that stride, that coat and hat going down the drive toward the road, and his heart would stop and even turn over. He (Ned) was eighty-four now and in these last few years he had begun to get a little mixed up, calling the middle-aged not only Master but sometimes Master Murry, who was the middle-aged's father, and Colonel too, coming once a week through the kitchen and into the parlor, saying: "Here's where I wants to lay, right here where I can be facing out that window. And I wants it to be a sunny day, so the sun can come in on me. And I wants you to preach the sermon. I wants you to take a dram of whisky for me, and lay yourself back and preach the best sermon you ever preached."

And Caroline too, whom the middle-aged had inherited too in his hierarchal turn, nobody knowing any more exactly how many more years than a hundred she was. But not mixed up, she: who had forgotten nothing, calling the middle-aged "Memmy" still, from fifty-odd years ago when that was as close as his brothers could come to "William"; his youngest daughter, aged four and five and six, coming in to the house and saying, "Pappy, Mammy said to tell you not to forget you owe her eighty-nine dollars."

"I won't," the middle-aged would say. "What are you all doing now?"

"Piecing a quilt," the daughter answered. Which they were. There was electricity in her cabin now, but she would not use it, insisting still on the kerosene lamps which she had always known. Nor would she use the spectacles either, wearing them merely as an ornament across the brow of the immaculate white cloth—head-rag—which bound her now hairless head. She did not need them: a smolder of

wood ashes on the hearth winter and summer in which sweet potatoes roasted, the five-year-old white child in a miniature rocking
chair at one side of it and the aged Negress, not a great deal larger,
in her chair at the other, the basket bright with scraps and fragments
of cloth between them and in that dim light in which the middle-
aged himself could not have read his own name without his glasses,
the two of them with infinitesimal and tedious and patient stitches
annealing the bright stars and squares and diamonds into another
pattern to be folded away among the cedar shavings in the trunk.

Then it was the Fourth of July, the kitchen was closed after breakfast so the cook and houseman had rallied, and that morning the
generations of her loins began to arrive, from her own seventy- and
eighty-year-old children, down through their great- and twice-great-
grandchildren, faces which the middle-aged had never seen before,
until the cabin would no longer hold them: the women and girls
sleeping on the floor inside and the men and boys sleeping on the
ground in front of it, Caroline herself conscious now and presently
sitting up in bed: who had forgotten nothing: matriarchal and im-
perial, and more: imperious: ten and even eleven o'clock at night
and the middle-aged himself undressed and in bed, reading, when
sure enough he would hear the slow quiet stockinged or naked feet
mounting the back stairs; presently the strange dark face—never the
same one of two nights ago or the two or three nights before that—
would look in the door at him, and the quiet, courteous, never servile
voice would say: "She want the ice cream." And he would rise and
dress and drive in to the village; he would even drive through the
village although he knew that everything there would have long
been closed and he would do what he had done two nights ago;
drive thirty miles on to the arterial highway and then up or down
it until he found an open drive-in or hot-dog stand to sell him the
quart of ice cream.

But that stroke was not the one; she was walking again presently,
even, despite the houseman's standing order to forestall her with the
automobile, all the way in to town to sit with his, the middle-aging's,
mother, talking, he liked to think, of the old days of his father and
himself and the three younger brothers, the two of them, two women
who together had never weighed two hundred pounds, in a house
roaring with five men: though they probably didn't, since women,
unlike men, have learned how to live uncomplicated by that sort of
sentimentality. But it was as if she knew herself that the summer's

stroke was like the throat-clearing sound inside the grandfather clock preceding the stroke of midnight or of noon, because she never touched the last unfinished quilt again. Presently it had vanished, no one knew where, and as the cold came and the shortening days she began to spend more and more time in the house, not her cabin but the big house, sitting in a corner of the kitchen while the cook and houseman were about, then in the middle-aging's wife's sewing room until the family gathered for the evening meal, the houseman carrying her rocking chair into the dining room to sit there while they ate: until suddenly (it was almost Christmas now) she insisted on sitting in the parlor until the meal was ready, none knew why, until at last she told them, through the wife: "Miss Hestelle, when them niggers lays me out, I want you to make me a fresh clean cap and apron to lay in." That was her valedictory; two days after Christmas the stroke came which was the one; two days after that she lay in the parlor in the fresh cap and apron she would not see, and the middle-aging did indeed lay back and preach the sermon, the oration, hoping that when his turn came there would be someone in the world to owe him the sermon owed to her by all who had been, as he had been from infancy, within the scope and range of that fidelity and that devotion and that rectitude.

Loving all of it even while he had to hate some of it because he knows now that you don't love because: you love despite; not for the virtues, but despite the faults.